News in a New Century

REPORTING IN AN AGE OF CONVERGING MEDIA

D1469819

TITLES OF RELATED INTEREST FROM PINE FORGE PRESS

Media/Society: Industries, Images, and Audiences, 2nd Edition by David Croteau and William Hoynes

---

THE PINE FORGE PRESS SERIES FOR JOURNALISM AND COMMUNICATION FOR A NEW CENTURY

Senior Editors: Shirley Biagi and Duncan McDonald
Consulting Editors: Marilyn Kern-Foxworth, Meg Moritz, and Leonard Teel

Facing Difference: Race, Gender, and Mass Media by Shirley Biagi and Marilyn Kern-Foxworth

Mediamorphosis: Understanding New Media by Roger Fidler

Covering the Community: A Diversity Stylebook for Media by Leigh Stephens Aldrich

Free Speech in the 21st Century by Robert Trager and Donna Dickerson

News in a New Century

REPORTING IN AN AGE OF CONVERGING MEDIA

JERRY LANSON

Emerson College

BARBARA CROLL FOUGHT

Syracuse University

PINE FORGE PRESS

Thousand Oaks, CA ■ London ■ New Delhi

For Infomation

Pine Forge Press
A Sage Publications Company
2455 Teller Road
Thousand Oaks, California 91320
Bus: 805-499-4224
Fax: 805-499-7881
E-mail: sales@pfp.sagepub.com

SAGE Publications Ltd.
6 Bonhill Street
London EC2A 4PU
United Kingdom

SAGE Publications India Pvt. Ltd.
M-32 Market
Greater Kailash I
New Delhi 110 048
India

Production Management: Melanie Field, Strawberry Field Publishing
Production Coordinator: Windy Just
Typesetter: TBH Typecast, Inc.
Cover Designer: Deborah Davis
Interior Designer: Yvo Riezebos Design
Copy Editor: Judith Brown
Proofreader: Linda Ruth Dane
Indexer: Katherine Stimson

Printed in the United States of America
99 00 01 02 9 8 7 6 5 4 3 2 1

Library of Congress Cataloging-in-Publication Data

Lanson, Jerry.
    News in a new century : reporting in an age of converging media / by Jerry Lanson and Barbara Croll Fought.
    p. cm.
    Includes bibliographical references (p.) and index.
    ISBN 0-7619-8506-9
    1. Reporters and reporting. I. Fought, Barbara Croll. II. Title.
    PN4781.L37 1999
    070.4'3—ddc21
                                          98-25449
                                            CIP

This book is printed on acid-free paper that meets Environmental Protection Agency standards for recycled paper.

DEDICATION

To Ethel Lanson, who taught her two sons to revere words.
To Allen Houston, whose calm editing style and clear thinking under
the harshest deadline pressures serve as an inspiration to colleagues.

—Jerry Lanson

To the outstanding journalists at News 4 *(WDIV-TV, Detroit), who*
taught me most of what I know about the news business.

—Barbara Croll Fought

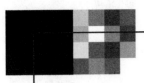

BRIEF CONTENTS

CONTENTS

CHAPTER 11   Lifestyles   162

ABOUT THE AUTHORS

JERRY LANSON

A writing coach and columnist, Jerry Lanson has taught journalism at seven colleges and universities. In January 1999, he joined the faculty of Emerson College as chair of its Department of Journalism and Public Information. He also has taught on the journalism faculties of Syracuse University, San Francisco State University, New York University and Boston University. Lanson is a former reporter for *The (Bergen County, N.J.) Record* and a former deputy city editor and bureau chief of the *San Jose (Calif.) Mercury News*. This is his second textbook. His honors include a National Teaching Award from The Poynter Institute for Media Studies. Lanson has two daughters, an extraordinarily patient wife, an insane golden retriever and a penchant for shouting, "Yes!" on those rare occasions he sinks a jump shot.

BARBARA CROLL FOUGHT

An associate professor in Syracuse University's broadcast journalism department, Barbara Croll Fought has specialized in the areas of Internet research and public access to government documents. Fought, a lawyer, teaches communications law as well as broadcast journalism classes. She is a former news researcher and special projects producer for *WDIV-TV*, Detroit, where she earned nine Emmys. In 1995, students at SU's S. I. Newhouse School of Public Communications chose her as professor of the year. Prospective students should know that Fought's name rhymes with *boat*. Her co-author has found her both unsinkable and unflappable.

Pine Forge Press is a new educational publisher, dedicated to publishing innovative books and software throughout the social sciences. On this and any other of our publications, we welcome your comments and suggestions. Please write to:

Pine Forge Press
A Sage Publications Company
2455 Teller Road
Thousand Oaks, CA 91320
805-499-4224
E-mail: sales@pfp.sagepub.com

Visit our new World Wide Web site, your direct link to a multitude of on-line resources: www.pineforge.com

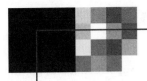

PREFACE

Another reporting text? With a few dozen others swirling around out there, it's not a surprising question.

But when we began talking about this book in 1995, something else surprised us. The definition and delivery of news were changing at a dizzying pace. Yet many textbooks clung to outdated and somewhat formulaic means of teaching students how to report and write news. Instead of taking the lead in educating a new generation of reporters, most journalism texts seemed stuck somewhere in the mid-1970s. They taught students to write by fact sheet. They were media-specific. And they seemed to suggest to would-be reporters that as long as they could follow the conventions of news writing and the basic standards of news gathering, someone else would provide the idea and angle of the story.

Too often, the method, the lesson and the content seemed out of date.

And so we talked some more. Why, we reasoned, not write a book emphasizing reporting skills? Why not show how technology has expanded the reporter's toolbox without discarding the well-tested tools already in it? Why not teach writing by taking would-be journalists through a writing process that begins with the inception of an idea instead of with an instructor's handout?

No one, it seemed to us, had written a book including all elements of that approach. Sure, since then, a flurry of specialized texts on the Internet, computer-assisted reporting and multimedia have hit the market. But none has wedded the reporting techniques and story approaches that have worked for decades past with the new realities of journalism. That is what we have set out to do in this book.

Our approach is based on several premises:

- The media are converging. Ten years from now, we believe vertical department lines separating print, broadcast and online departments in universities will fracture further if not shatter.

- Regardless of how news is delivered, the skills of effective news gathering will remain in demand.

- The Internet and computer are no longer frills but basic tools needed to report effectively.

- Reporters in the next century will need an understanding of how news is presented in all media.

- Reporters will find themselves covering news beats more broadly defined than those still practiced at more tradition-bound news organizations.

News in a New Century is primarily a reporting text. But we think its emphasis on the writing process makes it a valuable addition to the discussion of news writing as well. In Chapter 8, "Writing in Different Media," students will glimpse how reporters in different media struggle to craft a story on deadline and will see, by example, how the media are similar and how they differ. Throughout the book, we emphasize that good writing grows out of focused ideas and solidly grounded reporting and research.

This book is filled with hundreds of examples culled from interviews with dozens of reporters in print, electronic and online media. Reviewers have called it highly readable and praised its conversational style. We think its strength is its content.

DISTINCTIVE FEATURES OF THIS BOOK

Here is what we have done to make the book different:

- Combine all the elements of news gathering into a single text by focusing on the reporter's job in getting good stories, no matter how a story is delivered. To complement traditional research, sourcing and interviewing techniques, the book is filled with advice for surfing the Internet effectively for sources, information and stories.

- Fill a vacuum that now exists in the broadcast curriculum, where books focus on writing or production, with little coverage of basic news-gathering skills and beats.

- Deliver readable and user-friendly chapters that are comprehensive without being encyclopedic. Summary boxes help the hurried reader.

- Expand traditional definitions of news coverage and beats, putting less emphasis on institutions and more on the people affected by them.

- Address important issues of sensitivity in covering an increasingly diverse national community. Sections of the book key on interviewing across cultural lines and covering diverse populations.

- Introduce new research skills in using databases and computer-assisted reporting.

- Integrate law and/or ethics into each chapter, rather than relegating them to the end of the book where they're rarely read.

- Provide exercises and assignments that force students to identify the news, report it and then either explain what they've found (for introductory-level courses) or write stories (for second-level courses).

WAYS TO USE THIS BOOK

Right now, this book should appeal to instructors of traditional second-level and public-affairs classes for newspaper and radio/TV news majors. Students in these courses typically must come up with story ideas, research them, conduct interviews, get sound and/or video (in R/TV courses) and write or produce multiple stories during the term. Some of these courses are beat-based. Some introduce students to Internet reporting and the rudiments of computer-assisted reporting. Most build on the writing skills learned in a previous course that has emphasized writing in a laboratory setting. What's new to all students in these second-level classes is an emphasis on original reporting, information gathering, story development and analysis. Students in broadcast also may be introduced for the first time to the special technical challenges of reporting for television and radio.

We hope that this text eventually might serve as the cornerstone of a new kind of introductory course—one that puts reporting first. Reporting precedes writing in the newsroom. We think it should as well in the classroom, where boot-camp drills in the inverted pyramid tend to dull rather than develop the curiosity and persistence so critical for quality journalism.

ACKNOWLEDGMENTS

We'd like to give our special thanks to the faculty and staff of the S. I. Newhouse School of Public Communications at Syracuse University for their support and resources during this project. We also appreciate the research assistance given us by Deepa Bharath, Chris Pollone and Rana Said.

Thanks also to the staff and management of *NewsCenter 5 (WCVB-TV), New England Cable News, The Boston Globe* and *WBZ-AM* for allowing us to watch their organizations at work and shadow their reporters. And thanks to the dozens of reporters, editors, photographers and producers who took time in their busy lives to talk with us about how they approach their jobs.

The news business changes rapidly, and many of the reporters, editors, producers and videographers quoted in this book have moved on to new jobs and other news organizations since we interviewed them. For purposes of this book, we have identified most in the positions they held at the time they shared their insights and expertise with us.

Every writer needs an editor, and this book would not be what it is without the gentle guidance of Shirley Biagi. Nor would we have succeeded without the detailed critiques and helpful suggestions of the professors who reviewed the book:

R. Thomas Berner, *The Pennsylvania State University*

Sharon Bramlett-Solomon, *Arizona State University*

Steve Corman, *Columbia College*

Arnold Ismach, *University of Oregon*

Dianne Lynch, *Saint Michael's College*

Christopher H. Schmitt, *Santa Clara University*

Erna Smith, *San Francisco State University*

Paul Voakes, *Indiana University*

Special thanks go to Steve Rutter, publisher at Pine Forge Press, for his patience in awaiting this book and his insightful comments along the way.

Finally, thanks to our families for understanding when we disappeared on weekends, in early mornings or in late evenings to do some more work on "the book."

We would like to acknowledge and thank all the individuals who granted permission to reprint and use the photographs that appear in this book.

CHAPTER 1

Introduction

As a correspondent for the Fort Lauderdale, Fla., *Sun-Sentinel,* Ernie Torriero has visited the burned-out shells of black churches in the South and seen the charred hulls of bombed buses in Tel Aviv. He is a storyteller, a reporter who grew up with the best traditions of print journalism. But today, filing stories for his newspaper is only part of his job.

Sometimes, when his reporting is done, he'll call in updates on the news to the paper's audiotext service, a telephone headline system. Sometimes he files a version to the Internet site, the online service of his paper's parent company, the *Chicago Tribune.* Sometimes he readies himself to be interviewed by the all-news radio station with which his paper has an agreement. Other days he finds himself in front of a camera at the *Sun-Sentinel*'s cable television operation.

Ernie Torriero

"I really want to emphasize that this isn't just me," says Torriero, who has been named Florida's reporter of the year. "It's every reporter here. We want to be the sole information source. We're really getting away from the idea that we just sit here and write stories."

NEWS IS CHANGING

Sound a bit dizzying? Well, consider this: The revolution in new media technologies has just begun. No one is quite sure how most Americans will get their news a few decades from now. Sure, it's a safe bet that traditional newspapers, national television news operations and all-news radio won't vanish anytime soon. But there are plenty of new kids on the block, and others are threatening to move in.

Already it's possible to read customized newspapers in some cities, to view interactive multimedia news, to tune in to radio and television news 24 hours a day as it happens and then to dive into the news on hundreds of online outlets in as much depth as your appetite and time allow. And already most of those hot new online outlets seem to be little more than the primitive pioneers in a world of electronics that could soon wed the speed of cable and the interactivity of the computer to forge news outlets that truly integrate all media.

ABOUT THIS BOOK

In this book we won't attempt to predict how well the new forms of news media will catch on or exactly what form they will take. (If someone had given us the inside answer, we'd be out investing.) Instead, we will teach you the skills needed to operate as a news gatherer—a reporter—who, like Ernie Torriero, may have to produce news for several media at once. We'll do that by ignoring the traditional, and often artificial, barriers of form that separate print and broadcast textbooks. This book will concentrate on how to find interesting stories and gather quality content using everything from the old-fashioned interview to newfangled advanced searches on the Internet. We'll show how stories find their way into varied forms—in print, in broadcast and online. And we'll bring you the tips and techniques of reporters who gather news for all of them.

We think there are good reasons for doing this book differently from most journalism textbooks. For one thing, we believe it is likely the reporters of the future will end up working for more than one medium over the course of their careers. This book exposes young reporters to reporting techniques and their application in a variety of media.

For another, we believe that no matter what form news will take in the 21st century, reporters trained to find the best stories, discover them first and report them thoroughly will succeed, no matter where they work. That is why the emphasis of this book is on reporting, from the framing of an idea to its delivery to an audience.

In his textbook, "The Process of Writing News," R. Thomas Berner writes that news writing "is a process, 90 percent of which is not putting words on paper." We heartily agree.

Yet most textbooks on reporting and writing devote most of their space and energy to the 10 percent. They tell students a lot about how to write news. They tell those same students little about how to find, background, develop and frame news—skills without which writers have little to say.

WHERE STORIES BEGIN

This book starts with what we consider the logical beginning: where to find great ideas. It progresses through chapters that show how professionals in all media turn those ideas into stories that are authoritative, human and compelling enough to hold and inform their audience.

All these chapters are informed by one overriding philosophy: We believe reporting and writing news begins with thinking. Reporters chasing the same unfolding events ask themselves a series of questions. What's the news? What's the story? What information do I need? What approach should I take? How can I grab and hold my audience while staying true to the facts?

Reporters keep asking these and other questions as they gather the news. They challenge their own assumptions as well as those of others. They look for facts that tell and examples that show. They push for one more detail, one more interview, one more nugget that gets them closer to the truth. It takes more than luck to get there. It takes tireless work.

The chapters that follow will give you thousands of tips on how to think about and report stories so that those you write are indeed the "news" rather than the "olds"—a rehash of what everyone has done before. These tips will help you build pieces of information that result in stories others will turn to and talk about.

Only at the end of this book's first section, once you have a firm grounding in news-gathering techniques, do we introduce you to writing techniques. In Chapter 8 we will look at how various media approach telling the same story. We'll give you tips about organizing, shaping and layering stories for print, broadcast and online.

That chapter begins on page 96. But in a sense, you will have been writing as you read all the pages that precede it. That is because writing, we believe, is a process that begins at the inception of an idea. Great stories have three ingredients: great ideas, great reporting and great writing. Without the first two, the writing alone can't carry your story or capture your audience. As simple as that may sound, it is a fact often overlooked in the journalism classroom.

BEAT REPORTING

The second part of this book will take you beyond the fundamental skills of the reporter's craft to more specialized skills practiced in modern newsrooms. We will introduce you to covering **beats**—areas of responsibility in which reporters specialize. These beat chapters will take you beyond the crucial but sometimes confining skills needed to cover institutions. Already the phrase, "cover the beat and not the building" has found its way into newsrooms. Coverage of the so-called quality-of-life issues—health and environment, spirituality and community—has taken a prominent place alongside coverage of the actions of city governments, school boards, courts and police. All of our beat chapters emphasize this broader definition of news and news coverage.

If emerging research skills and the message of change are at the heart of this book, so, too, are the established and unassailable skills—from sound interviewing techniques to strong source development—that remain foundations for the reporter at work. The way people learn of the news could change rapidly in the multimedia decades ahead. And the resources reporters use to find information undoubtedly will continue to expand. But we'll bet the skills emphasized here will remain true. Interesting news, regardless of its form, will continue to rely on the goods you, the reporter, bring back to the office or tell from the field. It all starts by turning a curious eye toward the world.

CHAPTER 2

Finding and Framing Stories

Most reporters would have chalked it up as a lost night.

Boston Globe intern Manny Lopez had put nearly 100 miles on his car in search of Mo Vaughn, the Boston Red Sox first baseman. And now, for the sixth time, he'd struck out. Vaughn, who had gotten mixed up in a different kind of slugging contest—with a girlfriend's former boyfriend—wasn't to be found at a luxury condominium complex in Braintree, Mass. It later turned out he was at police headquarters.

Lopez went home without a story that night. But he didn't go home empty handed. Searching for Vaughn, he met a man who told him the condominiums were in a converted high school. What's more, the man and other residents had once been enrolled there.

Lopez liked the idea of former students returning to live where they'd learned their p's and q's. He called the management company, got more names, and tracked down a former teacher at the school who now lived in his old homeroom.

Lopez had his story. It began like this:

> BRAINTREE—When John LeRoy was a teacher at the old Braintree High School, students were not allowed to sleep in his homeroom class. For the last two years, however, LeRoy has done just that.
>
> *The Boston Globe*

Lopez is still a relative newcomer in the ranks of reporting. But he says six years of bartending taught him that many of the best stories are found with your ears.

"You learn to listen to people and find something interesting in what they say," he says.

Reporters who wait for assignments—dreaming of the day they'll get handed the Big Disaster, the Exclusive Interview or the Historic Moment—need to take a harder look at what the news business is really about.

"I find that a lot of reporters, especially younger television reporters today, expect things to be handed to them," laments Beth Willon, a veteran television reporter at *KNTV-TV* in San Jose, Calif.

"The best reporters never need to get an assignment," says Charles Sennott, a project reporter for *The Boston Globe*.

Nor do they find their big stories through luck. Like Lopez, they look—and listen—for them.

This chapter will emphasize ways of finding stories, like the one Lopez happened upon, that are not announced, that don't come packaged in a document, that aren't the intentional tips of a carefully cultivated source. In each of the beat chapters later in this book you will learn to report on basic news stories, from covering a fire to covering a city council meeting. But we believe, and will preach throughout this book, that the best reporters don't wait for news to happen.

As Donald Murray, dean of writing coaches, wrote in his book, "Writing for Your Readers" (see Recommended Reading): "A good way to measure the vigor of a newspaper is to count the number of good stories that were not produced by the calendar, the police radio, the competitor's newspaper, the publisher's second cousin, or the PR release."

The same applies to good radio and good television. As online staffs grow, it will apply to the new multimedia news outlets as well.

Curiosity, it is said, can't be taught. But thinking of ways to apply it can be. Join us and we'll show you. This chapter will help you to:

■ Understand the different news needs of different media
■ Categorize different types of news
■ Develop skills at finding fresh stories and approaches

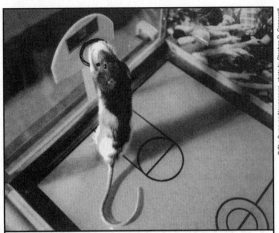

Good reporters don't merely listen. They find stories in the darndest places. We wonder: Just how do you teach a mouse to play basketball?

NOTICING THE NEWS AROUND US

Tony Melfi, a photojournalist (also called a videographer) at *WTVH-TV* in Syracuse, N.Y., was curious when he noticed what looked like a couple of security cameras mounted on 10-foot-tall towers alongside area highways. He alerted the assignment desk. While Melfi shot video, reporter Keith Kobland made some phone calls. The mini-towers, he discovered, were part of a new automated system being set up to monitor winter weather conditions, a story worth doing in a city that averages more than 100 inches of snow a year.

Melfi and Kobland always are attuned to visuals: For television reporters, finding the news means not only getting the information but also finding the sound and pictures to tell the story.

To Mike Sugerman, a radio reporter at *KCBS-AM* in San Francisco, the key ingredient is sound. He listens as he walks to work over the city's narrow, hilly streets. That is why he noticed the soothing sounds of a clarinet floating from a North Beach barbershop one day. The barber, he discovered, for decades had whiled away his slow times playing his clarinet. It was a nice feature—especially on radio.

"The sound is the picture in radio," says Sugerman, who has painted that picture at *KCBS-AM* since 1982. "It illustrates what you want to say."

If curious reporters wander with their eyes and ears, they also wander with their minds. They meander through offbeat and obscure magazines just as they would an unfamiliar neighborhood. They monitor talk radio. They take note of what themes or issues resonate with friends and acquaintances, bouncing ideas off each other to test and shape them.

"Some of our best ideas come from photographers and reporters just sitting around and brainstorming," says *WTVH-TV*'s Kobland.

Today's enterprising reporters have expanded their intellectual journey by wandering through new communities for ideas—those in cyberspace. There, reporters can mine different points of view on a story as easily as they can move from an electronic discussion group of the Religious Right to one rallying support for abortion rights (see

Chapter 4). They can answer questions about the performance of government or inequities in the courts by massaging massive amounts of data on their personal computers. And instead of taking a source to lunch, they can bring a brown bag and eat their sandwich while chatting with new-found sources and tipsters over e-mail (see Chapter 5).

"If you're not hanging out on a discussion group, you're not covering your beat," says Nora Paul, who trains journalists at The Poynter Institute for Media Studies in St. Petersburg, Fla., on how to navigate through the wealth of information and ideas available on the Internet.

Whether they are gleaned from new avenues or old, from a chat by modem or a conversation at a corner bar, good story ideas come from concentration and cultivation. They come to reporters who make connections between things they've heard and seen at different times. They come to reporters who look at more than the moment, who ask questions about what came before and what comes next. And they come to reporters who realize that the work of *finding* good stories is every bit as important as the work of reporting thoroughly or writing fluidly.

TARGETING AN ANGLE

Photographers can provide great pictures. Reporters can capture countless facts and details. Producers and editors can make language flow. But the same rule applies in news as it does in computers: garbage in, garbage out. If the story isn't worth covering, or if it's old, or weary, or overdone, readers, listeners and viewers will move on.

It is possible to think about and look at what's around you in ways that make it easier to find news that is fresh and interesting. What you are seeking is a new approach, a different **angle** to a story. Think photographically for a minute. Roy Peter Clark, a senior scholar at The Poynter Institute, talks of a magnificent, prize-winning photograph of slugger Babe Ruth right before his retirement. It is taken from the back and shows old No. 3 being photographed by a horde of other photographers. The picture worked so well because the photographer had found a fresh angle, an approach no one else was taking. Reporters can do the same.

Not all news needs a fresh angle. Much breaking news is built on facts—information of a fire, an arrest, a vote not previously reported. Broadcasters, in particular, rely on the immediacy of this information to hold their audience. But news is more than new information. Some stories, like that picture of the Babe, take existing information and cast light on it in ways that help readers, viewers and listeners understand. Stories can explain as well as inform, often by drawing connections between seemingly disparate events. Still other news looks beyond the blizzard of information in our lives and makes sense of smaller pieces, often through the eyes and experiences of people affected.

Earlier generations of reporters might have classified these stories as backgrounders, explainers, news features or slices of life. In the past, news was more narrowly defined, and there were fewer outlets for it. Today, the story that did not necessarily happen minutes or hours ago can be found nearly as often on the front page or at the top of newscasts as can the latest fire or murder.

But let's start at the beginning. The first step in covering any kind of story is understanding the ingredients of news. This will help you know where to start and how to approach the story, whether it comes over the transom or you are sent in search of it.

THE NATURE OF NEWS

News used to be simpler to define.

More than a century ago, an editor at the *New York Sun* opined: "If a dog bites a man, it's not news. If a man bites a dog, it's news."

That, of course, would still hold true. The *unusual* makes news. So does a good fight; *conflict* sells. It would help, of course, if this man was a local fellow and if he did this dastardly deed just a few hours ago. *Proximity* and *timeliness* are two other traditional measures of news. And it would help even more if either the man or his unfortunate victim were celebrities—perhaps the Budweiser dog or Lassie II. Because like it or not, *prominence* makes news. We are all gossips at heart.

But these days the world—and the news—is more complicated than whatever deviates from the norm close to home in the recent past or whatever smacks of celebrity. People expect the news to help them make sense of their lives, to help them learn more about the world, to help them make decisions.

To underscore this point, let's turn to a less frivolous example. "If a terrorist's bomb explodes in the World Trade Center, that's news," an exasperated professor once told a New York University journalism class years before that terrorist act actually took place. "If the building is standing, just as it is every day, that isn't news."

Surely any World Trade Center bomb fits all the conventional precepts of news named above. An added measure of that story's importance would be the bomb's *impact,* both in depth and breadth. People may be killed—the ultimate impact. Ghoulish or not, the more dead and injured, the bigger the story, the more prominent the play. A reporter measuring impact also would take account of how much property damage was suffered and who was inconvenienced.

These, again, are traditional measures of news. But in today's news world, it's no longer good enough to dismiss the thousands of people streaming in and out of the World Trade Center until a bomb explodes or something else goes really wrong.

Today, for example, readers and viewers hunger for what is known among journalists as *news you can use.* On an average day when the roads are a mess, the news you can use may be a map of the best way to get to the World Trade Center's garage while the city does maintenance work out front. It may mean a story about the city's hottest discount travel agent operating in the building. News you can use gives information the audience can act on directly—in this case, either by taking a different route to work or by booking a cheap ticket.

Consumers also want *news that explains* how the world is changing. Perhaps a reporter who h s sources in the World Trade Center has spotted a subtle trend—three or four companies have started on-site da care in the last month. Why? Is this a sign of the changing face of the business world? Or perhaps the reporter has noticed that the building's directory reflects rapid growth in consulting firms servicing clients who have downsized and replaced salaried workers with outsiders. Explanatory journalism helps us see trends and better understand how the world around us works.

Thinking about these categories of news can help answer two questions young reporters should always ask and be able to answer: Why should my readers or listeners or viewers care about this story? What do I need to tell them to make the story reasonably complete?

When reporters don't know the answers to these two questions, they often propose broad-ranging ideas instead of stories with specific angles or approaches that reflect something new, changing or downright unusual: a snarling man who goes after dogs, for example.

"I want to write something about women's college sports," a student might say. Or, "I want to pe a story about zoos."

OK. What story about women's sports? What story about zoos? These are broad ideas. The reporter needs an angle.

In looking for an angle, it helps to start close to home, something in the proximity of your reader or viewers. And it helps to be timely, to "come off" what's in the news.

How about the latest Supreme Court decision demanding true equality of funding for men's an women's sports on campus? How will it affect my local campus? Didn't we recently report that the city zoo open d a natural habitat for its gorillas? How is that working? How have the animals' behaviors changed?

With experience, journalists don't need to ask themselves what category of news a particular story falls into. But finding the best stories and angles continues to take thought. And there are ways to think that will improve your skill at originating good stories.

A DOZEN WAYS TO SEE THE WORLD

"Ideas," says Thomas Winship, former editor of *The Boston Globe,* "are the name of the game in daily journalism."

Reporters can never ignore the daily barrage of news that comes over the police scanner, the 24-hour news channel, the wire services. Good journalists listen to radio news on the way to work and the way home. They scan **daybooks**—wire service listings of the day's events—in search of an interesting story or the seed of an interesting idea.

But sometimes there are more interesting ways of covering the news than gravitating to the event itself. The reporter, for example, may not bother covering that press conference on a new grant for the battered women's shelter. Instead the event may serve as a **news peg**, a timely justification for looking at the challenges some women, driven from their homes by abusive spouses, face in putting their lives back together.

And reporters needn't wait for someone else to call a press conference before they tackle a topic. Some days are slow news days. The best reporters relish these to go after their own angles.

The rest of this chapter covers a dozen ways reporters can stay ahead of the crowd.

START WITH YOUR OWN EXPERIENCES

Mike Sugerman was aghast when the bill came. His young son had just had his tonsils removed. And the itemized hospital bill listed a $50 charge for a single diaper. Sugerman could have complained loudly. Or he could have paid and gone home in disgust. Instead, he asked why, and he turned the answer into a radio report for his station, KCBS-AM.

When Sugerman discovered he'd been charged for an entire pack of diapers, he put on his reporter's hat and began interviewing hospital officials. He did a story about how hospitals run up bills because they know insurance companies will pony up the money. It was an interesting insight into a medical system run amok.

"It's the stuff that comes out of your own life that people relate to the most because they also go through it," says Sugerman.

Sugerman's approach and his advice are sound. Plenty of things that frustrate us in our daily lives make interesting news for everyone. Cursing the construction on the way to work? Amazed at the rapid run-up in milk prices? Drawn in by the rich aroma of coffee shops cropping up all over? You might have a story.

Mike Sugerman

The trick is to notice what's new around you and to ask about it before some other journalist does.

READ EVERYTHING

The short wire story out of Oregon told of plans for a reunion of the crew members of the ill-fated Pueblo, a U.S. naval vessel captured by North Korea in the late 1960s. It would take place in San Diego, and some of the crew members quoted lived in northern California.

So Charlie McCollum, then an editor for the *San Jose (Calif.) Mercury News,* printed the story and assigned a reporter to look into it. When the reunion took place, a reporter from the *Mercury News* was the only media representative there.

Although editors at every newspaper and broadcast outlet scan the wires for breaking news, they're often too hurried to think what is behind or beyond the day's news. Yet many wonderful stories—like that of the Pueblo crew—

are as nearby as a stray paragraph buried in the steady stream of wire stories transmitted into newsrooms each day.

"You've got to read everything," says McCollum, a veteran who has recently returned to reporting. "And you've got to read AP [Associated Press] stories to the end because sometimes the lead is buried in the 15th paragraph."

The best reporters don't stop with scanning the wires. They read specialized newsletters and publications. They read government reports and budgets. They flip through magazines and peruse bulletin boards. They scan their own paper, listen to their own radio station, watch their own television channel's newscasts. Then they turn to the competition.

None of this is idle curiosity. It's a way for their minds to wander even while their feet remain firmly planted atop their desks. Reporters want to find new ideas before they percolate into the mainstream media, or new angles that make old news fresh.

Barry Bearak, then a national reporter for the *Los Angeles Times*, wasn't the first to write about drug dealers taking over apartment houses in New York City and terrorizing the law-abiding citizens who lived in them. But when he read about the trend in *The New York Times*, he found it a story worth telling. So he found a new way—a new angle. Bearak brought the story to life by recounting the tale of a Bronx building where addicts had stolen the plumbing fixtures to sell on the street and where the residents had organized to fight back.

Like McCollum at the *Mercury News*, he knew that a smaller, specific story about real people can create greater interest and have a greater impact than a piece filled with numbers but few faces. The story began like this:

> The parallels are haunting. John P. Royster, the father, and John J. Royster, the son. Both smart, both drifters, both spurned by a woman—both accused murderers.
>
> Set contrapuntally, the two stories seem too simple, and too cruelly fatalistic, the plot line of uninspired fiction. But as a fuller picture began to coalesce yesterday of John J. Royster, the 22-year-old man who the police said confessed to four bru-
>
> tal crimes, the most striking conclusion that surfaced was how a young man largely raised by his mother led his father's life.
>
> The father, interviewed yesterday in prison and speaking of his son's bright side, summed up the likenesses they shared concisely, "He's a chip off the old block."
>
> *The New York Times*

Go Wandering

We'll tell you this more than once: There is no substitute for getting away from the phone, fax and computer to see, smell and hear what's going on outside. Reporters often lament that they are too busy to look for fresh stories and fresh sources of information. Perhaps. But in a world saturated with information, those who forget that news ultimately involves telling fresh stories may find their viewers or listeners are too bored to buy their paper or turn on their broadcasts.

Wandering can be a great way to find news that no one announces and that has a human face. When reporters stroll through unfamiliar neighborhoods, chat with parents in the park, ask shop owners how business is, they usually leave with an unexpected story. As an editor at the *San Jose Mercury News*, one of this book's authors regularly gave reporters "wandering days," urging them to visit a place or a part of the city they'd never seen before.

One reporter who needed no prompting was Mike Cassidy, who has a knack for seeing stories all around him. Pass a house with handmade windmills in the yard? There's a story there. See a quirky street bearing the city's name? Another story. See someone still living in an area cleared out by airport expansion? Cassidy has written that one as well.

The new city ordinance had made some people plenty angry.

The Houston City Council wanted to slap tougher restrictions on sexually oriented businesses and the women who danced in them. So it required all the entertainers, many of whom operated for their own safety under pseudonyms, to display licenses with their real names and addresses for all the clubs' clients to see.

At *KHOU-TV*, Hamilton Masters learned of the heated fallout over the council's action by reading on the **Internet**, the new communications medium that has exploded from a government research network to a source of just about everything.

Masters, a reporter/producer and longtime computer hobbyist, regularly monitors the Usenet newsgroups *alt.Houston. general* and *alt.Houston.politics* to find out what people are talking about (more on these in Chapter 4). This wandering leads to news before it's announced.

KHOU-TV beat the rest of the local media in reporting about the stir over the new licenses. And it quickly followed with a second story. Someone, Masters discovered, had found a way of getting back at the council members for requiring the licenses. That individual had created a new Web site—with the home addresses and phone numbers of city council members and maps directing people to their homes.

Chris Swingle, a reporter at the *Rochester (N.Y.) Democrat and Chronicle* has used the Internet to solidify story hunches and give those stories scope. Swingle, who has worked a nontraditional "trends" beat, received a fax one day from a company whose business is reminding people not to forget their relatives' birthdays. Because she tries to avoid writing about individual companies, Swingle set out to see whether others were doing the same thing. She typed *birthday reminder* in the Yahoo! search engine on the **World Wide Web** and found a variety of services, along with the fodder for a good story (more on search engines in Chapter 4).

Swingle did the same when a friend told her she'd seen a furniture store with a throwback to the 1970s—inflatable furniture. Once again Swingle went to Yahoo! (a portion of the Internet) and typed *inflatable furniture* into the search slot. "It turned out to be a fun story with lots of photos," she recalls. And the story was picked up by the wires.

Some people have a knack for seeing what's right before their eyes, but you can develop the skill with practice. The senses seem to sharpen in unfamiliar settings. So drive a different route to work; sit someplace where people congregate; sign up for a local walking tour. A piece of news likely will sneak up and surprise you.

Just ask Tram Nguyen. During her first week interning at *The Boston Globe,* she was driving in a part of that city she hadn't yet visited when she spotted a Chinese funeral home. She checked and discovered it was not only new but also the city's first. She also learned that the city's growing Buddhist population had had difficulty finding anyplace that could perform burial services according to custom.

All that because she kept her eyes open on the way to lunch.

KEEP YOUR EARS OPEN

Reporters treasure their **sources**, the people to whom they talk on a regular basis to keep up with the news in their assigned area, or beat (see Chapter 5). Reporters call their sources routinely to ask, "What's happening?" The result can be tips—leads to stories. And strangers call with tips, too. The tip may be news of a blazing fire, an extraordinary teacher or an official with a penchant for taking "working" vacations at the public's expense.

The fact is, anyone can be a source, from the switchboard operator to the man Manny Lopez talked to in the condo-complex parking lot. That is why reporters are never hesitant to ask questions, show a genuine interest in who is talking, and listen to the answers. They are always filing away ideas, monitoring that inner voice that whispers, "That's a story," even as they pursue others.

It happens to Mike Sugerman of *KCBS-AM* news radio all the time. He was working on a documentary on the emotional and financial costs of violence when he rode to the hospital with a paramedic.

"He put on the red light and started bitching that no one pulls over any more," says Sugerman. "Well, that's a good story."

And a story he soon did.

Working on the same project, he discovered that doctors and nurses at a city hospital considered themselves in danger because would-be assassins sometimes walked the corridors in an effort to finish a job they'd botched.

That was a story, too.

LOOK FROM A DIFFERENT POINT OF VIEW

Sometimes reporters find stories by looking at a conventional event from a less predictable perspective, or point of view. Take a trial, for example. A reporter who doesn't go beyond the daily drama of who said what on the stand misses many good stories that can be seen by looking at events from a slightly different viewpoint. For example, the reporter might also choose to view the trial:

- Through the eyes of the victim reliving the crime
- Through the anguish of the suspect's family
- Through the talk in the neighborhood where the crime was committed
- By reading the faces and questions of jurors
- By capturing the drama of the dueling lawyers
- From the perspective of those who analyze evidence under a microscope
- From the carnival of media coverage

By looking for what makes people and institutions tick, reporters often find the best stories.

In following up on the arrest of John J. Royster, accused in a murder and three other vicious attacks in a New York City crime spree, N. R. Kleinfeld wrote a powerful follow story from the perspective of Royster's father. Here is how it started:

> The parallels are haunting. John P. Royster, the father, and John J. Royster, the son. Both smart, both drifters, both spurned by a woman—both accused murderers.
>
> Set contrapuntally, the two stories seem too simple, and too cruelly fatalistic, the plot line of uninspired fiction. But as a fuller picture began to coalesce yesterday of John J. Royster, the 22-year-old man who the police said confessed to four brutal crimes, the most striking conclusion that surfaced was how a young man largely raised by his mother led his father's life.
>
> The father, interviewed yesterday in prison and speaking of his son's bright side, summed up the likenesses they shared concisely, "He's a chip off the old block."
>
> *The New York Times*

MEASURE CHANGE

Who is moving to town and who is moving out? Have rents and housing prices pushed upwards on the east side? Are more students crowding lower grades? How much have teachers' salaries changed, and how does that compare to state and national norms?

Measuring change generates news. Too often, however, reporters stop with the numbers instead of giving them a human face. They write about reports, not the people behind them or the people affected by them. Stories that combine statistics and humanity have far more impact.

Edwin Garcia of the *San Jose Mercury News* realized the human side was missing when he saw a census chart in a rival newspaper. That story identified North Fair Oaks, a community about an hour south of San Francisco, as a place where Spanish had become so common it remained a first rather than a second language for much of the population. Garcia realized there was a story behind the numbers. He spent time in the community and wrote a story that captured its flavor—a story that, unlike the competition's chart, ran on Page 1.

"There was a chart and it was a good chart," Garcia said of the competitor's graphic, which measured the number of people who spoke Spanish in different communities in the Bay Area. "But I couldn't believe nobody had done a story on this specific community. I did a lot of door-to-door walking through the neighborhood to try to put a human face on what the numbers showed. I found out from that that there was a whole life (on the Peninsula) that people didn't know about. Maybe they do now."

Anniversaries of key events can provide a good news peg to measure change. Anniversaries allow comparison of present to past, making it easier to measure change.

The fact that a 20-pound striped bass can be caught near New York City these days would hardly make compelling news if the river hadn't been so heavily polluted just a few

Edwin Garcia, of the *San Jose Mercury News,* has learned to frame stories through the eyes of people who are living those stories.

decades ago. But it was, so *The New York Times* wrote a two-part, front-page series on "reversing pollution's toll." Here is an excerpt from William Stevens' first-day story:

> The scope of change is huge. Raw sewage no longer flows routinely into the river. Toxic contamination has been drastically reduced. There are no more summertime dead spots. People swim in the Hudson now. Recreational fishermen in charter boats dot the water.
>
> *The New York Times*

COMPARE AND CONTRAST

Voters in one suburb pass a curfew to keep teens off the street after midnight. Voters in another defeat a similar measure. Taken individually, these stories would barely be of passing interest to people outside the individual towns. But a story comparing the two towns and their opposite conclusions would have broader appeal.

Reporters should consider themselves in the business of looking for comparisons that stretch beyond the geographical or psychological boundaries of their particular beat. If one police department, for example, decides to get officers out of patrol cars and back onto street beats to prevent rather than investigate crime, a few calls can help a reporter provide **context**—a sense of how unusual or commonplace this action is.

By looking for comparisons and contrasts, reporters also can shed light on the difference between public perception and reality, as Margot Adler of *National Public Radio* did when she filed a report about New York's Central Park that began like this:

> The murder of a woman jogging in New York's Central Park last month confirms the view of many people outside the city that the park is a haven for urban predators.
>
> *National Public Radio*

But statistics, Adler went on, suggest it may be one of the city's safest places.

In comparing, reporters can stumble on patterns of action or behavior. They also can set out specifically to look for them.

Computers can help here, and that is why more newsrooms are devoting resources and training to computer-assisted teams and projects (See Chapter 4). By using a computer to help organize and evaluate hiring, promotion and salary records, for example, reporters can determine whether discriminatory practices have blocked the path of women and people of color in local government. They can review which government officials have rung up the highest travel expenses and which keep ringing up friends on work phones. Data can show patterns.

But reporters needn't rely exclusively on computers to notice relationships or to write about them. An individual daytime burglary in an affluent neighborhood may not warrant a story. But an alert police reporter might notice a pattern of such burglaries and check to see whether they are being carried out by the same suspect.

Stories that trace a pattern of action or behavior in several communities or places often are called **trend stories**. Trend pieces are broad in scope. A piece on efforts to get more police onto the streets, for example, might include the latest crime statistics and how they're changing. It also would include quotes from experts on criminal justice, local officials, shop owners and residents. In putting together the piece, the reporter would likely get video, sound or description as police walk the neighborhood, talking with people on the beat.

LOOK FOR THE LOCAL CONNECTION

News gains importance when it hits close to home. So **localizing** news—finding the local reaction to, or impact of, state, national and international events—is a staple of reporting. When the federal government closes down because Congress is bickering over a budget, readers in Houston, Texas, want to read about or hear stories about the impact on federal workers there, not in Washington.

If the wire services send out a story about students teaching their teachers how to get around on the Internet, any self-respecting news organization will check with local schools to see if the same thing is happening.

And when hundreds of thousands of black American men journeyed to Washington for the Million Man March, many local news organizations told the story through the eyes of participants from their own area. The *St. Louis Post-Dispatch,* for example, began its story on the day of the march like this:

> Christopher Taylor may be only 15, but today he joins hundreds of thousands of black men in Washington for what he hopes will be a historic day.
>
> . . . "This is a great way to help stop the social problems we have—gangs and drug dealers," Tay-lor said, as he waited to board a bus in north St. Louis. "We need a change in our community. We must begin to look at things differently."
>
> *St. Louis Post-Dispatch*

GET AHEAD OF THE CURVE

Too often, reporters are content to wait for the speech, the event, the meeting or the demonstration to write anything about it. **Previews** of predictable news, called **advances** in the print media, serve three purposes. They alert viewers, readers and listeners to the event in time to participate. They can help frame the debate and thus shape

LOCALIZING NEWS

Buying into the adage that "all news is local" doesn't mean that all reporters need to stay close to home or ignore the relationship of their community with the rest of the world. Beth Willon of *KNTV-TV* in San Jose, Calif., understood that well. It earned her a three-week visit to Vietnam and led to a 10-part series on the ties between that country and the city where she covered the news.

"Something that really hits you like a bolt of lightning when you talk to the Vietnamese in San Jose is how much their hearts are still in Vietnam," says Willon, who often found herself covering stories about the 50,000-strong Vietnamese-American community there. "That was one of the deciding factors to me in proposing the series. I could see there was this very, very strong tie."

With the help of a Vietnamese-American intern at her station, Willon spent more than a month preparing for her journey, timed to run around the 20th anniversary of the collapse of the South Vietnamese government.

Her stories were personal. They were visual. They were emotional. And they were highly local.

One looked at San Jose State University students who had journeyed to Vietnam to teach English, a language now mandatory in government schools but once forbidden. Another showed an orphanage. The nun who ran it had built it with money sent by her family in San Jose, a family 14,000 miles away whom she had not seen in many years. A third told the story of two couples returning to see relatives whom some hadn't seen since their childhood.

"I must have gone through every contact I had in town," Willon recalls. "That story was the hardest. Nobody here wanted anybody to know they were going back because it is still looked down on. They were terrified about backlash."

But Willon got her story. She accompanied a couple to the Mekong Delta, capturing on tape the reunion of a San Jose man and the father he had not seen in 20 years.

its outcome. And they enable reporters to deliver a more interesting perspective than that of public officials droning on in front of a microphone.

When officials in Mountain View, Calif., moved to require businesses to clean up graffiti on their property, *San Jose Mercury News* reporter Melody Peterson wrote about the persistent problem of tagging—and the anger of shop owners being told to deal with it—before the measure came up for a city council vote.

When the same council talked about banning massage parlors it said were nothing but fronts for prostitution, Peterson again got ahead of the competition. She talked to women who said they were legitimate masseuses caught in a nasty political mess.

FOLLOW, FOLLOW, FOLLOW

Every story leads to others, sometimes by the dozens. Take something as innocuous as a big winter snowstorm. The initial roundup likely will include information on how much fell, who was hurt, what was damaged, what was closed. Then the follows begin: stories about the economic impact, the rush to buy snow blowers and the cost crunch of clearing the roads; stories about the environmental impact, the animals deprived of food, the flooded low-lying areas, the salt and gravel runoff in streams; stories about skiing, sledding and the best snow sculpture around town; stories about those who love the snow and those who hate it. The list goes on.

One thing is certain: Any time major news breaks, editors will scramble the next day to see how they can carry the story to the next step. Reporters who come up with their own follow ideas not only are treasured, they're also left alone. They are not tapped to do the dull and predictable follow, like that cutest snowman story.

One way of following stories is to test the claims of those in power. Sometimes the system doesn't work quite the way they say it does.

When San Francisco's mayor told reporters that there were enough beds for the homeless in that city, Mike Sugerman didn't take him at his word. He tried to find a bed himself. "I waited six hours to get a number to come back and wait another hour," Sugerman recalls. "In fact, I didn't get a bed."

Follow-ups aren't confined to the first few days or first few weeks after a story appears. A Detroit TV station once slotted a "Follow Up Desk" segment to run twice a week in its dinner-time newscast. The reporter told viewers what had happened since a story first made news. Similarly, newspapers often run "Whatever Happened To" columns or stories marked "The Update File."

ALWAYS ANSWER THE QUESTION, "WHY?"

Reporters frequently report the resolution of events. They'll tell the story of an 80-year-old woman who earned a college degree or the story of the Olympic athlete who overcame polio to excel in crew. Too often, however, they forget to ask why. Why did that woman go after that degree? What motivated her? What obstacles did she face along the way? How did she overcome them? The answers typically make a far more interesting story than the mere bestowal of the award.

"Most news stories are endings without the beginnings attached," writes two-time Pulitzer Prize winner Jon Franklin in his book, "Writing for Story."

The "why" can make a story more newsworthy as well. And it can save lives. When the Loma Prieta earthquake in California caused the collapse of the Cypress Viaduct, killing several dozen people, subsequent investigations into the overpass design raised questions about the readiness of various roadways statewide to withstand a major earthquake.

By focusing on the why of a ValuJet crash in the Florida Everglades, reporters raised legitimate questions about everything from the transportation of hazardous materials to the adequacy of federal oversight.

When Dave Rummel produced a "60 Minutes" segment tracing how Illinois police had largely abandoned their search for a black family whose partially submerged car later was found less than a mile from police headquarters, he keyed not only on what happened but also on why.

"It was a story about police ineptitude and allegations of racism," Rummel says.

And true to Franklin's assertion, it was a story that Rummel started to follow after reading a one-paragraph "ending" in a newspaper.

BRAINSTORM

Two brains are better than one.

That is important advice to remember when you get stuck for ideas. As simple to do as it should be, reporters and their editors or producers sit down far too infrequently just to kick around ideas. When they do, they're too often desperate for a quick fix—a story to fill a hole for tomorrow.

To work, brainstorming needs to be free from such constraints. The best brainstorming needs some loose focus and complete separation from the twin monsters of time and criticism.

Pick a broad topic such as air travel, teen recreation, volunteerism. That's your loose focus. Get a half dozen people—the more diverse the better—into a room and start throwing out ideas. It might go something like this:

"What's killing me is the cost of flying to Peoria. It costs more to go to small cities than it does to go across the whole country. Why?"

"So I thought deregulation was going to keep costs down. Has it? How do fares compare with markups in other industries since the time of deregulation?"

"Let's look at what you get for the money, too. How many more people are they packing onto flights these days?"

"How about a piece on the art of choosing a seat in this age of no-leg-space travel."

"Speaking of comfort, let's do a mock five-star guide on airlines' food."

"Or figure out how they pick those movies they show. Man."

SUMMARY   FINDING FRESH STORIES

1. A checklist of what makes news includes timeliness, proximity, prominence, impact, conflict, the unusual and usefulness.

2. The best reporters don't wait for an assignment. They come to work brimming with story ideas.

3. Reporters who find good stories read voraciously, listen attentively and wander regularly to places they haven't been before.

4. Enterprising reporters nurture their curiosity. They're often asking why.

5. Covering the event isn't enough. Reporters should write about it beforehand, and then look for follow-up angles afterwards.

6. Good stories come from comparing and contrasting, identifying patterns and measuring change.

"That stuff is great. But when I fly I'm more worried about staying alive than lifestyle. I'd like to see if we can do a story inside the air traffic tower. What's it like to land all those planes?"

"Or to gather the courage to get on them. I'd love to get natural sound inside one of those classes for people who are afraid to fly."

You get the idea. This is pure brainstorming. For it to work, someone should jot down the list of ideas. All the participants should check any tendency to judge and criticize at the door. Only when the list is complete should those who put it together start to sharpen and focus, to set priorities on which stories should be done first and which are worth doing at all. Brainstorming sessions die the minute someone in the group rejects someone else's idea as "stupid."

RECOMMENDED READING

Brooks, J. *Searchable dates archive*. Berkeley, CA: The Daily Globe. [Online]. Available: **http://www.dailyglobe.com/day2day.html**.

Here's a quirky Net site listing observances and historical dates for each day of the year. Looking for a story on August 15? Well it's National Relaxation Day, National Failures Day and National Lemon Meringue Pie Day. Also the day that the first croquet tournament was held and the day the Berlin Wall was completed.

Hyman, V. (1998). *Follow your curiosity to find better stories*. St. Petersburg, FL: The Poynter Institute. [Online]. Available: **http//www.poynter. org/research/rwe/rwe_curious.htm**.

This list of tips on finding stories is directed specifically at broadcast journalists. "Go where the puck isn't," advises Hyman, who directs the broadcast journalism program at The Poynter Institute for Media Studies. She encourages reporters to use photographers as field producers and ask them at the end of interviews whether they have any questions.

Murray, D. (1992). *Writing for your readers*. Chester, CT: Globe Pequot.

This writing handbook, based on interviews with reporters from *The Boston Globe,* contains a marvelous chapter called "Seeing the Obvious." Murray is a great believer in the value of finding enterprise stories and fresh approaches. Other chapters are sprinkled with examples and tips on how to find both.

Zinsser, W. (1994). *Speaking of journalism*. New York: HarperCollins.

During the 1970s, author William Zinsser taught a course in nonfiction writing at Yale University. Many of his students went on to become journalists. For this book, he interviewed 10 of them about how they approach their work. Much of the discussion is about how they approach stories. One chapter's first sentence, from feature writer John Tierney, reads: "For me the biggest challenge in feature writing is to find the angle."

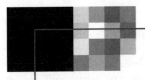

EXERCISES

A. NEWSWORTHINESS

1. Check the item with greater news value, all other things being equal, in each of the following pairs.

a. ____ Food bank begins annual holiday drive.

   ✓ Donor gives food bank month's supply of canned provisions, the largest single donation ever given in the city.

b. ✓ University hires first woman chancellor.

   ____ University fires first woman chancellor.

c. ____ Scientist isolates gene responsible for a rare hereditary disease, putting a treatment within sight.

   ✓ Scientist isolates gene responsible for a widespread hereditary disease, putting a treatment within sight.

d. ____ Naturalists spot flock of Canadian geese heading south for the winter.

   ✓ Naturalists spot pair of endangered American eagles in city park.

e. ____ Eighty firefighters take two hours to put out blaze in empty warehouse. Damage put at $350,000. No one is hurt.

   ✓ Twenty firefighters take 45 minutes to put out blaze in three-story tenement. Three children, ages 1 to 9, die of smoke inhalation.

f. ✓ Police announce street crime has declined by 50 percent in the city's toughest neighborhood since a citizens' patrol, working closely with officers, has begun nighttime patrols.

   ____ Liquor store in city's toughest neighborhood robbed of $325 in cash.

g. ✓ The girls' swim team in your town wins the league title.

   ✓ The girls' swim team in your town finishes second in the state.

h. ✓ A flood in your community leaves 10 families homeless and cuts electricity to 5,000 homes and businesses.

   ____ A flood in the Loire Valley leaves 425 French families homeless and cuts power to hundreds of thousands.

i. ____ The state legislature votes 127-114 to raise tolls on the state turnpike by 5 percent.

   ✓ The main street in town will be closed for a month for complete resurfacing.

j. ____ Local woodworking plant declares a jump in profits of 26 percent over a comparable period last year.

   ✓ Tax assessor announces all businesses and residents can expect their property taxes to go up 6 percent next year.

B. LOOKING FOR NEWS

1. Take a bus, drive or walk to a part of your town you have never visited. Using a street map, walk through the area, noting on a pad anything unusual that you see or hear. What might make a story, what catches your eye as unusual, where do people congregate? Discuss your findings with classmates.

2. Ask a public official or community activist to coffee. (It can be a man or woman. We will use both genders interchangeably in examples.) Ask her to describe her job, her goals when she took that job and how those goals have changed. Ask her what her greatest satisfactions are about the job and her greatest frustrations. Ask whether the subject has achieved what she set out to accomplish over the last year. If not, what are the biggest obstacles remaining to achieving those goals? Return with your notes and discuss with classmates whether the interview provided leads for a story or might be one in itself.

3. Go to a magazine stand or library and spend an hour scanning magazines you normally don't pick

up. Jot down any stories you find interesting or surprising. Discuss with classmates whether these stories could be localized, written about from the unique perspective of the community you live in.

4. Get a budget of the city or school district. Compare it to one from five years ago, looking for those areas that are most markedly different. Find out why they are different. If a program has been eliminated, expanded or curtailed, talk to people involved in it now and before it changed. Ask how things have changed, pushing for facts that measure the change, examples of how it affects people and quotes from the people affected.

5. Find an action by the U.S. Congress or the state legislature that has the potential to affect people in your community. First, using newspaper, broadcast or Internet accounts, read about what transpired. Then discuss how the events might be followed with an article from your area. Who stands to lose or gain by the government's decision? How might the effect of the government's decision be measured? Discuss possible angles and then report on one of them, either writing a story or a news memo when you have finished.

BRAINSTORMING

1. With classmates, discuss the following topics, listing five possible story angles, or approaches, for each. Remember not to judge ideas before all are stated. Only then should you prioritize and further define.

a. Stress

b. Diversity

c. Summer jobs

d. Volunteerism

e. College dating

f. Academic pressure/cheating

g. Computers in education

h. Academic bureaucracy

i. Campus safety

j. Sports and athletes

k. Thanksgiving

l. Memorial Day

CHAPTER 3

A Day in the News

It wasn't a day for Boston's history books. No tea parties or skirmishes on the green. Not even an infamous strangler. Just one miserable January day, one with enough snow to fray tempers, bend bumpers and strain city workers already reeling from the worst blizzard of the decade a few days earlier.

In a sense this Jan. 10 was just like—and just unlike—almost every other day in the news: unpredictable, unmanageable and uneven.

Such is the nature of news. It starts early, takes a nap and snaps your head back minutes before deadline. As hard as producers, editors and reporters try, it never seems to come out as planned.

This is a tough business, making sense of the day's events. For those of you who still think reporting is more glamour than gray cells and elbow grease, modeling may be a better option.

This chapter is designed to:

■ Build on Chapter 2 by helping you see how reporters in different media find and frame stories

■ Take you beyond book learning to show you, rather than tell you, what a day's news is really like

■ Chronicle the news at four news organizations in a single day

So come along and glimpse the patchwork of excitement, frustration, surprise and satisfaction that comes with tracking all good stories. On radio, on television, online and in print, the news of one nasty winter day is about to unfold.

THE MORNING'S STORIES:
SNOW AND MORE SNOW

4:45 a.m. Flo Jonic is used to waking people up; her day at *WBZ-AM* all-news radio starts at 3 a.m. So she doesn't hesitate as she punches in the number of a sleepy Kevin Sullivan, deputy commissioner of the state highway department.

"He drew the short straw," says Jonic, explaining that Sullivan is on call.

Jonic wants to talk about plow operators. They work 16 hours for every eight they're off, Sullivan tells her. And after several days of these monster shifts, they're getting mighty tired.

Jonic knows people on the scene give better interviews than bureaucrats struggling out of bed. So rather than airing the Sullivan interview, she heads for the roadways in search of plow operators.

By 6 a.m. she's ready to air the first of several versions of the story on snow removal. Each will use a different interview segment, called an **actuality.** But all have the same basic message: "If you see a plow," says Jonic. "Stay out of the way. These guys are awfully tired."

5:27 a.m. Click-click. < IMG ALIGN = bottom SRC + "/scvb/triangle.fig" > Jordan Marsh Department Stores will be renamed Macy's.

The symbols look like so much gibberish coming over Neil Ungerleider's screen. But they are computer coding that will change the icons, text and pictures for *5 Online,* the Internet news site for *NewsCenter 5 (WCVB-TV).*

Ungerleider codes in three regional news stories from The Associated Press (AP): the retailer that is changing names, firefighters who are requesting help shoveling out hydrants and reaction to Gov. William Weld's State of the State speech.

He adds the Celtics and Bruins scores, updates the weather forecast and is done in 10 minutes. The news stories will stay up all day, but the weather forecast will change hourly. That's what people are most interested in today.

6:58 a.m. Out in the suburbs, Foxboro is one place the roads are clear and traffic is moving. And that's a problem for TV reporter Leslie Gaydos. She thought she'd be going live for *New England Cable News'* "Early Edition" from an area hard hit by the morning snows, but Mother Nature isn't cooperating. So she improvises, something the staff at the lean 24-hour cable news operation has learned to do of necessity.

"If you come to an area where there's just no story, you just have to keep an open mind," advises Gaydos.

After a quick update of conditions, she plays the "comparison" angle, measuring this morning's snow—not much—against the last storm. Not the stuff of Emmys, no doubt, but it beats dead air.

8:00 a.m. In a sleepy *Boston Globe* newsroom, assistant city editor Patti Wen can afford to be deliberate as she checks the wires, reads a computer page listing events for the day and scans the overnight note from the night city editor. Tomorrow's paper won't hit the streets for 20 hours yet, and right now, there's nothing urgent to jump on.

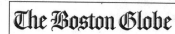

Wen knows that this morning's fender benders and tie-ups probably won't even merit fleeting mention in tomorrow morning's newspaper. When editors gather in a few hours to plan the day's assignments, they'll look behind such news as Weld's speech and ahead for stories that haven't yet aired on the city's broadcast outlets.

8:02 a.m. *WBZ-AM* radio reporter Flo Jonic has become a victim of the gridlock about which she's spent much of the morning reporting. A van has bounced off a snowbank and flipped on the eastbound Massachusetts Turnpike in suburban Newton, and she's somewhere in the line of cars backed up behind it.

"How bad is it?" asks Paul Connearney from the assignment desk. "Like a standstill?"

He barely pauses.

"How about you go live at 8:18?"

That solved, he pivots his chair to update a visitor on the rapid-fire pace of drive-time news. "We try to go after what's affecting people," he says. "And right now, that's traffic and weather."

Connearney is like a juggler who keeps talking with four or five burning torches in the air. He cruises the wires, keeps one ear to the police scanner and another to his staff—all while lining up the next newscast.

"Every half hour has to be different," he says. "We don't want everything repeated."

As news director at *NewsCenter 5* (*WCVB-TV*, Boston), Candy Altman is responsible for the content of the newscasts, as well as their graphic look and all the personnel who put the shows together. Her counterpart in radio is also called a news director. At the newspaper, the top manager is known as the editor or the executive editor.

9:33 a.m. "My friend is a teacher and she's totally depressed," says *NewsCenter 5* producer Mimi Wishner. "They're going to have to work till July."

Wishner's looking for a fresh angle, which is no easy task for her and the news crew as they start the morning meeting. Today is Wednesday and some have barely made it home since the first snowstorm Sunday.

Still, the ideas keep coming: ice dams on roofs, blocked emergency exits at schools, the impact of snow on airline and retail sales.

"What about young people getting heart attacks from their shoveling?" asks news director Candy Altman.

All heads turn to the intern with the medical unit. He also happens to be an emergency room doctor.

"I've never seen it," he says. But he adds, "The rule of thumb is if you don't normally do anything aerobic, you shouldn't shovel snow."

"Now, that's interesting," Altman says, as a producer pencils in the medical reporter for a "shoveling" story.

10:12 a.m. The snow hasn't slowed *Globe* education writer Karen Avenoso. School closings have given her a bit of time to schmooze with school officials in the search for news. And late yesterday, after five calls, she convinced a recalcitrant Boston school official to leak a report on why middle school kids leave city schools.

It had been due for release in two weeks—not soon enough for Avenoso, who is hustling to turn a six-month stint at *The Globe* into a permanent job.

"I got a little itchy," she says. "I'm from New York . . . I really don't like other people to get things first."

10:55 a.m. Mark Mills, *NewsCenter 5*'s money reporter, points to a jagged-line graph on a computer screen.

"Here's a snapshot of July to the present; this is one I can use," he says, referring to his TV story on home heating prices.

Mills found the graph on a terminal tucked in an alcove of *NewsCenter 5*. The terminal is linked online to *Bloomberg Business News,* a news service that sends out hundreds of articles daily.

"I always like to know a lot more than I'm going to need for a story," says Mills, explaining that if he understands the big picture, it's easier to pick out the best elements for his story.

11:03 a.m. David Armstrong knows Massachusetts liquor laws. So he's drawn the assignment at *The Globe* to make sense of Gov. Weld's proposal in his State of the State address to cut beer prices.

Armstrong did a series a year ago on the Byzantine ways of the Massachusetts Alcohol Beverage Control Board. Knowing the system, he realizes, is critical to writing about how it's changing.

"I could never do this story in a day without my earlier investigation," he says. "The biggest problem on a story like this is the learning curve."

He calls up his past stories from the library, checks his personal phone directory for old sources and goes to work.

11:04 a.m. Janet Wu jumps into *NewsCenter 5*'s unmarked beige Blazer and asks her videographer to head for the state house for a follow-up story on the governor's State of the State address. Her angle: the governor's new emphasis on education.

11:57 a.m. No one likes to inherit the competition's story, but it happens. That task is doubly nasty for Ric Kahn today. He's supposed to find some kind of a fresh angle on a juicy Brockton murder that *The Globe* relegated to a news "brief" and the *Boston Herald* played big. The victim was found in his own freezer.

Kahn is a pro at working the police. But he doesn't know Brockton, it's almost noon, and he can't reach the local police or the district attorney—the places he usually starts. He's facing a 5 p.m. deadline to file a "top," the first few paragraphs of his story.

"I'm totally in the dark on this one," says Kahn, a baseball cap pulled low over his forehead. "I'm not sure what I am going to do. Basically whatever I can get by deadline."

He heads for the door and, ultimately, the dead man's house.

MIDDAY: STORIES TAKE SHAPE

12:05 p.m. Not all news is done on the fly.

Tucked in a back office, up a spiral staircase from the hubbub of the newsroom, *NewsCenter 5* reporter/anchor Brian Leary is working on a series that won't air for a month. It's on problems with the mental health system.

"I can present research findings that show we've wasted $80 million and people aren't getting the care that they could have gotten," says Leary.

His research is done, but now he needs to make this into a television story. In such a sensitive story, the pictures and on-camera interviews he needs aren't easy to get.

Leary, who's also an attorney, has spent most of the day negotiating for permission to photograph a mentally handicapped adult.

"If this were a *Globe* story, it would have been published a month ago," Leary insists.

In-depth stories, however, take plenty of time to get into print, too. And each day, city editor Teresa Hanafin faces a balancing act, covering the day's news, planning for the weekends and keeping track of longer-term projects.

This morning, Hanafin has assigned general assignment reporter Matt Bai a weekend piece on the homogenization of Boston following the announcement that Macy's is renaming all Jordan Marsh stores—long considered Boston landmarks.

"It's the Walmartization of the world," Hanafin mutters.

Bai pulls old stories about the influx of chains and the buying out of various Boston institutions. He talks to reporters he knows have written on this subject in the past. And now he's preparing two lists of sources, those who can analyze the trend and those with a personal stake—the losers.

12:12 p.m. Two key sources for Janet Wu's State of the State follow-up story for *NewsCenter 5* are about to get away.

"Go, stop the elevator," videographer Bob Wilson urges her.

So Wu turns in midinterview, runs over to the elevator, sticks her foot in the door, and finds herself face-to-face with Senate President Thomas Birmingham and House Speaker Charles Flaherty.

"Oh guys," she says feigning innocence, "let me ride down in the elevator with you."

Once inside, her tone changes to mock sternness. "All right guys," she says. "Do we have to stop the elevator and nab you for an interview, or are you going to talk to me when we get out?"

Flaherty snaps his fingers. "I thought we'd get away," he says in mock exasperation.

12:28 p.m. The snow is sweeping down, and that's a relief for *New England Cable News* reporter Leslie Gaydos, stationed by now in the city of Lowell. When you're talking snow on live TV, it sure helps to show it falling. Unlike early this morning in Foxboro, this time Gaydos doesn't have to improvise.

"City crews are very, very busy today trying to put together some plan to make room for emergency vehicles and find somewhere to put the snow," she tells viewers.

12:36 p.m. At *The Globe,* education writer Avenoso and her editor leaf through the Boston city schools' report, trying to reconcile the numbers of those who left the system.

"Did those who left stay in the city or leave for the suburbs?" her editor asks. "That will be a key question."

Statistical stories always pose special challenges for reporters, and this is no exception. Avenoso knows how many 6th and 7th graders left the system. What's harder to judge is whether the figure, 600, is a lot, and whether those students are leaving for private schools or just moving away.

Her editor, Sara Snyder, urges her to spread her net wider. "You need a parent activist or the citywide education council to put it in perspective," she says. She knows Avenoso is avoiding top school officials so the competition, the *Herald,* doesn't get wind of her having the report.

"Just tell them, 'This is a figure I've got,'" Snyder suggests. "You don't have to say how."

12:42 p.m. *The Globe's* other education writer, Kate Zernicke, has pitched a lighter story for today, one that always intrigued her as a kid. She's toying with an opening for a story on how superintendents decide when to close school. One option is the superintendent who'd throw out his dog in the morning and call off school if the dog immediately came back. Another is a superintendent who vigilantly drove the roads in the early morning hours. One day, he ended in a snowbank without a cell phone. His was the only district to have school that day.

Zernicke goes with the snowbank.

12:47 p.m. A snowbank is the reason *New England Cable News* reporter Traci Grant is playing catch-up on her story. Her car ended up in one, and she missed the morning news conference on the upcoming 100th Boston marathon. Now she's looking for a way to humanize an otherwise dull story on the last 1,000 people picked today to run in the 37,000-strong field.

"I'd like to find the last man or woman they picked," she explains as she looks through the news conference videotape that an *NECN* photographer shot.

She scribbles down the last six people named at the news conference, grabs the 4-inch-thick Boston phone book, and starts calling anyone with the same name. On the 16th try, she finds a runner. But he won't agree to go on camera.

Twenty minutes later, she's saved. The man at the other end of the line got her answering machine message, the first he'd known he'd been picked. He's excited.

"There was a meeting going on down the hall," he told her, "and I just interrupted it and said, 'I just got accepted for the Boston marathon.'"

That's a scene to build her story around.

Traci Grant
Stamford CT

New England
Cable News

One reason reporters love the news business is because they have a front seat on history. They get to go places and meet people few others do. That thrill compensates for the days they are caught in a near blizzard or, as was Traci Grant in this photograph, doing live shots in the rain.

1:11 p.m. Michelle Johnson is "talking" to the online readers of *The Boston Globe* in a real-time chat at *Boston.com,* the online subsidiary of the paper.

"How have *Globe* reporters taken to *Boston.com*?" The question scrolls across her computer screen.

"The ones who are plugged in are very excited about it," she taps back. "The ones who aren't, don't really understand it enough to care."

What Johnson doesn't say is that *Globe* reporters, realizing online readers can help them report stories, have begun approaching her to post questions.

One question to online readers helped reporter Irene Iudica find sources for a story on "random acts of kindness." That prompted another reporter to post a question about where people swim in the winter.

Word, Johnson says, is beginning to spread.

1:16 p.m. Janet Wu is upset. She's just learned she missed a news conference two hours ago on the very topic of her story—the governor and education. Sen. John Kerry, whom the governor is running against in November, predictably lashed out at what he calls Weld's new-found interest in education.

Because of a mix-up at *NewsCenter 5,* no one told Wu about the news conference. Her competitors, of course, did know, and they have tape, an essential part of the story on TV. So Wu calls Kerry's press secretary and asks for five minutes with the senator.

"I know that he wants as much face (on-air) time as he can get, and he especially wants face time on the No. 1 station in town," says Wu, in recounting the incident.

1:46 p.m. Hurry up and wait. That's what the news business is often about.

Now at *New England Cable News* one wait has ended. The public relations office at Beth Israel Hospital has a man who just came into emergency after slipping on the ice and falling. He's willing to go on camera.

It's the interview medical reporter Cara Birrittieri needs to complete her piece on snow-related injuries.

"That's just what we've been waiting for for two days," says assignment editor Christen Graham.

2:29 p.m. "It's changed, it's evolving," *The Globe*'s David Armstrong says. He forgets to mention he's just dug up an angle that will land his alcohol pricing story on Page 1. The governor, it seems, only told part of his plan for liquor deregulation in his State of the State address.

Reporting his analysis piece, Armstrong has interviewed a state agency lawyer who tells him the governor wants the "three-license cap" to go. Armstrong knows that jargon from his earlier stories. So he knows what to ask next.

Yes, the lawyer tells him. That would mean any grocery store in the state could sell liquor, not just three stores per chain. The governor just hadn't gotten around to announcing that part of his plan yet.

The analysis can wait. Armstrong's been around long enough to know that reporters' agendas change quickly when bigger news comes along.

3:12 p.m. "We're OK. I've figured out the numbers," *The Globe*'s Karen Avenoso tells her editor. The most startling: 40 percent of the families who pull kids from Boston middle schools do so because they fear for their children's safety. "That's where I'm going to start," Avenoso says.

3:15 p.m. "How long is it?" asks *New England Cable News* producer Audrey Laganas, as she opens the door to the edit booth.

Traci Grant's marathon piece is set to air in less than an hour. And Laganas needs to know how long it will run.

Grant stares at scribbles on a yellow pad and tape editor Jerry Saslav madly pushes buttons. The air hangs thick with tension.

"We have no clue," says Saslav, with an edge in his voice. "We're not even sure we're going to make the show."

"Just let me know," says Laganas calmly, closing the door.

At 4:07, Saslav breaks into a sprint to run the tape to the playback machine. It makes air, with 30 seconds to spare.

MIDAFTERNOON:
IN SEARCH OF THE TOP STORIES

3:34 p.m. Twenty-one editors sit around a horseshoe-shaped table at *The Globe*, editor Matt Storin at its head. For metro, national, foreign, business, sports editors, it's time to sell their candidates for tomorrow's Page 1.

Walter "Robby" Robinson, who heads the metro operation, appears to like Armstrong's story.

"In addition to saving Joe Sixpack 75 cents on beer, every supermarket in the state could sell beer and wine," he says. "We have that alone."

Sports reports that next year's 100th anniversary of the marathon is expected to draw four times more participants than ever before. "It's monstrous," says editor Joe Sullivan.

Both stories will make tomorrow's Page 1 cut.

3:46 p.m. Clump, clump.

"You're listening to the sound of luggage wandering aimlessly around one of those baggage carousels at Logan Airport," Flo Jonic tells *WBZ-AM* listeners, in a taped report. "It's a common casualty of snowstorms: The bags get there, but the owners don't."

Jonic knew she'd found a good story when she spied more than 1,000 bags spread out in American Airline's baggage area. She also knows that the best way for listeners to "see" on the radio is to bring them to the site with natural sound.

4:01 p.m. Guy Morris, the organizer of that monstrous marathon, sits nervously on a raised chair in a corner of *The Globe*'s newsroom, facing a camera that will beam his face out over the *New England Cable News* network. He'll be joined by a *Globe* editor in one of four live interviews today from the *Globe* newsroom.

This one will be the paper's first "trifecta" in the era of converging technologies, notes Ande Zellman, associate editor of new technology. The marathon story will run in print on Page 1. It's already beaming over *New England Cable News* with a graphic "Around the Globe." And, says Zellman, part of the video will go online as the first moving pictures on the *Boston.com* Internet site.

"Everything is going to start merging," predicts Zellman, former editor of *The Globe*'s Sunday magazine.

4:40 p.m. With his tie askew, *NewsCenter 5* anchor Chet Curtis plops down before a newsroom computer to check the stories he'll read in 20 minutes.

After 23 years at the anchor desk, Curtis doesn't hesitate to edit his scripts. One piece on a mock trial involving Alan Dershowitz seems a bit flat, given the well-known attorney's flair. So Curtis types in a change. *Harvard Professor Alan Dershowitz will get the chance to STRUT HIS STUFF in a mock trial,* he writes.

DEADLINE

4:59 p.m. Deadline's approaching and metro editor Walter Robinson tries to keep the trains running close to schedule. "Karen," he asks Avenoso. "Is the top in?"

"Top's in," comes the reply.

Across town at *New England Cable News* the cry is, "Roll the open tape," as the 5 p.m. show begins with—you guessed it—snow.

5:17 p.m. Police reporter Ric Kahn has made it back from the Brockton murder where the victim was found in the freezer. He's a little late and a little frazzled, but despite being largely shut out by authorities, he has enough to put together a story for tomorrow's *Globe*. The court clerk wouldn't release the homicide complaint even though public records laws require it. The DA wouldn't talk. So Kahn swung by the house of the guy found in the deep freeze. A neighbor started talking. Kahn also tracked down the suspect's prior police record, checked out local voting records that give some basic information about the victim and his wife—even looked up the assessed value of their house.

"How are you going to approach it?" asks deputy city editor Sean Murphy.

"How did a street guy named Spider end up in the home of a couple of registered Republicans with an American flag hanging out their window?" Kahn shoots back.

Murphy half turns in his chair. "Don't hold out Republicans like they're a foreign species or something," he warns.

6:02 p.m. "NewsCenter 5 at Six" is already rolling and Page 1 of tomorrow's *Globe* is taking shape as the *AP*, used in part as a tip service for regional breaking news, sends a couple of paragraphs over the wire. A University of Massachusetts swimmer has collapsed during a meet.

7:15 p.m. David Armstrong awaits his editor's final thumbs up. It's been a good day. And there is a saying among reporters, "You are only as good as your last story."

"The key was knowing whom to call," he says. "It was strictly by touching base with these people that they coughed up this new information."

Tomorrow, his exclusive story will begin like this:

> Massachusetts residents may soon be able to buy beer and liquor at supermarket and warehouse clubs and at lower prices if a plan by Gov. William F. Weld . . . is approved.

EVENING: A STORY BREAKS

8:21 p.m. "Hey, did you guys see this," executive producer John Davidow yells out at *NewsCenter 5*. The wire story on his computer reads:

> HANOVER, N.H. (AP)—A star swimmer for the University of Massachusetts died of a heart attack Wednesday after collapsing during a meet at Dartmouth College.

Before the staff can finish reading, the phone rings. News director Candy Altman just heard the story on *WBZ-AM*. And a busy newsroom just gets busier in preparation for the 11 p.m. news.

Davidow tapes a phone interview with Dartmouth's sports information director. But he needs pictures. No luck in the station's archives, nor the network, nor a half-dozen TV stations in New Hampshire and Oregon, the swimmer's home state.

Finally, assignment editor Susan Griffin finds a black-and-white photo of the swimmer at the *AP* office in Springfield. She works out an elaborate and risky plan. She'll get *AP*'s Springfield office to feed the photo to the Boston *AP* office, divert a photojournalist there to shoot the photo on videotape, then rush to Quincy where the station's microwave truck happens to be, and feed it in.

It works, with seven minutes to spare.

8:40 p.m. *New England Cable News* producer Bob Keating can't get the swimmer's picture for his 9 p.m. cast. But he adds the story to his rundown, telling a writer to type out 20-seconds worth for the fourth segment.

8:44 p.m. This was the wrong day, free-lancer Brad Parks quickly decides, to have headed to the Dartmouth University library to "drool over geography books."

His answering machine blinks feverishly. *Globe* sports editor Don Skwar has called. So has Dartmouth's sports information director. A fax by his computer tells the rest: A University of Massachusetts swimmer has died on the Dartmouth campus.

Parks, a *Globe* sports intern the previous summer, sprints to his car, drives to Dartmouth Medical Center without cleaning an ice-coated windshield, and races inside.

He's 15 minutes too late. The University of Massachusetts team has left.

Parks has about 40 minutes until the first edition deadline. He tracks down the hospital spokesperson for some basics. He reaches a Dartmouth swimmer who tells him the dead swimmer was standing when he collapsed. He finds the hospital chaplain, who won't answer questions. Then, at 9:45, he calls *The Globe.*

Since sports editor Skwar hasn't heard from Parks, he's enlisted a staff correspondent to call the swimmer's hometown paper in Oregon and to track down the coach or athletic director.

No family, he instructs. There are ethical issues here. The parents may not yet know their son has died.

The correspondent is weaving the Oregon athletic director's remarks into a wire story when Parks calls.

Says Skwar: "I told the guy laying the paper out to allow for more room because we'd probably get stuff from Brad and that's when Brad called."

11 p.m. The story of the dead swimmer leads "NewsCenter 5 at Eleven": "Tragedy has struck a star swimmer from the University of Massachusetts tonight."

Anchor Natalie Jacobson introduces the taped story she's quickly pieced together with the photo, an interview with a local cardiologist, the phone interview from the Dartmouth official and graphics.

"It was obvious to us that this was the lead," executive producer John Davidow says later. "It was immediate, it was tragic, it was our state team, a young man—star of the team. This was obviously a big story."

At *The Globe,* a thorough story runs on page 38, inside the sports section.

"It probably would have made the (sports) cover on most days," says Skwar. "But it was an incredibly busy day. We had an exclusive that Jim Johnson was going to be named Miami coach, the Celts were playing, UMass was playing and was in overtime. You've got a Red Sox trade of major import, a columnist."

News is like that. No two editors see it exactly alike. News organizations play their own stories big. Some play breaking news harder. Others play to the emotions of their audience. The immediacy of television gives way to the reflection of print tomorrow morning. One thing is constant. News keeps moving.

The Boston Globe

THE PLOW AND STARS
Thursday: Sunny, 44
Friday: Snow in p.m., 44
High tide: 2:44 a.m., 2:45 p.m.
Full report: *Page 82*

THURSDAY, JANUARY 11, 1996

Numbers climbing in Boston

64

inches of snow have fallen on us this season, and more is expected tomorrow. Pages 25, 32.

Snow from yesterday's storm is added to a pile in Neponset.

37,000

runners, by far the highest total ever, will line up for the 100th Boston Marathon

By Bill Griffith
GLOBE STAFF

The 100th running of the Boston Marathon has taken on epic proportions: 37,000 runners are expected to gather in Hopkinton by noon on April 16 to begin the run to Boston. That's some 27,000 more than participated last year, and 36,886 more than ran in the initial race in 1896.

Boston Marathon officials had anticipated attracting 25,000 runners to the centennial event on Patriots Day, more than twice the number who participated in recent years, but they were snowed under by a reported 10,000 applications from qualified runners in the two weeks before the Dec. 31 deadline.

So the numbers continue to rise of all expectations. Race Director Guy Morse said yesterday that he expects about 24,000 qualifiers to compete, along with 5,000 runners whose names were selected in three lottery drawings over the last six months, 4,000 foreign entries, and another 4,000 competitors from local running clubs and charitable organizations.

Such runaway popularity can make for logistical nightmares, so to ensure that the 100th run finishes before the 101st begins, Boston Athletic Association officials have reconfigured and extended the area beyond the finish line on Boylston Street at the

MARATHON, Page 40

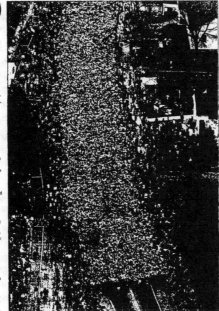

This typical starting-line crowd equals but a fraction of the field that will be in Hopkinton in April.

Democrats push health coverage

New proposal applies to all Mass. workers

By Richard A. Knox
GLOBE STAFF

In an effort to restart Massachusetts' stalled drive toward near-universal health insurance, state Democrats today will put forward a proposal that would require all employers to provide at least minimum coverage to workers – though not to their dependents.

The proposal, which its authors liken to a minimum-wage requirement for health care, would also expand state-funded coverage for uninsured children and subsidize some seniors' prescription drugs.

Passage of the plan – the Democrats' answer to a long-pending Weld administration health reform proposal – would put Massachusetts back on the map in health care reform. Main provisions of the 1988 landmark Dukakis universal health care law have never been implemented, and while some states have tried to reduce their numbers of uninsured citizens, state-based health care reform has languished in recent years.

But the Democrats' proposal won't overcome Gov. William F. Weld's opposition to requiring businesses to provide health insurance, as well as his antipathy toward new taxes.

Both Weld and state Health and Human Services Secretary Gerald Whitburg yesterday reiterated their

HEALTH, Page 29

Weld wants to open up liquor sales

By David Armstrong
GLOBE STAFF

Massachusetts residents may soon be able to buy beer and liquor at supermarket chains and warehouse clubs and at lower prices if a plan by Gov. William F. Weld to gut the regulation of alcoholic beverages is approved.

The radical proposal is advertised as a boon for consumers who pay among the highest prices in the country for beer and liquor, but critics say the plan could put small liquor stores out of business and foster corruption.

For Weld, promising to cut beer and liquor prices while throwing away layers of regulation could play well with the blue-collar Democratic voters he has targeted in his campaign to unseat US Sen. John F. Kerry this year.

The governor even highlighted lower beer prices in his State of the State address Tuesday night.

For the first time, aides to Weld yesterday said the governor's plan would include eliminating the long-time cap of three liquor licenses per company.

LIQUOR, Page 28

Report finds safety is concern of 40% who leave city schools

By Karen Avenoso
GLOBE CORRESPONDENT

About 40 percent of families who left the Boston public school system when it was time for their children to enter middle school said they did so because they feared for their children's safety, according to a report to the Boston School Department.

But the 1994 report, scheduled to be released later this month and obtained in advance by the Globe, also shows that the number of exiting middle-school students is significantly lower than many educators believed. The success of the exam schools, the report shows, has kept many students in the system and even attracted some parochial and private school youngsters back to Boston public schools in the seventh grade.

The study, conducted pro bono by the Bain & Co. consulting firm, shows that of the 9,200 city students eligible to enter grades six and seven, 600 – or about 7 percent – left the system to enter local parochial or private schools, or moved out of Boston.

The study, commissioned but never made public by former school superintendent Lois Harrison-Jones, focused specifically on students at

SCHOOLS, Page 20

Pressure by Mrs. Clinton is hinted in travel firings

By John Solomon
ASSOCIATED PRESS

■ Budget battlers sound ready to let voters decide. Page 3.

WASHINGTON – In the days before White House travel office workers were fired, Hillary Rodham Clinton pressed top presidential aides, including the chief of staff, to get the employees "out of there," FBI interviews and White House documents say.

"May 16 – HRC pressure," then chief of staff Thomas McLarty scribbled on a chronology of events the White House prepared a few days after the firings created a public uproar in May 1993. May 16 was three days before the firings.

Notes from a White House re-view of Ron Butler, an employee of the Arkansas company that took over part of the travel office business after the firings, suggest Butler also believed Mrs. Clinton named the workers fired.

"Said HRC very upset re misuse of funds and wanted them out of there," say the notes of Butler's interview, conducted as part of a subsequent internal review. "Misu" is short for misappropriation.

In the days before the firings, Butler talked to the key advisers who were involved in the decision that led to the dismissals, the notes suggest.

The documents obtained by the Associated Press provide additional evidence to support a memo by a White House aide released last week

CLINTON, Page 18

Patrick Buchanan

A firebrand refocuses

Second in a series of occasional profiles of the presidential candidates.

By Curtis Wilkie
GLOBE STAFF

CEDAR FALLS, Iowa – As the world order went through convulsions at the beginning of the decade, Patrick J. Buchanan, a product of the Cold War, made his own transformation. He began condemning the military interventions he had once cheered. He turned from a 100 percent free-trader into a "trade hawk." He even started calling himself a populist.

He kept, however, the raspy voice and wrathful pen that have been scourge to a generation of liberals. The commentator-candidate says a line from author Arthur Koestler that he used years ago – "One should either write ruthlessly what one believes to be the truth, or shut up" – is still "a pretty good maxim for Pat Buchanan."

In other words, Buchanan's message may have changed, but his persona hasn't. His followers adore as belligerency; some critics still consider him a bully and a bigot.

Campaigning the second time for

BUCHANAN, Page 8

Patrick J. Buchanan talks to workers in Madison, N.H. Tuesday.

Inside

CALENDAR: Outlet bound / AT HOME: The coloring line

■ Red Sox swap: Boston gets infielder Wil Cordero and pitcher Brian Eversgerd from Montreal for pitcher Rheal Cormier and two minor leaguers. Sports, Page 33.

Unmasking the Fabulous Sports Babe

LIVING/ARTS Page 49

TIPS ON REPORTING

Some stories collapse, some change directions. Planning helps, but so does flexibility. The best reporters know that lemons can always be turned to lemonade. Here are 10 lessons learned from a day in Boston's news.

1. Do your homework.   Check what's been written or aired before. Stories your news organization has run before provide names, threads to develop and angles you know you don't want to repeat. That's why *The Globe*'s Matt Bai starts his research on the homogenization of Boston businesses by looking through *Globe* stories published earlier.

2. Dive in.   You can't report without making that first call. *WBZ-AM*'s Flo Jonic made her first call at 4:45 a.m. Reporters who start early get the story.

3. Develop expertise in key areas.   If you know the system, it's easier to notice that it's changed. *The Globe*'s David Armstrong broke an exclusive story on proposals to loosen liquor sales laws because he understood the jargon and how the state Alcoholic Beverage Council worked.

4. Go to the scene; legs write stories.   Without visuals, television isn't television. Viewers could see the actual road conditions and traffic speeds on *NewsCenter 5*'s many live traffic shots throughout the day.

Janet Wu wouldn't have nabbed the legislative leaders if she hadn't been at the state house. Likewise, *WBZ-AM*'s Flo Jonic would have missed the lost luggage story if she hadn't wandered around the airport.

In print and in radio, where there are no pictures, detailed descriptions make the story.

5. Search diligently.   Stories are built on facts. And public records are repositories of facts. That is why Ric Kahn, of *The Globe,* started in district court, looking for the specific complaint against the man accused in the Brockton murder. That is also why he checked census data, tax assessment records and past criminal records. Public records give a story authority. More and more are being made available online (see Chapter 4).

6. Know your audience.   Reporters look for what affects their audience, not an audience miles away. The fact that

Philadelphia got more snow than Boston didn't matter to reporters looking at Beantown's traffic, business and psychological upheaval. Only *New England Cable News* spent significant time on road closures in Maine. "Local" for *NECN*'s audience means Connecticut to Maine.

7. Be flexible.   Reporters need an initial focus for their stories but must adapt as events unfold.

"The story didn't end up what I thought it was going to be at 11 o'clock in the morning," said Janet Wu, of *NewsCenter 5.*

She started out looking at the governor's position on education, but the unexpected interview with Sen. John Kerry turned the piece into more of a political analysis.

8. Check again.   *The Globe*'s Ric Kahn was at his desk late into the night checking a discrepancy in the middle initial of the man suspected of killing the man in the freezer. A little detail? No, a big one. Kahn wanted to make absolutely certain he didn't write about the wrong suspect.

It's scary how easy it is to make mistakes. Brad Parks later discovered the swimmer had been sitting when his heart attack hit. He changed the information, given to him incorrectly, for later editions.

The credibility of reporters rests on detail. To get those details right takes exceptional care.

9. Be thorough.   Always be thorough, but don't expect to be complete. Stories continue to evolve. Karen Avenoso knew what she didn't have when she wrote her story about middle school kids leaving Boston schools. She also knew she had made 60 phone calls in a single day and the story would leak out if she didn't go with what she had.

Among the missing pieces: how the middle school drop-out rate in Boston compared to that in other cities, how it affected parochial school enrollment, and what Boston schools planned to do about it.

10. Follow up.   Just as Armstrong and Wu looked for a second-day angle on the governor's State of the State address, Avenoso was back at work on her story the next day. The angle: Did crime statistics at middle schools warrant the fears of parents who'd pulled their kids out.

RECOMMENDED READING

Filoreto, C., & Setzer, L. (1993). *Working in T.V. news: The insider's guide.* Memphis, TN: Mustang Publishing Co.

Here's a look from the inside on what television news is really like, written by photojournalist Carl

Filoreto and reporter/anchor Lynn Setzer, both Emmy award-winning journalists. It's designed to help students decide if they want to work in television. The authors also give tips on how to get that first job.

Main, A. *The producer page*. [Online]. Available: **http://www.scripps.ohiou.edu/producer**.

You're sure to get several laughs, as well as valuable insights, into the world of TV news producing if you spend time at this Web site. The monthly newsletters include tales from the trenches by producers around the country. Also worth reading is Alice Main's *Producer's Book* with tips about TV news producing.

Robertson, N. (1992). *The girls in the balcony*. New York: Fawcett Columbine.

This account by a Pulitzer Prize–winning reporter tells how women broke the gender barrier at *The New York Times*. It traces the history of women at that powerful news institution and explains how a group of women, through their courageous actions, brought about equity in promotions and assignments.

CHAPTER 4

Gathering Information

Reporter Sean Coulthard arrives at work at *WCBS-AM* in New York City at 8 a.m. But by 5 a.m., his job has begun. His breakfast regimen includes a daily dose of news: *The New York Times, The Wall Street Journal, USA Today* and *The (Newark, N.J.) Star-Ledger.*

"You have to live and breathe the business or else you're not going to be a success in it," says Coulthard, who adds that he thinks about news just about every waking moment. That dedication explains why, just seven years out of college, he earned a slot working in the largest radio market in the country.

"The bottom line is backgrounding yourself," he says, "that's not just listening to the five-minute news at the top of the hour, but reading the local coverage in the Jersey and Long Island papers and the op-ed pieces in *The New York Times.*"

Coulthard says he has to be aware of what's happening because he never knows what story he'll cover.

Not all reporters are as disciplined as Coulthard in getting a jump on the day's news. But reporters' jobs would be nearly impossible if they had to start every story with no information on what has already been aired or published. Before anything else, reporters take steps to get up to speed on a story. That is called backgrounding, the first step in researching.

In addition to learning how to background a story, in this chapter you will learn:

- The significance of verifying information and using first-hand sources whenever possible
- Techniques for researching stories, including traditional methods using books and public records, and newer skills in using databases and computer-assisted reporting
- Tips for researching on the Internet

BACKGROUNDING

The best background information is the information you already know. There's no substitute for being knowledgeable about your community.

That said, few reporters have a photographic memory. They need to look things up. They do this by checking the files they've built for themselves, those of their news organizations, reference books and any of the slew of electronic references and libraries online.

Courtesy of WCVB-TV, photo by Molly Lynch.

The nerve center of *NewsCenter 5* (*WCVB,* Boston), like all television newsrooms, is its assignment desk. Here desk editors keep on top of breaking news, make beat checks and gather information for the newscasts.

The concept of backgrounding is simple enough. If reporters are to pass on intelligent accounts of what's new, they first have to look up what's old—what's come before. For example, backgrounding tells reporters covering a dispute over expanding a shopping center not only when it was built but also whether a similar dispute over its size took place at that time.

Backgrounding often takes only 10 or 15 minutes. It may be all the time a reporter can spare. Sometimes, on big or complicated stories, it takes hours or even days.

Backgrounding a story on an upcoming 10K race might be as simple as rummaging through a newsroom file for an article clipped a month ago showing the route through the city park. But backgrounding an in-depth piece on police efforts to crack down on drug traffic in that same city park might require reading a year's worth of articles or reviewing dozens of audio clips.

Reporters on a daily deadline typically might scan wire stories about a story that broke overnight or go online to read what a company that has scheduled an 11 a.m. news conference has to say about itself.

Most student reporters have access to the Internet, and often their newsrooms have some files or a wire service. They may not work with all of the resources discussed here until their first full-time job, but it's important to know what is available.

Topical Files

Good reporters build their own files. They clip stories about a topic and stuff notes from their stories together in file folders. One file might read "stadium" and contain information both on the new stadium being debated locally and other new stadiums across the country. Another file might be called "welfare reform" and contain articles on the fallout over welfare changes nationally and locally. If the reporter expects to do a series of stories on either of these topics, she might further segment her files, creating one on the new stadium's financing, for example, and another on its design.

The titles of topical files obviously vary from reporter to reporter and locality to locality. Some reporters fill several file cabinets with topical files in areas that interest them.

At broadcast stations and smaller print operations, most reporters work **general assignment**, which means they don't focus on one beat or topic, but cover all types of stories. In such newsrooms topical files also are kept in a central location for the entire news staff.

But don't rely on what's in the drawers at the college paper and radio station or what might (or might not) be at that first job. Start saving stories and tapes of interest as a student reporter. Get a stack of manila file folders. On each, mark a topic you are interested in or likely to be covering in the future. A student covering the university's health services, for example, might have a folder on stress, another on drinking, a third on health education. Someone covering the region's environment might mark folders: recycling, lake cleanup and endangered species.

Whatever the topic, the folders provide a place to drop stories of interest, notes from broadcast news and information off the Internet. Radio and TV reporters also might jot down numbers of tapes so they can pull them to get file video or sound.

Some newsrooms also organize background information in a **future file**—a file drawer or computer folder with files for every day of the year. For example, the March 23 file might contain information about the upcoming city council vote that evening on a proposed bike path. It would alert the reporter assigned to cover city council that day.

Future files and topical files are essential in other ways. They provide:

- Names of key players and sources
- Background information for building interview questions
- Context that can be woven into a story
- Perspective, so the reporter doesn't chase an angle done last week

ETHICS ATTRIBUTION

Reporters often use information from wire services and television news feeds in their stories. That is considered ethical when the news organizations have contracted with those wire services and news feeds to use their material.

A radio station subscribing to the AP wire, for example, could broadcast an AP story reporting that the university president will announce her resignation at a 10 a.m. news conference.

That same station, however, should not air that story as its own if it is broken by an enterprising reporter at a competing news organization. That would be plagiarism, such a serious offense in some places that a single incident leads to dismissal.

Standards vary. Print reporters often complain that their radio counterparts, operating on tight morning deadlines, do little more than "rip and read" their stories on the air.

Many news organizations are beginning to require careful attribution of the news source, even if it is not required in a contractual agreement. In other words, after announcing that the university president will resign, a radio reporter might say, "The Associated Press reports that . . . ," so listeners will know where the information came from.

Attribution isn't necessary for commonly known information. You needn't attribute a city hall press release to the mayor or credit a church bulletin for telling you that Christianity was founded on the teachings of Jesus Christ.

The purpose of attribution is to clearly state where information originated. It is a way to let readers, listeners or viewers judge whether the information is credible and authoritative.

By using attribution, reporters still can't vouch for accuracy of information. That's why every reporter should go to the original source. Some broadcast journalists in Atlanta learned that the hard way.

The *Atlanta Journal-Constitution* reported in a front-page story that Atlanta was the most dangerous city in the United States, based on calculations number crunchers at the paper made from FBI crime statistics. Many of the radio and TV stations in the city regurgitated the information on air without checking the numbers. It turned out that the paper inadvertently left out about a dozen cities, and Atlanta wasn't No. 1. The stories led to red faces and a round of retractions later in the week when all the media outlets had to admit they'd goofed.

CLIPS AND ARCHIVES

Most news organizations file previous stories systematically. When such files exist, reporters routinely check them before going out on assignment.

In newspapers these "old" stories are called **clips** because they used to be clipped by hand from the newspaper and then filed. In radio and television they're called the **archives** and include scripts and tapes. Today, in all but the smallest of newsrooms, reporters find them by searching through the newsroom's computer system.

For example, a reporter assigned to do an anniversary story on a historic hotel badly damaged a year ago in a fire might search using the name of the hotel and the word *fire.* Up would come all the stories with those terms. To see every article or script written about the hotel since the fire, a reporter might type the name of the hotel only.

A few newsrooms—and classrooms—aren't yet computerized. Journalists who still work in the typewriter age might have to hunt through file cabinets for articles and scripts or dig out tapes and listen to the story.

NEWS SERVICES AND OTHER MEDIA

Like Sean Coulthard, most reporters are news junkies. By monitoring other media and news services, they know what follow-up angles others are reporting. They'll also learn details to help them shape the story they're covering. A consumer reporter writing about home buying might check a **news service** such as the AP wire to see if the Federal Reserve increases interest rates as expected. A TV reporter setting out on a story about the reaction of local immigrants to a coup d'etat in their home country will watch a network **news feed**—video sent by satellite—to learn more about the situation and know what pictures are available for the story.

READY REFERENCES

Reporters find that ready references assist them in gathering background information, checking facts or finding contacts. These books contain names, addresses, historical information and statistics. Some of the most common references are described here.

If these references aren't handy in the newsroom, they can be searched at the public library or through a phone call to a reference librarian. Librarians are often a reporter's best friend. Don't overlook them.

Phone books: The familiar paper phone book contains much more than phone numbers and addresses. Look for information on community services, the arts, even the seating chart at the local stadium. CD/ROM phone books now cover the entire country, and phone books on the Internet, while not comprehensive, are often helpful in finding an out-of-state source.

Reverse directories: Reporters use this reference (also called a crisscross index) to find a phone number when they have a street address but don't have the name of the person living there. Or if they have only a phone number, they can find the name and address of the person whose number it is. Streets in the directory are listed alphabetically with the house numbers numerically ordered under each street. Each address is matched to a phone number. Elsewhere, phone numbers are listed numerically with the accompanying street address. Some Web sites offer similar services.

Reverse directories are particularly helpful in covering fires, disasters and crime stories. For example, if you hear on a police scanner that there's a fire in the 3200 block of Water Street, you can use the reverse directory to find the names and phones for residents on that block and call them for eyewitness accounts.

Local directories: Police departments, hospitals, social service agencies and a wide range of government entities publish handy booklets that contain organizational information, names, addresses and phone numbers. Many publish the information online. If an escaped pit bull bites a child, you might look in a county government directory to find the local animal control officer.

Maps: They're available in paper and book form, online and on CD/ROM. You can discover where Timbuktu is (Mali) or how to drive to the industrial waste plant across the county. On the Internet *Yahoo! maps* will sketch out the map of that neighborhood.

Almanacs: These are full of facts on everything from how to reach The Songwriters Guild Foundation (New York City, (212) 768-7902) to the biggest news stories in the year you were born.

Encyclopedias: You can learn about the peregrine falcon (an endangered species), the chador (a cloak worn by Islamic women) or thousands of other entries from A to Z. You won't find many of these 15-volume sets in newsrooms—most reporters search them on CD/ROM.

Media stylebooks: "The Associated Press Stylebook and Libel Manual" and similar guides tell much more than whether or not "senator" is capitalized (it's not unless before a specific senator's name). The stylebooks also explain such things as the difference between Christian evangelicals and fundamentalists (the first group emphasizes sharing one's faith; the second believes the Bible is literally true). And they provide such information as who compiles the Index of Leading Economic Indicators (U.S. Commerce Department).

Dictionaries: Yes, spelling is important. Dictionaries also help you background unfamiliar or technical terms when you are preparing for a story. Broadcasters check dictionaries regularly for pronunciation.

The Virtual Reference Desk, an Internet site maintained by librarians at Purdue University, offers a master index linking reporters to dictionaries, thesauri, calendars and much more.

BACKGROUNDING ON THE INTERNET

We can't resist passing on a few more backgrounding tips using the Internet. It is, after all, the newest gadget in the reporter's toolbox. If you're not familiar with the Internet and its technojargon, stop for a moment and read the Internet primer in Appendix A. To find the Internet addresses of sites boldfaced in the text, see the box, Clipboard. There's a similar box in every chapter that mentions Internet addresses in the text. At the end of each chapter, the Recommended Reading section contains a few master sites that are great jumping-off points to all types of resources.

Later in this chapter we will take you through the steps of using the Internet for research on specific issues or topics. Here are some ways to get up to speed on the news or on a company or government agency that is making news.

- News from across the country and around the world can be found at directories such as *AJR/Newslink*. Reporters visiting there can connect to more than 7,000 electronic news sites.

hot research

Hong Kong Bird Virus

- **Bird Flu Outbreak**
  "http://www.scmp.com/news/special/birdflu/index.asp"
  These updates about the H5N1 influenza virus come from The South China Morning Post. The H5N1 virus, formerly found only in birds, has been identified as a cause of influenza in Hong Kong.

- **News Bulletin**
  "http://www.info.gov.hk/dh/new/bullet.htm"
  The Hong Kong Department of Health is also posting updates about the virus.

- **Hong Kong Hospital Authority**
  "http://www.ha.org.hk/newsroom/index.htm"
  The Hospital Authority is monitoring the situation and providing information about the management of Influenza A in Hospitals.

- **Bird-to-Human Influenza**
  "http://www.outbreak.org/cgi-unreg/dynaserve.exe/avianflu.html"
  David Ornstein's resource page is part of Outbreak, an online information service addressing emerging diseases.

- **Centers for Disease Control and Prevention**
  "http://www.cdc.gov/"
  The CDC, an agency of the U.S. Department of Health and Human Services, offers summaries about influenza conditions in the United States. They also have information about influenza prevention.

At the Web site of The Poynter Institute for Media Studies, reporters find ready links to do research on a hot story. Staffer David Shedden selects a topic each week (here, it is a rare virus), finds the best resources on the Internet and then prepares an index with links to the best information.

- Need to find out about a company? Use the address: *www.companyname.com,* but fill in the name of an actual company. For example, if you want to see if McDonald's has a site (it does), type *www.mcdonalds.com.*

- Standard address formulas can help you find nonprofit organizations, too. Type *www.nonprofitname.org.* For example, *www.redcross.org* is the Internet address for the American Red Cross, the group that collects blood and responds in emergencies.

- Try *www.cityname.state.us* for city government sites. But again, be sure to plug an actual city and a state ZIP code abbreviation (for example, *www.syracuse.ny.us*). A reporter might use city sites to check the agenda for a council meeting, review the city budget or check the latest list of what residents can recycle.

Topical briefings on geographic regions or issues appear many places on the World Wide Web (that is what "www" stands for). ***Poynter Online,*** run by The Poynter Institute for Media Studies in Florida, offers "hot research," with new topics weekly. When airline safety became a big news story after a ValuJet plane crashed in the Everglades, Poynter Online had an index with **links** (highlighted words to click on) that connected readers to other Web sites. One link took readers directly to the airline's **home page** (the first page of an Internet Web site), another to an informational site on the Everglades, a third to the Federal Aeronautics Administration and others to aviation databases. All had the potential to provide background for a reporter working on some aspect of the air safety story.

PBS' Online Newshour provides transcripts and background information on national and international topics. Suppose a reporter is assigned to interview a Bosnian refugee family arriving in town as part of a local church resettlement program. He could click on the ***Newshour Online Backgrounders*** site to learn about the government, geography and economics of the country.

RESEARCHING IN DEPTH

It was late in the afternoon. *WCCO-TV* reporter Jonathan Elias was schmoozing with Minneapolis police officers when one tipped him that police had tracked down a serial rapist who'd been terrorizing single women in recent

SUMMARY

BACKGROUNDING

1. Background yourself on the story by reading your news organization's clips or archives and your own topical or future files. Look for information on what's come before and what needs follow-up.

2. Monitor news services and other news organizations' stories to see what's been done on the subject.

3. Use references or online sources for a brief overview of a topic or issue.

4. Make a list of people to interview, using your personal phone directory, your news outlet's list of contacts and tips from other reporters. Ready references, from the phone book to city directories to the Internet, can expand your list.

5. Continue to monitor the competition as well as national and regional news outlets as you write.

weeks. Elias immediately called other police contacts to get more. He got a suspect's name, but with two different spellings.

It was time to call *WCCO-TV* reporter, Alan Cox, fondly known in the newsroom as "Mr. Techie."

"Run everything on him," Elias told Cox.

Cox has gathered enough government records to make the station a leader in using computerized files (see box, Learning from the Pros: Compiling Databases).

Cox typed both spellings of the name into three databases—prison records, court records and motor vehicle records. Up came a match: a man by the same name with a previous record of sex crimes.

Soon Elias was able to confirm with sources that Cox had found the right guy. Cox, meanwhile, began assembling everything he could about the suspect: his criminal history, his lengthy court record and several places in Minneapolis where he'd lived.

In just a few hours the reporters had enough information for the lead story of the 10 p.m. newscast. The anchors opened the show:

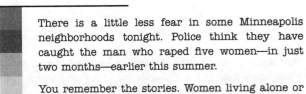

There is a little less fear in some Minneapolis neighborhoods tonight. Police think they have caught the man who raped five women—in just two months—earlier this summer.

You remember the stories. Women living alone or with their children—three in northeast Minneapolis, two on the south side—attacked in their homes. Police tracked their suspect across the country and arrested him tonight in the town of Long Beach, Mississippi.

We're going to begin our coverage with Jonathan Elias—who's out at the suspect's last known address here in the Twin Cities.

WCCO-TV

Elias ad-libbed his story live using the information from the databases to chronicle the man's criminal record.

The other stations in town, which didn't have the sophisticated computer records of *WCCO-TV*, carried a short story, based on a police news release, saying an unnamed person had been arrested.

It was no contest.

"I can't duplicate in any way, shape or form what a police reporter does," says Cox, the research expert, "but working together we're able to take it to another level."

Taking a story to another level is what reporting is all about. First comes backgrounding. It tells reporters what came before. Then comes researching, the quest for new information.

Research includes what reporters call shoe leather: going to the scene, knocking on doors, working the phones and whatever else it takes to talk to the right people. We'll talk about those techniques in the next two chapters and the chapters on beat reporting. For now, we'll concentrate on the ways reporters use the Internet, documents and databases to find hidden information, uncover the source nobody found before or piece together disparate information to tell the big story the competition hasn't yet figured out.

INTERNET RESEARCH

Odds are you've already used the Internet, not only to get background information for a story but also to get an interactive, multimedia glimpse of the news put online by hundreds of news organizations. There's a good chance some of you will work for one or more of these online news operations some day. For now, however, consider the Internet a wonderful research tool.

Jim Walrod uses it daily. He's the assignment manager at *WINK-TV*, Fort Myers, Fla. Walrod tapped into the Internet as Hurricane Erin bore down on Florida. Walrod wanted to find out how bad the hurricane season would be.

He remembered a professor at Colorado State University would be releasing a forecast any day but didn't remember his name or number.

So he logged onto the Internet through America Online and used the search program to pull up the address for the university. He traveled to the university's site, found the meteorology department and soon located the professor's name and e-mail address. Soon he was tapping out a short e-mail message to the professor and the public relations department, asking for the latest report and a live interview.

The PR office faxed him back a news release in which the professor said the season would be worse than predicted earlier.

"We had that on our 9 o'clock update—two hours before the AP even moved the story," said Walrod.

The Internet isn't yet a magical information warehouse that easily displays the exact fact you want. It can be slow, frustrating and sometimes misleading. Remember: Anyone can put information online. Some sites—those with the suffixes .gov and .mil—contain information from the government and the military. Others, such as .edu, have information from university scholars but also from sophomore pranksters. Be careful.

It would take us more than a few pages to teach you how to be sophisticated and efficient researchers on the Net. But the following tips will give you a good start.

SEARCH A TOPIC USING AN ENGINE

A **search engine** is a Web site with a searching function that hunts through the Internet for key words you designate. You type key words into a form provided, click the "search" button, and in seconds the program will identify all the sites, or **hits**, where the term or terms you requested are used. When you see a listing that looks promising, you just click on it and zip over to that site.

Suppose, for example, there's a controversy at the middle school about whether too many boys are being medicated for attention deficit disorder. A reporter could use *AltaVista*, a search engine, and type *attention and deficit and disorder*. When one reporter did this, AltaVista returned thousands of sites with those terms, but fortunately the first address that popped up was for Children and Adults with Attention Deficit Disorder, a national organization dealing with the disorder. At the group's home page, that reporter found articles about the disability, help for parenting, services and local chapters.

This example shows a downside to these search engines—they often return way too many hits, many of them not relevant. The best tip: Read the help guide for that search engine to learn how to refine your search. For example, you can type a phrase rather than separate words, putting it in quotes: *"attention deficit disorder"*. Then you can further narrow the search by adding *and "support group"*. This means you only want sites with both phrases. Finally, you can ask to look only at sites active the previous three months. Suddenly your list of thousands is narrowed to about 40.

SEARCH A TOPIC USING A SUBJECT INDEX

Sometimes reporters find it faster to go to a subject index where librarians or others have catalogued Web sites by subject.

Suppose local Native Americans are complaining that the U.S. government is planning to relocate their ancestors' graves. A reporter could use the subject guide at the *University of Michigan Library Subject Resource Guide.* By clicking through a series of links, from "Government" to "American Indians" to "Legislation Affecting Native Americans," the reporter would land at an Internet site that explains a bill pending in Congress to require permission from Native American tribes before graves are moved.

Several news organizations have put up such indexes just for reporters. One of the best is *Facsnet,* run by the Foundation for Communications. It lists more than a dozen topics, from agriculture to sports, to help reporters start on their research trek.

CLIPBOARD — INTERNET SITES MENTIONED IN THIS CHAPTER

AJR Newslink	www.newslink.org	Tile	www.tile.net
Alta Vista	www.altavista.digital.com	University of Michigan Library Subject Resource Guide	henry.ugl.lib.umich.edu/ libhome/rrs/selector
Deja News	www.dejanews.com		
Facsnet	www.facsnet.org	The Virtual Reference Desk	thorplus.lib.purdue.edu/ reference
Newshour Online Backgrounders (PBS)	www.pbs.org/newshour/ background.html	Yahoo!	www.yahoo.com
Profnet	www.profnet.com	Yahoo! maps	www.proximus.com/yahoo
Poynter Online	www.poynter.org		
Reporters Committee for Freedom of the Press	www.rcfp.org/foi.html		
Student Press Law Center	www.splc.org		

For a more complete list of Internet resources to help with research, see Appendix B. Update this list at http://web.syr.edu/~bcfought.

SEARCH MAILING LIST AND USENET POSTINGS

When reporters want to find various opinions on a topic, follow trends or find people with specialized expertise, they often **lurk** (read messages) on electronic mailing lists or Usenet newsgroups, the bulletin-board-like part of the Internet (see Appendix A).

Mailing list messages tend to be more professional and focused. The postings arrive directly in the reporter's e-mail once he's subscribed to the mailing list. To find a mailing list on a specific topic, reporters use a directory on the Net, such as *Tile*, which allows a key-word search. Let's say you cover county government and one of the key issues right now is whether to privatize the emergency medical service. You might want to read what emergency medical technicians are writing about it. Plugging *paramedic* into Tile doesn't score a hit, but *emergency and service* tells you about the list EMERG-L and how to subscribe.

Usenet newsgroup postings are similar to mailing lists but tend to be more raucous and less reliable. Reporters also access them differently. Mailing list messages come to those signed on to the list through e-mail, but reporters see Usenet postings on the Internet using a newsreader program built into Web **browsers** (the software used to travel the Internet).

When she was a reporter at *The (Nashville) Tennessean,* business reporter Heather Newman regularly read the discussion among Saturn car owners on a newsgroup, *rec.autos.makers.saturn,* because the plant is located just outside Nashville.

Reporters who don't want to read a newsgroup daily, as did Newman, can search Usenet postings for specified terms using a search program such as *Deja News*. By typing *emergency medical technicians,* for example, reporters can get a list of messages from various newsgroups on which people have posted thoughts about EMTs. Deja News provides the date and subject of a message, the newsgroup it was posted to, and the e-mail address of the writer. Any of these messages can be read by clicking on them. Reporters also might want to note which newsgroup posts messages on a topic of interest and watch that group.

Heather Newman

NETWORK WITH OTHER REPORTERS

It's amazing how many good Samaritans online offer practical tips to the reporter in need. Several mailing list discussions can link you to experts at other news organizations.

Jon Whisenant, editor of *The MoJo Wire* (the Internet site of *Mother Jones* magazine), posted this query on NICAR-L, a mailing list discussion run by the National Institute for Computer-Assisted Reporting:

> I'm trying to locate a geographical breakdown of government dollars. How much money each state, county, census tract received in government fund-ing, that sort of thing. Is there a one-stop source for this kind of info?

The same day, Griff Palmer, of *The Daily Oklahoman,* wrote back:

> The U.S. Census Bureau's Web server provides the Consolidated Federal Funds Report, a pretty good breakdown of federal spending by state, county and place, summing federal grants-in-aid, assistance to individuals, salary and wages, and procurement contracts. A variety of information about spending by state and local government units is also available from the Census Bureau.
>
> Census Bureau's URL is: www.census.gov. The URL for the Consolidated Federal Funds Report is: www.census.gov/govs/www/cffr.html.

Another netizen (short for "good citizen of the Net"), Ray Robinson of *The (Norfolk) Virginian-Pilot,* later chimed in and told Whisenant how to get the reports on CD/ROM from the Census Bureau.

Reporters often jump on lists to share research tips even without being asked. CARR-L is the computer-assisted research and reporting list, run by Professor Elliott Parker of Central Michigan University. One day CARR-L carried a posting from the *Palm Beach Post*'s Larry Lipman, who offered a gem he'd found while mining on the Internet:

> I discovered an excellent site at the University of Indiana's Prevention Resources Center. Among the postings is the annual "Monitoring the Future" survey of drug use among 8th, 10th and 12th graders conducted by the University of Michigan. The site is at: http://www.drugs.indiana.edu/statistics/mrf/.

No doubt lots of reporters added the address to their lists of **bookmarks**—lists of World Wide Web sites they visit frequently—so they'd have it handy for future research.

Although reporters are always cautious about tipping their hand on a story to the competition, most aren't afraid to ask for some advice from out-of-town reporters with whom they're not competing.

Student reporters should take note, however, that professionals get upset if they think students are trying to take the easy way out and begin their research with a "help" posting via e-mail. So don't try a generic request like, "My professor just assigned me to do a story on seat belt recalls, where can I go on the Internet?" Make sure you've put work into the research—traditional and online—before you turn to others for help. Also, monitor the mailing list to get the flavor of the discussion before you jump in with your request.

RESEARCH USING BOOKS AND DOCUMENTS

The computer is a powerful reporting tool. It certainly isn't the only one. Until the very recent past, reporters didn't have the luxury of cruising the Net to get documents, press releases and background material to find sources or to interact with colleagues. But they still broke big stories. They still uncovered dirt. They still amassed a powerful array of facts, even though it couldn't match the breadth of today's computer-aided work.

For example, David Burnham covered criminal justice for *The New York Times* a few decades ago, long before the computer became a reporting tool in his newsroom. He couldn't analyze the disposition of thousands of robberies

ONLINE PRODUCING

Colleen Green says her boss calls her a "hunter and gatherer of information." As a producer/reporter for the *Star Tribune OnLine,* an electronic newspaper in Minneapolis, Green's beat is the Internet.

Green and other *OnLine* staffers adapt many of the stories from their sister publication, the *Star Tribune,* for the online edition. But they also add lots of information the paper doesn't have room for, making it an interactive site for readers who can get as much or little news as they choose. Readers subscribe to the electronic publication and usually read it online from their home computers.

"I get out on the Internet, hunt around for useful information and then gather it, whatever that entails, for our service to use to supplement stories or just to provide any background information," explains Green.

The kinds of skills Green uses are the same ones reporters use to research their stories. And as the Internet explodes, more jobs like hers are sure to be advertised.

Green gets story ideas by checking the **budget**— the daily list of stories the newspaper reporters at the *Star Tribune* are working on. One day her eyes caught an item saying reporter Larry Oakes was writing about the 20th anniversary of the sinking of the freighter, The Edmund Fitzgerald, in the icy waters of Lake Superior. Green knew of the mysterious incident, popularized in a song by Gordon Lightfoot.

"I thought this would be a great story for me to find some supplemental information for," she says. "It has a local focus, it has appeal, and it's a 20-year anniversary."

Green slotted the story for the online edition's metro page and set out on her Internet hunt to find what else she could add to Oakes' story. First she went to a popular Internet site, **Yahoo!**, where she typed in the key words *Edmund Fitzgerald* to search Internet sites containing those words. Green got back 10 hits. One by one she went to each of those sites to see what they offered. She picked three World Wide Web sites to add to *Star Tribune OnLine,* based on their look and content.

One site, put together by students at Michigan State University, told about the recent raising of the ship's bell. The other two also were from universities. One showed a tour of Lake Superior lighthouses; and the other ran the lyrics to Lightfoot's song. In about an hour, Green had done her research, selected the sites and designed the pages.

in New York to see how the criminal justice system handled the crimes. But that didn't keep him from a story. Burnham asked police for a random sample of 100 people arrested for robbery a year earlier. He tracked all the cases through the court system and discovered only one had been convicted. His methods would be considered outdated today, but his message is an important one that still holds up.

"Don't be a highly paid stenographer," he admonished students in a visit to Syracuse University.

If you're doing a piece on a particular topic, learn the system and its expectations. Then start measuring where it falls short and why. It's a mental process measured not in megabytes, but in gray cells.

When documents aren't online today, reporters still have to do what Burnham did in the old days—comb through paper files. Investigative producer John Trafalet, *WXYZ-TV,* Detroit, paged through 10 years of minutes from the Detroit police commissioners to pull the names of police officers who'd been suspended. The information formed the foundation for a three-part series by reporter Shellee Smith, "The Class of 1985," which showed how one-third of the officers hired in 1985 ended up going bad—charged with crimes ranging from stealing to manslaughter.

Journalists in the past also relied on libraries—the one at the newspaper, the public library down the street or the federal government depository library an hour away. Many reporters still do.

As a student reporter you probably think doing time in the library will be over once you graduate. Not so, says Don Gonyea of *National Public Radio.* When he was preparing a half-hour documentary on the 1937 sit-down strikes in Detroit, Gonyea spent a whole day at the Wayne State University labor archives picking through documents, bits of paper, meeting notices and shop flyers.

PUBLIC RECORDS LAWS

One of the best ways the media act as a watchdog on government is to follow paper trails to see how government officials are making decisions, allocating money and paying bills. That's possible because of federal and state open records laws.

The federal Freedom of Information Act provides that records kept by federal agencies should be open to the public. At the state level, similar laws are usually titled with the terms "open records," "freedom of information" or "sunshine law." (See The Legal Line box in Chapter 10, page 142, for information on open meetings laws.) Most laws cover public records kept in electronic form, on video or computer tape as well as in printed form.

WHAT'S COVERED

Whether at the federal or state level, open records laws provide public access to records found in government offices—most records, that is. One Michigan inmate tried to get the blueprints of the state prison where he was housed. He didn't succeed. Here are few other commonsense exemptions:

- Private personal information, such as the results of a soldier's HIV tests, done at a veteran's hospital.

- Trade secrets, including the formula for a new life-saving drug listed in confidential papers at the Food and Drug Administration.

- Law enforcement records that might jeopardize a person or investigation, such as the name of the undercover officers on the drug unit.

- Contract bids, such as the janitorial contract to clean the county office building. A competitor might use this to underbid a rival.

- Negotiation documents, such as the appraisal of a farm that the city wants to buy for an incinerator or the city's strategy in bargaining with the bus drivers' union.

Exemptions in one state aren't always exemptions in others.

WHO'S COVERED

What's considered a government agency also differs among the states, although generally the laws pertain to the administrative branch of government—city and county offices, state agencies and federal departments and agencies. Congress doesn't come under the federal Freedom of Information Act, and many legislatures have exempted themselves as well. Access to court records may come under a state FOI law, court rules or another statute.

We can't harp on it enough—know what your state's laws allow. Many government employees don't know the law and will erroneously prevent you from peeking into their file cabinets.

HOW IT WORKS

Reporters get records in two ways. They usually go to the office where the records are kept and ask for them. Often a letter isn't needed; an oral request will do. One tip: Don't be belligerent; a little sugar and patience go a lot further than threats or a recitation of your rights. But should an ornery bureaucrat simply refuse to respect those rights, don't quit there.

(continued)

"It ended up as only a couple of lines in the story, but it helped me feel more comfortable when writing the whole piece because I'd spent time with those original documents," Gonyea recalls.

Historical materials, film and tape are often researched the old-fashioned way.

ORIGINAL RESEARCH

Reporters aren't academics trained in statistical analysis or data collection. But it is not unusual for them to be guided by experts to do original research firsthand. Sometimes it's the only way to get the information.

Elizabeth Marchak of *The (Cleveland) Plain Dealer* coaxed a co-worker into sitting at the Cleveland airport one whole day copying down the tail numbers of all the planes that landed and took off. She then compared those tail numbers to a database of Federal Aviation Administration maintenance records and discovered the FAA didn't have maintenance records on some planes for more than two years. What started out as a story about the safety of planes in Cleveland soon mushroomed into a much bigger story about how the FAA doesn't have a handle on which planes are safe.

(continued)

You can write a letter to the head of the office (or the FOI officer, if one is designated), citing the appropriate state or federal freedom of information law and stating the specific records you want. Letters are best if you can't get to the office, if you have a large request, or if you expect the agency will have to screen out some exempted material from the records. See the **Student Press Law Center** Web site for sample letters.

Usually anyone can look at the records, but if you want copies, you often have to pay the cost of duplication. Most laws require the agency to give you the records within two weeks. However, the U.S. Justice Department is so understaffed it might take more than a year to respond. That leaves the reporter with little recourse other than to find the documents through a source.

BLOCKED ACCESS

When agencies won't release records, news organizations must sue to get them. *The (Baton Rouge, La.) Advocate* sued when the coroner's office wouldn't release information about a man accused of killing his brother. The paper ultimately got the documents, which confirmed a tip that the killer had a long record of mental illness and had been committed to a state institution for treatment several times. Although the information came a couple months after she wanted it, police reporter Melissa Miller says the suit set an important precedent for future requests to the coroner.

OTHER RECORDS LAWS

FOI laws aren't the only laws that require the government to release information. For example, one federal law requires colleges receiving federal funds to publish campus crime statistics. The Internal Revenue Service requires nonprofit organizations (charities, colleges and the like) to file financial information.

TIPS

Here are some tips, gathered from seasoned FOIA users, for getting records:

- Figure out who in government might keep the data you want and what specific record includes the information.

- Remember the laws cover records that exist, so you can't ask the agency to compile information for you that it doesn't regularly keep.

- Ask for the records first before writing an FOI request. Sometimes a letter starts a more formal and time-consuming process than is necessary.

- If you get turned down, be persistent. "Reporters need to know how to pry this stuff out on their own," says Max Jennings, editor of the *Dayton (Ohio) Daily News*. "Negotiate first, before you get the lawyers involved. It saves money and it simplifies things."

- Enlist newsroom management to help open records. *The (Raleigh, N.C.) News & Observer* requires all reporters to alert a supervisor when they've been rebuffed in getting public documents. Then managers help figure out the best technique to get the records. This policy helps editors keep tabs on just how open government is.

- Be persistent and creative. If you can't get the records from one office, think of what other agency might keep the data or whether the information is reported to a higher level of government.

Here's a sampling of what Marchak explained to readers:

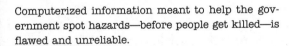

Computerized information meant to help the government spot hazards—before people get killed—is flawed and unreliable.

Thousands of mechanical breakdowns, perhaps nine of every 10 affecting the nation's 294,000 aircraft, never are reported to the Federal Aviation Administration the way regulations require, a study of records shows.

The (Cleveland) Plain Dealer

Marchak wouldn't have had the story without the original research at the Cleveland airport. It was the only way to get the tail numbers.

DATABASES

Marchak's story was also aided by use of a database of government records on airplanes kept by the FAA. **Databases** are simply computerized collections of records that can be easily searched. But they are oh-so-valuable.

TRACING PEOPLE

If there is one type of research reporters do repeatedly, it's checking a person's background. Here are 10 types of records to help in that quest:

- Drivers' licenses and motor vehicle records (available in many, not all, states).
- Birth certificates, which give middle names and parents' names and occupations.
- Marriage licenses.
- Court filings, including divorce records, small claims court records, civil suits, criminal cases and bankruptcy filings.
- Real estate transactions.
- Voter registration lists.
- Professional licensing records, kept for jobs ranging from lawyer to beautician.
- Telephone company directory assistance. (Ask for several cities so the operator searches the area code rather than one city.)
- College alumni offices.
- Pet licenses. (Those who won't give their address to anybody often list it with the city in case their pet gets lost.)

Who is the biggest keeper of databases? If you guessed the U.S. government, you're right. Government offices house vast numbers of documents, from elevator inspection reports in county offices to plant safety records at the federal Occupational Safety and Health Administration. Not all government records are computerized on databases, but more and more are added daily. Under public records laws, nearly all of these files are available to the public, including reporters (see earlier box, The Legal Line: Public Records Laws).

Increasingly, commercial companies, called **vendors**, are putting together databases of scholarly journal articles, newspaper stories, radio/TV transcripts or collections of medical articles, for example.

Whether they come from government or private companies, databases can help reporters:

- Track companies or people
- Find specific records or statistics
- Analyze volumes of records for summary information and trends
- See the context of a topic
- Read other perspectives on an issue
- Fact-check information
- Locate managers, experts or complainants

Reporters access databases in two ways: either by dialing into a remote computer where the records are stored or by purchasing the database and loading it on their newsroom's system for quick searching.

IN-HOUSE DATABASES

Remember the story earlier about using computer records to trace the serial rapist? What Alan Cox of *WCCO-TV* has done in gathering thousands of government records and reformatting them on disc and CD/ROM for the newsroom computers is an example of in-house databases (see box, Learning from the Pros: Compiling Databases).

Newspapers are often far ahead of their radio and TV counterparts in this new level of research. King of the hill is *The (Raleigh) News & Observer,* which boasts more than 300 such in-house databases and adds or replaces several each week.

In the Pulitzer Prize–winning series, "Boss Hog," reporters used databases of campaign contributions and government phone records to track the ties between pork producers and legislators. And after analyzing state trooper citations, they told readers how much they could drive over the speed limit without being pulled over by the State Highway Patrol (9 mph).

Reporters can also mine their databases for some lighthearted stories. The paper ran one article on the superstitious nature of North Carolinians—40 percent fewer couples tie the knot on the 13th of the month. That came from researching a database of marriage licenses.

"We want to use computer assistance every time the value added to the story exceeds the cost," says Pat Stith, *The News & Observer*'s editor for computer-assisted reporting. "That means we'll use computer assistance to add a 10th graph to a story, if we can do it in a hurry."

If news organizations choose not to go through the hassle of transferring the records themselves, they can buy them already formatted and cleaned up (inaccuracies and inconsistencies corrected). Many turn to the National Institute for Computer-Assisted Reporting at the University of Missouri. One of the popular databases NICAR offers is a CD/ROM of campaign contributions from the Federal Elections Commission.

Newspaper reporters should think of their computerized bank of past stories, public notices and advertisements as valuable in-house databases. They can be treasure troves of information to research people, from business promotion announcements to bankruptcy notices, and from real estate transactions to the police blotter.

David Milliron, at the *(Fort Myers, Fla.) News-Press,* was working a story about a 6-month-old who'd been shaken to death. He had the name of the father, who had been arrested for the crime, but little else. Using that information, he searched for the birth announcement in the paper's database of old stories and found the child's name, the mother's name (different from the father's) and the date of birth.

Another advantage for those who work in print: Policies at some newspapers allow reporters to find hard-to-locate people through the marketing department's subscriber database. Many people who keep their phone numbers unpublished give them out when they subscribe to the paper. Reporters at the *St. Petersburg (Fla.) Times* used the subscriber list extensively to track down some of the area's richest residents for a series, "Who in the World Lives There?"

But this raises ethical issues. Should subscribers, who provided their phone numbers and addresses to get a newspaper, be visited by reporters using that information for a very different reason than it was offered? As more and more information becomes available from more and more sources, the number of such questions can only multiply.

ONLINE DATABASES

If reporters don't have the databases they need right in the newsroom, they can use a computer, modem and telephone line to dial into a remote computer to get the information. For example, some reporters can dial in (via modem) directly to a courthouse computer to find the history of a forgery case and the next scheduled court date.

Suppose the local hospital has just announced that it is a trial site for a promising new breast cancer drug. A reporter could track the drug's history and clinical trials through the National Cancer Institute's modem-access CancerLit database, which contains almost a million references and abstracts of articles about cancer.

More and more database owners are moving their information to the Web for easy searching. But often the same database is available in several ways. For example, Uncover is a database index of over 17,000 periodicals, mostly in the sciences and social sciences. Reporters can search it by **telnet** (a computer-to-computer connection using telnet software), but they can also read it through CompuServe (a commercial online service) or on a Web site. Once reporters find the articles they want, Uncover faxes them out.

Many news outlets subscribe to databases with articles from media publications and transcripts of TV newscasts. *National Public Radio*'s technology reporter Dan Charles needed details on a five-year-old Colorado crime for a story on digital fingerprinting, so he enlisted *NPR*'s whiz librarian, Kee Malesky, to find any newspaper stories about the homicide.

Malesky decided the best place to look was Nexis, a dial-in database to which *NPR* subscribes. Because she knows the tricks of fast searching on Nexis, which contains articles from hundreds of newspapers, Malesky found two stories for Charles in just a few moments.

COMPILING DATABASES

WCCO-TV reporters easily access the following records in their newsroom. Beginning reporters can use this as a model for setting up databases in their newsrooms.

- **Airplane tail numbers** from the FAA and a vendor. Useful in aviation stories or when planes crash.

- **Census data** for Minnesota from the U.S. Census Bureau. Contains all types of demographic information, such as how many VCRs are in homes or how many unwed couples live together.

- **Court records,** criminal and civil, from the county. Useful in tracking cases or in seeing how many times a defendant has appeared in court.

- **Criminal history records** from the Minnesota Bureau of Criminal Apprehension, including information on charges, convictions and sentences a person has faced.

- **Death certificates** back to 1983 from the Minnesota Department of Health. Helpful in tracking disease trends or investigating the most frequent cause of death by age.

- **Fatal traffic accident data** from the National Highway Transportation Safety Administration. Useful in tracking common causes of crashes or where accidents routinely occur.

- **Political campaign contributions** from the Federal Election Commission and the Minnesota Ethical Practices Board. Helpful in finding who is contributing to whom.

- **Prison records** since 1978 from the Minnesota Department of Corrections. Used to find out where a convict is housed or what types of offenders are living in what prisons.

- **Property records** from the county and from a private subscription service covering the region. These tell who owns what residential and commercial property and can be helpful, for example, in checking who stands to benefit from a new shopping development or sports arena.

- **Public employee lists**—including names, hometown, pay rate, job title and date hired—from the state, county and city. Helpful for stories about who is running the government or for stories analyzing, for example, whether pay is equitable for men and women.

Malesky asked the service to give her all the stories with certain key words, called **search terms**. Her search terms included the names of two Denver newspapers, the victim's name and the word *fingerprint* or *kidnap*. But to further limit her search to truly relevant articles, she asked that the terms appear near to each other and that they appear several times in the articles.

Other common news databases used by journalists are DataTimes, DIALOG, Dow Jones News/Retrieval, MEDIS (medical journal articles) and Westlaw (law cases and articles). Some, like Nexis, provide full text; others offer abstracts or bibliographies.

Such research can really make a story when you're on deadline, but these commercial databases can be expensive—some cost upwards of $100 per hour. So it pays to learn how to get on, get what you want and get off quickly.

COMPUTER-ASSISTED REPORTING

The proliferation of databases, especially those with government records, has led to one of the most powerful research tools now becoming standard in newsrooms—**computer-assisted reporting**. Some reporters use CAR to refer to anything they do on a computer. For this book, we're defining CAR as using a computer to analyze records—from fairly simple calculations of the increases in city budget line items year-to-year to complex analyses of millions of Medicare payment records.

CAR helps reporters get new information to plug into stories. Sometimes by crunching numbers, journalists learn things even the experts don't know. Or the numbers point them to a new angle or provide support for an interviewee's arguments.

In this book, we can't teach you the rudiments of becoming a computer-assisted reporting pro—that's another course and another book. But we can expose you to the ways computer-assisted reporting is used. It can:

- Examine trends over time. *Are police confiscating more or less heroin than five years ago?*
- Verify or refute claims. *Is the state senator correct when he says he's brought more than $500,000 in government aid to the district?*
- Rank items from best or most to worst or least. *Here's the city intersection where the most accidents occur.*
- Compare parts with the whole. *How does the voter turnout rate in a suburb compare to the state average?*
- Compare similar entities. *Are property tax assessments the same in neighboring suburbs?*

"Reporters have to be info-savvy in ways they never did before," says Nora Paul, library director at The Poynter Institute for Media Studies. Increasingly, newspaper editors are listing CAR skills as a requirement for reporting jobs. On the radio/TV side, managers are now waking up to the fact that CAR skills help their reporters compete with print reporters, who always outnumber them.

"As we become a more and more computer-based society, that's where the news is," says Alan Cox, of *WCCO-TV,* Minneapolis. "I don't think we as broadcasters can cede to print people a corner on this type of news."

Such number crunching is only the start to a story. The numbers can merely show correlation, not cause. For that, reporters use the traditional reporting tool of talking to people. For a series on airline safety, Beth Marchak of *The (Cleveland) Plain Dealer* and a colleague traveled to six cities and interviewed more than 100 people.

"The numbers help tell the story, but if you can't find any human drama, you don't have the story," she says. "Good quotes still make the story."

VALIDITY OF SOURCES

When it comes to numbers in a computer-assisted project and information found online or, for that matter, in reference books, reporters always need to evaluate whether the information is accurate. In an age of instant access, it's easy for misinformation to be passed from story to story and, each time, be incorrect. Anyone, as we've said before, can put up a Web site. The fewer layers of editing, the more room for error.

Professor Christina Hoff Sommers, of Clark University, checked out a statistic appearing in many media: that 150,000 women die from anorexia in the United States each year. Sommers traced the number back through several publications to a newsletter of the American Anorexia and Bulimia Association that mentioned 150,000 sufferers, not fatalities. Checking further, Sommers found the National Center for Health Statistics reported only 51 deaths from anorexia nervosa the previous year.

"Data has always had errors—human and otherwise—and has always been used to manipulate people," says Nora Paul of The Poynter Institute.

Debbie Wolfe, newsroom technology training coordinator at the *St. Petersburg (Fla.) Times,* reminds reporters not to get so enamored with the Internet that they believe everything on it.

"I don't trust anything I see," says Wolfe. "I corroborate it with information that I know is correct."

She tells reporters not to drop information wholesale into their articles or scripts. Because it's there doesn't mean it's accurate. Her tip: Check with an expert in the field, a news librarian or other printed sources.

Knowing the source helps in evaluating the information. If it's a government statistic from a government manual or government Web site, it's probably more reliable than a contrary number printed in an old clip.

"Use your own news sense and what you feel safe with," says Wolfe. "Take the information and bounce it off another person whom you trust."

Tracking information to the original source is one way reporters can verify it. A **primary source** is a firsthand source—the doctor who conducted the research and explained it to a reporter, or a government study that a reporter read cover to cover. A **secondary source** is one step removed—a researcher who told you what the other

RESEARCHING

1. In-depth research helps reporters gather new information for the story, see the big picture and build a foundation from which to develop questions and pursue new angles.

2. Reporters who want to sharpen their competitive edge are increasingly looking online for government records, company profiles or the latest discussion on a current topic. The best reporters know the quick tricks for searching whatever resources they have—a database, CD/ROM or the Internet. But technique isn't everything. Good answers, by computers or people, require smart questions.

3. Computer-assisted reporting is the hot new skill that news managers want in reporters they hire. Such skills include finding stories hidden in database records, verifying sources' claims by pulling out the real numbers and analyzing information too voluminous to go through by hand.

4. The adage "If your mother says she loves you, check it out" is true. All information garnered through research must be verified. Go to primary sources and evaluate what you've found.

doctor found, or a magazine article reporting on the government study. Reporters should attempt to get a primary source whenever possible.

Here are other key questions in evaluating information:

- Who is the source or researcher?
- How credible is the source?
- How was the information gathered?
- How timely is the information?
- Does the source hold a bias or have a vested interest? Finding out who funds the sources goes a long way toward answering this question.
- Does the result of a poll (or a study) confirm or conflict with past results? If it conflicts, why?

One last tip about accuracy: All information changes quickly. Be sure to note the date, time and address for an item posted online and the publication date of something in print. And remember, books, in particular, often don't appear until a half year or more after the information was gathered.

RECOMMENDED READING

Access to electronic records. (1994). Arlington, VA: Reporters Committee for Freedom of the Press.

This 30-page booklet gives a good introduction to electronic records, how to get them and what the costs might be. The best part is a state-by-state review of the law on electronic access so you'll know what you're entitled to receive. See other publications and sample FOIA letters at the Reporters Committee for Freedom of the Press Web site: **http://www.rcfp.org**.

Houston, B. (1995). *Computer assisted reporting: A practical guide.* New York: St. Martin's.

Brent Houston, executive director of Investigative Reporters and Editors, has written this helpful guide for beginning reporters. He covers database managers, spreadsheets and online resources to help in news stories, along with stories showing how reporters are using them.

Paul, N. *Computer assisted research: A guide to tapping online information* (3rd ed.). St. Petersburg, FL: The Poynter Institute for Media Studies. [Online]. Available: **http://www.poynter.org/car/cg_chome.htm**.

This online resource is an easy-to-understand primer on the Internet, commercial databases, commercial information services, directories and much more to help reporters make better use of computers in research. Nora Paul is the library director at The Poynter Institute and continually updates this guide.

Reddick, L., & King, E. (1997). *The online journalist.* (2nd ed.). Orlando, FL: Harcourt Brace.

This is the best textbook out now that gives an overview, with detailed instructions and examples, of how reporters are using the Internet.

Weinberg, S. (1995). *The reporter's handbook* (3rd ed.). New York: St. Martin's Press.

This book is at the right hand of every investigative reporter, but it's also a must for any reporter

doing enterprise and in-depth stories. Steve Weinberg, a well-known investigative reporter and former head of Investigative Reporters and Editors, has packed this full of detailed information on 16 beats, including records to get, structures of organizations and how things work. Plus, it has chapters on working sources, using documents and organizing for a big project.

Wendland, M. (1999). *Wired journalist: Newsroom guide to the Internet* (3rd ed.). Washington, D.C.: Radio Television News Directors' Association Foundation. [Online]. Available: **http://www.rtndf.org/programs/century/wjforward.html**.

Available in book form or on the Internet. Although it's written for broadcast reporters, all journalists will find this user-friendly guide helpful in getting started. Mike Wendland, investigative reporter at *WDIV-TV,* Detroit, makes it sound like fun, as he's packed it full of anecdotes and examples.

EXERCISES

A. BACKGROUNDING

1. A total solar eclipse will take place in your city next week. You've been asked to write a story in advance of the event. How do you prepare yourself to conduct interviews with a scientist at the local university who will do research on sun spots during the event?

2. The chief of police has called a press conference in two hours to comment on charges that his officers roughed up a local teen-ager while arresting him after a high-speed chase. The charges were made and reported in the media yesterday. How do you prepare?

3. You have to get to the nearest federal courthouse to look up a civil case that is coming to trial. Write out the directions.

4. A wire service advancer (an alert to an upcoming story) says the Southern Baptist Convention is meeting next week in your city. Someone else tells you the big topic on the agenda is "inerrancy." How do you prepare for coverage? What information do you find and where?

5. A celebrity (pick one) is coming into town tomorrow. Research his or her biography in preparation for an interview.

B. FINDING CONTACTS

1. You're assigned an adopt-a-pet feature story. How do you find the name and address of the dog pound?

2. A tipster calls in and says the cops are raiding a drug house down the street (the 3200 block of Main Street). How do you find the names of other persons who know what's going on?

3. You're assigned a story on the problems with the local recycling program. Find four local people and one national expert to interview.

4. Local churches are collecting clothing and money to send to victims of a recent disaster overseas. The distribution is being coordinated by Church World Service. Find the phone number and address.

5. An exhibit of Monet's paintings is about to open at the local art museum. Find the names and numbers of three persons to interview.

C. RESEARCHING

1. The state legislature will be voting tomorrow on cuts to the state's welfare program. Find out how many persons were on welfare five years ago compared to today, as well as the total cost of the program then and now.

2. Check real estate records at city hall to find out what your dean, department chair and/or professor paid for their homes. Check an online database to see if you can find how much your parents (or another relative) paid for a home. Write a memo detailing how you found the information.

3. Research one beat, or area of coverage, and write a chapter for a class "Beat Book," which all the students in your class can refer to as they report stories the rest of the term. Find at least two sources who can give you a history and summary of this beat. Each chapter should include an overview of the beat, a brief historical perspective, a summary of ongoing stories, a calendar of future events or decision dates, and 10 sources (people, paper, online) whom students might need to call to do class assignments.

4. Find a story for which you need state or local government records. Write a freedom of information request for the documents (see sample at the Web site of the Student Press Law Center). Before you send it, call or visit the appropriate agency and ask to see the records. Prepare a presentation for the class outlining the steps you took and the response.

5. Select a story out of the daily paper that you think would be good for an online edition of your local newspaper. Using the Internet search sites listed in Appendix B, find three relevant sites that you could link to your online local story. Write a memo telling why that story is good for the online edition, how you found the Internet sites, and why those sites would be of interest to your online readers.

D. VERIFYING SOURCES

1. How many countries exist in the world? Check several sources (ideally, text and online references) to determine the correct number. What did you find? How do you explain any discrepancies?

2. A news release says the Amazon River is the world's longest. You think it may be the Nile. How do you find out? Which is it?

3. A wire report talks about the growing clout of women in the U.S. Senate but doesn't say how many women senators there are. How are you going to find out? What's the number?

4. Read or listen to local news and note a statistic used in a story. Find the original source for the information using ready references, online sources and the telephone.

5. Call the local rape crisis center and get the figure of the number of women raped each day, nationally. What's the source? Check newspapers or magazines for the same statistic. What do you find? Which number would you use in a story and why?

CHAPTER 5　Cultivating Sources

Tom Flannery has turned up some big stories snooping around the little piece of Pennsylvania covered by the 50,000 circulation *(Lancaster, Pa.) Intelligencer Journal.* He has twice won the state Associated Press Managing Editors Award, seen his stories chased by the elite national media and served as a consultant on ABC's "Nightline." So what's the secret of his success?

"If I had to put my finger on one reason for my success, it would be my ability to develop, keep and work sources," says Flannery.

Flannery might add that these sources often have led him to documents that serve as the factual evidence he needs to publish his investigative pieces. Documents, too, can lead reporters to people who serve as sources.

But winning the trust of sources can't be done by reading their words in print. Flannery's foremost advice: Get out of the office, meet people away from the pressures of a breaking story and remember that every one of them might help you some day.

How reporters ask questions and what they ask certainly influences the quality of the answers that come back (see Chapter 6). But the best journalists often get the best information not because of a clever question but because of the long hours they've spent finding key people, getting to know who they are and learning what makes them tick.

That is what the work of "sourcing" is all about. In this chapter you will learn how to:

- Identify different types of sources
- Develop sources
- Find and keep the best sources
- Work out ground rules of attribution with your sources

ANYONE CAN BE A SOURCE

Contrary to the image of the classic book about the Watergate scandal, "All the President's Men," most reporters don't rely on sources who skulk around garages and go by the name Deep Throat. Usually there is far less mystery and intrigue to finding the people reporters interview in developing stories.

"I consider everyone I meet a source," Flannery says. "I am never without a business card."

Reporters intent on hobnobbing only with the rich and powerful shut off plenty of avenues of legitimate news. Judy Rakowsky knows that well. She covers the federal courts for *The Boston Globe.*

"I strike up a conversation with every stenographer, every clerk," she says. "There are court watchers in the courtrooms. That's what they do all day. I know them all by name. Some of them stop by every day. Some call me. So even though I can't be everywhere at once, I've heard who was in the building, who went before the grand jury, what's going on in so-and-so's court."

From defense attorneys to drug enforcement agents, Rakowsky talks to people not only in formal interviews but also at the newspaper stand, on the elevator and in the hallway. She's relaxed and personable. She's also chasing the news.

"You can't do your job all by records, that's for sure," she says. "By the time [documents] get recorded, your deadline might be past."

If anyone in the hallway or elevator might prove a source, so might contacts in communities reporters "visit" on the Internet. There, reporters can find sources who don't have offices and don't list their businesses in the yellow pages. The most highly placed source at city hall, for example, won't be much help if you're beginning research on the spread of the straight edge movement—those rockers who have sworn off drugs and drink. The straight edgers themselves will be. But where do you find them?

You could type *straight edgers* into **Deja News**, a search program for Usenet, the bulletin-board-like part of the Internet (see Chapter 4). Your query would prompt several dozen hits with messages from teens about the straight edgers' lifestyle. Many give their e-mail address, full name and phone number.

No need to call the first one. By lurking (reading messages) on a straight edge newsgroup, you'll learn more about straight edgers' interests. You also might hear from one in your own community.

ALL SOURCES AREN'T EQUAL

Some people are experts; they're trained in a specific area or have studied it extensively. Others can share personal experiences that experts have studied but not lived through. Still others merely voice strong opinions.

All can be sources for stories, but all play different roles. A reporter arriving at an accident scene, for example, will get the official account of what happened from a police officer, not the first bystander she runs into. The officer presumably is trained to provide accurate and authoritative information. A survivor of the accident could provide a much more personal and emotional account, but that account won't be complete and may well be biased. This isn't to suggest that reporters won't interview the survivor. Naturally, they will. But that person will primarily provide drama and firsthand details. The survivor won't be relied on to give definitive information about whose fault the accident was or how fast different vehicles were traveling.

Reporters make the same kinds of distinctions in countless stories. People in authority don't always tell the truth: Witness the videotapes that showed police beating Rodney King. But even though reporters shouldn't take official accounts as gospel, they should start with them, if for no other reason than that public officials are entrusted to serve the public. Officials are paid to gather facts. A person who happens to be wandering by is not.

There are exceptions to getting the official version first. They occur more frequently in investigative pieces. A reporter investigating complaints of beatings in the county jail, for example, likely will gather evidence from prisoners, their attorneys and public records before confronting the jailers.

SOURCE VARIETY BUILDS BETTER STORIES

Regardless of the story, one lesson is constant: The best stories—on everything from the changing face of a neighborhood to a new program to keep kids in school—are built on information provided by a variety of sources and a variety of types of sources. The reporter who interviews only the administrator of the new school program won't have a clue what kids going through it actually think. The reporter who interviews 15 kids but no administrators won't know what the extent of the drop-out problem is or how the school is attempting to combat it.

Stories need facts. These often are provided by someone in authority, such as that administrator, a fire chief, a statistician, a social worker or city council member. Stories need knowledgeable, impartial assessments of those facts. These, in turn, often come from experts outside the government or organization that provided the initial information. And stories need specific, human examples. The best come from the mouths of people who have experienced rather than observed, from those whose lives exemplified whatever issue the reporter is exploring in a story.

Years before Bob Dotson of *NBC News* became what he calls a "second-generation [Charles] Kuralt," he was learning the lesson that real people make stories special. One day, teamed with photojournalist Darrell Barton, he was sent out to cover what he describes as a "grade C" tornado story in Oklahoma. No one had died and no one had been injured. But the twister tore up several homes. Many news crews would have been satisfied with a standard and predictable news segment—a camera sweep of the damage and an earnest mayor or governor asking for federal disaster relief. What Dotson calls "paint by the numbers stuff."

Instead, Barton worked in close, watching and getting to know the people sorting through the wreckage. He settled on an older fellow and followed him as he dug through what was left of his house.

"Well, the fellow finally found what he'd been looking for," Dotson recalled. "He pulled out this big hunk of pink goo, held it up and said, 'Well, [the twister] got my teeth but it didn't get me.'"

Then he smiled a big toothless grin. The story's lasting image, its **close**, was set in stone by a source who didn't appear in the city hall directory.

BUILDING SOURCE LISTS FROM SCRATCH

When Ann Scales moved from Texas to Boston to join the staff of *The Boston Globe,* she knew little about her new city. She wasted no time in changing that.

"I spent a lot of *Globe* money taking people to lunch," recalls Scales.

During those lunches she talked with people—new sources—about who they were, what they did and what concerns they had about their city. Scales says she always came away with a little more knowledge—and a list of other people to contact.

In the long haul, there's no substitute for meeting would-be sources face to face. But lunch takes time, so Scales looked for other ways to build up her Rolodex. When she read, for example, a pen was never far away. Often she stopped to pop another would-be source into her list of people worth knowing.

"I collect names," she says simply. "Names can be very useful to me."

And when she met people informally, at parties or on a story, she collected cards as well. "Find out what people do," she urges young reporters. "I think of reporting as detective work. You want to talk to enough people to build your case."

Like detectives, reporters always have to talk to plenty of strangers. And like detectives, reporters are most efficient when they move quickly to the most knowledgeable strangers rather than spending hours with the first person they happen to meet. But the best information is likely to come from people who already know you and trust you.

THE PSYCHOLOGY OF SOURCING

The more a reporter knows about a new source and the greater the empathy that reporter can convey, the better the odds of developing a lasting relationship of mutual respect.

People talk to reporters for a variety of reasons. Some sources are high-minded: They want the truth to be told. Some are vicious: They want to do in another person. Still others are ambitious or egocentric. But many are merely interested in the topic they're being asked about or are engaged by the person doing the asking. When these people are convinced a reporter's interest is genuine rather than manipulative, they are more likely to open the door and invite the media in. The same is true of sources who are just plain scared.

"Very few people have to talk to us," Rakowsky says. "So I guess I go into everything thinking about why. Why should they talk to us?"

The answer, like the source, varies. It may be because that source's point of view isn't getting out. It may be because the reporter has challenged a source's intellect. It may be that the reporter has engaged that interview subject as a human being.

"I try to show a bit of myself," Rakowsky says.

Charles Sennott, a special projects reporter at *The Globe,* says, "You can't just be about gathering information."

The line, however, is a fine one. The reporter who loses objectivity, whose friendships or loyalties distort or skew the news, is a reporter headed for trouble. Or, as Rakowsky adds, "It still has to be clear that you're not their friend."

That said, reporters shouldn't treat the people they interview as mere conduits of information. The best reporters know this. Many have an "A" list of a few dozen key sources whom they'll call every week or two to develop a relationship that lasts beyond the give-and-take of any one story. They chat with these sources about their hobbies, swap tales about families, send along stories or tapes on which the sources have been helpful.

"Stay in touch with people," Rakowsky counsels. "The thing that people really don't like is if you only go to them when you want them to spill their guts on something that's tough for them. Find a way to touch base."

Flannery of the *(Lancaster, Pa.) Intelligencer Journal* says he operates by a golden rule. "I ask myself, 'How would you like to be treated if you were on the other end of it?'"

By investing time when news isn't breaking, smart reporters save time when it is.

"I can call people at 3 a.m. and get a comment because people know me," Flannery says. "They know what I look like. They've seen my eyes. I am not a voice on the phone."

Herb Weisbaum, a *CBS News* consumer reporter, sounds a similar refrain: "When the big story hits, and there are 35 messages sitting on the desk [of key sources], you want to be the one call they return right away. You're involved with them all the time, so when you really need them, they're going to return your call."

Often the best sources, those with whom reporters have established lasting trust, don't wait to be asked. Frequently, they pick up the phone to offer new **tips**—nuggets of information that either are news or lead to it. Some tips to newsrooms do come from strangers. But find a reporter who regularly breaks news and you've likely found a reporter who has built a strong list of sources and who keeps in touch with those people.

FINDING THE BEST SOURCES

It's one thing to build trust. But how do you find the best sources? How do you develop a source list with breadth and depth? Here are some ways to start.

FIND OUT WHO HAS BEEN INTERVIEWED BEFORE

Rare is the story subject that's never been covered. When reporters take on a new topic and face a blank slate rather than familiar sources, a good starting point is to check out who has been interviewed on the subject in the past (see Chapter 4).

This can be overdone. The media are accused, sometimes justifiably, of always returning to the same "experts" instead of finding new ones. Still, a reporter scrambling to find a leading expert on the bond market might well check a database of *Wall Street Journal* articles for good leads. Or she might hop online and search ***TotalNEWS***, a search engine and directory to 1,200 online publications.

BUILD A CONTACT LIST

Smart reporters build their own contact list, chock-full of the names and numbers of sources. Sean Coulthard of *WCBS-AM* kept his contact list on his laptop computer and printed it every few weeks as a backup in case his computer crashed.

"Every single story that I do, every phone call I make, every number on a press release, every business card I get, I put into my Rolodex at the end of the week," he says.

Reporters often keep sources on file not only alphabetically by name but also under the subjects on which the source can be of help. And don't settle for office phone numbers. News breaks on weekends and in the evening. Always ask for home numbers, car phone numbers and pager numbers.

Source files are more effective if they contain some information about each person. Then when you call, you can ask, "How's your tennis game?" or, "Did your son make the starting football team?"

"I try to jot down [sources'] personal interests," says Nina Kim, who has covered police, suburban communities and city hall for *The (Syracuse, N.Y.) Post-Standard.* "I jot down where they live, work, their spouses' names, their birthdays. These things personalize my interactions with them."

REMEMBER THE PERSON AT THE NEXT DESK

Many newsrooms provide a source list on the newsroom computer system with listings by subject areas, such as "airport," "recycling" or "water pollution contacts." Such lists give reporters a quick reference of whom to interview for a story on unfamiliar turf. Other news organizations, such as *Newsday* on Long Island, require reporters to compile beat books that list sources. Alas, building great sources is never as simple as talking to the last reporter who covered what you do. Each reporter's best sources grow out of an intangible called personal chemistry. Some people hit it off. Others don't. That said, a five-minute chat with a colleague who has written a story on a similar subject still may well save you a five-hour search for sources. If you are starting a new beat, take the last beat reporter to lunch.

PUBLIC RELATIONS PEOPLE CAN HELP

The give and take of news has changed since an era, not so long ago, when journalists disdained all public relations types as "flacks," and they in turn seemed more intent on blocking the door than in helping reporters get in the right offices. More often than not today, PR practitioners help link reporters with the people they need to interview and help them find useful background information.

In calling a PR representative, make it clear what kind of information you need. And explain that you want that information directly from the person with the best firsthand knowledge, not filtered through a PR release or statement. A cautionary note: While information from many public relations people can be substantive and useful, it always should be scrutinized. PR people are paid to portray their organizations in the best light. They are a starting point for news, not an ending point.

USE ONE EXPERT TO FIND OTHER EXPERTS

Once you find an expert to interview, don't walk away or hang up the phone without asking these two questions: "If you were looking for advice or authoritative information on this subject, whom would you call?" And, "Whom do you respect in your field who takes a contrary point of view to yours?"

This technique can quickly expand your source file.

Also, don't overlook your source's expertise in directing you to paper sources. Ask, "How does the office document these types of complaints?" or, "What other studies do you consider worth reading on this subject?"

One Source Can Open Doors to Another

When Sennott of *The Boston Globe* arrived in Oklahoma City to cover the bombing of the federal building, he already had the name of a key law enforcement source, thanks to a good contact in the same agency in Boston who told Sennott to call the man and use his name as a reference. Sennott had worked with the Boston source on earlier stories; he also joined him regularly after work for a drink.

"It's not only important to save phone numbers and to treat people well, it's also important to stay in touch," Sennott says. "You never know when a similar story will happen and you'll need someone's expertise again."

Start Locally, Then Look Beyond

Whether the issue is welfare, the flat tax or organic farming, the local university may have someone who can answer your questions and suggest other sources. But you shouldn't make that local university your final destination. Local experts often help lead you to the real experts, the people they turn to when seeking information in their fields. By making that extra call, you'll have a more authoritative story.

Out-of-town experts are easier for print, radio and online reporters who can use a quote, phone interview or audio computer file in their stories. But television reporters need not whine that they can't use out-of-town experts because they must have pictures and sound. They can still interview these sources by phone and integrate the information into their scripts.

Find Instant Help Online

In a burgeoning online world can be found several directories of expert sources. One favorite of reporters is *Profnet*, which links journalists to professors and experts at more than 800 institutions in 17 countries. Reporters can check the directory at the Profnet Web site or send an e-mail query. It's then forwarded to public relations officers worldwide who e-mail or call the reporter to suggest an interviewee.

Profnet helped Christopher Mele and Paula McMahon of the *(Middletown, N.Y.) Times Herald-Record* pin down information they needed for a voter-fraud story. They uncovered more than 170 instances of people with the same name and birth date voting in the same election in two different New York counties. What, they wondered, was the probability that there could be so many twosomes with the same name and birth date living within 70 miles of each other. Mele plugged the terms *odds* and *probability* into the search function at Profnet and found the name of Dr. Bruce Bemis, a math professor at Westminster College, Salt Lake City. Bemis confirmed Mele's hunch: The numbers were beyond the laws of chance; something was amiss here.

Many public relations firms, organizations and publishers have put source directories online. For example, reporters who want to find a lawyer in a certain specialty or even track down one by name, use the ***West Legal Directory***. Sometimes companies list employee directories on their Web sites or provide "reply" or "feedback" buttons on their home pages that reporters use to track down a source.

CLIPBOARD   Internet Sites Mentioned in This Chapter

Big Book	www.bigbook.com	TotalNEWS	www.totalnews.com
Deja News	www.dejanews.com	West Legal Dictionary	www.wld.com/client/
Four 11	www.four11.com		Welcome.asp
Profnet	www.profnet.com		

If you have a source's name and hometown and want her phone number or e-mail address, Internet phone books such as **Big Book** or **Four11** might help, but they aren't yet one-stop shopping. Using telephone directory assistance or calling people for their e-mail addresses is often faster.

Look for People Who Live the Story

Remember Bob Dotson's toothless tornado survivor? Some people talk about issues. Others live them. Students building houses for Habitat for Humanity are a lot more interesting—and, on television, more visual—than Habitat's directors sitting in an office talking in general terms about the experience. That piece on the growth of volunteerism wants to key on the volunteers themselves. On the flip side, kids who spray-paint walls will have more to say and show about what they do and why they do it than cops, who can give some general comments on the problem.

Finding sources who don't sit in offices takes time, often much more time than the interview itself. It's an investment good reporting requires.

"It's absolutely critical that young journalists get out of the newsroom," says Flannery of the *(Lancaster, Pa.) Intelligencer Journal.*

To Get the Best Stuff, Don't Start With the Boss

Madeleine Blais, who perfected her craft for *The Miami Herald* before leaving to teach, gives this advice to reporters: "Never interview the mayor."

She is exaggerating, of course. But nine times out of 10, people don't make it to the mayor's office, the executive boardroom or the school superintendent's chair by making waves. Bosses generally play within the rules, and those rules don't invite them to blab to the media. Sure, when crime statistics show a sharp drop, the sound bite or quote likely will come from the mayor or police chief. If you're looking at whether a city's police are outgunned by street gangs, other people besides the mayor and his handpicked chief can give you a more knowledgeable and more honest assessment.

Push Beyond Your Own Experience

As newsrooms push to diversify their coverage, some have ordered reporters to **mainstream**—to seek out and establish source lists of women and minorities to include in stories. At such a news organization, a story on emergency room care would be more likely to include the opinions of African-American, Latino and Asian-American doctors and nurses, not just white doctors and nurses.

There's a reason for this practice, as controversial as it's been in some newsrooms. We all—white, black and brown; rich and poor; straight and gay—tend to look toward our own communities. Studies demonstrate this—studies that show women and minorities are dramatically underrepresented on news pages and in news reports put together under the direction of managers predominantly white and male.

The best reporters guard against this tendency to cover only what they know and interview only those they know. These reporters seek out sources who didn't grow up in their community, go to their college, worship in their church or synagogue. They consciously reach out to broaden their own horizons (see Interviewing Across Cultural Lines in Chapter 6).

Don't Run With the Pack

"Zig when others zag," is how Sennott of *The Boston Globe* describes it. Too many reporters are so intent on getting the official line at press conferences that they spend entire days waiting for events they could just as well watch on live television or read in wire service reports.

A relaxed smile can help broadcast reporters cut through the nervousness of sources intimidated by a camera and microphone. Here, Pam Cross of *NewsCenter 5*, Boston, conducts an interview.

Sennott avoided these press conferences when he was sent to Union, S.C., to write a piece about Susan Smith after she confessed to killing her sons. Instead, he found the bar where she went the night before her sons died and an African-American community angered by early reports that the boys had been killed by a black man Smith had invented.

"The media came in here and made Union in the image of how they thought a small town should be, and that's what the townspeople gave you. . . . But that is not what Union is," the head of the local NAACP chapter told Sennott. "The truth of this town is very different, and not all of it is very pretty."

No one offers those kinds of insights at press conferences. Knowing when to run with the pack and when to leave it is particularly challenging for television and radio reporters. Needing sound bites and visuals, they can't play catch-up the way print reporters can. But no matter what the medium, reporters content to show up only where everyone else is won't distinguish themselves.

Honesty and Respect Go a Long Way

The night three teens were killed in Newton, Mass., Sennott would just as soon not have called their families. But these were exceptional kids, and *The Globe* wanted to write a profile about them for the next morning's paper.

So Sennott did call and found himself talking into an answering machine. He apologized for disturbing the family in its grief. And he explained that his purpose was to write a portrait of the teens for the next day. Two of the families called back.

The lesson: If you treat people courteously, they may talk even in situations when you don't expect them to. Reporters should never assume a person won't talk to them. On the other hand, it's highly unethical to browbeat people at times of grief.

"Every story is its own unique situation," Sennott said. "The primary things are to be upfront, honest and direct as possible. There's nothing harder than to try to get information on deadline from a stranger. That's the toughest."

Save Time to Meet New People

Reporters are busy people. Unless they carve out time to meet new sources, that task becomes a part of their job relegated to "when I get to it" status. And that may mean never.

One way to counter the constant demands of news is to set aside an hour to meet at least one new source each week. Breakfast meetings are ideal because they take place before anyone's day becomes overwhelming. Meetings that are not built around specific stories give reporter and source a chance to relax. They often can provide valuable insights into a person the reporter may be interviewing by phone next week.

GROUND RULES

Beth Willon's daughter was eight months old when a Superior Court judge in San Jose, Calif., gave Willon a choice: Reveal her source on a key piece of evidence in a murder trial or go to jail. Willon, like almost all self-respecting reporters, chose jail. The source of her report on *KNTV-TV* in San Jose was off-limits. She was spared by a higher court's ruling.

THE IMPORTANCE OF ATTRIBUTION

In many cases the identity and credibility of the source is central to the meaning and value of a story. For example, consider this sentence:

"The growth of China's military presents a serious threat to the security of the United States."

Is that news? Without attribution, this statement represents a reporter's opinion—one that may or may not be true. Viewers and readers would balk at such a sentence, unattributed, in the midst of a news story. They are used to certain standards of **fairness** in American news: They expect that news is based on facts, not reporters' opinions, and that news contains a range of views, clearly identified.

In the example, the identity of the speaker—the source—is central to the value and perception of the news. Let's say the statement was made by the head of the local American Legion. Would it be news? Possibly, in a small market. But it surely wouldn't top the 6 p.m. newscast. The source lacks

demonstrated expertise and might have an ax to grind. Regardless, the local head of the Legion doesn't have a thing to do with setting U.S. policy toward China.

But if the same the statement were made by the president before both houses of Congress, it likely would lead the news. Why? Presumably the president will present evidence. But the very fact that he makes such a charge and has the power to suggest policy changes as a result, makes it big news. Reporters still won't take it as gospel. They will look for those with opposing viewpoints and those who can explain the disagreement. They won't, however, ignore what the president has said.

The information—a statement—is the same in all three cases. Only the source has changed. That's why viewers and readers demand to know where information comes from, not merely the information itself.

Nothing is more sacrosanct in the world of reporting than a promise made to a source. Reporters who lose their reputation for trustworthiness lose the fundamental tool of their craft: credibility with the people who give them key information, sometimes at considerable risk to themselves (see box, The Legal Line: Protecting Sources, Notes and Tapes).

Reporters rarely have to choose between jail and protecting the identity of a source. Often, however, they have to deal with tricky negotiations with sources over whether those sources will appear on the air (in the case of television), whether they will be identified by name in a story and, in some cases, whether their information can be used at all.

Nonetheless, reporters should not readily grant sources protection from attaching their names to the information they feed the media. Information that is not sourced is less credible. Sometimes it is less ethical, because it allows figures who remain in the shadows to make accusations that place others in a bad light. This can make the accused, and an audience with a high sense of fairness, equally angry (see box, Ethics: One Internal Critic's View).

On the Record

Reporters generally assume the information they receive is **on the record**. It can be used without restrictions and attributed by name to a specific source. One exception to this rule is in interviewing people who haven't talked to the media before. In this case the advisable and ethical course for a reporter is to make it clear that the information is for a story and that the source may be quoted by name.

"I have no qualms with taking a step back, especially with someone who isn't very sophisticated, and saying, 'You aren't talking to your brother here. I'm working on a story, and I'm going to use what you say,'" says Flannery of the *(Lancaster, Pa.) Intelligencer Journal*.

Clear, upfront discussion of the ground rules becomes paramount on long, sensitive stories that require extensive interaction between reporter and subject.

ONE INTERNAL CRITIC'S VIEW

There was a time when Geneva Overholser was editor of her own newspaper, *The Des Moines Register*. By the late 1990s she had taken a different job: as ombudsman, or independent internal critic and reader representative, for *The Washington Post*. And when stories about the relationship between Bill Clinton and Monica Lewinsky broke, she spoke for readers in expressing concern about the paper's heavy reliance on anonymous sourcing.

"This story has readers complaining about anonymous sources in new numbers and with new passion," she wrote, as accusation after accusation poured out of President Clinton's relationships with Lewinsky and other women.

Overholser noted that there was reason for the public's concern. She cited a study showing that only 16 percent of *The Post*'s reporting in the story's first few days was based on named sources, a considerably lower percentage than in *The New York Times* (53 percent).

Quoting from the report by a group called the Committee of Concerned Journalists, she wrote, "The anonymous sources in this story—even those close to events—might have an ax to grind and needed to be treated with greater discretion than many of the stories demonstrated. What's more, the reporting rarely explained the possible bias of any anonymous sources that might have colored the reliability or completeness of what they were offering."

Should *The Post* and other media have relied on so many anonymous sources? Did the media have a responsibility to at least identify whether these sources came from the independent counsel's office, the president's staff or the Republican majority in Congress? Should members of the public leave issues of credibility in the hands of journalists, relinquishing their own rights and abilities to sort out the degree to which charges and countercharges can be believed?

Reports after the Lewinsky story broke showed a public clearly disgruntled by the media's performance. A poll by the Pew Research Center for the People and the Press found that nearly two-thirds of the people surveyed said the media had done "a fair or poor job" of carefully checking the facts.

But after Overholser's column ran, *The Washington Post*'s managing editor Robert Kaiser defended the paper's performance and attempted to explain the difficult choice journalists make between being first and being absolutely forthright with readers.

"We realize that we strain relations with readers when we ask them . . . to trust us and our unidentified sources. But we are left in this position once we decide that our first obligation to readers is to give them as good and as timely information as we can. And that is our decision, almost always. Informing the reader comes first."

When Jack Thomas of *The Boston Globe* spent a week living with an Alzheimer's patient and her husband, he wanted it crystal clear from the outset that "I wanted the tape recorder, me and the reader with them at the most god-awful moments."

That agreement allowed a sensitive, highly personal portrait that otherwise might have proved impossible.

In breaking news, there also are many reasons reporters work hard to get information on the record. Knowing the source lends credibility, authority and a sense of balance to a story. Some news organizations, such as the *San Jose (Calif.) Mercury News,* have policies against reporters quoting unnamed sources who use anonymity to criticize someone else. In such circumstances it becomes too easy for the anonymous critic to take potshots.

NOT FOR ATTRIBUTION

Reporters sometimes have little choice but to get and use information from those who don't want their name associated with it. In the case of Willon's reports on the murder trial, for example, the judge had imposed a gag order—a ban against trial participants speaking to reporters. Had Willon's source spoken on the record, he or she would have risked going to jail. Sometimes sources with crucial information—about sexual harassment on a military base or the junkets the mayor keeps taking at government expense—risk losing their jobs if they go public. Sometimes they risk losing access to information that reporters seek. In all these cases, reporters likely will protect their sources and work out ground rules for identifying them that fall short of naming them.

PROTECTING SOURCES, NOTES AND TAPES

Suppose you are working in the newsroom one day when the local police come barging through the door, wave a search warrant in your face and ask for one of your tapes. That's just what happened at *KOMU-TV,* Columbia, Mo., the commercial station run by the University of Missouri. Would you know what to do?

NEWSROOM SEARCHES

The police wanted the audiotape of a phone interview that an accused murderer had given to a student reporter the day before. During the interview, the man had talked about the crime; so, obviously, the tape was valuable to the prosecutor. He asked a judge to sign the search warrant. The judge did.

What the judge and prosecutor didn't know, and every reporter should, is that newsroom searches are usually illegal. The Privacy Protection Act of 1980 forbids the police from searching a newsroom unless (1) there is probable cause to believe a news employee was involved in a crime, (2) the seizure is needed to prevent injury or death, or (3) the material is about to be destroyed.

This doesn't mean that prosecutors will never get the evidence. It just means that they have to get a **subpoena**, which is a legal document ordering a person to come to testify or to turn over evidence at a certain place and time. But the media can go to court to fight a subpoena, a tactic not possible with the search warrant.

CONFIDENTIAL SOURCES

Beth Willon of *KNTV-TV,* San Jose, is one of many journalists who have refused to turn over tapes, notes or names of sources—especially if they've promised confidentiality. These reporters know sources won't talk to them if their information ends up in the law's hands.

Increasingly, people in law enforcement or parties in lawsuits are reaching out wider and wider to figure out the names of the media's confidential sources. They're subpoenaing credit card transactions, airline receipts and telephone logs. An Illinois sheriff got records of calls from newsroom phones at the *(Peoria, Ill.) Journal Star* after reporter Omar Sofradzija refused to give up the name of his confidential source for a story on problems in the sheriff's department. The paper was never notified but learned about the subpoena from a source. After the paper sued, the sheriff agreed not to use anything from the records and gave all the copies back to the paper. Since then the newspaper has written to all its communication providers, alerting them to notify the paper if they get subpoenas for newspaper records.

Not all reporters are as fortunate as Sofradzija. Some subpoenas require reporters to testify, even when they've promised confidentiality to sources. If they don't, the judge can cite them with **contempt** (disrespect for the court) and order them to jail. Reporters are most often forced to testify when they've witnessed a crime or are called before a grand jury. Judges say the need to solve crimes outweighs the reporter's First Amendment rights. In many states, before the reporter is forced to talk, the prosecutor has to prove that the information the reporter has is necessary to the cause of justice and can't be found anywhere else.

Giving up a source's name presents an ethical as well as legal dilemma. Numerous reporters have gone to jail rather than give up a source.

"Reporters should serve as watchdogs of government, not an arm of government," says Lisa Abraham of *The (Warren, Ohio) Tribune Chronicle.* "I believe in that point very strongly—obviously to the point that I am willing to go to jail for it."

And Abraham did just that. She holds the record for the most days a reporter has spent in jail in the 1990s—22. She refused to talk to a grand jury about her interviews with a public official.

"I think that the reporter's job in society and the role of the journalist is being undermined every time the government tries to use us as its secret police force," Abraham told the Toledo chapter of the Society of Professional Journalists.

SHIELD LAWS

Reporters in 28 states have some protection from giving sources' names under shield laws, which "shield" reporters from having to give up their information in many circumstances. But the laws vary greatly from state to state, and they don't all cover the same people or the same information.

Here are some tips for reporters dealing with confidential interviews:

■ Know your news organization's policy on confidentiality and whether prior approval from an editor or news director is needed.

■ Make sure you and the source understand exactly what information is confidential and for how long.

■ Know whether the state where you work has a shield law and specifically what it covers.

■ When you're confronted with a search warrant or subpoena, contact your media attorney immediately for advice on how to handle it.

CULTIVATING SOURCES

1. Consider everyone you meet as a potential source.

2. Choose a variety of sources—from experts to ordinary people—so you get both a range of opinions and specific, human examples.

3. Get help in finding sources from newsroom contact lists, online sources, colleagues and public relations practitioners. Let one source lead you to two others.

4. Don't take everything a source tells you as gospel. Evaluate the source's bias or perspective and corroborate the information with documents or other sources.

5. Make sure you and the source work by the same ground rules—know when information is on the record, on background and off the record.

Once again, however, reporters should have good reason before allowing a source to provide information that is **not for attribution** by name, also called **on background**. Even when prevented from identifying a source by name, reporters must establish that individual's credibility to the highest degree of specificity possible. An anonymous attack on Newt Gingrich, for example, wouldn't be worthy of being aired or printed. If, however, that attack came from a "senior Republican senator" (rather than "a source") and if it were corroborated by "two Republican staff members," the story likely would run. As a rule, unattributed charges, when run at all, must be corroborated by at least two other responsible sources.

OFF THE RECORD

Sometimes sources want more than their names protected. They don't want the information they provide used in a news report at all unless the reporter independently develops the information without disclosing the original source anywhere along the line. This is what the term **off the record** means (although some sources erroneously say they are off the record when they merely mean they want to be on background). Investigative reporters will develop and use such sensitive sources to steer them toward key information that can be found on the public record.

Elizabeth Marchak, an investigative reporter with *The (Cleveland) Plain Dealer* who has done extensive work on airline safety, says such sources are crucial to her success.

"Several of my sources are sort of feeder spots for me," she says. "I ship things to them and they'll say, 'I've heard this and you should check this out.' Invariably they are right."

The tips are off the record because Marchak never reveals that someone has pointed her in the right direction, nor does she ever use the information without tracking it down in documents elsewhere.

"I work extensively with documents and extensively with data," she says.

Off-the-record interviews do little for most reporters, however, especially when chasing stories or breaking news.

Elizabeth Marchak

RECOMMENDED READING

Bennett, K. *Sources and experts.* St. Petersburg, FL: St. Petersburg Times. [Online]. Available: **http://sunsite.unc.edu/slanews/internet/experts.html**.

News researcher Kitty Bennett from the *St. Petersburg (Fla.) Times* has compiled a master list of organizations that have put their directories of experts on the Web. The list ranges from Big Ten experts to resources for Canadian journalists to the online version of the Yearbook of Experts, Authorities & Spokespersons.

Black, J., Steele, B., & Barney, R. (1995). *Doing ethics in journalism* (2nd ed.). Boston: Allyn and Bacon.

This ethics textbook is filled with real-world examples of the kinds of dilemmas reporters find themselves in. The chapter devoted to source-reporter relationships comes with an ethical checklist that covers everything from basic ground rules to the advice "do not abuse naive news sources."

DeSilva, B., & Mura, J. (1996). *The straight scoop.* Hartford, CT: The Hartford Courant.

Subtitled *An Expert Guide to Great Community Journalism,* this textbook, compiled by the staff of *The Hartford Courant* is filled with tips on finding sources and stories on topics from housing to "how to get more than grief from the cops." Chapters 27, 31 and 32 provide helpful tips on developing and working sources.

Ricchiardi, S. (1998). **Standards are the first casualty.** *American Journalism Review.* [Online]. Available: **http://www.newslink.org/ajrricchiardi.html**.

This article chronicles the collapse of conventional sourcing standards during the first days of the Bill Clinton-Monica Lewinsky scandal and examines the issue of how news media standards are under siege in an age of instantaneous news.

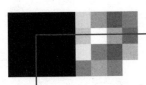

EXERCISES

A. RESEARCH

1. Find the name, telephone number and e-mail address of a person in your area who might provide answers to these questions:

   a. How many languages are taught in the high school?

   b. What is the largest immigrant population in the county?

   c. How many false alarms were called in to the fire department last year?

   d. What movie had the longest run at the local theater last year?

   e. What was the county unemployment rate last month?

   f. At what age should a dog have its first parvo virus vaccine?

   g. How much has tuition gone up at your university in the last decade?

   h. How many men and how many women get athletic scholarships at your university?

   i. Where is the nearest United Methodist Church, and how many are there in your community?

   j. Has air quality been improving or getting worse in the last year?

B. BRAINSTORMING

1. Talk with a classmate to list potential sources for each of the following stories. Then discuss your list in class, looking for ways to expand it.

   a. The city's only public bus company announces that it will eliminate some routes and curtail others because of financial difficulties.

   b. An increase in rabies among wild animals has been reported in your county.

   c. A small private plane crashes at a local airstrip, the second such fatal crash in a month.

d. The local school board proposes a $500,000 bond issue to upgrade technology in the school system.

e. A suspect in a murder trial who has spent most of his life in jail chooses to represent himself in the courtroom.

f. A blistering heat wave has caused a run on air conditioners, bottled water, fans, backyard pools and any other way to stay cool.

g. The local college has hired a new women's basketball coach.

h. An anti-abortion group in the area is planning a parade next Saturday.

Lorraine Kee operates in a world of big men and big egos. As a sports reporter for the *St. Louis Post-Dispatch,* she covers the city's professional football team, the St. Louis Rams. Kee knows that sports stars have perfected the art of the stock answer. So before approaching players for extended interviews, she looks for an added edge. She steps back and observes.

"I tend to watch players for a while, to see what kind of people they are, how they conduct themselves," Kee says. "You look for those little details [about players], and then when you sit down with them, they're kind of flattered. It tickles them that you already know about them."

Elizabeth Marchak of *The (Cleveland) Plain Dealer* reads voluminously about her interview subjects. She figures she'll not only be able to show sources that she is prepared but also will have a sense of what they're willing to say from what they've said on the record before.

Bob Dotson makes his living reporting before a camera at *NBC News.* But he often keeps his notebook in his pocket and camera at bay when approaching a stranger on a sensitive story. Reporting for the broadcast media can by nature be more intrusive. People who are reluctant to talk with print reporters may well be even more gun-shy of cameras and tape recorders. That's why Dotson tends to ease in.

"People hate questions," he says. "So if you can bring them to the point you want without asking a question, they'll answer the question you didn't ask."

That's when the videotape needs to roll.

No matter what their medium, whom they interview or what techniques they choose, the best reporters know interviews start long before the subject comes to the phone or answers the door.

To avoid interviews that start and end with, "Get out!" reporters plan ahead. And when they walk out the door or hang up the phone after the interview, they quickly review what they have, what they've missed and where they need to go next.

Interviewing is a four-step process: getting ready, getting the interview, getting good answers and sorting out what you've got. This chapter will walk you through all four steps. It also will:

- Discuss the special challenges of cross-cultural reporting
- Offer tips on how to take good notes
- Explain some of the special issues and problems involved in television interviews, e-mail interviews and using a tape recorder in interviews

GETTING READY TO INTERVIEW

How much and in what way reporters prepare for an interview will vary depending on the nature of the story and the importance of the interview subject.

When fire trucks race down the street toward city hall, the reporter whose instinct is to wade through files of old fire stories and previous interviews with the fire chief may be out of a job tomorrow. The right instinct here is to head straight to the scene, collar the chief and ask, "What happened?" Research on other fires at the site can come later.

Lorraine Kee

But if the mayor has just appointed the first woman in city history to hold the job of fire chief, the reporter headed to an exclusive interview should know a good bit about her and the department before showing up.

In short, when there's time to prepare in journalism, there is no advantage to walking in the door cold. That's equally true in covering the local sports team, the latest scientific discovery or the intrigues of city government.

"Doing your homework means talking to other people, reading clips, observing, talking to relatives, teammates, coaches. I try to do all that before I sit down," says Kee of the *Post-Dispatch*.

KNOW HOW THINGS WORK

A sports reporter would never presume to cover a football game without knowing the rules. Why, then, do some reporters attempt to cover trials without knowing the rules of evidence or the procedures for cross-examination?

"If you don't know how things work, you're not going to get anything but a nuts-and-bolts answer, and you're going to want more than that," says Judy Rakowsky, who covers federal courts for *The Boston Globe*.

Learn the system. That is the first thing any reporter covering a story should set out to do.

By knowing how things are done, Charles Sennott of *The Boston Globe* developed a key piece of his story the day a bomb ripped through the World Trade Center in New York. Throughout the day, reporters could only speculate whether a bomb or some type of gas leak had caused the explosion. At midafternoon, Sennott talked off the record with a member of the city's bomb squad. His source couldn't say whether a bomb had ripped through the building but did tell him how investigators would begin to determine the answer. Sennott learned that investigators would use cotton swabs to pick up traces of chemicals at the blast site. If these showed signs of nitrates, it would be a strong indication of a bomb, he was told.

That information about how a bomb squad works allowed Sennott to ask the right question later that day: Had tests found traces of nitrates? "At least," he said, "we were able to report that the earliest tests proved positive."

KNOW THE PURPOSE OF THE INTERVIEW

Just what do you need from the director of public works? Quick verification of how much the city has spent on trash pickup this year? A 10-second sound bite on a contract dispute with trash collectors for the evening news? A lengthy background session explaining how a new recycling program will work? Or a confrontational interview pinning him down on just why the firm that has collected trash for the last decade never made the lowest bid and always hired his relatives?

By knowing the purpose of an interview, reporters also can determine how much time they need. Interviews are not open-ended affairs. Once you know what kind of information you need, you should have a sense of how long the interview will take and let your subject know. The people reporters interview are busy people. If you get in the door by promising you'll need only 10 minutes, don't try to steal an hour—at least not if you hope to interview the same subject in the future.

Plan the Direction and Pace of the Interview

Good interviewers respond to what people tell them. They don't pull out a list of questions and read it like a bulldozer flattening a row of pine trees to build a new highway. Even so, interviews are anything but purely spontaneous events.

"I try to have the answers to the questions I ask before I ask them," says Tom Flannery of the *(Lancaster, Pa.) Intelligencer Journal.*

Dotson of *NBC* says he starts thinking of his interview questions the minute he gets an assignment. He writes a checklist that includes every question he needs answered and every picture he thinks he'll need to show his story.

"It's a mental game I play so that I don't overlook something."

Before confrontational interviews, some investigative reporters rehearse their questions and the possible answers. Eric Nalder, who has won two Pulitzer Prizes for *The Seattle Times,* says he imagines a successful interview during his morning shower. "I always assume people will talk to me," he says. It is a confidence builder.

Nalder and many other reporters do jot down questions or single-word reminders of the questions they'd like to ask. It helps to organize their thoughts. By rehearsing key interviews, reporters can anticipate answers and come up with more questions.

"When you go into an interview, you want to be a little surprised," says Jack Thomas, master of the long profile at *The Boston Globe.* "But not a great deal."

Choose the Interview Method With Care

Print, radio and online reporters can just as easily conduct interviews by phone as in person. It always saves time. The telephone is a powerful interview tool for gathering facts, a quick reaction quote, background information from a source who already knows and trusts you (see Chapter 5). The phone and the Internet likely are the only tools available for interviewing an expert in Washington, D.C., on immigration policies or that college kid who has just biked 3,000 miles across the country. Showing up in person would take too long and cost too much.

But to establish trust, to get a sense of a source's eyes as well as words, to break down barriers and to achieve the most candid exchange, there is no substitute for being there. The reporter looking for a revealing profile of a controversial young minister will not conduct the interview by phone or online.

Choose a Revealing Location

Where should the interview take place? Should you interview the pastor in the sanctuary after her Sunday sermon? Should you interview her at a drug treatment program where she volunteers her time? Should you interview her at home, where she is raising two adopted children as a single mother? Or should you interview her in all three places?

The print reporter might choose all three locations because of what they reveal about the clergywoman's different interests and commitments. Observation during the interview can be as telling as the answers to questions (see Chapter 7).

For an in-depth story, television and radio reporters almost certainly would choose all three: Natural surroundings are essential to get the sound or pictures that are just as important to their stories as the words. Even for a daily story, someplace natural that "shows" the minister in picture or sound would be far better than a sterile studio.

The point is that interview locations are not chosen at random. Geoff Stephens, a producer for *NBC*'s "Dateline," says he avoids the sterile hotel room interviews used too commonly in network newsmagazines. So in a murder story that involved people in the horse industry, he interviewed one woman in front of a stables, atop her horse.

Likewise, Jack Thomas of *The Boston Globe* likes to meet his subjects at a place that tells him something about them. That's why he interviewed a jazz-playing housewife in her home and at a club. That's why he always has his interview subjects pick the restaurants where he meets them. That's why he arranged to help transport architect Ben Thompson by ambulance back to his creation, Boston's Faneuil Hall, to interview him.

"It gives texture," Thomas says of an interview's location. "It also gives readers a greater sense of understanding and exposure."

GETTING THE INTERVIEW

Let's start with the obvious: Once you're ready, dive in. The truth is, even some experienced reporters don't. They rustle around for that last bit of background. They make one more trip to the water fountain.

Why? Because making a cold call on a subject you're just getting a handle on can be a bit intimidating. It is also very much a part of any reporter's job. No matter how much you plan, no matter how good you are at research, the time will come when you simply have to pick up the phone and ask questions to which you don't know the answer.

"On the first couple of calls, you're always going to sound a little stupid," counsels Matt Bai of *The Boston Globe*. "You have to sort of offer yourself up, to admit what you don't know. People are usually willing to help out."

The trick is to start early enough and to build enough of a head of steam so that by the time you reach your key sources you will know enough to ask the best questions. Or, should you reach that key source early, you will have time to call back and sharpen the information you've gathered.

Veteran reporters will tell you that much of the day is spent simply getting through to people. They may put out six calls in the morning, fret for a while and then get three calls at the same time about an hour before deadline. Some days are better, of course. And not every story is turned in a day. Some must be reported and written in minutes; others offer the relative luxury of a few days. A few stories take weeks and months of preparation.

More often than not, broadcast reporters and producers need to set up interviews in advance, even when they are racing to get ready for the 5 p.m. news. They need pictures, they need sound, they need the right location. No sense sending out a crew if they can't get the right interview or the OK to shoot. Print reporters, too, sometimes call first to set up the interview in person or by phone later. Frequently, however, they are ready to start the interview the minute the source comes on the line.

Getting through to the right person can be the toughest part of any reporter's day. Here are some tips that should make it easier.

KEEP CALLING

The number of messages piling up on your would-be source's desk is a clear measure of your urgent need to reach that person. No reporter worth her pay makes a single call and sits back waiting for an answer.

"Be persistent," says Elizabeth Marchak of *The (Cleveland) Plain Dealer*. "Sometimes people will talk because they want to get me off their back."

Esther Davidowitz, who free-lanced for major women's magazines for years before entering the ranks of editors, recalls that the frequency of her calls increased as the days before deadline grew shorter. "If necessary, I'd call every half hour," she says.

GET TO KNOW THE GUARDS

Reporters who ignore the person sitting at the desk outside the inner office won't get far in their professional life. Instead of squabbling with secretaries and receptionists, reporters should cultivate them. ("Boss is in a bad mood today, huh? I know the feeling.") These people can be your best friends or your worst enemies. They're people just like you. Remember that.

Always learn the name of the person at the other end of the line or the other side of the desk. Then when you call back or come back, be sure to address that individual by name.

GET HELP IN PLEADING YOUR CASE

Sometimes reporters will turn to an intermediary—another reporter, a friend of the potential source—to set up an interview. It might be your daughter's dance teacher, who is a good friend of the person you need to reach; or the police officer whom you've worked with before, who tells his captain you can be trusted.

With a bit of cultivation, that intermediary can turn out to be the personal secretary with whom you've taken time to talk.

TRY AN END RUN

Busy sources tend to come to the office early, work through lunch or stay late. By calling early or late, you can often catch the boss answering her own phone, instead of the secretary, who has instructions to fend off all callers. Calling early has another benefit. The person at the other end isn't likely to have meetings scheduled yet and may be able to answer your questions on the spot.

KEEP A FOOT IN THE DOOR

Once you've gotten through to the person you want, don't allow yourself to be brushed off easily. The reporter who meekly hangs up in response to, "Sorry, I'm just too busy right now," is too easily dissuaded.

There are many ways to turn around a reluctant interview subject. You might try appealing to his vanity. "Dr. Schultz. I've heard no one in your field has as global a vision as you. I'll keep my questions to 10 minutes."

Or try showing your smarts. "That's a disappointment, Dr. Schultz. I was fascinated by your journal article last month suggesting that global warming initially could result in colder temperatures in some regions."

Or try standing tough. "Your opponent has charged that you are circulating phony polls to damage his reputation, Mrs. Koh. In fairness, I'd like to give you a chance to respond. But if you choose not to, the story will run anyway."

When all else fails, just keep talking. Eric Nalder of *The Seattle Times* says when reluctant sources decline to answer questions, he simply talks to them about something else.

"When people are closing the door on you, all you really have to do is to get them talking about anything—anything."

Once a source was closing the door in his face when Nalder looked down and said, "You've got a poodle? I've got a poodle." Nalder said he then "told a poodle story" and before long was invited inside.

Even when the answer is no, be polite. Sources may not be able to talk the minute you reach them. Just be certain you've set up a time that will work for an interview before you sign off.

JUST SHOW UP

"You always have to calculate the element of surprise," *The Boston Globe*'s Judy Rakowsky says.

Faced one day with the task of interviewing a corruption case witness who'd had enough of the press, Rakowsky decided to forgo the phone and surprise him at work. "I knew he wouldn't talk to me on the phone," she said.

GETTING PEOPLE ON TAPE

Radio and television reporters may have difficulty getting people to talk on mike. Sometimes it's because they feel inadequate or fear embarrassing themselves. Most times, with some affirmation and encouragement, they will talk. Here are some tips on how to nail a broadcast interview.

- Take time for a proper warm-up. Establish rapport by chatting before the tape rolls. Empathize. Introduce the videographer (if there is one) and explain how to talk in the microphone or whether to look at the camera. Spell out clearly what the story is about and how that person fits into the story.

- Explain that it's important to get and present as many sides to the story as possible. Tell the person the audience really needs to hear the facts firsthand, rather than from the reporter.

- Find a reason the person would want to do the interview. A crime victim or a patient may be able to educate others or help save a life. Relatives of a person who just died might want the world to know the wonderful person she was. Another person may want to set the record straight or expose a problem.

- Give the interviewee a general idea of the questions you're going to ask. Some reporters resist giving out questions beforehand, thinking it will limit spontaneity. But remember, people want to sound good and look good on camera, so they'd like to think through an answer before the tape rolls. If you end up with an answer that sounds rehearsed, tell the interviewee and ask the question again.

- Find out why someone is reluctant. One woman wouldn't let a camera crew come to her house because the carpet had just been ripped up and the floors looked awful. Once the producer promised they wouldn't shoot the floors, she said, "Fine."

- When you come up against interviewees who are essential to the story, but reluctant, remind them that you are trying to do a fair story—you'd rather not say, "So-and-so wouldn't talk to us." Make sure they know that even if they don't talk, you're still going to do the story.

Few people are downright rude when you catch up to them face to face. The president of San Jose State University hadn't sat down for an interview with the *San Jose (Calif.) Mercury News* in many months when Mike Cassidy tried to talk to her about the school's decision to eliminate its once prestigious track team. He called several times in the morning but got no response. Then he showed up in her office, told the secretary he was in no hurry and waited. He got the interview.

And showing up doesn't only mean at the office. The best local reporters know what bar or restaurant city council members and police officers repair to after work. Whatever the time of day, it's easier for sources to hang up on a reporter than to push past one sitting or standing beside them.

If Your Source Is Skittish, Consider Sending a Note

Sending a would-be source a letter or an e-mail note can pave the way for a subsequent phone call. This is not an advisable idea when your deadline is hours away. But on longer-term projects, letters or e-mail messages allow you to explain why you want the interview and why the source should talk to you.

GETTING GOOD ANSWERS

Some years ago, on the 50th anniversary of the onset of the Great Depression, *NBC*'s Bob Dotson found himself facing the toughest interview of his career. He'd flown halfway across the country to Modesto, Calif., to talk to a woman whose face had come to symbolize those hard times. But she had no interest in talking.

Florence Thompson never had been sent a print of "Migrant Mother," a picture that had captured her as a young widow, comforting two of her five children and pregnant with a sixth as she migrated westward from the dust bowl of Oklahoma. Her resentment at the media still festered when Dotson caught up with her decades later at her trailer. She threw him out.

Dotson drove into town, bought a glass of iced tea and drove back, taking a seat on Thompson's porch.

"After a while she looked out and said, 'Are you guys still here?'" the veteran reporter recalls. "I said, 'Yes, we came here all the way here from Oklahoma,' which was true."

It also, Dotson knew, might give him an opening. The two began talking about the state where Thompson had been raised and Dotson's wife was born. Dotson didn't try to take notes or shoot pictures. He never asked a question.

"Finally she said, 'All right, I'm going to give you two minutes, but that's it,' and that's what she did."

Every interview situation poses its special problems. Sometimes there are many ways to lead a subject where you want to go; sometimes there's just one. But as the story of Florence Thompson shows, genuine interest, coupled with polite persistence, carries reporters a lot further than the brash bullying of the TV detective.

Ann Scales (third from right) joins other *Boston Globe* reporters and editors in interviewing President Bill Clinton at the Waldorf Astoria, New York City.

Dotson had engaged a human being, not pestered a source. It earned him a short and powerful interview.

"She said, 'You know, I tended bar, I worked in the field, I scrubbed floors in a hospital, I did everything I could to keep my kids alive. I remarried and we ended up with 10 total. And every one of them went through school and has a job.'"

"Did you ever lose hope?" Dotson asked.

He remembers the answer.

"She said, 'Son, if we'd lost hope none of us would be here.'" Dotson recalls. "She'd obviously been thinking about it for a very long time."

How do you get interview subjects to share what they've been thinking about for a long time? Here are some tips for getting people to talk, on the air and off.

GETTING STARTED

Ease in, show an interest, show yourself. There are many ways to start an interview; some depend on what you want, others on how and where the interview takes place.

NAMES, TITLES, AND PRONUNCIATION COME FIRST

No matter what the subject, reporters should nail down two things at the outset of an interview. How does the person being interviewed spell his or her name? And what is that person's title? Broadcasters have a third question right off the bat—one they make sure they get on tape. They'll ask, "How do you pronounce your name?"

These questions can be asked with a light touch to help break the ice. "Let me ask you the really tough questions first. Would you spell your name for me and tell me your exact title? And how do you pronounce it?"

Notice that the reporter asks the interview subject to do the spelling. That is far more accurate than to say, "You spell Sarah with an *h*, right?" Sometimes when we're not quite tuned in to a question, all of us tend to simply answer, "Yes." That includes Sara.

IF THERE IS TIME, START WITH AN ICE BREAKER

When reporters get too wrapped up in the information they want, they forget how the person across from them feels. It is likely that individual is at least a bit nervous.

"We run into an awful lot of people who are scared of us," *The Boston Globe*'s Judy Rakowsky says.

That's why in face-to-face interviews reporters' first few questions are intended to get the interview subject to relax rather than to disclose critical information. Clearly, there are exceptions to this: The reporter at a fire, at the scene of a fatal accident or at a tense press conference gets to the point—no chitchat here. Get the facts and get out of the way. But at least as often, it pays to build your source's comfort zone.

"Great picture—your kids?" might be the first question asked of the high school principal you are interviewing in his office.

"Have any trouble getting here? Thanks for taking the time," might be how you greet the angry community leader who came to your news organization's office to vent about the city's police.

Whatever your exact words, it pays to start most face-to-face interviews with comments or questions that show an interest in the person rather than just in what that individual has to say. Sometimes the answers can reveal a detail about the person's life that will prove useful in the story (see Chapter 7).

DON'T DILLYDALLY WHEN YOU'RE NOT EXPECTED

Reporters who catch up to a busy source for an unscheduled phone interview should get right to the point. This is no time to chat about the weather. It is a time to show that you are prepared, particularly when dealing with experts who likely will measure the reporters who approach them by how much they know.

"You have to establish that you are on the same footing with them," *The Boston Globe*'s Rakowsky says. "Sometimes you do that by throwing a few pointed questions so they know you are on the ball."

LISTEN AND CARE

It's one thing to hear the words people speak. It is quite another to listen to what's behind the words, to respond to the speaker as a human being, to show that you are genuinely interested and care. These are skills that take interviews below the surface.

"It's really basic. It's listening and empathy," says Rakowsky, who has interviewed all types while covering the courts. "I don't think the bare bulb and the old interrogation routine does us much good. Because we don't have subpoena power."

WATCH FOR NONVERBAL CUES

Reporters can listen with their eyes, says Cliff Hebard, a former supervising editor at Syracuse, N.Y., newspapers and a consultant in the field of active listening. A good listener measures how things are said, what's left out, whether the speaker keeps shifting his eyes, whether his arms and legs are folded tightly or he's sitting relaxed.

"A lot of times, I see reporters just trying to get information rather than trying to get a sense of what's going on," says Charles Sennott of *The Boston Globe*. "If you're asking a police officer about an investigation and he seems frustrated, maybe he is. The last thing you want to do is badger him. The right question might be, 'Are you frustrated by this case?'"

In radio, a good interviewer will note the nonverbal cues a source is giving him so the audience is aware. During an interview on homosexuality in Russia, *NPR* host Daniel Zwerdling took note of his interviewee's body language as he asked a question.

Zwerdling: So at the official level there are no pronouncements by the government that we're going to forbid discrimination against gays . . . you're shaking your head no to all of this . . .

National Public Radio

Zwerdling not only took his audience to the interview but encouraged the person being interviewed to explain why.

ENCOURAGE WITH YOUR OWN CUES

Try this experiment with an unsuspecting friend or family member. As he or she talks, slouch in your chair, stare at the ceiling, look bored. It won't take long before the conversation crashes. Then consciously try active listening techniques during a different conversation: Lean slightly forward, nod your head, encourage with your eyes. The difference in the other person's reaction will amaze you.

"This is a human relationship between two people," Hebard says. "Too often it gets reduced to a more limited kind of exchange, a purely journalistic exchange. In my opinion that's not enough."

STAYING IN CONTROL

If an interview is a human exchange, that exchange typically is not equal. The interviewer ultimately has a purpose: to elicit information. There are tricks to keeping an interview on track.

FRAME QUESTIONS TO CORRESPOND TO THE ANSWERS YOU NEED

When reporters want facts, they ask specific questions. For example: "You say you expect the merger will result in 'some downsizing.' How many people do you expect to let go and in what areas? Will they receive any extended benefits? When will the first layoffs occur? Will you help those laid off to find other jobs?"

These are **close-ended questions**. They focus on a specific answer—a number, a yes, a no. They make for miserable quotes and sound bites. But they also tend to cut down on obfuscation and generality.

The same reporter, seeking to look behind the scenes at a wrenching restructuring, might take a very different approach: "What options did you consider before deciding you had to lay people off? What kinds of market pressures are leading to so many layoffs in industry this year? How did you feel when you stood in front of your staff to break the news?"

These are **open-ended questions**. Open-ended questions can't be answered with a yes or no. They are asked not so much to establish fact but to elicit opinion and explanation. They begin with words such as "why" or "how" or "what," which are intended to draw out a source and give insights into that source's thinking. Open-ended questions can help reporters gain a broader understanding or perspective on a subject. They also are asked when reporters want powerful quotes or sound bites so that listeners or readers hear what interview subjects have to say in their own words.

IF THE ANSWER IS INCOMPLETE, REPHRASE THE QUESTION

People rarely talk in perfect quotes or sound bites. Sometimes they get distracted in midthought. Sometimes they'll explain just enough to leave you confused. This is the danger of a cookbook approach to questioning. The reporter who follows a recipe of questions likely will be thinking of the next question instead of listening to the answers.

Listen. If the answer isn't clear, rephrase the same question or ask for further explanation.

"Make the person work," Jack Thomas of *The Boston Globe* says. "When you don't challenge, you frequently end up with quotations with no edge to them."

SIMPLE QUESTIONS ARE BEST

You've seen the press conferences. The politician, trying to divert the heat from a hostile line of questions, calls on Joe Longwind, a local reporter who is just thrilled to be on national television. And Longwind just can't shut up.

"Senator," Longwind begins. "A lot has been said and written lately about your stance on casino gambling in this state. I'd like to ask you two questions. Do you or do you not support casino gambling, and if a similar measure were to come before Congress proposing national oversight of casino gambling, can you see circumstances under which you might support it or your party would support it?"

What happens? The senator surely ducks question one, unless he considers it advantageous to answer. The viewer on television or the listener on radio, meanwhile, has gotten completely lost.

Even if he's not on TV, where viewers can see that Longwind is a windbag, he's not off the hook. He's made it clear to the person he is interviewing that he is confused at best and easily manipulated at worst. By asking such a convoluted and cumbersome question, he has lost control of the interview.

It seems easy to ask one question at a time. Why then are so many press conferences muddied by endless multi-part questions? Look to them as an example of how *not* to conduct yourself.

A popular children's book came out a few year's ago titled "Simple Pictures Are Best." The same is true of questions. Simple questions are best. If you have trouble framing a simple, and single, question, it's a good sign that you are not sure what you want to know. That's why thinking through questions ahead of time helps, as long as you aren't so wedded to the list of questions that you forget to listen to the answer.

SILENCE IS GOLDEN

Bob Dotson was interviewing a Vermont botanist for *NBC*'s "Today Show" when the give-and-take suddenly died away. The photographer was panning a roomful of stuffed birds the man's father, also a botanist, had collected years ago. Dotson didn't fill the silence; it just hung there. Suddenly the man, German born, blurted out, "Did you know that I found the Red Baron after he was shot down?"

"Stuff like that happens all the time," Dotson says, referring to the seductive power of silence.

Try it. Sit down at a table with a friend or acquaintance and consciously keep your mouth shut. It won't take long before the other person is filling the silence. Silence makes most people uncomfortable. That is precisely why strategic silence in interviews can be effective in getting the reticent source to say more.

"People always answer in threes," Dotson says. "They give you the answer they think you've asked for. Then they explain their answers. Then, if you just hold it a beat, they say, 'Well dummy, that's why I killed my wife.' People hate silence. You've got to give them a chance to fill it."

IF YOU KNOW YOUR FOCUS, TECHNIQUE WILL FOLLOW

Entire books have been written on interview strategies (see Recommended Reading at the end of the chapter). A reporter, for example, might start with broad-based questions and then ask more and more specific questions to catch a politician in a contradiction between his present statements and past actions.

Q *Congressman, what kind of policy would you support for welfare reform?*

A I think we need to set a three-year limit for anyone on welfare but then help those people prepare for useful jobs in our market economy.

Q *What kind of help do you have in mind?*

A A combination of job-training funds and social service support such as child care. But there has to be a clear cutoff.

Q *Has this always been your view?*

TOUGH INTERVIEWS

Here are the top tips of Elizabeth Marchak of *The (Cleveland) Plain Dealer* in preparing for and carrying out tough interviews:

- Know what sources have said to other reporters and the context in which they said it.

- Visualize your story. "What," she asks, "are the issues the person needs to cover for you?"

- Ask key questions in more ways than one. And always ask them.

- Let your source do the talking. "Big-shot investigative reporters fill up a lot of space in an empty room. That's not what you want to do."

- Be tough only when being nice doesn't work. "I'm not afraid to do it, but I do it selectively," she says.

A Yes, I've always backed a humane and rational shrinkage of our welfare system.

Q *Why then did you vote to abruptly end all job-training funds for welfare mothers three years ago?*

Memorizing specific techniques, however, is far less important than finding your interview's focus. If you know where you want an interview to lead, the path you should take will become clearer.

"It's a matter of thinking about your story," *The Globe*'s Rakowsky says. "What can this person add to your story? Are you looking for a quote? For an opinion? For facts? Is this the person who is going to say, 'I'm going to get that guy,' or is this the person who will give the emotional response from the family?"

GET THE FACTS AS YOU GO

Except in particularly tense or emotional circumstances, reporters nail down specific points raised in an interview as they go. Consider this statement by a source: "There's an excellent study by the Pew Foundation on that. It found that 65 percent of the public doesn't think it has enough of a voice in the news."

The green reporter might dutifully write down the quote and regurgitate it back to readers or let it air unchallenged and unqualified. But what does it mean? How was the figure arrived at? What's the correct name of the foundation? Whom does it represent?

Reporters are not stenographers. Their job is to make sense of what that source is saying. Assuming the interview was not live, here are a few questions a reporter might ask in response to the sample statement:

- Is that P-E-W or P-U-G-H?
- Is that the full name of the foundation?
- Do you have a copy of the report?
- Do you know where I might get one?
- How was that figure arrived at?
- How does it compare to earlier polls on the subject?

PUSH FOR SPECIFIC EXAMPLES AND INFORMATION

No matter what the medium, good questioners probe for specifics to bring a story to life. Several approaches are particularly effective in drawing out answers that show rather than merely tell. Here are some examples:

Q *You said that walking helps you write. Can you give a specific example?*

A Why yes. The figure of the father in my last short story came to me in the middle of a short walk around the block last week. I thought I was heading to the convenience store to buy orange juice, but by the time I got home two hours later I'd created a new character.

Q *You said the wind was loud when it blew through. What did it sound like? Can you compare it to something specific other people might be familiar with?*

A It sounded like an express train hurtling past a crossing gate at full speed.

Q *What evidence can you provide that the program is helping to keep kids in school?*

A To be honest, none yet. We have anecdotal evidence that some of the participants are more excited about their classes, but the drop-out rate hasn't changed.

Stories are built on facts: The question about evidence tries to dig out specific information that measures a general claim.

Stories are built on example: Specific tales or anecdotes make information clearer and easier to understand. Interview subjects don't always offer examples unless they are asked for them.

Stories are built on vivid quotes that appeal to the senses: Nothing confuses an audience more than a reference to something they don't understand. By asking interview subjects to compare the unfamiliar to the familiar, the interviewer can appeal to the audiences' senses (see Chapter 7).

KEEP CONTROL, BUT DON'T GRAB THE SPOTLIGHT

Think for a moment of an interview's possible direction as a series of roadways leading off a busy intersection. The reporter's job is to provide the road map she wants the interview subject to follow. That's very different from taking over the car.

Interviewers who try to steer the car—who constantly interrupt, who try to put words into people's mouths, who antagonize and who offer their own opinions—may put on a good show. But they'll come away with a lot less information.

Sure, reporters should follow up when the answer isn't clear. They should challenge sources to explain, to elaborate or to reconcile inconsistency.

"In an interview, you frequently have people jump from [point] A to C, and we lazily let that happen," Eric Nalder of *The Seattle Times* says. "We lose a lot of information that way, and frequently we don't realize that until we sit down to write."

Still, the reporter's role is to draw out the person talking so that the gaps of information or logic are filled. The reporter's job is not to promote a point of view or argue an opinion.

"I don't learn anything when I'm talking," says Tom Flannery of the *(Lancaster, Pa.) Intelligencer Journal.* "As a reporter, you ask something and then keep your mouth shut. You sit back and let them talk."

Keeping quiet while the person is talking is especially important for radio and TV reporters who otherwise will have difficulty editing a tape filled with their own "um-hms" and questions that cut off the ends of answers.

ASK AS IF YOU PRESUME YOU'LL GET AN ANSWER

It's one thing to be polite. That's good. It's another to be meek. Reporters who apologize for their questions before asking them might as well not bother with the question.

Here are the key tips of *NBC*'s Bob Dotson in interviewing for television:

Bob Dotson

- From the moment of an assignment, start jotting down the questions you want to ask and the pictures you want to shoot.

- Look for information that allows you to write "to the corners of the pictures." For example, the text of a story on a blizzard needn't say the snow buried cars. The visuals will show that.

The sound will show that the wind howled. The picture won't show how many hours it took the mayor to drive 10 miles.

- Avoid making people defensive with abrupt, staccato questions. The best questions often are those you don't ask directly. For example, "Sounds like it was a tough decision" or, "I bet you never expected that to happen." Empathy goes a lot further than interrogation.

- Give people time to fill the silence. They will.

- Write as you gather information. That way, you will know what gaps you need to fill during interviews.

- Always think about where your story will end. Listen for that one sound bite or detail nothing else in the story can top. Once you've picked out the close, the rest of your interviews can focus on material that leads there.

- Be flexible. Stories often end up in a different place from where you thought they were heading when you started.

Ask, "Are you making any progress in the contract negotiations?" Don't ask, "I know you're not supposed to say anything about these talks and you probably don't want to, but can you tell me whether any progress has been reached in the negotiations?"

Guaranteed, the answer will be no.

BE FLEXIBLE

It happens frequently. The school superintendent, midway through an interview about a proposal for all-day kindergarten, lets slip that she'll be retiring in three months. The head of the state's toxic waste program, discussing a longer-term story about environmental cleanup technology, shares his concern about a threat to the drinking water supply in your community.

Prepare as you might, interviews can bring big surprises. Always be prepared to pick up on a better story than the one you're working on. Always be prepared for information that disproves your suppositions.

"If you are too concerned about getting your questions answered, you may miss the biggest jewel of the interview," Rakowsky of *The Boston Globe* says.

The same thing can be true if you are too concerned about looking stupid. Pride can't be a factor in this business. Sometimes reporters have no time to do their homework. Sometimes an interview takes a direction the reporter didn't expect. Sometimes reporters get confused. Whatever the reason, if you don't understand something, say so: "Lt. Allen. I'm really sorry, but I'm not clear what agency you work for" or, "Dr. Smithson, what do you mean when you say his T-cell count is low? Just what is the T-cell count? How does it explain his condition?"

The worst thing you can do as a reporter is to return to the newsroom with gaps in your notes that you knew about but were afraid to ask about. Few are the reporters who can sit down to write without thinking of another question to ask a source. Never make the list longer on purpose.

Wrapping Things Up

Interviews should end with purpose. This is the time to tie up loose ends, check your understanding of the facts and pull out all the stops.

SAVE THE TOUGH QUESTIONS FOR LAST (BUT ALWAYS ASK THEM)

"Did you put in all that overtime to assure a bigger retirement?"

That's not how you'll start an interview with the city bus driver who tops the list of workers paid the most overtime last year. For one thing, you'll intimidate your interview subject before establishing any trust. For another, he'll probably get up and walk out.

"If you ask without context, you'll shock the person into not answering," *The Boston Globe*'s Thomas says.

Even worse, however, is to leave an interview with the tough questions unasked. At best, you'll end with a story that's incomplete. At worst, your reticence could result in a serious breach of ethics. The bus driver accused of padding her overtime hours to assure a cushy retirement has a right to hear and address that charge; so does the teacher accused in a lawsuit of physically intimidating his students. Whatever the charge, the person accused should get a real chance to respond, not a cowardly phone call at the last minute that becomes a "declined to comment" in the story.

"A big thing in this business," says Rakowsky, "is being able to go and confront people, even if they say, 'Well, you're wrong.' A big complaint about reporters is that they come in at the 11th hour and ask, 'What are you going to say about this?' That's not fair."

ASK IF YOU'VE MISSED ANYTHING

"Is there anything I've missed?"

"Is there anything you would like to add?"

Those should be two of the last two questions a reporter asks. The answer may well be no. The questions, in any case, implicitly make the interview more fair and more complete.

SUMMARIZE WHAT YOU'VE GOT

As an interview ends, it helps to summarize what you've learned.

"Do you mind if I just go over what I think your key points have been?" you might say.

Restating the interview subject's main points does several things. It can draw out further comment. It can also protect you from making embarrassing mistakes. Any misunderstandings should be caught right here.

EXCHANGE PHONE NUMBERS

"Can I have your home number?"

"I invariably like to double-check things, so is there someplace I can reach you this evening when I'm writing?"

"Can I give you my phone number in case you'd like to add something? My e-mail address?"

Each home number you get as a reporter is a small savings account in the world of deadlines. So think ahead. Rather than scrambling through the phone book at 9 p.m., be upfront with your sources. Sure, some may say, "No, I'll call you." But few sources, if any, will resent the reporter who says, "I'd like to check back with you because I like to get things right."

Of course, there's a side benefit. The next time a story breaks after hours, your new source's home or pager number already will be on hand.

KEEP LISTENING WHEN THE FORMAL INTERVIEW ENDS

It's uncanny. Ask experienced reporters when they get some of their best stuff, and they'll tell you it's the minute the camera stops, the tape recorder clicks off, the pen gets stuffed back in their pocket.

People seem to relax when the formal interview ends. People, that is, besides the reporter. She continues to listen closely because a comment made in passing as she stands to leave can sometimes trigger a whole new line of thought.

"I've had interviews continue for an hour after I've shut my notebook," says Tom Flannery of the (Lancaster, Pa.) Intelligencer Journal.

But don't deceive the person you are interviewing here. If someone's comment brings up a new line of questioning or offers a great sound bite, be upfront: "Hey, mind if I jot that down?" or, "I'd love to get that on tape."

SORTING THINGS OUT

Fine wines should age in their barrels. Interviews should not yellow in reporters' notebooks or shrivel on tape. One simple mistake can trash an excellent interview: procrastination.

Don't wait until after lunch to check back over what you were just told. There are several reasons:

- Many reporters have trouble sorting through their own handwriting. By going over an interview immediately, you are much more likely to remember what was said so you can translate your own hieroglyphics.
- It's easier for reporters to spot and fill gaps in interviews right after they've finished than it is hours later. A quick review of notes tells a reporter what's still missing and where to go for it.
- The best reporters begin to write as they gather information. It saves time by focusing what work is left to do. A quick review of interview notes or tape also allows the reporter to pick out powerful sound bites and quotes, identify key facts and see the picture that's the perfect close.

One TV news director required reporters to use an audiocassette during all interviews. That way they could play the tapes as they drove back and pick their sound bites so they were ready to write when they hit the station's doors.

SPECIAL ISSUES

Some issues of interviewing deserve a little more attention than a quick tip. Our thoughts on cross-cultural interviewing, note taking and other specialized issues of interviewing are presented in the following sections.

INTERVIEWING ACROSS CULTURAL LINES

Raul Ramirez, by his account, grew up as a "lower-class kid in Havana." But when he arrived in the newsroom of the San Francisco Examiner years ago, colleagues didn't think twice about asking his help in understanding the customs and cultures of the largely Mexican Spanish–speaking population in the area. They simply assumed that with his Spanish surname, he'd know the answer.

"Someone came up to me and asked, 'Is Cinco de Mayo about Mexican Independence?'" he recalls, referring to a holiday that actually marks the victory of outmanned Mexican troops over the French in an 1862 battle in Puebla. "I didn't know anything about it but it sounded good to me. I said, 'yes.' Of course, I was wrong."

Ramirez, who is news director at KQED -FM in San Francisco, says today he would have the confidence to answer the question honestly. But, he said, then he felt the pressure many minorities feel—both in the newsroom and as

Raul Ramirez, news director at *KQED-FM,* San Francisco, frequently lectures on the subject of cross-cultural reporting. Here are his tips for avoiding typecasting, which can misrepresent an individual, and interviewing blunders, which can shut an interview subject down.

Get beyond labels and look at differences within groups. "You have to be aware of the internal diversity of each ethnic group and even each religious group," Ramirez says. "Be aware that people aren't necessarily in the same place in respect to their group."

Realize that interviewing takes different forms in different cultures. Working in Japan, Ramirez discovered that he often had to discard the American practice of asking direct questions. Blunt questions and blunt answers were considered rude. For example, he got nowhere when he asked a Japanese general about what pressures long-standing bitterness between Japanese and Russians would place on efforts by the two countries to work together. Finally, after three direct questions brought no answer, Ramirez said, "Tell me something about the attitude of Japanese to Russians." This, he said, allowed the general to say several polite things before criticizing the Russians.

Be aware of each culture's nonverbal cues. In Thai households, it is rude to cross your feet and point the sole of your foot at another person. In Japanese communities, it can be insulting to walk into a house with your shoes on. People in some cultures avoid direct eye contact, not because they are being evasive but because that is the polite thing to do.

Reporters interviewing across cultural lines need to be restrained, Ramirez says. "It just means being much more aware of yourself and how your actions can be interpreted and misinterpreted."

Look at yourself from the vantage point of the interview subject's experience. "Not everyone cherishes the 15 minutes of fame we want to give them," Ramirez says. "There are a lot of people in this country who have grown up in a culture where being in the news media is nothing but trouble."

Suspicion of the media is not limited to immigrants either, he said. "A lot of minorities have a feeling that the news media tend to distort, to mischaracterize and, at best, to misunderstand. As a reporter, you have to be aware this could be a factor."

Confront your own cultural or racial stereotyping. "As a reporter, you should not bring your own baggage with you," Ramirez says. "We don't do it walking into the halls of government. Why should we do it walking into people's hallways?"

Take extra care in interviews that demand translation. Reporters who use a translator need to interview the translator before allowing him to transmit and translate their own questions. Does the translator have a point of view, an ax to grind? Does the translator have a command of the idioms and dialect of a particular subject's speech?

A tape recorder can help here. It allows the reporter to bring the interview back to the newsroom and verify its meaning with colleagues or friends who speak the language or know the culture.

interview subjects. They bristle inside at being asked questions that don't apply to their culture, Ramirez said. At the same time, however, they often feel subtle pressure to represent an entire race.

"There are 27 countries in Latin America, and each has its own views, set of rules, assumptions about religion," says Ramirez. "And I barely know about Cuba. But over time I've had to learn more in the newsroom under the assumption that at some point I'd be asked."

Few reporters would be ignorant enough to seek out an interview with an oceanographer on the latest breakthrough in gene therapy. Sure, the oceanographer is a scientist, but all science isn't alike. Why, then, don't reporters hesitate when asked to "get reaction from the African-American community" to a dispute over a proposed ethnic studies class at the local high school? Just who represents the African-American community? Or the Asian-American community? Or the Latino community? Or any community? It's a question reporters don't ask often enough. The answer, of course, is no single individual, no single perspective, no monolithic point of view.

Newsrooms in all media have pushed somewhat harder in recent years to diversify their staffs so they reach and begin to reflect a more diverse audience. For some managers, this effort reflects a greater understanding of the need for the news media to serve more than the upper-middle-class, largely white community from which most of them come. For most managers, however, diversifying is a business decision. As the United States becomes more multiethnic and multiracial, would-be readers and viewers won't waste their time or money on newscasts or papers that don't reflect any understanding of their own lives. They will—and have—shifted their attention, and money, elsewhere.

More diverse ideas should percolate up in more diverse newsrooms. Because try as they might to represent all of their audience, most journalists draw heavily from their own experience. Nonetheless, all good reporters should and will be pushed increasingly to conduct interviews beyond the limited perspectives and exposures of their own upbringing. Just as white, suburban-bred reporters should be able to interview inner-city, black construction workers, Asian-American reporters should be able to connect with teens at a Latin dance club.

That said, when reporters interview across cultural lines, they should be aware they are doing so. It can take a little more time and a lot more sensitivity (see the box, Learning From the Pros: Cross-Cultural Reporting).

TAKING NOTES

"It's hard enough to listen and ask questions. How on earth do I take notes, too?"

Every beginning reporter has asked this question. Every honest one, anyway. The others just think it.

The art of note taking starts with what you leave out. Reporters are not transcribers. Few know shorthand. None write down everything their interview subjects say. Why should they? Key facts, compelling quotes, interesting examples—these are the things reporters listen for like a piano tuner hones in on middle C.

Radio and TV reporters, of course, want to get those pithy sound bites on tape. Listeners and viewers have to hear and see the speaker talking. Reporters often sit so they can see the counter on the recorder and jot down the number when they hear a good sound bite.

Whether print or broadcast, the principles of selection are the same. Quotes and sound bites should be short and sharp. They need to stand out. They're the salsa on the chips, the icing on the cake, not a lecture on the ingredients. Quotes add flavor to a piece; they don't provide its central poundage. And rarely, in print or broadcast, do they run for more than a sentence or two. When they do, it may well be an indication the reporter needs to paraphrase part of the material and save for quotation only what grabs.

Consider this hypothetical quotation by a high school music teacher after the school board passed a very lean school funding measure:

> *"This isn't merely an austerity budget. It is a budget that simply ignores the role music has long played in our school. It cuts our instrument acquisition budget by 87 percent. It eliminates our budget for band trips. And it wipes out our budget for new band uniforms. How am I going to live with this budget? I'm not. I may have to melt down the tubas and sell them as scrap metal."*

Would a reporter write all that down verbatim? Absolutely not. Should a story or tape use the entire statement? No, again. In the story, the information on what will be cut would be paraphrased:

> *The teacher said the budget cuts ignore the school's historic commitment to music. It will eliminate band trips, new uniforms and most new instruments.*

That sets up a much pithier and more powerful quote or sound bite:

> *"How am I going to live with this budget? I'm not. I may have to melt down the tubas and sell them as scrap metal."*

Even when reporters are selective in what they write down, taking notes can be taxing. Most reporters develop their own shorthand: "2 d., 3 i." might mean two dead and three injured in an accident. Reporters also leave out articles ("the," "a"), some vowels and other little words without which they can still read their own writing: "Twister hit nr. S-end, flttned 3 hses," might take the place of "The twister hit near the south end of town and flattened three houses." And, again, they pick and choose what they write down at all.

Figure 6.1 shows a page of notes reporter Nina Kim took for the *Syracuse (N.Y.) Herald-Journal* to do a short story on one police department's program to welcome residents home from vacation with a report on when police had driven by to check their property. She was interviewing a resident who had come back from Florida.

Some people talk very fast. Reporters have three options when the answer outraces the pen. They can ask the person speaking to slow down. They can let the room fill with silence as they catch up on their notes. Or they can ask a "throwaway question"—one they don't really need the answer to—as a way of masking their mad scramble to catch up.

WHEN TAPE RECORDERS MAKE SENSE

If you're in radio, tape recorders always make sense. It is a medium that "shows" through sound, that appeals to the imagination, that brings us the voices at the scene.

Print reporters generally turn on the tape recorder in selective situations. In most cases, the deadlines of breaking news dictate against recording long interviews on tape. There are at least three times when the tape recorder gains importance: at highly sensitive interviews or events, during lengthy projects and when writing extended profiles.

When the president of the United States announces plans to send troops to Bosnia, dozens of reporters will attend the press conference. None wants to be the one to get a single word the president said wrong.

FIGURE 6.1 Translation: "Neighbors asked if we knew someone in the police department because they were up here every day, two times a day."

And when the investigative reporter sits down across from a restaurateur and accuses him of using horsemeat in the ragout, she wants the answers on tape. The restaurateur may choose to sue, charging among other things that his words were misconstrued. The tape provides insurance.

Tapes make sense, too, at those times in reporters' careers when they spend two months rather than two hours on a story. These stories can be tough to keep track of, involve lengthy interviews and demand follow-up.

Finally, the tape recorder allows reporters to avoid writer's cramp when writing extended profiles. A profile is a story about a person or place. In longer-form profiles, reporters sometimes let quotations run much longer than in daily news stories. The subject's words reveal the subject.

THE LEGAL LINE | TAPING INTERVIEWS

When a source has given permission for taping or the recorder is in plain view, there's usually no legal problem. But what if the source doesn't know of the taping?

Laws in several states prohibit secret taping by anyone, including reporters. Other state laws say as long as one participant (the reporter) knows of the taping, it's OK. So it's very important for reporters to know the law of the state in which they're working.

Federal law requires radio and television reporters who want to air a telephone interview to alert interviewees before they turn on the tape recorder. But similar notice isn't required for face-to-face interviews, because the interviewee sees the recorder.

A cautionary note: Tape recorders have a bad habit of breaking down at the most inopportune times. Before you use a tape recorder, always pop in new batteries. And carry an extra set. Finally, even if you're taping, take notes as well.

INTERVIEWING BY E-MAIL

It's awfully tempting to jot down some questions on a computer screen and then zap them off into cyberspace. There's no negotiating with secretaries, no repeated callbacks to catch your source in the office, no fine-tuning of the question that wasn't quite answered. But interviewing online is a temptation that generally should be avoided.

Sure, e-mail has its advantages. It costs less than the phone. The quotes you'll get back, even if canned, probably will be more carefully crafted and may be more thoughtful. And if you are dealing with a computer-savvy source, it might be the most practical way of tracking down that person on the road, late at night or out of the office.

But questions sent by modem generally are the method of last resort for conducting anything approaching a candid interview. Quite simply, you don't know who is answering your questions, you can't engage in any spontaneous interchange and you are more likely to get the kind of canned responses that leads most reporters to reject the so-called quoted material written by press agents for releases.

Interviewing, as this chapter has discussed, is a process of establishing human interaction. A good interview relies on rapport and on reading face-to-face or at least voice-to-voice cues, nonverbal as well as verbal. All of these get lost in the silent world of the Web. E-mail is best used as one more way of getting through to a source. Once you've succeeded, pick up the phone. Or better yet, show up in person.

INTERVIEWING ON LIVE TV

Live broadcast interviewers don't waste time.

Dan Mountney of *WDIV-TV* in Detroit says the first question must be the most important one—the one viewers want to know most: "If it's a murder, who did it or how did the person die," he explains.

Selecting the right person for the interview is also key for live hits. If reporters need a rundown on the rescue efforts after a chemical plant explosion and only one deputy fire chief is available, there's no choice. But if reporters are looking for a reaction to the explosion from neighbors living in the area, they might have 20 to pick from.

"I can tell in 20 seconds whether they're going to be good on live TV," Mountney explains. "I like to find somebody who has self-confidence and is fairly articulate, someone who has a certain energy level."

Because time is such a consideration, Mountney usually briefs the interviewee on the topic and on how long the interview will run.

"If it's a cop, for example, it's helpful to say, 'Hey, I'm going to ask you about what you found when you got here, what's the latest on suspects and what the motive might have been. And we just want to hit these bing, bing, bing.'"

While he never rehearses a live interview, he says it's helpful to give interviewees a sense of the story, especially if it's their first time on live TV. They're usually nervous. Here are Mountney's suggestions for handling three common problems in live shots:

- The interviewee who rambles: Gently interrupt with, "In other words you mean that . . ."
- The interviewee who freezes: Have a backup plan, something else to describe or some other element of the story to tell.

INTERVIEWING

1. Interviewing starts with careful research. Think about what questions you'll want to ask and what answers you might get back. But realize your questions may change depending on the answers you get.

2. Nailing down an interview requires persistence and, sometimes, repeated calls. Use intermediaries to get through, call early and late, and don't hesitate to just show up. Sometimes it is the best way of getting your questions answered.

3. Interviewees give better answers when they sense they are talking to someone with a genuine interest in them and their area of expertise. People don't like to feel as if they are being interrogated. Ease in, especially when interviewing face to face.

4. Subjects open up more when the reporter listens carefully, keeps eye contact, gives nonverbal cues and rephrases statements from the interviewee.

5. Most interview subjects will add more if you aren't in a hurry to ask the next question. Keep the focus on the person being interviewed. Don't offer opinions. Do allow for silences.

6. Interviewing people of other cultures takes time, sensitivity and openness.

7. Reporters always leave an interview with a phone number where the interviewee can be reached later for more questions or clarification.

■ The interviewee who keeps talking when time is up: Nod, hoping the person gets the visual cue and stops. If you have to interrupt, apologize with, "I'm very sorry, but we have to move on" or, "I'm getting cues we have to wrap this up."

One final tip: Planning the location of the live shot is as important as the interview.

"Early in my career I was live at the Fourth of July fireworks," Mountney recalls. "As soon as we went live in the middle of this crowd, the mob just went *whoosh,* trying to get on camera. I got knocked to the ground and the mike went flying."

Mountney says in similar situations now he gets up on top of the live truck or moves to a position away from the crowd. If the bright lights attract the crowd, he asks the photographer to go with low or no light. And sometimes he works without a TV monitor so the crowd behind him won't see themselves and mug for the camera.

RECOMMENDED READING

Biagi, S. (1992). *Interviews that work* (2nd ed.). Belmont, CA.: Wadsworth.

Based on interviews with print and broadcast reporters, this short, well-organized book covers all aspects of interviewing, from "How to Get Organized" to "How to Write What People Say." It also contains excerpts from stories that resulted from the interviews the reporters described to Biagi.

Steele, B. *The bummer beat: TV reporting on tragedy and victim.* St. Petersburg, FL: The Poynter Institute. [Online]. Available: **http://www.poynter.org/research/me/et_bumer.htm**.

Few assignments are harder than contacting the family of someone who has just died or the witnesses to a horrid accident. Steele, the director of The Poynter Institute's Ethics Program, shares the stories of television reporters and some concrete suggestions about how to get the story without violating basic ethical principles.

EXERCISES

A. HONING ANGLE AND APPROACH

1. Interviews need a clear purpose, an angle of approach. Without it, the person being interviewed is likely to take control, or the interview will meander all over the place. Jot down three possible angles for each of the topics that follow. Then choose one person to interview for each angle. List 10 questions you would ask each source in roughly the order you think you'd ask them. You may choose to use the Internet or library resources to look up similar coverage.

   a. Students call a hunger strike on campus, demanding the hiring of more professors of color.

   b. An animal rights group in your community spatters blood on the windows of a furrier, the fifth incident like it in three months.

   c. It is the first day of spring.

   d. Residents of your community are expected to hand the city council a petition signed by 400 people tonight protesting plans for a huge new medical center immediately adjacent to a widely used piece of parkland.

   e. The head of the community's volunteer corps is back at work today. She quit her job a year ago when doctors said her chronic back pain would put her in a wheelchair soon. Now she's pain-free after using alternative treatments including meditation, acupuncture and a vegetarian diet.

B. ASKING THE RIGHT QUESTIONS

1. Write a list of questions you would ask in each of the following situations. Then order the questions. Finally, note whom else you would want to talk to.

   a. Juwala Wright isn't your average college freshman. Two years ago, when you first met her, she organized classmates to build a home for a Laotian immigrant family sponsored by her church. Now she has decided to run for city council. She's angry that her community has joined the growing number that have imposed curfews on all those under 18 years old from dusk to dawn.

"We need more constructive things for kids to do—a youth center, a town pool, a police athletic league—not more bars to put across their windows," she said last week in announcing her candidacy. "I want to represent the young and the young adults in this community to bring about constructive change. And I'm appalled by an electorate so apathetic that the same council members run unopposed year after year."

Today Wright wants to sit down with you for a longer interview. She's mad. Why? Her opponent, Boothe Hadfield, had a few words about her at last night's council meeting. "I understand a young do-gooder plans to tell us how to run this town," he said. "Considering I've been on the council since the year before she was born, I welcome the challenge. In fact, consider this an open invitation for Ms. Wright to come by. I'll show her what a budget looks like and talk to her about the hard compromises it takes in running this place."

You'll be sitting down with Juwala Wright in an hour. What do you want to ask her?

   b. It was supposed to be a senior prank, a smoke bomb planted in an outdoor fountain the last week of school. But something went wrong. The smoke bomb packed enough gun powder to shoot out flames 15 feet. Eight kids were burned, two of them badly enough to be hospitalized. And police say it is a miracle no one was killed. Allen Lowry, first-chair violinist in the city's youth orchestra, now is facing the possibility of jail instead of a full scholarship to the Juilliard School of Music. He has been castigated by parents and classmates, defended by friends who say it was a tragic mistake, interviewed by police. Now he wants to tell his side of the story. You've been sent to conduct the interview.

   c. It was one weird storm. Winds of 75 miles an hour, lightning, 5 inches of rain in two hours, flash floods. Jill Barlett and Amy Durand, two 16-year-old Scout leaders in training, couldn't have watched it from a worse spot. They were less than 500 feet below the summit of Mt. Baldy with just a few boulders to huddle against while lightning crashed into the mountainside feet away. Then they found the bridge over Baldy Creek washed out and the creek too high to cross. The temperature dropped to near freezing, and they kept warm through a sleepless night by huddling under pine needles and rubbing each other's feet and legs to keep their circulation going. Rescue teams reached them yesterday, the following afternoon. And, because you sat up with their parents the night before, you are about to get the first interview about their adventure.

C. INTERVIEWER AT WORK

1. Write stories or memos based on the following interviews. In order to assess note-taking technique or interviewing techniques, students might be asked to supply notes from these interviews, or to tape the interviews.

   a. Interview the head of women's athletics at your school about what efforts the school has made to comply with the requirements of Title IX of the Educational Amendments Act. Does she believe the school is in compliance? If so, why? If not, why not?

   b. Interview a foreign-born student on your campus about cultural differences between his or her native country and the United States.

   c. Interview a newly sworn-in citizen in your area. Find out why the person became a citizen and how hard it was to achieve citizenship.

   d. Interview the animal control officer in your community. Focus on the funniest things that happen on the job.

   e. Interview someone who works the graveyard (midnight to 8 a.m.) shift. What is it like when the rest of the world works days?

   f. Find someone who repossesses cars and interview him about his line of work.

   g. Interview someone in computer support at your school about the growth of computer use on campus.

   h. Interview a travel agent on the changes in vacation plans over the last decade.

   i. Interview a city council member about the five greatest challenges facing the city in the next year.

   j. Talk to the city budget director about the difficulties of budgeting for overtime, whether the overtime budget has grown and why or why not.

D. INTERVIEWING ONLINE

1. Using Deja News on the Internet (www.dejanews. com), find Usenet groups for the following topics. Read some of the postings on each topic. Then, by e-mail, request an interview with someone who interests you. If the person agrees, ask a series of questions by e-mail. Write up the results as a memo or short profile. Finally, evaluate the strengths and weaknesses of this form of interviewing and discuss in class.

   a. Someone who builds and flies hang gliders

   b. A Latin dancer

   c. A cowboy poet

   d. A massage therapist

   e. A gardener who raises scented geraniums

CHAPTER 7

Using Your Senses

MILWAUKEE—For weeks the residents of the Oxford Apartments, a beige cinder block low-rise in a weathered North Side neighborhood, knew something was terribly wrong in their building. The stench of rotten meat wafted through the corridors. There was the occasional hum of a buzz saw and cursing and rumbling in one of the second-floor apartments.

What the residents did not know and could not have imagined was that the tenant in Apartment 213 had been storing the body parts of as many as 15 men in his one-bedroom apartment.

The New York Times

Isabel Wilkerson who won the 1994 Pulitzer Prize for feature writing, surely wouldn't include her story on the arrest of one Jeffrey L. Dahmer in a portfolio of her best writing and reporting. The story ran inside *The New York Times,* a paper that rarely plays crime big. And by the time the paper's subscribers read it, Dahmer's arrest was more than 30 hours old.

That, however, did not keep Wilkerson from pulling readers into her story. She knew how to take them to a scene she'd never witnessed—through the eyes and ears and noses of those who had.

It is hard to overstate the power of the senses. Think back to your childhood. Your strongest memory likely won't be grandma's quote; it could be the smell of her fireplace, the way she touched your shoulder, the image of her smile, the taste of her favorite stew. The senses leave an imprint. They appeal to our imagination. They strike an emotional chord.

Recognizing this, the best journalists don't settle for stories cobbled from facts and quotes—stories that keep the reader or listener or viewer in their homes instead of at the scene. The best journalists take you there, either on their own or with the help of those they interview.

This chapter will give you:

- Examples of how to use all your senses, or those of eyewitnesses, to capture the small, specific details that bring a story to life
- Examples of how picture and sound shape stories in the broadcast and online media
- Guidelines for deciding which images, details and dialogue are the best to gather and use in a story
- A sense of the importance of a sixth sense: place, the often elusive "where" of a story

IMAGES

Whenever possible, go to the scene to record the sensory images at a fire, at a mountaintop retreat, in the old poet's home or on the riverboat casino. In television, "there" is often seen through the lens of the photojournalist.

In radio, it is heard through sounds that tickle listeners' imaginations. In print, words must bridge the distance from scene to reader.

Finding images takes patience and time. Every reporter's instinct is to get the news. But whether in the court-room, at the crime scene or some other place, reporters need to pause when possible to observe what is going on around them. Observation is hard work. It is a skill that takes just as much practice as interviewing. Only by pausing to observe will the court reporter notice the juror wiping away a tear as an investigating officer describes the murder scene. Only by looking up from her notepad can that reporter notice the tremble in the defendant's knee or the bored expression on the judge's face. These are the kinds of telling images around which great stories are built.

VISUAL IMAGES

"We don't have smell. We don't have feel. But we do have sight and sound," says Lane Michaelsen, news director at *KHTV-TV,* Little Rock, Ark.

Michaelsen, who has three times been the National Press Photographers Association's photographer of the year, uses both sight and sound wisely. He thinks before he shoots. What will bring this scene to viewers? What will capture the essence or the emotion of the story?

He recalls, for example, covering the story of a family whose house had burned to the ground after being struck by lightning. "What memories have you lost?" he gently asked the woman who had lived there. Three stuck out: pictures of a son who had died, a record collection, her grandmother's piano.

Such images, told through the woman's words, would have saddened those who read this story in print. Radio lis-teners surely would have heard the emotion in her voice. But Michaelsen could also enlist the power of pictures. He photographed a picture frame in the rubble, the picture burned away. He found a melted record, its cover still identifiable. He zoomed in on a string amid the rubble from the grandmother's piano. He took the viewer to the scene.

SOUND IMAGES

As a veteran photojournalist for *WUSA-TV* in Washington, D.C., Kline Mengle has learned that sound can be as powerful as pictures.

"Without the sound, the picture loses 75 percent of its impact," says Mengle, who counts 15 Emmys among his awards. "What I do is consider what would make this story real to me if I were sitting home in an easy chair."

On radio, of course, listeners "see" exclusively through sound. That is why Mike Sugerman, a radio reporter at *KCBS-AM* in San Francisco, always looks for natural sound that places listeners where he is.

That sound may come from the crackle of a police radio at a crime scene, the sound of the puck and the crunch of bodies at a hockey game, the whip of a casting rod at a mountain lake, the hammer of a gavel as a court pro-ceeding begins.

"I often liken it to a canvas," says Sugerman. "The sound is the paint. It's the color, and my script is white. Some-times white is good. But (sound) can place a listener where you are. It's the theater of the mind. One of the great things about radio is that everyone sees a different picture."

WORD IMAGES

Julie Sullivan paints her pictures with words, sometimes accompanied by still photographs.

"If you don't see it, it doesn't happen," Sullivan, a reporter for *The (Spokane, Wash.) Spokesman-Review,* says of her own responsibility as an observer. "If you don't observe it, it isn't reality as far as the story is concerned. I defi-nitely am aware of the five senses."

Sullivan, like Isabel Wilkerson, also is aware of the powerful imprint senses leave on people's memories. Her skill in coaxing sensory images from interview subjects has helped her win national awards for her nonfiction story-telling.

"If your senses aren't available," she says, "you have to ask [interview subjects] to use theirs. You have to have them do the work."

That is just what Worden Bishop did 50 years after D-Day when Sullivan got him to talk about the remarkable diary he kept. It is a story Sullivan never would have heard had she not observed a curious collection of paper tags in Bishop's bedroom. Her story in *The Spokesman-Review* began like this:

> The war diary of Worden Bishop is 73 pages long, each page a tag pulled from the fuse of a bomb.

LOOK FOR THE DETAILS

The reporter who comes back with a notebook full of facts and quotes and not a single detail of scene has missed half the story. David Arnold started as a photographer before making his mark as one of *The Boston Globe*'s better storytellers.

"Writing," he says, "is about observation."

What Arnold means is that nonfiction writers can't tell compelling stories unless they return to the newsroom with notebooks filled with snippets that will create a scene for readers. Here is how Arnold started a lighter story about a Boston spy business:

> A sign above the doorbell warned patrons they were subject to electronic surveillance. This was the New England Spy Center, Inc. Three steps inside, clocks on the wall told the time in Moscow, London, Los Angeles, Boston, Tokyo.
>
> The visitor penetrated deeper, the James Bond theme pulsing through his head. Suddenly he found himself on five television monitors, their cameras concealed in a book, a clock, a beeper, a cellular telephone, a thermostat . . .
>
> "Hello. May I help you?"
>
> His name was John. He wouldn't give a last name. Wouldn't talk much about his background either. Cryptic business, being co-owner of what apparently is the region's only full-service spy store catering to the needs of paranoids.
>
> *The Boston Globe*

Detail. Had Arnold not noticed the number of steps, the different clocks, the television screens or the way they were concealed, he couldn't have put them in his story. And it would have been a lot duller.

Arnold undoubtedly noted other details he did not include. For example, he left out the texture and color of the carpet. It would have been a detail worth selecting, however, if the carpet had been a collage of famous spies.

Capturing detail is not only the domain of the print reporter. Those who work with camera or tape recorder also jot down details. The broadcast equipment won't capture everything. And it is the reporter's role to keep track of which scenes and moments—captured in sound and on screen—are most vital to the piece.

As he goes out to report for *WCBS-AM* in New York, Lou Miliano gives his story shape by thinking of the sound he'll use and how he'll use it.

"I will visualize the story before I go out on it," he says.

For example?

Lou Miliano

"This afternoon I'm going to a theater on Long Island to do a piece about how theater has changed. I've already envisioned starting the story off in the city with the sounds of Broadway behind me. Maybe then the story will cut to birds tweeting in the background and something like, "This is also theater . . ."

Miliano says that sound, like words, must have a point. Just as too much detail or description can bog down a print story, so can too much sound or confusing sound bog down a story on radio.

"I regularly find reporters trying to incorporate sound without providing a reference. You'll hear something in the back going 'click, click, click,' but you don't have a clue what the sound is."

He adds, "I find there's a fine line between sound for sound's sake and sound as a way to actually show the story."

Finding details that show something special about the scene requires the same concentration of the television photojournalist. It means getting beyond the routine video just as the reporter must get beyond the routine question.

"You've got to be single-minded toward your goal," said Mengle of *WUSA-TV.* "Some cameramen are so busy paying attention to the competition that they don't come up with anything on their own."

LEARNING FROM THE PROS — PICKING THE RIGHT DETAILS

It's one thing to look for details and take note of them in reporting. It's another to figure out which of those myriad details to use when you write an article or script.

"What," the reporter asks, "should I include?"

The answer to that question alone could fill a different text—one on telling stories. Here are a few tips that should help the reporter in filling up that notebook.

1. BE SELECTIVE.

When Roy Peter Clark wrote "Three Little Words," a painful and compelling tale of "trust, betrayal and redemption," he drew a single excerpt from the diary of a St. Petersburg, Fla., woman whose husband had died of AIDS.

On the day her husband died of the disease, Clark notes, "She could manage only subject, verb and date: 'Mick died 3/3/93.'"

The unusual series, which was cut into 29 short, readable segments in the *St. Petersburg Times,* left out plenty of other details that undoubtedly were in the diary. An entry on an afternoon at the kids' soccer game, for example, wouldn't have been applicable.

Reporting is like that. Most of the information doesn't fit the framework. It's not unusual for reporters to leave 90 percent of the information in their notebooks.

Even fascinating details don't belong unless they are on point in a story. Clark, a senior scholar at The Poynter Institute for Media Studies and a writing coach, has a rather bloodthirsty phrase for getting rid of gratuitous gems: "Kill the babies." His babies are precious details that simply don't help tell a story.

2. BE SPECIFIC.

One day Julie Sullivan sailed high in a balloon, overcoming her terror of heights to capture a story she wished she hadn't had to tell. Her day—and perhaps her life—was saved by a passenger who had a cigarette lighter buried in her purse. The light was essential because the "striker"—a gadget that gives off a spark to ignite the burner that heats the air for the balloon—had been left behind.

Sullivan's story, however, didn't just say someone had "a lighter." Her savior dug around for "a $1.09 Bic lighter." The reporter had tracked down the lighter's brand and cost because she knew such specificity is more vivid and, in the case of the low-cost, low-tech Bic lighter, more informative.

When *National Public Radio*'s Don Gonyea told the story of the last days of the Detroit Arsenal Tank Plant, which churned out tanks for the U.S. effort in World War II, he didn't merely say, "The factory is mostly empty now." He left listeners with a sense of its vastness: "1.2 million square feet of cold cement floor."

With the help of the last few remaining workers, Gonyea looked back at the plant's history. He not only told that

(continued)

Mengle likes to bring the camera in tight. For example, there was the scene he captured in a tough city neighborhood while shooting a five-part series on crime. On the ground was the victim, blood running from his head. There was sound, the shouts of detectives yelling into two-way radios. The image that sticks with Mengle, however, is that of a toddler, standing behind the police line.

"I panned up from the body lying there to a little boy about 3 in his pajamas, holding his mother's hand with a football in his other hand. To me this shot said it all. What's his future in a place where you see this kind of thing all the time?"

Some photojournalists, Mengle cautions, lose the urgency of the news looking for pretty shots. He recalled the story of a winter fire in which the photographer shot so many pretty shots of ice forming where water hit the building that the drama of the event was lost.

Regardless of the medium, knowing what to leave out is often the hardest lesson to learn.

LISTEN FOR DIALOGUE

Reporters are used to training their ears to pick out pithy quotes and sound bites that change the cadence of a story and convey a sense of energy. But in real life, people don't talk *at* each other. They talk *with* each other. That is why short segments of dialogue prove much more effective than quotes in bringing the audience to the scene.

(continued)

President Franklin Delano Roosevelt visited but also described the scene: "FDR spoke from a temporary balcony some 30 feet above the factory floor."

Such specificity helps the listener "see" the scene.

3. BE SPARING.

Our entreaty to use the senses should not be mistaken for an invitation to "be expressive." Descriptive reporting requires careful observation and then spare reconstruction of what was observed.

Julie Sullivan and other exacting nonfiction writers use no unnecessary words. She writes primarily with nouns and verbs. Her sentences are short; her images vivid and specific. This is from a series of stories on the dilapidated Merlin Apartments in Spokane:

Joe Peak's smile has no teeth.

His dentures were stolen at the Norman Hotel, the last place he lived in downtown Spokane before moving to the Merlin two years ago. Gumming food and fighting diabetes have shrunk the 54-year-old man's frame by 80 pounds. He is thin and weak and his mouth is sore.

The (Spokane, Wash.) Spokesman-Review

"I've got no problem not using stuff in my notes," Sullivan says. "I try to look at [my work] as a painting in relief. I try to stand back and say, 'This is what really matters. This is the one true part.'"

It is that part that she includes.

Says Lou Miliano of *WCBS-AM* radio: "We have time for so few words that you have to be brief and exact in your use of language. I will spend considerable time in the truck thinking about one word that is the right word instead of three or four in its place."

4. BE THERE (WHEREVER "THERE" IS).

Sullivan's stories use a close-up lens. That's how she started with Joe Peak's smile. Getting that close to subjects takes patience, curiosity and the ability to convey genuine interest.

"Being in somebody's space is often critical to these kinds of images," she says. "I don't think you have to be in somebody's bedroom. But, if an hour into the interview, they might want to go into the bedroom to get something, you follow them."

National Public Radio's Gonyea drove out to that nearly empty tank plant to interview the last guard of workers. This allowed him to hear and describe the buzz of factory lights high above and to record the echo of heavy machinery being loaded in the mostly empty plant.

No matter what the medium, reporters have greater impact on their audiences when they take the time to capture the scene through natural sound, a vivid shot or the still photographer's eye.

Good dialogue, captured in a reporter's notebook or as natural sound, conveys the whole array of human emotion. And unlike a quote, it shows rather than tells. Dialogue can put the reader or listener in the courtroom, the classroom, the clubhouse. It can do something else too few news stories do: Make the audience smile.

Yet dialogue rarely finds its way into the news. This may be because of space and time constraints or the instinct to question rather than eavesdrop. Perhaps it is the recognition that capturing dialogue requires an exceptionally good ear and, in print, a fast pen as well. Whatever the reason, we think it's a shame dialogue is hard to come by. It needn't be long to be good.

Here is an example from an article Michelle Guido of the *San Jose (Calif.) Mercury News* wrote after she spent a few weeks posing, with the principal's permission, as a student in a San Jose High School.

"You new here?" asked the guy who sat in front of me in speech class. He had long, dark brown hair he would flip backwards on my desk. I nodded.

"Where you from?" he asked.

"New York. I just moved here."

"Yeah. I could tell there was something different about you," he said, glancing at me sideways. "I can tell by your writing . . . You write big. Girls around here write really small."

San Jose (Calif.) Mercury News

REMEMBER THE SIXTH SENSE: PLACE

It was a horrible place, one that shook Julie Sullivan as much as it did the Spokane contingent she accompanied to a Romanian orphanage. Still, her description of the scene was spare and understated. She let the scene speak for itself.

The Romanian orphanage looks abandoned. Half the roof is gone, glass chips sprinkle the walkway, concrete walls peel paint like old skin.

Inside is a hallway 60 yards long and the 13 Americans who enter are forever changed when they come out.

The floor is slick, sticky and slick, a wetness sliding under shoes from days-old urine, fresh feces and decades of neglect. In the greenish light are children, ages 3 to 8.

They are naked. Their heads are shaved.

Skin gathers at their bony elbows and hangs there. A boy scratches sores that lace his body from his buttocks to his heels, so does the girl next to him. They jump at the visitors, screaming . . . so loud that one girl covers her ears.

The (Spokane, Wash.) Spokesman-Review

Each night, in her bed, Sullivan would write down every scene and image she could remember. Back home, when she wrote, she knew the story would grab readers if she showed them what she saw and touched and heard, rather than merely telling them the reactions of those she accompanied.

"You have to orient readers," she says. "To give them a sense of what they are seeing. I always have tried to give people a sense of place."

That is why KHTV-TV's Michaelsen typically starts with the wide-angle set-up shot. It lets viewers know where they are. He began a story on a neonatal intensive care unit with the harsh sounds of a busy place—the beeping of infant monitors and the cries of the babies themselves. Only then did the reporter weigh in with, "It's hectic here."

"The natural sound," says Michaelsen, "shows that it's hectic here. That all reinforces the reporter's first line."

In contrast, Michaelsen ended the piece, which was about a harpist who visited the unit twice a week, on a peaceful note. The harpist can be heard playing "Silent Night." The final shot is of an infant, curling his tiny hands into contented balls, on the last note.

A sense of place plays a big part on the radio as well, says Lou Miliano.

"I did an enterprise piece on the flourishing used car market," he recalls. "I'd slap my hand on the hood of this Chevy. Slap my hand on the hood of this Audi. The listener knew the sound and knew just what I was doing. Now they could see me standing in front of the used car lot. I had to add that sound to let them see me.

"I'll add visual references," he says. "I'll say, 'Look at that sign up there: Zero percent financing. We can finance anything.' Now the listener can see that sign."

Miliano also believes in taping his narrations where the news is breaking so that listeners have a sense of immediacy and place.

"I don't like disembodied voices," he said. "When you are on the street, the microphone is different from a studio mike. Your voice is flatter. It's not as full as it is in the studio."

Television reporters give their audience a sense of place by going live to the scene.

And on the street, of course, there is action. "If I'm doing a story about the fight against triple-trailer truck routes, I will do phone interviews with people, but the story will be done on the Long Island Expressway and weave the natural sound with the telephone tape."

If radio is about seeing, Miliano said, reporting for radio is about hearing what will put listeners on the scene. "You've got to be able to hear a story to bring it across on radio. For the audience to be able to see on the radio ultimately takes a reporter with sensitive ears."

BRING THE ROUTINE TO LIFE

Using the senses to show rather than tell can unearth interesting tales on even the seemingly mundane assignment.

Told to cover a water rate hike when he worked at *KARE-TV,* Minneapolis, Michaelsen headed for the YMCA pool, where he could capture the action of kids jumping into the water and the words of mothers about to pay higher bills.

USING THE SENSES ONLINE

They're called producers and most of their shifts are spent surfing the Internet rather than out in the field. But online journalists, such as Pat Sullivan of *Mercury Center* in San Jose, Calif., do their best to bring readers to the scene in a different way.

The morning after a blistering fire burned three homes to the ground and badly damaged two others, Sullivan was at work at 5 a.m. putting fresh photographs from the scene online. When Microsoft mogul Bill Gates spoke with the *San Jose Mercury News*' editorial staff, one of Sullivan's co-workers at *Mercury Center* was in the room, recording the event with digital audio so that the site's visitors could listen in. Streams of video are not far behind.

As use of online news sites explodes, their staffs remain lean and their technology the Model T of what it will be in the 21st century. But fasten your seat belts. Change is coming fast.

SUMMARY

USING YOUR SENSES

1. When it is possible, go to the scene. When it is not, get someone who was there to describe it to your audience.

2. Take time to observe. Reporting is more than studying documents and asking questions. Note what you see, hear, smell, taste and touch. Convey that to your reader.

3. It is usually more effective to focus in detail on one person than to write in generalities about lots of them.

4. Bring viewers, listeners and readers a sense of place. Capturing dialogue often helps to do this.

5. Use detail, but use it selectively and sparingly. Only use those details that advance the audience's understanding or appreciation of the story.

6. Descriptive detail has a place in all stories, not just features, magazine segments or projects.

"You are personalizing your story and humanizing it," he said. "That brings it to life in a way the meeting can't."

In Spokane, Wash., Sullivan was given the routine task of advancing a series of lectures by the Alzheimer's Association of Eastern Washington. Many, if not most, reporters would have dismissed the event in a paragraph or two. Sullivan sought to show why the lectures were important. She gave Alzheimer's disease a human face, not only by telling of people who had suffered through the disease with a loved one but also by showing what it was like.

Working on a two-day deadline, Sullivan found and told the story of a prominent local couple, a love story that had ended in the husband's death after an agonizing decade in which his Alzheimer's disease eventually left no trace of the prominent city council member and Mormon bishop he had been.

Sullivan interviewed his widow in a sterile office. Then, the next day, she asked to interview her at home. It was there that the reporter noticed keys hanging beside the widow's door. She asked about them, listened closely and ended with this detail about the wife's struggle to care for her deteriorating husband:

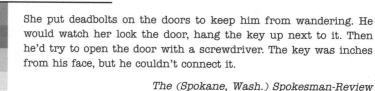

She put deadbolts on the doors to keep him from wandering. He would watch her lock the door, hang the key up next to it. Then he'd try to open the door with a screwdriver. The key was inches from his face, but he couldn't connect it.

The (Spokane, Wash.) Spokesman-Review

RECOMMENDED READING

Clark, R. (1998). *How do you learn to tell stories in journalism.* St. Petersburg, FL: The Poynter Institute for Media Studies. [Online]. Available: **http://www.poynter.org/research/rwe/rwe_tellstory.htm**.

This checklist provides exercises to help reporters become better observers and listeners and to evaluate how well their own news organizations are doing.

Harrington, W. (1997). *Intimate journalism: The art and craft of reporting everyday life.* Thousand Oaks, CA: Sage.

Harrington has brought together examples by some of America's premiere storytellers in this work. Their common thread, says Harrington in two introductory essays, is that they capture and celebrate everyday life. Some of the basic techniques he talks about include "thinking, reporting and writing in scenes; gathering real-life dialogue and gathering telling details from our subjects' lives." The stories throughout this book show how the masters do just that.

Scanlan, C. *Best newspaper writing*. St. Petersburg, FL: The Poynter Institute for Media Studies.

This book, published each year by The Poynter Institute, contains the stories of the winners and runners-up of the American Society of Newspaper Editors competition. In addition to their stories are interviews with the authors and essays by the editor, most recently Christopher Scanlan, a talented writer and the director of the institute's writing program.

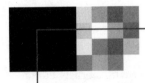

EXERCISES

A. PASSIVE OBSERVATION

1. Go to one of the places listed below and observe for 30 minutes or so. Listen to dialogue, look for details that bring the scene to life, note unusual smells. When you return, write a short scene— 150 words should do—that captures where you were and that might be used within a story. There are two rules here: You may not conduct interviews, and you may not write about what you felt. Simply convey what you observed.

   a. A coffee house

   b. A diner

   c. A sporting event

   d. A bus stop

   e. A playground after school

   f. A hospital emergency room

   g. An amusement park

   h. An accident scene

   i. An aerobics class

   j. A courtroom

2. Go to one of these places and record natural sound that would help bring readers to the scene in a radio or television piece.

3. Go to one of these places and either shoot video that captures the place or note what pictures you would shoot.

B. PERSONAL REMEMBRANCE

1. Write an essay about a memory from your past. Comb your memory for details that can place your reader in the story you are telling. As you construct your essay, jot down at least three scenes that will show the story. Do you recall any dialogue? If so, try to re-create it.

C. CRITIQUE

1. Review a story in print, on radio or on television. Discuss what details the reporter included and what was left out. Jot down five pieces of specific information that might have been included to better draw you to the scene.

CHAPTER 8

Writing in Different Media

Writing coach Don Fry likes to tell the apocryphal story of the young reporter's encounter with a crusty editor.

The two peer across the street from the paper's dimly lit offices at a sign taped to the window of a small local stand.

"Fresh fish sold here," it reads.

"What's wrong with that sign?" the editor asks gruffly.

The reporter stares, dumbfounded.

"Do you think they'd be selling rancid fish?" the editor snarls, striking a line through the word "fresh" on a replica of the sign in front of him.

"And where else besides 'here' do you think they'd be selling this fish?" he continues, striking a line through that word as well.

"Now," he asks the pale young reporter. "What else is wrong?"

Silence.

"Well," the editor snorts, striking a third line through the word "sold." "You don't think they'd be giving the fish away, do you?"

Fish.

It is a tale worth remembering when you sit down to write news on deadline. When news breaks, regardless of the medium, reporters look for ways to get straight to the unvarnished center of a story's message. The news comes first. And it comes lean.

Oh sure, there are real differences among news media. Print reporters, for example, write in the past tense since their accounts are permanent records and often come out the following day. Broadcast reporters, eager to convey a sense of immediacy, write in the present tense. Recognizing that listeners and viewers can't refer back to their fast-moving stories, they also put attribution—the identity of their source of information—at the beginning of sentences. And they keep their sentences short and active.

Radio reporters paint visual images with words and sound. They deliver their audiences up-to-the-minute immediacy. Television reporters tie their words in some way to the picture on screen. They can show and tell.

Everyone faces constraints of time and space. But time on the air is much more precious than space on the printed page. So ideas must be kept simple.

Online reporters also think in short takes—a computer screenful. But they've got all the space in the world to link readers to everything from related stories and original documents to places where readers can talk back.

Ultimately, the different media diverge not only in how each course of news is prepared but in how many courses—the *layers* of a story—are delivered and at what pace. Print reporters and their online counterparts offer more layers—sidebars, graphics, fact boxes—to audiences who may already know the news but don't fully understand its context or know its details.

Indeed, the news in all media these days is getting sliced and diced into more and more courses. In broadcast news, however, these courses all move pretty quickly—a three-sentence headline on radio, a facts graphic on TV, one angle on the 5 o'clock newscast, another angle at 6. In print and online, the layering can be a more complex stew, offering related stories of different subjects and lengths for the information-starved.

But strip aside these differences and the goal of breaking news—the main course of the news business—remains the same: fish. So when you sit down to write breaking news, think this way:

F—forget

I—incidental

S—stuff and

H—hit the news straight on.

This chapter will introduce you to the techniques of writing for broadcast, print and online media. On the pages ahead, you will read:

- How radio, television, the newspaper and an online service told the story of a brush fire that threatened a California town
- How you can better organize your writing process, regardless of the medium for which you are working
- How to humanize and follow stories once you've gotten the basic news
- Why and how new media are different

THE STORY OF A FAST-MOVING FIRE

Thursday, Aug. 8, was proving a bad day all around. As warm winds blew through the dry brush of the Santa Cruz Mountains, a wall of flames suddenly swept through the scrub and California oak near the city of Los Gatos. Fire crews scrambled on land and in the air. And reporters struggled behind them.

News, it seems, likes to break at the most inopportune times. This fire began its spread during rush hour, as daytime reporters wrapped up their shifts, commuters sat at a standstill on roadways, and radio and television news producers finalized the lineups for their nightly newscasts.

Dispatched to the fire by *KCBS-AM* news radio, reporter George Harris found himself trapped in traffic for nearly an hour. His station relied on its traffic helicopter pilot to fill in with live news until Harris, one hand on the wheel, the other on a cell phone, finally began describing the scene in Los Gatos at about 5:40 p.m.

Reporter Betsy Gebhart from *KNTV-TV* in San Jose had better luck, at least at first. She made it to downtown Los Gatos an hour earlier, only to run into difficulties with her cell phone and transmission signals. Hungry as she was to move closer to the fire, she and her photojournalist stayed tethered to their TV truck. Producers feared they'd lose the already finicky signal and in any

The Los Gatos, Calif., fire obliterated a handful of houses, like the one pictured here. Swift action, chronicled by reporters in this chapter, saved the town.

case didn't want to abandon the fire command post with no second crew in place to back up Gebhart. In the end, the best visuals—critical to all television—had to be borrowed from *KTVU-TV* in Oakland, with whom *KNTV-TV* has a reciprocal agreement.

At the *San Jose Mercury News,* Brandon Bailey began the task of building facts to write the main news story for the next morning. Each time he started, it seemed, the computer system crashed. It was one of the paper's worst production nights in memory.

In the end, all three reporters prevailed. Their stories weren't artistry, just the stuff of basic news. There are times, of course, when reporters can put in the extra effort to recut a radio actuality (sound bite), recast a lead, rework the script to better fit a visual. But in the real world of news, writing is craft, not art. It must be done on tight deadlines—sometimes minutes, rarely much more than an hour or two.

The following sections are designed to show you how a half-dozen writers and reporters pursued their craft on one story in four different media. This chapter is about writing, but as we've noted often before, we consider writing and reporting inseparable. You'll see this in some of the comments of the reporters as they discuss how they put their stories together.

So join us as we take you from radio to television to print to the online world in the story of a fire. You'll notice some similarities and some differences in the tips to help you write for the different media. One similarity in particular sticks out: All the reporters interviewed for this chapter knew their stories could have come out better and could explain exactly how. If only they'd had a little more time.

THE STORY ON RADIO: *KCBS-AM*

News of the fire filled the 6 p.m. report on *KCBS-AM.* The lead story, recalls editor Frni Beyer, "was sort of a team effort," cobbled together by writers in the studio working with reports from the field. It began like this:

At least two homes have burned in a multiple-alarm fire off of Highway 17 in the Santa Cruz Mountains in Los Gatos.

The fire broke out about four o'clock just north of the Cats Restaurant near downtown Los Gatos. The fire quickly consumed several acres of brush. Firefighters appeared to get the upper hand—but then the flames blew out of control. And since that happened, at least two homes have been burned and several others remain threatened.

Fire officials have ordered evacuations of the Meadows Convalescent Hospital, Wood Road, Broadway and Fairview Avenue.

KCBS-AM

Thirty seconds. That is an average-length lead story in the world of radio news. It's a world in which what gets left out of the story is every bit as important as what gets in.

"You just have to learn to condense what's needed in a story and get rid of the junk," says news writer Michael Bower, who worked with Beyer and reporters in the field in constructing the Los Gatos fire coverage. "Get rid of words like 'very.' 'Very' is very worthless. You just need what happened."

What happened, he adds, had better be clear, catchy and accurate.

"Grab people at the very beginning," Bower counsels. "Give them a reason to keep listening."

That is why the news here is not that "a fire broke out." It is that "two homes have burned." Writing news, regardless of the medium, means looking for impact.

Radio reporters face other challenges:

- **They want to lead with what's newest.** By 7 the same evening, the *KCBS* anchors had updated the lead on fire damage and recast it in more active language:

A wind-whipped fire has burned at least two homes and a total of five structures near Los Gatos in the Santa Cruz Mountains.

- ***They must keep things simple.*** The shortest sentence in the 6 p.m. fire story was eight words. Only one, the first, was more than 20. Radio reporters keep things concise. They write with verbs. They strip their sentences of clauses.
- ***They must weave sound and words creatively to bring the scene alive.*** Natural sound—sirens and the shouts of officials checking IDs at the fire line—captures the action. Radio reporters also use their words to help the audience "see." In his live report from the field immediately after the news summary, reporter George Harris brought listeners what he heard and described what he saw.

I'm at the very edge of this fire. You might be able to hear the helicopters overhead. It is a very smoky scene as another bucket of water is dropped on the fire.

"I had a terrific boss who once told me, 'Just describe everything that you see and take me to the scene,'" Harris recalled later. "I've always based my coverage on that concept. I want to engage the listener's mind and imagination."

RADIO WRITING TIPS

News rarely is as neat as the writing rules in a textbook. Here are tips on writing for radio. Let's see how many were followed in the Los Gatos fire story.

BE CONVERSATIONAL

"What we need to do is tell the story like you'd tell your best friend standing next to you," explains Bower, the *KCBS-AM* writer. "It's kind of like saying, 'Hey, did you hear about the big fire in Los Gatos this afternoon?'"

Radio reporters write like people talk. Notice how conversational this sentence is: "Firefighters appeared to get the upper hand—but then the flames blew out of control."

BUILD THE STORY AROUND COMPELLING SOUND BITES

"It's amazing how effective you can be if you allow yourself to get out of the way," says Harris, one of the *KCBS-AM* reporters. "I always think in terms of people. People have something interesting to say. It's my job to get out of the way and let them tell the story."

The sound bites of radio, called actualities, are interspersed throughout reports. Harris and other radio reporters typically use actualities to carry a story and convey its drama. In picking actualities they look for opinions, feelings and firsthand accounts. The nuts and bolts of the story, the facts, go into the reporter's narration.

Faced with instantaneous deadlines at the fire, the *KCBS-AM* crew relied on live interviews instead of taped ones to carry the drama.

The Internet has brought a new dimension to new writing. News organizations' Web sites, such as this one for *KCBS* radio, allow for constant updates, layers of information and a mix of media never seen before.

HOOK YOUR LISTENER IN THE FIRST FEW WORDS

KCBS-AM listeners are going to be more interested in a fire that burns houses than one that merely breaks out in the brush:

 At least two homes have burned in a multiple-alarm fire off of Highway 17 in the Santa Cruz Mountains in Los Gatos.

Radio has to compete for its audience. Most people tuned in are also turned to other tasks. They're driving their car or warming lunch for the kids. The radio can become background noise unless the news commands attention.

"Rather than saying, 'Governor Wilson signed a bill,'" explains *KCBS*' Bower, "let the top say, 'From now on, new mothers will be able to stay in the hospital two days instead of one. That after Governor Wilson signed a bill.'"

Bureaucratic phrases such as "signed a bill" make for dull copy. Who cares? Radio reporters recast leads to measure the impact on people.

CONVEY A SENSE OF ORDER IN A WAY THAT MAKES FOR GOOD STORYTELLING

People can't reread on the radio, so each element must flow from the one before.

"Move the story forward," says Bower.

Once the lead is set, the second point must be closely related. A reporter can structure a story in many ways, but each should have a beginning, a middle and an end.

In this *KCBS-AM* story the first sentence summarizes the big news. The next four sentences explain how things got bad. It starts at the beginning and moves forward.

 The fire broke out about four o'clock just north of the Cats Restaurant near downtown Los Gatos. The fire quickly consumed several acres of brush.

Firefighters appeared to get the upper hand but then the flames blew out of control. And since that happened—at least two homes have been burned and several others remain threatened.

WRITE FOR YOUR EARS, NOT YOUR EYES

Radio stories are meant to be heard, not read. That's why you'll hear a low murmur in any radio newsroom as reporters and writers practice the copy aloud.

Reporters know to keep one idea to a sentence. Simple writing also means few numbers and no unfamiliar names.

Read the preceding excerpt from the story aloud. Notice how the short sentences make it easier to follow what happened. Now read this sentence aloud:

Firefighters appeared to get the upper hand over the fire, which broke out about four o'clock just north of the Cats Restaurant near downtown Los Gatos, but then the flames blew out of control destroying at least two homes and threatening several others.

Can you see why simple sentences are best on the air?

GIVE LISTENERS A VISUAL IMAGE

"I can't stress enough the importance of painting very clear word pictures on the radio," Beyer says.

Word pictures show listeners what they can't see. They engage the imagination and convey the intensity of a scene.

"I see a lot of thick brown and black smoke," George Harris reported. "It is carrying toward the downtown area."

USE NATURAL SOUND UP FULL

Another way to bring listeners to the scene is to let them hear the activity that is abuzz there. So radio reporters allow their stories to "breathe" for a few seconds by inserting segments of natural, or wild, sound that's occurring on the scene.

Such sound inserts take creative editing on the fly or good coordination between the reporter in the field and the producer back at the station. The reports on *KCBS-AM* might have been more compelling if reporters had recorded the sound of water-carrying helicopters flying overhead or the orders of officials turning pedestrians away from blocked-off streets.

MAKE EVERY WORD TELL

"We're brief," is how Bower puts it.

"Be direct, clear and concise," says Beyer.

Active verbs drive sentences. Verbs are active when the thing or person doing the acting appears in the sentence before the verb.

- "fire burned homes . . ."
- "fire broke out . . ."
- "fire consumed . . ."
- "fire officials have ordered evacuations . . ."

The verbs here are serviceable but not exceptional. "Consumed" conveys the fire's force. So did another verb, "races," used in the station's tease before the story began:

> At least two houses have been burned and several others are threatened as fire races through the Santa Cruz Mountains into Los Gatos.

BE CLEAR, NOT CUTE

A lead that reads, "It has been a bad day for Smokey Bear" would obscure the news and set a tone inappropriate for a story that tells about people losing their homes.

No cutsey language. No cliches. But radio reporters do strive for clever writing that pulls the listener back into the story. They look for words that "tickle the ear."

LET LISTENERS KNOW THE SOURCES OF INFORMATION

KCBS-AM didn't do this well in the lead story, although attribution was implied in this sentence:

> Fire officials have ordered evacuations of the Meadows Convalescent Hospital, Wood Road, Broadway and Fairview Avenue.

After the newscast, however, the station interviewed key authorities, including the spokeswoman for the Santa Clara County Fire Department and a battalion chief for the state.

When attribution is used in radio, it comes at the beginning of a sentence, for example, "Fire Chief John Jones says the fire is 50 percent contained," not, "The fire is 50 percent contained, Fire Chief John Jones says."

Likewise, anchors and reporters must always introduce the person who is speaking before the actuality comes up.

USE VERBS THAT SHOW IMMEDIACY

Note that Jones' comment above is in the present tense ("says"), not the past ("said"). Radio writing should update the listener with the latest events. That's why radio writers use the present tense or the present progressive ("is saying") most of the time. The same is true in television.

ANSWER THE BASIC QUESTIONS

Sometimes space and time limit you to little more than headlines. But at least know what listeners probably will want to know. The easiest way to do that is to ask yourself, "What would I want to know if I lived in Los Gatos?"

"To me it's important to convey some of the hard numbers," says Beyer. "Has anyone been hurt? Is the fire threatening or damaging homes? And where is it going? People want to know, 'Do I have to get out of my home, or what?'"

Those kinds of immediate answers only radio can provide. Interestingly, the story atop the 6 o'clock news didn't say where the fire was headed. It's quite possible the answer wasn't clear.

"The information kept changing," recalls Harris, who got a late start because editors thought the fire was under control earlier. "This thing was so intense I personally thought it was going to take downtown."

THE STORY ON TELEVISION: *KNTV-TV*

By the 11 o'clock news, some semblance of order had returned to Betsy Gebhart's day. She knew firefighters had gained the upper hand over the fire. She knew her transmission signals were reaching the station and her audience. She knew *KNTV-TV* had finally, belatedly, gotten two more crews to Los Gatos. And she knew, like it or not, that her producers had gotten hold of some better video than the stuff her photojournalist, ordered to stay put at the station's truck downtown, had managed to shoot.

It had not been a good day. But that didn't matter now. Gebhart's job is to give viewers the news. They don't care about what reporters didn't get. They want to know what happened.

The report began with anchor Mary Babbitt reading over a shot of flames licking at the framing of what was a home:

Homes destroyed and lives disrupted as a brush fire sweeps through the hills of Los Gatos.

Anchor Doug Moore took over as the video cut to a helicopter dumping water through the smoke-filled skies.

It's the most devastating fire to hit the Los Gatos area since the terrible Lexington fire back in 1985. Beginning our Team 11 coverage tonight is Betsy Gebhart. She's live in Los Gatos.

Gebhart stood in front of a roadblock, as close as she'd gotten all day to the fire she'd have liked to chase without the tether of her station's video truck.

| We're here on North Santa Cruz Avenue near the base to Wood Road. This is a hilly street where the fire threatened and destroyed numerous homes. | The road is still closed off to residents. The fire continues to burn at this hour, but it is 100 percent contained. |

Like all television reporters, Betsy Gebhart likes to look at and log available video before she writes her script. For one thing, she understands that the dominant video image drives television news. For another, she has been taught to write to the corners of pictures, not repeating everything the viewer sees, but not contradicting it.

On this evening, that wasn't possible. The truck in which she and her photographer had raced to the scene wasn't equipped for editing. And besides, some of the best video was footage others had shot. So Gebhart wrote her script as best she could, relying on her segment producer at the station to match her words with the best available pictures. Another team effort, imperfect to the reporter perhaps, but just plain news to the viewer.

The newscast producer slotted Gebhart's story as a **donut**, or insert—a taped story run between a live open and tag by the reporter. It was one of three reporter stories that night on the fire. Here is how her script went.

VIDEO	AUDIO
Gebhart live on camera at roadblock	(Gebhart live ad lib) We're here on North Santa Cruz Avenue near the base to Wood Road. This is a hilly street where the fire threatened and destroyed numerous homes. The road is still closed off to residents. The fire continues to burn at this hour—but it is 100 percent contained.
(Taped story begins) WS (wide shot) aerial of fire and wind	Natural sound up full (three seconds of wind and fire)
MS (medium shot) of blowing smoke whipping through trees Pan (movement right to left) of sky	(Gebhart narration) The fire was reported just before four p-m above the Cats Restaurant on Highway 17. And wind-whipped flames spread smoke toward the town of Los Gatos.
WS zoom to CU (close-up) of a burning house CU firefighter running with hose Pull-back to burning home	At least four large, expensive hillside homes were destroyed. Several streets were evacuated—Wood Road, Broadway, Fairview, Manzanita and Overlook. 200 residents fled homes.
MS ground flames and fire trucks	Also evacuated early on—400 to 500 people in the Los Gatos Meadows Nursing Home.
MS of officer	(Sound bite: Sgt. Mike York, Los Gatos Police) Most were very, very cooperative. They grabbed a few things and left their homes almost immediately. The fire was moving on them pretty rapidly and they saw the smoke coming. And they moved out pretty rapidly.

VIDEO	AUDIO
WS aerial of hills and smoke MS of firefighters spraying water on the smoking ground Pan to smoldering ground	(Gebhart narration) Santa Clara Fire estimates only 15 acres of wild land was charred. But much of it was timber that hasn't burned in at least 100 years.
MS of fire official	(Sound bite: Don Jarvis, Santa Clara County Fire Department) Our biggest problem here was access. We could not get people to all areas of this fire because of the steep terrain and the limited roads. The wind was heavy during all stages of this fire. Our initial dispatch was double that we normally send, and we called for additional resources right away. But we could not catch up to this fire. The wind was pushing it faster than we could move it.
WS of helicopter dropping water on the fire	(Gebhart narration) When six air tankers and four water-dropping helicopters made their way onto the scene, firefighters took the upper hand fairly soon after. There were reports that downed power lines caused the fire—but the fire department is not sure whether that was a result of the fire—or the cause of it.
WS of burning forest WS of helicopter flying over (End of taped piece) Gebhart on camera	(Gebhart live ad lib) Whatever happened, 44-hundred residents lost power for a certain amount of time this evening. One update—the C-D-F is now reporting at this hour—six homes were destroyed in the fire, another two partially damaged. Temperaturewise, it's cooled down quite a bit here. The winds have died down too. The fire department says that was another key to getting control of this fire. They are expected to get the fire out by midnight tonight. Reporting live in Los Gatos, Betsy Gebhart.

TELEVISION WRITING TIPS

The *KCBS-AM* and *KNTV-TV* stories are similar in two ways:

- Both rely on short, conversational sentences. Broadcasters write for the ear: "I try to think like I'm talking to my cameraman," Gebhart says. "I would do that in a conversational way: 'Here's what's going on. Five people are evacuated, all these roads are closed off.'"
- Both begin with a summary lead and then branch off to tell various aspects of the story.

Here are some other things Betsy Gebhart tries to do when writing for television.

START WITH THE STRONGEST VIDEO

"You go with best picture," Gebhart says. In fire stories, that means flames. That's why *KNTV-TV* began its story with a picture of a burning house. Editors cut back to that house later as Gebhart told her story.

The second-best picture? Leave it for a closing shot and build the story up to a strong conclusion.

BUILD SEQUENCES FOR GOOD STORYTELLING

The best stories are constructed around video sequences—three or four related pictures that tell a ministory in themselves.

Gebhart's taped insert (the part of her story edited on tape and aired between her live introduction and live on-camera ending) started with a sequence of fire pictures. These included an aerial view of the raging fire in the hills, a shot of smoke billowing in the trees and a pan (moving shot) from right to left of the smoky sky. When the reporter doesn't have time to show every view of the fire, a few selected shots in sequence condense the action and tell the story.

WRITE TO THE PICTURES

Gebhart planned her script so the pictures of the burning houses would be up when she related that "at least four large, expensive, hillside homes were destroyed." When she spoke of "wind-whipped flames," the picture showed blowing smoke.

"I started in radio and moved to television," Gebhart says. "The hardest thing for me was to learn to write to pictures. I was much more informational. Now I can write out a script, and in the left-hand margin I write, use this shot, use that shot."

While she wants to refer to the pictures, she doesn't want to become a play-by-play announcer. It would insult the viewers if she narrated the shots, "And now the flames are licking the roof, and now a firefighter is running to move a hose." The viewers are already seeing that. Instead, most TV reporters use a concept called "touch and go." They "touch" the video by mentioning what's on the screen and then "go," or write away from the pictures, telling viewers information the video doesn't show.

KEEP THE STORY MOVING

Pacing is particularly important in television. Viewers bore easily. No one wants to hear the reporter drone on for 40 seconds. Notice in Gebhart's script how she threads her narration around sound bites and keeps each element fairly short. Boring but important details shouldn't be dumped in one spot in a story. Reporters try to keep each bit of narration and each sound bite to around 12 seconds.

Good pacing also means varying the shots and the length of shots. In the case of the fire, of course, Gebhart had no control. But she gave an example: "Vary your shots. If you're talking about a school, don't just show the school. Get in the classroom and show the kids at work. That's much more interesting. Look over the kids' shoulder as they're writing. Try to use something that is action-oriented."

LOOK FOR GOOD SOUND TO PUNCTUATE AND HUMANIZE THE STORY

The two firefighters, Mike York and Don Jarvis, convey the frenzy of fighting a fast-moving fire in human and conversational terms. They were at the scene and thus lend a sense of immediacy that Gebhart can't.

The editor or producer picking the shots back at the station chose to show both men as they spoke. Had better video been available, it might have been used over the second half of Jarvis' sound bite as he spoke of the steep terrain and the firefighters' struggle to "catch" the fire.

Natural sound is just as important in television as it is in radio. Under all the pictures in the fire story you hear the low murmur of the sound on the scene—the whir of the chopper blades and the hum of fire truck motors.

Gebhart's story begins with three seconds of natural sound of the fire and the wind in the hills. Such natural sound turned up full is a good pacing technique in letting the story "breathe" for a few seconds. If she'd had the right sound on tape, she might have put in three seconds in the middle of the piece of a firefighter yelling, "We've got to get these people out" or, "Get some water over here," to punctuate the drama of the story.

MAKE THE STAND-UP AN INTEGRAL PART OF THE STORY

Gebhart was live at the scene, so she didn't need to include an on-camera narration, called a **stand-up**, in her taped piece. These usually appear in the middle or at the end of a story. Reporters learn to ad lib these quickly because they shoot them while covering the action and before the full story is written.

Reporters use stand-ups in at least three ways: to give information for which there's no video, to make a transition from one angle of the story to another or to demonstrate something.

ALWAYS THINK OF THE AUDIENCE

Gebhart says keeping the audience in mind helps her think about what information to report on different newscasts.

"I try to picture myself in this situation as a resident or a homeowner and I ask, 'What would I want to know?'"

She checked off the answers: homes burned, acres burned, streets closed. "I know that in South San Jose no one cares about Manzanita Road. But someone who lives there certainly cares about Manzanita Road."

THE STORY IN PRINT: *SAN JOSE MERCURY NEWS*

By the time Brandon Bailey's editor asked him for help, the *San Jose Mercury News* had dispatched two reporters to the Los Gatos fire. It was 5:30 p.m. and Bailey's task would be to take "feeds" from reporters and write the main story—not for the next hour's newscast or the 11 p.m. news, but for the next morning's paper.

As the story developed through the night, he began to realize his job, as is often the case for newspapers in an age of instant communication, would be very different from merely recounting the news. Bailey wanted his story to have context, to explain that this fire had scared people badly because of even worse fires not so many years before.

He didn't realize this right away, of course. First Bailey used the reverse directory (see Chapter 4) to call shop owners in Los Gatos. He flipped from one television channel to another to see what the scene was like and what people were saying. He read about big fires in past years, such as the Lexington fire, which had burned an extensive area near Los Gatos in 1985.

Brandon Bailey

It was a tough day to concentrate. The newsroom computer crashed twice, taking reporters' notes and stories with it. Reporters in the field were stuck in traffic. The *Mercury News* hadn't gotten anyone near the flames. But Bailey knew his deadline would remain 10 p.m., no matter what obstacles got in the way.

So, as he read and talked and watched, he thought. Like all good reporters, he was crafting his beginning, his **lead**, as he worked. Sometime after 8 p.m. he approached his editor.

"I wanted to have one of those conversations which was, 'OK. Here is what I'm thinking about as a lead and tell me if I'm off the mark.' It was a serious fire, but it was pretty clear it wasn't going to be the Oakland Hills fire [which burned hundreds of homes]."

"I asked myself, 'Why is this a big story?' The sense I had was that it was big because it was scaring people because they remembered the Lexington fire and they remembered Oakland Hills."

Realizing this, Bailey suggested a double-barreled lead—far too complex for radio or television, but helpful to a reader trying to understand the fire the next day. The lead would say the fire was a bad one. But equally importantly, Bailey said, it would get across that it heightened fears because of past experience. Here is how his story began:

A fast-moving wildfire destroyed six homes in the tinder-dry hills above Los Gatos Thursday. It threatened the downtown commercial district, raising uneasy memories of past disasters and provoking a massive response from firefighters on land and in the air.

Like all reporters, Bailey wanted his lead to do three things: sell the story to readers, summarize its news, and set its tone and direction. That is why he started writing the lead even as he still was collecting information.

"I guess I sort of made a decision that I needed to work out what the lead would be and the rest would be sort of like putting together the pieces of a jigsaw puzzle," he said. "I knew there would be some color [from the scene]. I knew there'd be some official fire department stuff and a little bit of chronology. But the first thing was the lead."

Bailey also knew he would have a lot more space than his broadcast competitors to fill. *KCBS* radio wrapped up its **reader**—a story read by an anchor—in just about 100 words. Gebhart's *KNTV-TV* package stretched to a few hundred. Bailey would write more than 1,000 words for an audience that likely would wake up well aware of the fire's headlines. His job would be to bring some sense, order and detail to events. In the heat of deadline, that can be one of the print reporter's biggest challenges.

What follows is a condensed version of Bailey's story.

[handwritten margin notes: "was actually 4 — at time supposedly 6 — could have attributed # of homes destroyed."]

A fast-moving wildfire destroyed six homes in the tinder-dry hills above Los Gatos on Thursday. It threatened the downtown commercial district, raising uneasy memories of past disasters and provoking a massive response from firefighters on land and in the air.

More than 4,500 households lost power and rush-hour traffic was thoroughly snarled on Highway 17 and Santa Cruz Avenue, where downtown workers and residents milled around outside in the stifling hot afternoon heat. *[handwritten: elaborating on the where]*

They watched as flames approached as close as 200 yards, while a fleet of water-toting airplanes and helicopters roared overhead. The cause of the fire, which burned about 15 acres, was unknown late Thursday, but officials had not ruled out arson. *[handwritten: massive response details]*

"It's been like a war zone since 3:30 this afternoon.... We've been sitting on the deck just watching these orange buckets fly overhead every 40 seconds," said downtown resident Skippy Purdy early Thursday evening. *[handwritten: Quote to capture drama]*

Echoing other longtime residents, Purdy said the scene was far too reminiscent of the disastrous Lexington fire, which burned 14,000 acres and destroyed two dozen homes in 1985. *[handwritten: tells of past disasters]*

"This is the second time we've seen this town burn," explained Purdy, who lives a block from Santa Cruz Avenue. "It's not that comforting—especially when you drive toward your house and see the flames, and it looks like they're in your front yard." *[handwritten: is fire ing still burning?]*

Authorities contained the fire by 6:30 p.m., but they said the first two hours of the battle were difficult, with flames fanned by winds gusting up to 22 mph. *[handwritten: no, contained fire, how contained]*

"The wind was pushing," said Santa Clara County Fire Capt. Don Jarvis, "and we couldn't catch up..."

... Temperatures stayed in the mid-90s Thursday despite forecasts that it was supposed to cool down.

At the fire's peak, there were 200 firefighters and 50 engines deployed, with 33 of the engines in use, said Jarvis. *[handwritten: this is how contained]*

Six closed-wing air tanker planes dropped fire retardant, and four helicopters doused the blaze with water from Vasona Lake mixed with fire-retardant foam. One air attack coordinator oversaw the aerial operation. *[handwritten: this how contained here's massive response]*

(continued)

[handwritten bottom margin: indirect attribution, shows delayed to a lot of people]

"The one good thing about this fire was that there was no other fire burning in the area, competing for resources," Jarvis said. "Everything was available for us up and down the state."

Officials counted themselves lucky that they stopped the blaze after it destroyed six homes—including four valued at between $500,000 and $1 million apiece—and partly burned two other buildings. They had evacuated 200 residents along Wood Road and neighboring streets, as well as 240 residents of a retirement complex, using ambulances to transport elderly residents to the First United Methodist Church of Los Gatos. *details on burned houses*

No injuries were reported.

Officials said the fire started around 3:30 p.m. in the heavily overgrown hills about 500 yards north of the Cats restaurant, a local landmark that sits alongside southbound Highway 17. The flames burned northward, never actually threatening the restaurant.

At one point, however, firefighters closed southbound Highway 17 to through traffic because the fire was so close to the highway that they had to fight it from the road surface.

"We had to protect our people working on Highway 17," Jarvis said.

He said the fire was considered contained by 6:30 p.m.

Nonetheless, he said, officers planned to spend the entire night monitoring the scene.

chronological

There were scattered reports of power lines down in the fire area, but Jarvis and firefighters didn't know whether the downed lines were felled by the blaze or might have caused it.

The fire was particularly difficult to fight because it was on a steep hillside slope, heavily wooded with brush and timber. Jarvis estimated that the area hadn't burned in at least 100 years. Access was also a problem because dead-end streets made it difficult for firefighters to get a good angle on the blaze, Jarvis said.

"This fire had a lot of potential to be disastrous because of the weather, the terrain, the homes and the heavy fuel," Jarvis said. . . .

San Jose Mercury News

back to why such a bad fire - setting up the quote - wants to end w/ good quote

PRINT WRITING TIPS

Here we'll take apart some of the pieces of Bailey's story and hear him talk about the newspaper writer at work.

CRAFT THE LEAD

Most writers start with the lead. They recognize that it informs everything that follows. The lead grabs the reader. The lead summarizes the key points of the story. The lead establishes what's to come. Most print leads, like broadcast, last a single sentence. But there are exceptions, as was the case with Bailey's fire story.

"I ended up with something pretty unusual these days, which is a two-sentence lead," Bailey said. "The first sentence was your basic *AP* lead. The second sentence raised the sense of past fires that provoked the massive response."

As important as leads are to writing, the lead shouldn't be all consuming. Spend too much time crafting the lead and you'll be exhausted by the time you need to frame the rest of the story. A tip: If the lead tends to take too much of your time, try to write a theme sentence. It will still focus your article by summarizing the main points. But it will do so without the pressure to word the lead perfectly. Then you can write the rest of the story and come back to smooth out the lead.

The theme sentence here might have been, "A fire destroyed six homes and raised fears of past disasters."

WRITE AS YOU REPORT

Reporters don't wait until they've gathered all their information before they start thinking about the shape of their stories. Often, consideration of what the story will say shapes the nature of late questioning and makes the reporting process more efficient. For example, Bailey knew he wanted to use Purdy's quote—"This is the second time we've seen this town burn"—high in his story because it elaborated on his lead. In newspaper jargon, the paragraphs after a lead that develop the main theme are referred to as **lead support**.

LISTEN TO YOUR WRITING

Broadcasters aren't the only ones who do this. Enter any newsroom and you'll see the best writers mouthing their stories to themselves. That is what Bailey did before he filed.

"I read it out loud to myself to make sure there was something of a rhythm there: a short sentence and then a longer sentence."

Bailey's first sentence also contains alliteration, the repetition of the letter "h," which makes it more pleasing to the ear ("six *homes* in the tinder-dry *hills* . . .").

SIMPLE SENTENCES ARE BEST

Another lesson the best broadcasters can teach and print reporters sometimes forget is to keep sentences simple. A piece of advice: The more clauses packed into a sentence, the harder it is to read. Study after study has found that stories with a lower average word count are easier to read.

Vivid action verbs help, too. The fire *destroyed* six homes. It *threatened* the downtown. It *snarled* traffic.

At times, we are all tempted to pack too much into one sentence. That's what Bailey initially did in writing a lead.

"At one point I was trying to squeeze all that into one sentence, which wasn't going to work," he recalled.

CONTEXT IS IMPORTANT

"You can't just provide some facts," Bailey said. "You've got to put a larger picture around it because many people will already have seen those pictures and seen those basic facts by the next morning."

That larger picture is called context. It is historical or background information important enough to include high in many print stories. Context allows print stories to be wiser, to use the advantage of more time to place events in the perspective of what has come before or will come next.

The context here is the "uneasy memories of past disasters" and an explanation in the fifth and sixth paragraphs of what those disasters were.

OUTLINE

Newspaper stories demand more of readers than the typical broadcast version. The newspaper story lasts longer. It contains more information. That means writers must be well organized if they hope to hold readers from beginning to end.

Organization is tough on-the-fly. Your eighth-grade teacher was right: Outline. We're not talking about the lengthy, rigid outlines of a term paper. But jot down key words and phrases. Bailey might have written.

   Lead

   Context about fire

   Support paragraphs about impact

   Support paragraphs about fire

   Details about fighting the fire

   Chronology

Good news writing is linear. The writer never has to double back. Can you find places where Bailey doubles back in his account? What might be done to prevent that?

Good news writing also is logical. It moves naturally from one theme to another. When writers are forced to make an abrupt turn, it is important for them to provide **transitions**—signposts that tell readers they are changing directions. Here is an example:

> The flames burned northward, never actually threatening the restaurant.
>
> At one point, however, firefighters closed southbound Highway 17 . . .

The transition here—"At one point, however"—is written to alert the reader that the sentence will say something that seems to contradict the previous sentence.

LOOK FOR WORD PICTURES

Print reporters have neither moving pictures nor sound. They bring readers to the scene with their own observations (see Chapter 7) or the vivid quotes of someone who was there. Bailey was disappointed with the quality of description he got back from the scene.

"I would have liked to have more description from up close to the fire, because that is after all what the story is about," he said.

Still, he tried to create a word picture of the community high in his story with this paragraph:

> . . . downtown workers and residents milled around outside in the stifling afternoon heat.
>
> They watched as flames approached as close as 200 yards, while a fleet of water-toting airplanes and helicopters roared overhead.

USE A STRONG QUOTE HIGH IN THE STORY

A quote helps bring readers to the scene. It also changes the cadence of writing, introducing another voice. This was Bailey's fourth paragraph:

> "It's been like a war zone since 3:30 this afternoon. . . . We've been sitting on the deck just watching those orange buckets fly overhead every 40 seconds," said downtown resident Skippy Purdy.

BE AS COMPLETE AS POSSIBLE

Good stories answer readers' questions, even when the answer is, "I don't know."

One of the first questions readers would have about the fire is what caused it. Bailey didn't have the answer, but he still provided an answer high in the story:

> The cause of the fire . . . was unknown late Thursday, but officials had not ruled out arson.

ATTRIBUTE KEY INFORMATION

The facts, especially in fast-breaking disaster stories, have a nasty habit of changing. That is why it is wise to attribute all factual information to the source that provides it. Bailey's lead says flat-out that six houses were destroyed. That is what he was told. The next day, however, that number was revised downward to three. Because Bailey didn't attribute the information in his first-day story, readers might mistakenly have thought he made an error instead of officials.

THE STORY ONLINE: *MERCURY CENTER*

Brandon Bailey had even more to worry about that night than crafting a great newspaper story. He had to scramble to feed that ever-hungry sibling of the newspaper, its online news operation. It was just getting into the breaking-news business.

When it first came online in the early 1990s, *Mercury Center*, like most newspaper online operations, had been completely divorced from the daily gathering and play of news. But since 1996 that has changed.

Online journalists now sit among reporters and editors in the main *Mercury News* newsroom. They go to news meetings. And they push to break big stories as they happen. So before Brandon Bailey ever typed the next morning's lead, he had filed a nuts-and-bolts overview for *Mercury Center* so that the paper's online readers could read about the fire at the same time they were hearing about it on the radio.

"It was just like the old days when the paper had a p.m. [afternoon paper]," Bailey recalled. "They said, 'Look, we need to give up-to-date information for our readers.' So they're saying, 'Hey, can you give me a lead for our home page, and I'm thinking, 'I don't even have a lead for tomorrow.'"

Such are the new pressures of online journalism on even veteran newspaper reporters. Bailey filed the basics. He didn't keep the exact copy but recalls it went roughly like this: "There's a fast-moving fire in the hills above Los Gatos tonight. It has burned at least three homes. There's umpteen firefighters out there. It's still not under control. There's a huge traffic jam and people filling the streets to watch the flames from downtown Los Gatos."

Sound a bit like radio?

"The Internet is pushing us back toward 24-hour publication again," Bailey said. "There's starting to be more signs of papers putting the news on the Net first."

He discovered that again the next day. Operating on six hours of sleep, Bailey updated the information on the number of homes that burned. He also found out that firefighters had fixed the cause of the fire on an electric company distribution line.

Once again he filed his basic information, short and sweet, to the paper's online operation. It included nothing but the facts, like an old-fashioned *AP* story. This time the words were crafted by *Mercury Center* online editor Patricia Sullivan and grafted online atop the story that had appeared in the morning paper.

"If we want, we are going to be able to recover the sense that we have the news first," Sullivan said of online publications. "The question is, 'How often do we want to rush to judgment?' There is a heated internal debate about this. Reporters have to have time to report and editors have to have time to think about editing. We don't want to become the wire."

Except, perhaps, on the biggest stories.

Online writing is changing fast. But this much is already clear: The Internet can offer everything from headlines on its splash page (first page) to extensive, in-depth links to related information. Mistakes can be fixed instantly. Readers can comment immediately and provide tips. New maps and graphics can appear. And widespread use of sound and video are increasingly commonplace.

WRITING FOR NEW MEDIA

It's foolish to discuss writing online without first mentioning what is perhaps the key difference in the medium: Online journalism by definition is interactive.

"Interactivity is providing the public with a much larger piece of the pie, and it's making your whole staff accessible to a whole lot of people," says Jon Katz, who writes an online column for the Internet magazine *HotWired.*

Beside his column on the HotWired site sits a forum called "Threads."

"It's devoted almost exclusively to trashing me," Katz says. "I sometimes go on Threads and defend myself, and sometimes I don't."

In traditional news forms, editors and reporters have seen their role either as experts or the conduits of information from experts. Reporters provide readers and viewers with information. The flow is one way. By contrast, writing online is closer to a conversation than a lecture. To use the new medium effectively, Katz says, the journalist must be far more open to engaging readers in discussion and, sometimes, to using them as resources of information.

Interactivity in online writing can be as simple as giving readers an e-mail address to which they can respond. It can be as complicated as creating data sets that readers can personalize to find out what the crime rate is in their particular part of town. And it can be as vocal as an unruly town meeting, in which members of the audience berate as well as listen to those on the podium.

Although all online journalists should consider how interactivity will be built into their stories, the first step is producing stories to which the public will want to respond.

"The first thing we tell students is to throw out all the rules," says Leonard Sellers, a San Francisco State University journalism professor who is researching a book on writing for the online media. "What we train them for in print journalism is a linear form of narrative, and that's gone. This is a nonlinear format."

Stories online don't have beginnings and endings as much as they have layers of depth. And they go beyond words, to words, pictures, graphics and sound working together.

"Students have to start thinking not as wordsmiths, but as wordsmiths and camera people and sound people," Sellers says. "They have to think—and it's an ugly word—of writing in *chunks* to break down the story."

Sellers gives his students three basic rules for writing online.

1. No story can be more than one computer screen long.

"People do not scroll on the computer," he says. "Students have to write so tight that it's the closest I've seen in years to wire copy. It really has to be quite lean to work well."

That lean writing might link to other pieces of the story, which are tightly focused in their own right. A one-page summary of the Los Gatos fire, for example, might link to a page summarizing the last bad fire in the area, a map showing where the fire began, a graphic showing who is involved in fighting the blaze, a video showing the firefighters at work, and sound cuts from people who've been evacuated and the fire chief.

Accompanying the one-screen main story might be a plan or word map showing the hierarchy of other elements linked to the site.

2. No links in the text.

Sellers finds the practice of dropping links into stories—something that's widespread on today's Internet—to be an invitation for readers never to get to the end of a story. He has a point. Stories, he says, need links. But they should be at the end so that readers aren't invited to leave the news before they've absorbed it.

"If you provide links in the text, every reader eventually is reading Ethiopian labor statistics," he says of people's propensity to get lost while wandering through the Net. "They don't know how they got to them, and they don't know how to get back."

3. Different media on the screen must work together.

Just as the television reporter can't write away from the pictures on the screen, today's online reporter must coordinate the words with all the other available story elements. It can be, and will be, quite a challenge to coordinate audio, video, graphics, words and original source material in a way that links them together logically and accessibly.

"It's almost like you've got a story and it's all sidebars," Sellers says.

But since these sidebars can't all run on the same page, the need for journalists to play gatekeeper—to prioritize or layer the news, to set up logical connections that go deeper and broader—continues to grow.

Sullivan did a lot more on her early morning shift than wait for Bailey to file a four-paragraph update. She posted a map with the precise locations of homes destroyed. It hadn't appeared in the morning paper. And she put up photos, several of which also hadn't appeared in print.

"None of this was on TV," she said. "It is nice to be able to say, 18 hours later, this is exactly where the houses were destroyed. We had a better map, we had more photos, we had fresh stories, and that pretty much continued throughout the day."

But the online site offered more than new information. It provided depth—links, for example, to a series on past problems the electric utility had had keeping underbrush cut back near its lines.

"We always ask, how can we make this story a Web story," Sullivan said. "And we answer that in layers—photos, graphics, library files. Certainly, whenever we get fully equipped in video terms, we'll have to think about that, too."

BEYOND THE BASICS OF NEWS

Reporters covering the fire in Los Gatos didn't dance around the facts. The news was compelling, immediate and powerful. Such stories cry out for lean, direct stories that deliver information. But also on the palette from which the news writer picks colors are the hues of humanity. Reporters are in the business of telling stories, not merely conveying facts. Often those stories are found on the perimeter of big stories. They also turn up in **follow**, or second-day, stories. The next two sections will look at one perimeter story and one news follow.

HUMANIZING THE NEWS

Beth Willon told her story for *KNTV-TV*. But the techniques could have worked equally well in radio, print or online media. Willon framed her story about the evacuation of 400 people from the Meadows Retirement Home around one person. Frances Teal was celebrating a special day when the fire struck.

Teal was the third person Willon talked to when she arrived at the First Methodist Church in Los Gatos shortly after 6 p.m.

"It was her birthday and she said, 'I certainly didn't order this,'" recalls Willon. "Instinctively, I know when I've got a good sound bite."

Willon already was writing her script in her head. So she asked her photographer to shoot a wide-angle shot of Teal as she was led into the building, moving slowly on her walker.

Later Willon ran into Teal's nephew, searching for her in the confusion. The video was rolling when they were reunited. And Willon had what print reporters sometimes call bookends—a story whose beginning and end are framed around one person's story.

Beth Willon

Teal served as a microcosm for a bigger message in another way. She conveyed the frailty and courage of the older people Willon had been interviewing.

"My whole point was to visualize how vulnerable these people were and later show how strong they were through their comments," she said. "[Teal] didn't look panicked, but she looked vulnerable and frail."

Willon's story went like this:

VIDEO	AUDIO
MS (medium shot) of Teal being led into the church on a walker	(Two seconds of natural sound of party)
MS of another angle of Teal walking	(Willon narration) Frances Teal's 83rd birthday almost went up in smoke. Tonight she began spending it as an evacuee from a Los Gatos retirement home.
CU (close-up) of Teal talking	(Sound bite: Frances Teal) Everything is there and it's my birthday. I said, "I didn't order this."
MS of woman evacuee led to car MS of man in wheelchair next to car MS of two evacuees talking outside	(Willon narration) Meadows Retirement Home residents were quickly taken out as the smoke and flames spread near Wood Road. They were shaky, but calm.
CU of Bert Toevs	(Sound bite: Bert Toevs, evacuee) After all, we're pretty elderly folk and we've been through a lot. And so, I think people were very calm, very well ordered. Things were well organized.
MS of woman pushed in a wheelchair MS of five people in circle talking MS of woman pushed in wheelchair as two people stand up from bench	(Willon narration) Using wheelchairs and walkers, they were brought one by one to the First Methodist Church of Los Gatos, given food and temporary shelter until many were taken to area hospitals for the night.
MS of Willon in front of church	(Willon stand-up) So many of the seniors here are on daily medication, and they had to leave it behind when they evacuated. So workers had to go back and try to find it.
MS of Dreger	(Sound bite: Youwanda Dreger, volunteer) They were able to go back to The Meadows and retrieve the medical files and boxes of medication.
MS of Elardo	(Sound bite: Carrie Elardo, The Meadows) We have people with diabetes, heart problems. Right now we're trying to get insulin and medication from The Meadows. Paramedics went back up there to get the medication cards. We did have one man comatose so we had to send him out.
WS (wide shot) of evacuees going into church	(Willon narration) They found their medication but not their families. Frances Teal was afraid no one would know where she was.
MS of Teal at dining table inside	
MS of Teal sitting at a table	(Sound bite: Frances Teal) I have no idea. I'm kind of waiting till my family—they live in Sunnyvale—turn up and find out the news of what happened to us.

VIDEO	AUDIO
	(Willon narration)
MS of two teens and man walking into church lobby	But her concerned nephew and his family immediately started looking for her.
	(Sound bite: Mike Harvey, Teal's nephew)
MS of Harvey	We headed. toward her facility and the smoke was there. We turned on the radio at that point and heard about the fire, and then the police were moving us. So we were quite worried. We thought maybe it was right nearby.
	(Willon narration)
Pan as teens run to Teal and hug her	In the end they made their way to the church—
Zoom to MS of Teal kissing teens	reunited and ready to take Frances home for her birthday. In Los Gatos, Beth Willon, KNTV.

Willon had about an hour that night to log her video and write her script. She couldn't have made it, she said, had she not thought of her visuals and sound bites while in the field. Her other tips:

- **Start with one person.** Willon didn't begin her piece with a wide shot of a large crowd or dull copy; she picked out one person, Frances Teal, and found something unique about her—she was having a birthday.

- **Use that person as a springboard into the situation.** Once viewers meet Teal, Willon can use her to exemplify the problems of everyone. After viewers hear Teal say, "I didn't order this," Willon says, "Nobody did." She then generalizes from Teal's story: "Meadows Retirement Home residents were quickly taken out . . ."

- **Think about pacing.** Willon started her story with short, lively sentences and only then worked to convey specific information.

- **Choose words carefully.** Cliches are easy to grab onto on tight deadlines, Willon acknowledges. She tries at least to use them consciously. Willon liked the double meaning of "up in smoke" and went with it. Notice the alliteration in "wheelchairs and walkers" and "reunited and ready."

- **Leave viewers with a strong visual and verbal image.** In television, the close counts as much as the lead.

Much of this advice holds in other media. In writing news features, one person's story can carry a broader message. Strong quotes and other human elements should grab readers before they are hit with a bundle of facts. And the ending should come back around to the person in the lead.

RECONSTRUCTING EVENTS

When Brandon Bailey came to work the day after the fire, his editors wanted him to look back, not forward. They asked him for a tick-tock—a chronological narrative of the previous day's events.

"The second-day story serves a different purpose," Bailey said. "By then everybody knows what happened. There was a fire. There was an evacuation. They got it under control. We started talking about how. . . . It's a pretty conventional device, recounting what happened in chronological narrative form."

It's conventional, but effective. Chronology can be a powerful tool in telling stories. Rarely do first-day stories begin at the beginning and end at the end. But as we've seen even when news breaks, there is a place for chronology after the basic news has been laid out. On subsequent days, chronology works even better.

Here is how Bailey's second-day story began:

When state Department of Forestry Capt. Steve Espe saw the flames rising from a steep hillside next to Highway 17, he knew the first arriving firefighters were going to need help.

The brush fire had only scorched a quarter acre just south of Los Gatos when Espe's helicopter and a trio of Santa Clara County fire engines converged on the scene. But a strong wind seemed to spring from nowhere, pushing the fire up the steep slope and quickly out of reach for the ground troops who struggled to climb after it.

Knowing the blaze was heading straight for a cluster of hillside homes, Espe called for more air support, while a county commander radioed for a second wave of fire engines to attack from the other side of the hill.

"We ordered an extraordinarily heavy response," Espe said. "But every time (the fire jumped), it would spread another quarter of a mile."

For three hours, according to firefighters, police and residents of the area, the fire moved like a wind-borne freight train—leaping canyons and consuming homes—while leaving a dense cloud of smoke in its wake.

But although they failed to save three homes, the combined state and local forces managed to avoid a much larger disaster through a combination of quick action, massive response and a healthy dose of luck. This is the story of how that happened.

San Jose Mercury News

In writing a chronological piece, keep several things in mind:

- *Find a lead that conveys tension and foreshadows what's to come.* In this case, Espe knew right away that he faced trouble. His decision to call in help proved crucial.
- *Look for action.* Espe is flying toward the fire in his helicopter.
- *Look for humanity.* The stories of individuals often carry big ideas better than the voice of the reporter-essayist. "It was really important to have a human, to-the-ground perspective right away," Bailey said.
- *Make sure you have a "nut" paragraph.* Chronologies need a paragraph that resolves a lead and makes it clear to readers where the story is going. The last two paragraphs in the excerpt of Bailey's story serve that purpose. These are the nut, or focus, paragraphs of Bailey's piece. They establish its theme.
- *Once you've hooked your reader and focused the story, let it tell itself.* "I have in the back of my mind some experts in writing who came to the *Mercury News* and said that average readers like chronology," Bailey said, "that they find chronologies the easiest way to digest some pretty complicated information."

ORGANIZING YOUR WRITING PROCESS

For all the differences in reporting and writing for different media, one similarity holds true: The best reporters in all media think about and shape how they'll tell a story from the moment they get an assignment. That thinking is where writing begins.

The Poynter Institute for Media Studies in St. Petersburg, Fla., runs writing and reporting workshops for journalists in all news media. The emphasis across the curriculum is on the *process* of writing. And the point Poynter coaches regularly make is that the writing process starts with the inception of an idea. Great writers plan. They frame an approach to their work as they work. They adjust the frame as they find new information, focusing and refocusing as they report. (In television, that reframing likely involves thinking of what additional video the story needs.) By the time great writers sit down in the newsroom, they'll likely know what the story is and where they plan to begin. It's no accident.

Think about it for a minute. What are the three ingredients to a great story—a great idea, great reporting and great writing. Yet beginning reporters in all media regularly make the mistake of trying to build a riveting story after they return to the newsroom. Often it's not possible. Why? They haven't considered the most compelling way to approach the idea. They haven't bolstered that approach with specific, detailed reporting (see Chapter 7). What they lug back in breadth of material—lots of sources reacting to an event, for example—they lack in depth—specific examples of how that event affected real people. Their problem is that they haven't thought in advance what the story is and how to tell it.

Let's say the state legislature is going to debate a bill to cut off all public assistance to legal immigrants who are not citizens. You could sit through the debate, taping or writing down the words of various legislators. Or you could find a family, newly arrived in this country and struggling to get by. The aid might make the difference between that family's survival or collapse. Which story do you think is more interesting?

Here's the best advice we can give you in this book about reporting and writing: Leave time to think.

And think not only about what people or facts or quotes your story will need. Visualize the story itself. Think about how the story can best be told. Frame it. Remember the Pulitzer Prize–winning picture of Babe Ruth mentioned in Chapter 2? Photographer Nat Fein thought he'd get a better picture of Ruth's retirement from the back, where he could capture all the other photographers shooting the Bambino from the front. By doing so, Fein was able to reflect the history of the moment. His decision proved the right one. Guaranteed: It wasn't a picture taken by accident.

TEN STEPS TO THE BEST STORY

Here are 10 steps to take in assuring a better story. None involves putting words on screen or paper, but we consider them tips on writing.

Step 1: Plan in advance. Keep the following points in mind as you plan:

- Think about your audience. Who are you telling the story to and why should they care?
- Think about the news. What's important here? Whom does the story affect?
- Think about the story. Is there a way of telling the story that will give it more power and impact than merely to recount the facts?
- Think about scenes. How can you show this story—in visuals, with sound, with dialogue, through anecdotes?
- Think about scope. How much time do you have to tell this story? How much work can you get done in the time you have? (It is often more valuable to give one example in depth than to get many similar, shallow comments.)

Step 2: Discuss your plan with your editor, another reporter or your photographer. Let someone react to your thoughts.

Step 3: Write a theme statement that says specifically how you plan to approach the story. For example: "Since arriving in this country from Bosnia, Rolfe and Hieke Ventner have each worked two minimum-wage jobs. But should the legislature vote next week to cut off their eligibility for food stamps, they don't know how they'll feed their seven children. The Ventners are among an estimated 600,000 working poor in the state who will be affected."

Step 4: After doing background work, make a list of what video, sound and information you need for the story (see Chapter 4). Ask yourself these questions:

- What types of sources should I call?
- Do I need experts, regular people or both?
- How many points of view need to be represented?
- Who can best represent the different points of view?
- How can I find those people? (The Internet can help.)
- What reports or documents do I need?
- Who has those reports or documents?
- What video, audio, still photographs or graphics do I need to tell the story better?
- What am I missing?

Step 5: Challenge your theme statement throughout the reporting process. In other words, keep your focus. Ask yourself:

- Is my story honest?
- Does it best convey the news?
- Have I found something more interesting?
- Has the direction of the story changed?
- Do I have the information, the video, the audio, the graphics needed to pull the story off?
- Given the information gathered, how should the story change direction?
- What am I missing?

Step 6: Talk through an approach to the story before you write or build it. If your boss is too busy to help, talk to another reporter. By thinking about the approach at the "front end," you'll avoid much painful editing.

Step 7: Block out the major points you want to include. Bailey of the *Mercury News* was right: Outline. The best way to do this is to keep related material together. Take the audience from one place to another, one topic to another, one person to another. News doesn't work as a collage.

Step 8: Whenever possible, look for quotes, facts and examples to bolster each major point. The quotes say it. The facts demonstrate it. The examples show it.

Step 9: Know where you want to end. An ending shouldn't be an accident. Some writers tell stories about people who have overcome internal or external obstacles. And they don't give the punchline—tell what happened—until the end. This technique borrows on fiction writing.

Sometimes the ending is answered by the question, "What comes next?" Sometimes it can be found in the single most powerful image—visual or verbal—that captures the story.

Step 10: Try writing your story through without your notes. This also might be step 7, depending on the complexity of the story and your confidence. In the end, however, the story isn't in your notes. It is in your head.

RECOMMENDED READING

Block, M. (1997). *Writing broadcast news—shorter, sharper, stronger.* Chicago: Bonus Books.

Melvin Block, revered by broadcasters, has updated this popular writing book with even more examples and practical tips. Chapter titles include "Dozen Deadly Don'ts" and "The Ing Thing (and other wrong things)." It's one of those books you want to read cover to cover and then take down every few months as a refresher.

Fidler, R. *Mediamorphosis: Understanding new media.* (1997). Thousand Oaks, CA: Pine Forge Press.

Roger Fidler, a former newspaper journalist turned techie, knows as much as anyone about recent technological changes in communications and what's ahead. Here he demystifies the new media and talks about how they will influence mainstream media in the future, including what's ahead for writers.

Lanson, G., & Stephens, M. (1994). *Writing and reporting the news.* Fort Worth, TX: Harcourt Brace.

A succinct, step-by-step look at writing news for print media, this book also includes a condensed chapter on writing for broadcast. Its strengths are the breadth of its examples, its organization and its exercises.

Poynter Online. St. Petersburg: Fla: The Poynter Institute for Media Studies. [Online]. Available: **http://www.poynter.org/home2.htm**.

Home to some of the brightest minds in American journalism, The Poynter Institute runs seminars for writing, editing, producing and designing in all news media. Its Web site enables visitors to search for articles by topic and draws on a marvelous library of staff and guest contributions, ranging from Chip Scanlan's "Storytelling on Deadline" to Donald Murray's "Real Writer's Don't Burn Out."

Zinsser, W. (1995). *On writing well* (5th ed.). New York: HarperCollins.

Perhaps the most enduring contemporary book on nonfiction writing. To Zinsser, writing is a "transaction"—a conversation between two people. It needs sturdy, spare and specific words to work, he says, adding that "clutter is the disease of American writing." Witty and instructive, this book is a must-read.

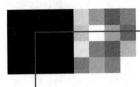

EXERCISES

A. ANALYZING NEWS WRITING

1. Compare radio, television, online and print accounts of a major trial or police story in your area.

   a. Look at how attribution is used and how it differs in different media. Discuss in class whether you think attribution was used well or poorly, and why.

   b. Compare the same accounts looking at the use of quotes (print), sound bites (television) and actualities (radio). How do the lengths of the quotes compare? What about their placement? Where does the first quote appear in the story? What is its role in the story?

   c. Compare how leads are approached in the different media. Do they stress the same information? How do they differ in the way the information is presented? Which do you like best and why?

   d. Does the script or the written paragraphs that follow the lead answer the questions the lead raises? Does the story follow logically for you in answering your questions as reader or listener? Why or why not?

2. Select two newspaper stories, one that you liked and one that you soon abandoned, that run at least 12 inches. Evaluate why you read one and didn't read the other by asking the following questions about each.

   a. Did the lead grab your attention? Why or why not?

   b. How long was the lead?

   c. Did the lead concentrate on the most interesting information in the story?

   d. Did the story following the lead develop the themes, facts or issues the lead focused on? If not, what did it do instead?

   e. Were your questions as a reader answered in the order you wanted them answered? If not, what happened instead?

   f. What is the average sentence length in the story? Do sentences seem tight and active?

   g. Did the writer use a succinct, powerful quote high in the story? How are quotes used throughout the piece?

   h. Does the story move logically from one idea to the next?

   i. When the writer changed subjects, did she use signposts—transitions that told you, as reader, that a new subject was about to begin? These can be anything from single words, such as "meanwhile," "however," "afterwards," to phrases, such as "a few hours later" (time), "behind the building" (place), "across the room" (direction).

   j. Was the story authoritative? Did it provide specific information to make its point?

   k. What did you like best about each story? Why?

   l. What did you like least? Why?

3. Tape the 5 or 6 p.m. newscast of a local television station. Then analyze two stories done by reporters: the one you liked best and the one you liked least. Ask the following questions:

   a. How does the story start?

   b. Is there a strong visual image?

   c. Is the reporter's style conversational?

   d. Can you follow the information in the story? Why or why not?

   e. Does the writer give information that complements the videos you are seeing?

   f. Does the information go beyond merely repeating what your eye sees?

g. What techniques does the reporter seem to use in telling the story?

h. How does the reporter bridge from one idea to another?

i. Does the story leave you with a lasting image? Why or why not?

4. Compare the coverage online of two national news Web sites. How does the coverage differ? How is it similar? Is the writing style different? The use of sound and visuals? Which links contribute to the story and which seem a distraction? Why?

B. WRITING NEWS IN DIFFERENT MEDIA

1. Clip a major news story from your campus newspaper.

   a. Write down what graphics, maps, documents and other online links you would establish if you were to put that story on your own Internet news site.

   b. Presuming you were to tell the same story on radio, how would you write the lead differently? What actualities would you go after? Does the story lend itself to natural sound?

   c. Television reporters write to their strongest video. What video do you think a photographer should shoot to tell best the story you clipped?

How might you lead a television story if you had that video?

2. Find a story on campus or in your community and report it thoroughly. Write separate versions that you would use for print, radio, television and online media. If possible, bring a tape recorder to the scene and record actualities you would use and natural sound. Build the radio story around those audio cuts.

3. Cover a story on campus or in your community. Instead of writing a story, outline how you would approach it. First write a theme sentence that captures the news. Then outline main points you'll use in the story in the order they'll appear. Once you've done this, write a story for the medium of your choosing. When you are done, discuss whether the outline helped you build the story and, if so, why.

4. Find a story you have difficulty sticking with in a newspaper. Read it aloud to your classmates and discuss its use of language. Is the language conversational? Is the story told as you would tell a friend? Try rewriting the story with various constraints. In one version, force yourself to include no more than 20 words in a sentence. Look for active verbs. Tell a story. Then read the version aloud. Discuss whether it is an improvement and why or why not.

CHAPTER 9

Building a Beat

Mike McGraw and Eric Nalder are soft-spoken men. They are patient men. And they get results.

McGraw, of *The Kansas City Star,* and Nalder, of *The Seattle Times*, have other things in common. Both are senior investigative reporters for their papers. Both won print journalism's most coveted prize—the Pulitzer—for looking into huge agencies of the federal government and showing where they were failing the public. Nalder's Pulitzer was his second.

McGraw and Nalder developed into award-winning reporters after years of learning, and applying, the basics of beat reporting. It is as beat reporters that they began honing a skill needed by beat and investigative reporters alike: the ability to penetrate the organizations that affect readers' lives.

Whether you will cover cops or courts, schools or civic life, sports or business, no skill will count more than the ability to dissect the key organizations at the core of most major beats. Even on some of the new, less institutionally centered beats cropping up in American newsrooms—beats that cover the aging population, the Internet or lifestyles, for example—stories born on the street and from noninstitutional sources ultimately lead back to institutions that regulate, monitor and keep statistics on who we are and how we live.

KNOW THE RULES

Put simply, you won't file knowledgeable, authoritative stories on any beat unless you learn how the system works. Some of the best and sexiest stories grow out of mastering how the system is supposed to work and then pointing out where it is falling short. That takes hard work and a mind-set McGraw and Nalder periodically share with reporters at journalism conferences.

For one thing, both men read voraciously.

"I don't read novels," says McGraw, who was part of a team that won a 1992 Pulitzer Prize for investigating the U.S. Department of Agriculture. "I read General Accounting Office reports and Inspector General reports."

"You can only see the grays, when you read the rules ahead of time," says Nalder, whose last Pulitzer in 1997 was for following the trail of misused federal Bureau of Indian Affairs funds.

Both men also build strong and extensive source networks that help them look at the organizations they investigate from inside and out, and from the cellar to the boss's pile-carpeted office.

McGraw says he always looks for ways to enter these buildings through side doors. There he finds the people who do the work instead of those top-level bureaucrats and chief executives who are expert at putting the most positive spin on their organizations.

It was through side-door discussions with union workers that McGraw unraveled one big clue to the space shuttle Challenger's explosion. Contractors building shuttle parts had laid off quality control workers and instead were giving workers bonuses for certifying the quality of their own work.

"I didn't hang around at press conferences to find out Challenger had 10,000 fewer quality control checks than other shuttles," he says.

Nalder likes to find out what's going on inside an organization by talking to those outside. For example, many people who work within any organization are licensed elsewhere. Lawyers are licensed; so are doctors, real estate agents, bail bondsmen and cosmetologists, to name a few. Finding the licensing board is one more way of peeking behind an organization's facade.

"Licensing boards are marvelous places for reporters because they're where people have to go and say who they are and what they do," Nalder says.

In approaching an organization, Nalder always starts his reporting with questions. Here are some of his favorites:

Eric Nalder

- Who are the players?
- What are the rules?
- How are things done?
- How can the organization be manipulated by those who work in it?
- Who are its potential victims and how might they be affected?
- Who are the regulators?
- Where are mistakes recorded?
- Where is spending recorded?
- Who knows the story, and how can I get it?

No matter where they are looking, both men understand that the best stories often are found in the contradictions between appearance and reality, the world that organizations promise and the world they deliver.

"It is like putting a puzzle together," McGraw says. "OK. Here is how it's supposed to work. But who would benefit if it worked another way? What kinds of signs would I see? Unless you are open to that kind of thinking, you won't find how an organization works."

Mike McGraw

KNOW THE TERRITORY

Michelle Guido faced a different problem when she invented a "teen" beat in the mid-1990s. Her puzzle wasn't getting to the heart of an organization at the center of her beat. It was figuring out the beat's very boundaries.

"It was the whole notion of taking an entire segment of the population and realizing we only wrote about them in very specific ways—when we wrote about juvenile crime and when we wrote about school. And we weren't writing those stories for teen-agers. We were writing them for their parents."

Faced with no source file, no institutional memory and no single core organization, Guido says she "spent a lot of time flailing around." She talked to kids in community centers, in the mall and in juvenile hall. She talked to kids about gay rights and abortion rights and city-imposed curfews. She hung out with them on Friday night and visited places they went to chat on the World Wide Web.

"I learned that I'm old even though I don't think I am," said Guido, who at the time was in her mid-20s. "I did a story on slang. I didn't know any of their terms." She wrote a front-page feature on the fear that groups of teens face even if engaged in harmless activities. She wrote about their cyberworld and their social life.

In some respects, Guido's approach to beat reporting is a long way from that of Nalder and McGraw. But then, some of the new beats—about the way we live and who we are—at first glance seem pretty far removed from the records-based, institutional reporting at the core of many public affairs journalism classes. Around the country today, there are reporters covering beats called "Relationships," "Family" and "Diversity." As touchy-feely as they may sound, these are serious sources of news. What is more important, for example, than the impact of divorce on a young family's life or the struggle of a new immigrant group to find a home, work and respect?

In the chapters that follow, we will tell the stories of both beat traditionalists and those who've stretched the definition of news far beyond an institutional setting. We believe they can learn from each other, and you, our reader, can learn from both.

Michelle Guido

No matter what your assignment, beat coverage should never stop at the boundaries of key institutions. Reporters who don't regularly look beyond the institutions of power to people out on the street miss a major part of their mandate. By the same token, reporters of the most amorphous beats should never forget the institutions that affect the lives of those people about whom they are writing. On the family beat, that might be family court, social service agencies, domestic abuse centers, religious organizations and a host of volunteer groups. On the teen beat, Guido looked to neighborhood and community groups who helped keep teens out of trouble and a system that dealt with them when they slipped.

"When you cover a beat that has no infrastructure, it's hard to find a place to start," she warned.

We believe a good place to start is in the institutions of government, education, justice, community and charity. All play a role in whether different people in different situations will succeed or fail. That's why we think the first step in building any beat is to find out who sets the rules and to read those rules. Next, figure out how they might be manipulated and who might try. Read on for ways to get started.

TEN WAYS TO BUILD ANY BEAT

1. **Learn the system.** Read everything you can get your hands on: organizational charts, annual reports, budgets, histories, ethics codes. Then set up off-the-record coffees with people who can explain how things operate. Get them to talk about their jobs.

2. **Look backward.** Gather a year's worth of clips or tapes. Look at what has changed, what stories were never followed and what stories were barely covered in the first place.

3. **Look forward.** Covering a beat takes organization. Start by filling a calendar with nothing but the key meetings of official and unofficial organizations you are responsible for keeping tabs on. You'll never have time to cover all the meetings on your beat. By knowing when they are scheduled, however, you will know when to place a call to a source. Once your calendar is ready, start a future file with slots for every day of the year. Then take 60 seconds after you finish each story to ask yourself what follow-up stories will be needed when. Tuck a reminder in your future file under the right date.

4. **Go there.** Whatever your beat, spend time there, formally and informally. If you cover schools, check out the high school play or jog on the track after school. The person next to you just might be the gym teacher.

5. **Get organizational directories.** Current directories will tell you who does what today. Dated directories will tell you who used to do what. Comparing the two will tip you to who has left, who has moved sideways, who has moved up and who has moved down. Look for the same last names. Relatives perhaps? Stranger things have happened.

6. **Build a source file.** Keep every number you get and always ask for more (home numbers are invaluable). Catalogue sources by name and area of interest or expertise. Hand out your own card like candy at a Halloween party.

7. **Never stop at the top.** The "little people" sometimes know more than the people at the top. They almost always are more willing to share what they know if you show you care about them and the job you are doing. Introduce yourself to secretaries and clerks, janitors and security guards. Then take the time to get

acquainted. Learn something about their spouses and kids. There are no more loyal sources than those who too often are seen as invisible.

8. **Read bulletin boards.** That chart for United Way donations can tip you to the names of activists within an organization who know what's going on not because of their rank but because of their involvement. Bulletin boards give home numbers for the supervisor selling a car, they plant the seeds of quirky stories, they capture the tone and mood of the community or organization where they appear.

9. **Follow the money trail.** This may be ninth on this list, but no piece of advice is more important. Money does indeed make the world go round. Find out who controls the purse strings and what is inside the purse. Gather governmental financial data such as budgets, payrolls and expense reports. These are public records, even if public officials don't always gladly part with them.

10. **Think about who is affected.** Every court agreement, new law, school award, scientific advance or setback affects real people. The news is much more than the facts about an issue. Look for the people who will feel its impact. Tell their story.

CHAPTER 10 | Civic Life

Whether we live in Kansas City, Mo., or Kalamazoo, Mich., Reading, Pa., or Redwood City, Calif., voters in our communities elect public officials whom they expect to keep the streets safe, the trash picked up, the parks tidy, the building rate moderate and local taxes low.

Nothing, of course, ever quite works as planned. Sometimes public officials reward their friends, their supporters or themselves. Sometimes their efforts dissolve into bickering. Sometimes they do their best but simply run out of money. And sometimes they actually come up with better ways of solving a specific problem.

More often than not, the public isn't paying much attention. Voting is on the decline. Most public meetings take place before a handful of onlookers. Confidence in government is at a low ebb. But whether people are tuned in or not, civic life—the actions of public officials, private organizations and involved individuals that affect the greater community—remains at the heart of daily journalism and the notion of community itself.

If anything, the nature of civic life reporting has broadened. Traditionally, government stories emanated from those in power. Reporters routinely worked the seams, the divides that separated Republican from Democrat, conservative from liberal, one department of bureaucracy from another.

Much of government reporting still revolves around developing sources inside bureaucracy. But today the best reporters understand that covering civic life means a lot more than covering city hall. Readers, viewers and listeners are demanding that news be reported and measured in ways that directly affect their lives. That means the story about the new garbage contract has to look beyond who beat out whom. It also should tell consumers whether the new trash hauler will change the rules for recycling, whether consumers will need different kinds of trash cans and whom they should call for more information. Put another way, the audience of news today wants to know less about the infighting of inside players and more about the impact of government on everyday life. They are less interested in who is winning in city hall than in whether they are winning in their neighborhoods.

"When we go out to cover the city council, we try to find someone who has been affected by it," says Doug Fox, who has covered politics for *WFAA-TV* in Dallas for more than two decades. "We try to humanize and try to make government news and information relevant to people's lives. 'Well folks, cuts in the budget may mean the end of midnight basketball. And in Dallas-Forth Worth midnight basketball happens to work.'"

Some news organizations have gone a step further than seeking out those affected by the actions of government. They've realigned beats to put more reporters in neighborhoods and fewer in government institutions. And they've sought ways to capture grass-roots community debate and, sometimes, to put themselves squarely in the middle of it (see box, About Public Journalism). Others are changing the breadth of the beat by sifting through and finding news in the enormous quantities of computerized data generated by government (see CAR and Civic Life, later in the chapter).

In this chapter you will:

■ Follow reporter Nina Kim as she makes the rounds getting started on a civic life beat. Her process of meeting the players, learning the rules and exploring how things work can be adapted on any beat.

- Find out how to handle basic stories stemming from press releases, meetings, budgets and audits.
- Eavesdrop as some of the best print and broadcast reporters tell you how they cover politics.
- Discover that the best enterprise, or reporter-generated, stories well up from your own curiosity and observation.

GETTING STARTED ON A CIVIC LIFE BEAT

In Nina Kim's first year out of graduate school, the Syracuse (N.Y.) Press Club chose her from among the city's promising young reporters to receive its newcomer award. In her second year as a reporter for the *Syracuse Herald-Journal,* Kim helped topple a mayor by writing about his actions in toppling his neighbor's trees without permission to give himself a better lakeside view.

These stories were made possible by the trust Kim had built over a year of covering the tough, tightknit community of Solvay, a blue-collar village of about 7,000 where the cop on Main Street likely is related to someone in the planning department and where just about everyone is related to someone who worked for the Allied Chemical plant before it closed in the mid-1980s. The way Kim approached the beat is a good lesson in how to build from the ground up.

LEARN THE TERRITORY

Kim started by establishing a sense of context. She knew that it's difficult, if not impossible, to make sense of what lies ahead without a firm grasp of what happened before. She scrutinized everything she could about Solvay—previous stories, the newspaper's computer databases, even the state's Web site, where she tutored herself in municipal and property law.

At the historical society she learned that the village's older residents were primarily immigrants from Italy and the Austrian Tyrol. Then she figured out that their descendants—fourth- and fifth-generation small-business people—still ran the village.

"They were the ones controlling the people in politics," Kim says. "They were the ones who put the mayor in power."

Nina Kim

FIND OUTSIDERS
WHO KNOW THE INNER WORKINGS

Kim applied an important lesson: One of the best ways to find out what's going on inside government is to find those on the outside with close ties.

She got to know the former village comptroller, a man who could explain the flow of money in the community. He helped her understand financial documents she used in a story about the village attorney, who was attempting to advise the village on choosing between two electric power companies at the same time that he was advising one of the power companies. Another source, a disgruntled member of the old boys' network that ran the village, the Commerce 2000 Club, helped her sort through the intricate web of relationships in the community. She then roughed out a genealogy chart, showing who was related to whom and who was beholden to whom.

"In any small community, there are always people in the know," Kim says.

She discovered there also was a "gossip center." In Solvay, that center was McKenna's Luncheonette, a place where the local power brokers routinely gath-

ABOUT PUBLIC JOURNALISM

The question of how much to involve readers, viewers and listeners in shaping the news became a hot issue in the 1990s. Proponents of what has become known as civic or public journalism say it is crucial for reporters to interact more regularly and directly with "just plain folks" to reengage citizens in both the news and public life. Public journalism efforts have ranged from sponsoring "community conversations" that tap their audiences' views to helping to mediate community disputes.

To critics, public journalism threatens to erode the lines of objective reporting by encouraging reporters to become participants in news rather than observers of it. Critics also question whether constant reader feedback and advice take the journalistic skills of analysis, synthesis and news selection out of the hands of reporters and transform reporters into stenographers, assigned to take note of the nebulous "public view" rather than to help shape it.

The debate gets muddied in part because public journalism projects vary widely. In North Carolina, for example, reporters for print and broadcast news outlets jointly polled citizens on what issues they considered most important in the 1996 Senate race. Reporters then pressured the candidates to address these issues instead of setting their own agendas. Reporters for different news media have teamed up on similar if less extensive election news projects in cities across the country.

While these projects aren't without their critics, this form of public journalism falls closer to the mainstream than some other efforts, which thrust newspapers into a community-organizing role. For example, *The Wichita (Kan.) Eagle*, a leader in the public journalism movement, organized "The People Project" to address violence, crime and education issues in urban neighborhoods. The paper joined a local television and radio station in not only covering these issues but also sponsoring "idea exchanges" to help citizens deal with the problems.

In Michigan, the *Detroit Free Press* sponsored a public forum featuring the attorney general to highlight issues of violence against children and began a fund-raising campaign to help disadvantaged children. And in California, the *San Jose Mercury News* trained citizen volunteers to observe the legislature at work and make the voices of citizens heard.

These kinds of activities have led critics to question whether advocates of public journalism can distinguish between covering the news and creating it.

---

ered. So Kim started eating breakfast there. ("People recognize you. You become a regular and people talk to you very naturally.") She befriended one of the waitresses, whom she could call and ask, "I was wondering if you've heard any good gossip in the last couple of days?"

She scoured bulletin boards in and out of village hall, looking for new names and interesting people.

GO WHERE THE ACTION IS

While Kim was building ties outside of village hall, she also was building them inside. Each week, she visited all municipal offices at least once, stopping to chat and hand out her business cards to those she didn't know. She made sure to get to know the head of each municipal department—finance, highways, electric—realizing that these were the people the council turned to for advice.

And she went to lots of meetings—"planning boards, zoning boards, club meetings—the senior citizens, the historical society, the Neighborhood Watch." All of these didn't produce stories, but to Kim that didn't matter.

"I'd go just to find out what the major issues were," she says. "They're also great because you meet the people really involved in the community."

FOLLOW THE PAPER TRAIL

As she began to feel confident, Kim dug deeper still, sorting through property records at the county courthouse to see who owned what property and how much. She discovered, for example, that the police chief, considered by some the most powerful individual in the village, had almost all his property holdings listed in his wife's or children's names.

SUMMARY   GETTING STARTED ON A CIVIC LIFE BEAT

1. Read about the municipality's history and peruse your news organization's files—big-issue coverage, databases, source lists, notes from other reporters. Then fill in the gaps.

2. Make regular rounds through city hall as well as places where those in the know gather. Talk to regular people, from secretaries to waitresses, bus drivers to shop owners.

3. Talk with the people who know about government but aren't in it. People who provide tips are as important as those who provide quotes.

4. Be visible at a wide range of meetings whether you are covering them or not.

5. Ask the community's records officer or clerk for an inventory of all records compiled by the municipality. That way, when you need to track something, you'll know where to look.

Such records can be complicated, and Kim admits she was "a little frightened" when she started looking around. But, in Onondaga County, she discovered that records had been computerized to give a reasonably easy road map to property deeds, property transfers and real estate mortgage information.

"It's great information," she says. "Even if you don't use it right away."

In the end, it was a source—a member of the village board—who tipped Kim to the story that brought down the mayor and finally established her as a credible reporter in the eyes of a suspicious citizenry.

"She told me, 'Word is the mayor has cut down his neighbor's trees.'"

He had cut down dozens of trees, it turned out, and without the neighbor's permission. It was an act, Kim recalls, that "showed enormous arrogance."

She knew Mayor Mario DeSantis would sidestep her calls, so she nabbed him in a place he couldn't get away—the city's main square after he played in a band concert.

Why, she asked, did you cut down the trees?

"He came right out and said, 'I wanted a better view of Onondaga Lake,'" Kim recalled. "That story broke open the entire community. After that I got calls every day."

A lucky story? Hardly. Kim got it because she'd spent a year getting grounded in the community. There are no shortcuts.

DEVELOPING SOURCES

After two years of covering the Texas State Legislature, Alan Berg knew he was beginning to make sense of it all.

"This session I think we did better in giving proactive instead of reactive coverage," says Berg, who works for *WFAA-TV* in Dallas.

The reason? Berg had made more headway in "peeling layers of the onion"—his analogy to the way reporters build sources and expertise. The way Berg sees it, covering the state house isn't that different from covering city hall. It's just a lot bigger.

"If you think of the city council as seven to 15 people, we've got 151 members of the House and 31 members of the Senate. You've got all these personalities. You've got divisions between rural and urban. You have divisions between inner city and richer areas."

LAYERS INSIDE GOVERNMENT

Peeling layers of the onion is a good way to look at the process of building sources at all levels of government. The top layer is always obvious. Each November, voters go to the polls to elect officials. If you dust off your junior high school civics text, you'll recall that they come from three branches of government—executive (president, governor, county executive, mayor), legislative (Congress, state legislature, county legislature, council) and judicial (judges at all levels). Officials in these three branches see the world from somewhat different perspectives and serve to check and balance each other. Theoretically, at least, all are accountable to the electorate. So it is important to record their promises, to measure their practical achievements and to sort out their goals.

Alan Berg

Practically, however, elected officials are more accountable to some people than to others. Beneath that first layer of the onion can often be found those who really wield power—the shadow government of folks like members of Solvay's Commerce 2000 Club or the contractors who win and lose bids for municipal services, developers who win and lose battles to rezone land, lobbyists who win and lose battles to amend bills. Following their tracks can lead to a better understanding of how government works and to some darn good stories.

It was a lobbyist, for example, who tipped Berg to the fact that a bill proposed to ostensibly regulate smoking statewide actually was backed by the tobacco industry because it would have superseded local ordinances that were stricter in some cities. With the help of a source and financial disclosure filings required by the Texas Ethics Commission, Berg established who the big lobbyists pushing the bill were.

"I hit that list and started taking pictures of these guys in the halls, asking, 'What does Phillip Morris expect for the $75,000 it is paying you?'"

He filed another report on industry's battles to give itself special breaks on utility bills. Here is how that report began:

(Anchor) The Texas Senate today began debating a bill that would deregulate the utility industry by the year 2002. Supporters say it would lower everyone's utility rate, but others wonder whether big business would profit at the homeowner's expense. Channel 8's Austin Bureau Chief Alan Berg reports.

(Alan Berg) Even though large plants and refineries pay less for their electricity than homeowners, they decided they could get an even better deal in an open market.

So these companies began pushing for deregulation. Utilities in turn want to protect their 16-billion dollar monopoly in Texas. Between them the two sides hired more than 250 lobbyists and spent each other to a standstill. Then the public utility commission dropped a bomb. . . .

WFAA-TV

There are other layers to peel. Just as the state bureaucracy has its various department heads and bureau chiefs overseeing different levels of regulation, each department in county government and city hall is headed by a director or commissioner who usually serves as the person to turn to for official policy and reaction. Beneath that layer are the people who do the real work—inspectors in the field, mechanics in the bus yard, budget analysts in the city manager's office.

"Underneath the director of planning there's likely to be a planner one or planner two who is working day to day with what you're reporting on," says Mike Shear, who covers Prince William County, Va., for *The Washington Post.* "They're likely to be more comfortable talking with you."

And, he might have added, they're likely to be more knowledgeable.

Layers Outside Government

If the issues of civic life cascade down to the people who live under government laws, they also bubble up. Reporters who realize this define the news differently and turn over another layer of sources.

Holly Heyser had covered a half-dozen municipal governments when she set up the "Listening Post" for the *San Jose (Calif.) Mercury News* during the 1996 presidential election. Her job was to solicit opinions and write stories about how ordinary people felt about the election. One story began like this:

Anger about special-interest money in campaigns.

Disgust with the two-party system. Desire to spare future generations from the national debt. Concern for the environment. Occasionally a sense that things really aren't as bad.

The opinions that Silicon Valley residents have shared with the Listening Post this year have been incredibly diverse. But if one thing stands out, it is this: You fervently want your voices to be heard in the nation's political debate.

San Jose Mercury News

As public life reporter for *The Indianapolis (Ind.) Star,* Bill Theobald has redefined the nature of covering community. Instead of spending his time inside city hall, he spends it seeking out informal centers of public discourse—from neighborhood associations to volunteer groups.

That message not only changed election coverage at Heyser's paper but also changed her whole vision of covering government. She listened more carefully to the concerns of residents when she began covering the city of Mountain View after the election, an approach she's continued to follow since moving to Virginia to cover the statehouse for *The (Norfolk) Virginian-Pilot.*

Whereas in the past, she had tended to wait until an issue found its way onto a council or agency agenda, Heyser listened when residents complained about sharply escalating rents. She recognized their concerns were news, even though government was in no hurry to react.

"This is putting more faith in what I heard from people instead of saying, 'You are never going to get rent control so I'm not going to write about this.'"

As public life reporter for *The Indianapolis Star,* Bill Theobald rarely goes inside city hall at all. He defines his public journalism beat as an approach to reporting that looks for news in the unofficial centers of civic dialogue instead of the official centers of public pronouncement. He believes that by looking for people who are involved in community but not elected to run it, reporters can get a better handle on stories as they develop.

"By the time it gets to the city council a lot of people already know about an issue," Theobald says. "If you can get to those primary places where people are already talking about things in the community, you're going to have a lot better coverage a lot faster."

His sources may coordinate volunteer efforts at a local senior center or run a church group for kids. They may dish out food to the homeless or have a stake in rebuilding a neighborhood.

"I started to do stories about the way neighborhoods solve problems or the way communities help people out," Theobald says.

One series looked at people making a difference in their communities. It began with the story about an elderly woman who served as an unofficial clothes pantry/food pantry, serving as a liaison between the disenfranchised and formal volunteer groups:

Officially Pearline Johnson's resume is short and fairly nondescript:

Crime Watch block captain.

Neighborhood organization member.

Yet those two titles barely begin to capture what the effervescent woman means to her Near-Eastside neighborhood.

"Pearl is the mayor," says Frank Watson, who lives across from Johnson's home in the 1700 block of Brookside Avenue. "Without Pearl, nothing works right."

With Pearl, the neighborhood kids all have a grandma—one who can give out advice but also wields a firm hand. And struggling families—black, white and Hispanic—have a place to get some clothes and something to eat.

The Indianapolis Star

Next Theobald planned to take a hard look at the volunteer organizations and charitable organizations that play a larger and larger part in civic life as government downsizes.

"We're investing a lot more responsibility in these groups, but we don't really cover them," Theobald says. "Our coverage of the United Way is the same as everyone else, which is 'Hooray for United Way.'"

He hopes to change that, peeling back one more layer of the onion of civic life reporting.

PEOPLE TO SEEK OUT

It's impossible to catalogue all the sources on any beat. These lists of people to seek out, and those in subsequent chapters, are meant as a starting point.

SOURCES INSIDE MUNICIPAL GOVERNMENT

The "little people"—the animal control officer or the cop on the beat—can tell you a lot. Here, however, is a list of the key players nearer the top.

THE MAYOR AND CITY COUNCIL

Know the form of government. In big cities, being mayor is the most powerful job in local government. In smaller cities, the mayor often works part-time and is merely an equal among council members. In towns and villages with a part-time council and mayor, the real power often lies with an appointed city manager.

Typically, there is an odd number of council members. Some cities profess to have nonpartisan government, but usually there are thinly veiled political divisions on any council. Look for them.

CITY ATTORNEY

The city turns to the city attorney for legal advice. Attorneys attend most council meetings and know about lawsuits filed by and against the city.

CONNECTING WITH THE COMMUNITY

For student reporters, whose lives revolve around campus life, it's often difficult to know how to connect with community residents. Here are suggestions from Holly Heyser of *The (Norfolk) Virginian-Pilot* on ways to find out what concerns regular people and to develop them as sources:

■ Find out who sorts and logs the letters to the city council, planning board and other agencies. Then read those letters. "It allows you to get ahead of the curve instead of waiting two years until an issue raised becomes an agenda item."

■ Find ways to help people "be better citizens." One way is to write about governmental issues before elected officials meet to discuss them. Print reporters can include a box telling readers when and where the meeting will be held.

Reporters in all media can give out phone numbers and e-mail accounts, encouraging the comments of viewers, listeners and readers.

■ At meetings, look to the audience instead of just who is on stage. "We spend too much time listening to the politicians," Heyser says.

■ Make a practice of talking to people around town. That is easier if you shop in the town you cover, get your hair cut there, talk to regular people when you go to lunch. "Talk to panhandlers as well as the cops," Heyser says. "Ask them what's going on, what's interesting you. That pays off big."

■ Never throw away a name or phone number.

CITY MANAGER

Generally, this is the most powerful appointed official in government. The manager coordinates the work of all city departments and is the liaison between elected and appointed officials.

CITY CLERKS

The city clerk keeps the official and unofficial agendas of the city. He or she, for example, would know who is suing the city, what contracts it has handed out and what came up at the last council meeting. City clerks can be extremely valuable sources.

Proposals for development and changes in land use and rezoning are logged by the planning board clerk. As suburban coverage gets more attention in the media, so will development issues. The pace and planning of growth are central issues as populations sprawl across the country.

AUDITORS

Whether elected or appointed, auditors are always important. Audits look at how money is spent and how well government has performed in putting programs in place. An audit, for example, might look at how the city has dispersed funds and whether it has met its goals in building a redevelopment zone downtown.

FINANCE DIRECTOR

Someone has oversight of the annual budget. Take that person to lunch early. You'll want to know the budget cycle and system. Win this person's trust and you'll also know who is vying with whom for power and dollars.

DEPARTMENT HEADS

Whether it's the head of urban redevelopment or the superintendent of public works, department heads tend to run their own fiefdoms. Deputy department heads often spend more time with the rank and file and have a better sense of the actual work being done. This is equally or more true in the state bureaucracy.

TAX ASSESSOR

You'll want to know how the tax rate is set and how to look up property values. The tax assessor oversees that process. He or she knows who the big landholders are and how much land values rise or fall when their zoning changes.

OTHER GOVERNMENT SOURCES

News in Lawrence, Kan., or Duluth, Minn., sometimes grows out of decisions made at the county seat, in the state capital or in Washington (see Localizing, later in the chapter). For this reason, it is important to establish key sources at other levels of government. A few are listed here.

COUNTY EXECUTIVE

In the same way a strong mayor oversees a city, the county executive oversees county government. County executives oversee staffs that are parallel to those of city government. There are county clerks, county legislators, county planning boards and a myriad of offices with department heads. New municipal reporters should soon find their way to the county building to pick up a budget, a directory of county workers and a basic understanding of where city and county responsibilities overlap. Municipal and county reporters talk regularly.

ELECTED OFFICIALS (COUNTY, STATE AND FEDERAL)

Know which elected officials represent your city, what committees they sit on and what issues they concentrate on. You can't always drop in on these folks; they don't always answer their own phones. But even the most imperious congressional representatives do visit the districts they represent. Tag along and listen to what their constituents are telling them. That debate over tougher driving rules for 16-year-olds might seem a whole lot less remote when a contingent of Mothers Against Drunk Driving shows up at your legislator's local office.

CONGRESSIONAL AND LEGISLATIVE STAFF MEMBERS

The people you likely can reach are the elected officials' staff members. Start with press secretaries. But also find out what staff members work for the committees your U.S. representative or state legislator sits on. Staff members often craft the language of legislation and tend to be much more knowledgeable than the elected officials.

LOBBYISTS

Larger cities have their own lobbyists, even if they have a fancier name, such as "legislative liaison." These people track legislation of special importance to local government and, therefore, of special importance to you. Other lobbyists can affect your community. Ask yourself: Are the businesses, tax groups, environmental groups or others in your community represented at the statehouse?

REGULATORS

That city-run water company has to send monthly tests on water quality to some state engineer. Find out who that person is. Whenever city services are regulated by state law, someone at the state level will be watching.

SOURCES OUTSIDE GOVERNMENT

Those in public office aren't the only people who wield power. Here are some other influential sources.

CONTRIBUTORS

In the age of computerized records and laws that dictate disclosure of political contributions and contributors, it is becoming easier for reporters to track those who subtly, and not so subtly, try to shape the direction of government. At the federal level, the Federal Election Commission requires candidates to file quarterly, not only how much they've raised but also who has made contributions. State and local laws vary. Start by looking for a state or county board of elections.

CONTRACTORS

In the old days of city political machines, the mayors and party bosses, as a reward for loyalty, packed the city payroll with patronage workers—people doing jobs for which they might not be qualified or which weren't needed. Today clean-government laws and tighter purse strings have made it tougher to create no-show jobs. The result, says Bob Crawford of Chicago's *WBBM News Radio 78,* is a new form of "pinstripe patronage." Chicago's council members, called aldermen, now reward their friends by awarding them lucrative contracts.

"They give all sorts of contracts to the big contributors," he says, "concessions at O'Hare Airport, consultant contracts, paving contracts."

Tip: When a big contract comes up in your municipality, talk to the contractors on the losing team.

INTEREST GROUPS

All communities have their share of advocacy organizations with agendas and concerns reporters should learn about. Some look out for the interests of seniors or taxpayers. The Chamber of Commerce represents the business community. Other organizations advocate fair treatment for people of color or battered women. Compile a list. Then start with the executive director and public information person in each organization. Remember, however, if you want more than official policy, you'll have to go a few rungs lower on the ladder.

NEIGHBORHOOD ASSOCIATION MEMBERS

The burning issues in the community often can be heard first in neighborhood associations. They sometimes spring up around a cause that mobilizes a community within a community: support for a teen-age recreation center or better street lighting, opposition to street widening or a new apartment complex. Neighborhood associations can take on some pretty sticky issues.

THE RELIGIOUS COMMUNITY

People attending churches, mosques and synagogues do more than work on personal faith issues. They run youth groups and food drives. They own buildings and schools. They lead volunteer efforts and, sometimes, take political positions. Clergy have as good a sense as anyone in a community about the concerns of those in their flock. They're a far more likely source than the local tax collector to alert a reporter when an elderly man is being forced from his home for failure to pay back taxes.

CHARITIES AND VOLUNTEER GROUPS

As government dollars get ever tighter, the role of charities and volunteer groups in civic life—from those that organize after-school sports in city parks to those that adopt highways and roads to clean—becomes increasingly important. There are serious stories here. Charities raise money, lots of it. Some spend it well on the people they are seeking to help. Others spend it to sustain themselves.

GOVERNMENT WATCHERS

Sociologists, urban planners, political scientists, economists—these are just a few of the expert observers who follow the workings of local government. These people can offer an analytical overview when the city's bond rating

CONFLICT OF INTEREST

Civic life reporters sometimes have to make tough choices between the demands of their jobs and their personal lives, but some things are clear. No reporter would argue that it is all right to run for the city council that he is covering. That is a clear conflict of interest. The reporter serving in government couldn't avoid furthering or damaging his political agenda in the way he chose to cover or not cover certain stories.

Less clear cut sometimes are issues of perceived conflict. Should a reporter live in the community she covers? Most editors would argue yes. Living in a community opens up a whole range of informal sources that a reporter from out of town would be less likely to meet, such as neighbors, members of a church congregation or book group, the owners of the local liquor store and dry cleaners. But what happens if her next-door neighbor turns out to be next year's candidate for mayor? It gets sticky. Even if a reporter can distance herself from any real conflict in coverage, others in town might perceive a conflict.

Herbert Lowe of *The Philadelphia Inquirer* knew all about these sticky issues when he agreed to cover his hometown, Camden, N.J.

"One of the reasons I had in my mind resisted covering the beat was these potential conflicts of interest," he said. "I understood the potential conflicts and I wondered how that would work. Twice a week I would see somebody I had known in high school whom I didn't recognize. A person who was appointed city councilman on an interim basis was my debate team partner in high school."

Lowe, who is upfront about his desire to see the economically depressed city rebound, at times felt a subtle pressure from editors to be tougher. And, as an African-American covering a largely black community, he also felt pressure from community members to cut the city a break. "As a black reporter covering a black town, there's an expectation that you will understand and you will, I guess, protect."

Striking a balance was challenging. When he was asked to leave a meeting of the Nation of Islam, Lowe recalls, he stood up and said the meeting should be open to the public because it was being held in a public building. He was thrown out.

"That one act," he says, "showed [my bosses] that I was not 'one of them.'"

On another occasion, he recalled playing basketball in a city park, where some of his sources could "watch me as a young black man as opposed to a reporter."

Lowe believes he has struck a healthy balance in his coverage.

He recalls: "I remember one guy came up to me once and said, 'When we read things in the paper, we know it isn't all good. But when we read your stuff, we can see the good in our city as well.'

"I think I've covered this town like I would cover another town," he says. "I've trusted myself, my integrity. Now will I care about another town as much I do about Camden? I doubt it."

---

is raised or lowered because of how prudently or imprudently money is handled. They can help evaluate how the city's new public transit plan measures up against cities the same size. And if they can't, they can help steer you to those who can.

Some government watchers, known as gadflies, make a point of hounding officials they think aren't serving the public. Gadflies generally are passionate private citizens who show up at many meetings. Their opinions need tempering and their "facts" need to be checked. But they can be great sources for the reporter.

SOURCES ON THE NET

Appendix B of this book lists source and resource guides on the Net. You will find your own favorite sites in the community you cover. That is what reporter-producer Hamilton Masters does at *KHOU-TV* in Houston. Two newsgroups in particular, *alt.houston.general* and *alt.houston.politics,* have led him to some good stories (see Chapter 2). Once by monitoring the local chat online, Masters found that people were mad about changes in local cable coverage.

"The cable company had cut a couple of things loose," he recalls. "It was worth a story."

Masters also has used the Internet to localize major stories from just about anywhere. "There are Texans all over the world," he says. He found a Houstonian in Kobe, Japan, after the devastating earthquake there.

Masters cautioned that surfing the Net is no substitute for wandering the city's streets. "It's just another tool to monitor what's going on," he said. "You read the paper, you listen to the radio. You talk to people. This is another way of doing that."

Find out if your community has its own Web site. Find out if there are news groups that deal with local issues.

THINGS TO READ

Good civic life reporters become experts at the art of skimming. There is never enough time to read thoroughly everything that crosses their desks.

"I don't wander through documents like I'm reading a book," says Dave Migoya, an investigative government reporter for the *Detroit Free Press*. "The documents are there to give me an idea. I'll get a tip a big lawsuit is coming up or I'll glance at contracts and say, 'Who are these guys?'"

The printed and online material that civic life reporters screen can be broken into three categories: background material, basic documents and online links. We've touched on some of these materials under Getting Started on a Civic Life Beat. We'll elaborate on others under Basic Stories. From the next three sections, you can start a checklist of what to look for.

BACKGROUND MATERIAL

The landscape of a geographic beat comes clearer with a good map. You will also need:

- A good local history.
- U.S. census data from the local library or **U.S. Census Bureau** Web site.
- Agency directories with flow charts, titles and phone numbers.
- Old council minutes. See who shows up for votes and who doesn't. Look for alliances.
- Resumes of key officials.
- Organizational newsletters. Get on the mailing lists of anyone who prints one, from the Chamber of Commerce to the state association of tax assessors.
- Information on the workings of government, such as the city charter, bid procedures, ethics code, zoning regulations, or master plan for future development.

BASIC DOCUMENTS

Government generates endless reports, studies and documents. These are available to the public. Get them. The most useful ones are described here.

BOND PROSPECTUS

All cities, public agencies and other public entities that have borrowed money—and that includes just about all of them—have a bond rating based on their assets and their overall fiscal health. This information can be found in a bond prospectus. It must be certified, which makes it a good reference point against which to check other city handouts. The prospectus includes everything from information on lawsuits that the would-be borrower is engaged in to detailed accounts of a city's debts, reserves and property holdings.

"It is probably the best last-word source," says Rose Ciotta of *The Buffalo (N.Y.) News*. "They are not supposed to play games with those." To get a bond prospectus, check with the chief financial officer for the city or county.

GOVERNMENT PAYROLLS

Asking to see government payrolls may raise some eyebrows, but they are gold mines. In most states you'll not only get the name, title, age and salary of every city worker, you'll also find out things such as who worked the most overtime and who spent the most time in court. Payrolls can be helpful in covering breaking news. When a backhoe accident sent reporters at the *St. Paul (Minn.) Pioneer Press* scrambling to find someone who drove the machines, the paper's database of county employees quickly led them to the man who had operated the backhoe.

"If the city golf course is being badly run, you can find the names of the course keepers," says *Pioneer Press* reporter Dan Browning.

SITE PLAN APPLICATIONS

Proposals for major development bring with them a host of questions. What will the impact be on traffic, air pollution, public safety? Will the building be an eyesore? Who is the developer and who is the owner? Instead of waiting until the public hearing for answers, read the site plan applications as they arrive at the planning department.

GRANT APPLICATIONS

When local governments see a problem that needs fixing, they often ask the county, state or federal government for help. Grant applications signal a community's priorities, summarize its problems and serve as a source of news themselves.

BUDGET

The annual blueprint for how the city gets and spends money says a lot more than how much taxes are rising or falling (see Basic Stories, later in the chapter).

OTHER RECORDS

Local government overflows with other documents that can lead to compelling stories. Some information, such as property records and voter registration records, is beginning to appear online in some locations. Some of it also is being loaded into in-house databases at more computer-savvy newspapers. Records to look for include:

- Voter registration records. Try the county board of elections, which gives addresses and phone numbers for those who don't list their numbers.
- Audits. These tell reporters how effectively government is meeting its goals and spending its money (see Basic Stories).
- Lawsuits filed by or against the city. They can be found at the county courthouse or in the city attorney's office.
- Inspection reports on restaurants.
- Property records showing what the city or an individual owns, what its appraised value is and who holds the mortgage.
- Contracts for services renewable without bids.
- Building permits for new construction.
- Travel and phone expense reports filed by city officials.

WEB SITES

"Once you learn where to go on the Internet as a government reporter, it can save you hours of what would otherwise be endless telephone calls and leaving messages on answer machines," says Michael Shear, a county government reporter for *The Washington Post*.

One day, for example, Shear needed to find out the history and background of a law that allowed the state to release the names and addresses of sex offenders.

"I went to the **Virginia General Assembly** Web site where they actually have a bill tracker," says Shear. By typing in the bill's number, he quickly found the history he needed. When he doesn't have a bill's number, he can search by key words.

One of the ways Shear keeps up with what's happening in Prince William County, Va., is to tap into a home page run by one of the county supervisors.

"She has a variety of things I use on a regular basis, such as a hot issue tracker. And she incessantly links to other documents that are helpful," says Shear.

You'll be surprised how much you find at government home pages. Many municipalities have their own sites, as do most state agencies and legislatures, and nearly all federal agencies. We won't list them all here. We won't list even a small fraction. The sites at the end of the chapter (see Recommended Reading) are listed because they are megasites. Using them, you can find links to thousands of governmental sites.

For the new searcher, it makes sense to start big and use links to narrow your search. Just remember, bring lunch, and perhaps dinner, too. Neil Reisner of *The Miami Herald,* for example, will tell you that the U.S. Census Bureau site alone is filled with so many riches that an enterprising young reporter could forge "a perfectly wonderful career" on it.

Thomas is the name of the U.S. Congress site. It's named after Thomas Jefferson but is linked to a lot more states than America's third president knew about. If you have hours to read the speeches of your local congressperson, Thomas will link you to the full text of the *Congressional Record.* It'll tie you to the full text of bills before Congress, by number and by title. It'll link you to the home pages of the White House and all key federal agencies.

Expand beyond the government sites and look for those from citizen groups and public interest organizations, Shear says. When county officials were debating building a massive freeway in Prince William County, he regularly read an Internet site put up by a neighborhood activist group, CARD—Citizens Against Roads for Developers. There he found the group's latest arguments against the superhighway, along with details on upcoming meetings, strategies and environmental studies.

Those assigned to cover state or federal election races might start at the site of **Project Vote Smart**, a national non-profit, nonpartisan organization that since 1990 has tracked the positions, voting records and campaign finances of thousands of candidates at the national and state levels. Its Web yellow pages provide a detailed guide to the organization's database and describe links to thousands of other political information sites on the Internet. Those looking only for campaign expenditures might start at the home page of the **Federal Election Commission**.

The potential list is endless, so we'll leave you with these for starters. Keep this is in mind: Anyone can put up a Web site. And even publications listing the best sites can have an agenda.

Take HomePC, which posts its list of the top 500 sites each year. Toward the top of its best political sites for 1996 was one for the Concord Coalition, "a nonpartisan, grass-roots organization dedicated to eliminating the federal budget deficits." Though the list also included the Democratic and Republican parties and opinionated sites for conservatives and Republicans, it did not mention a single one run by those who thought the budget deficit wasn't so bad after all.

CLIPBOARD   Internet Sites Mentioned in This Chapter

Congressional Quarterly	www.cq.com	Thomas (Congress)	thomas.loc.gov
Federal Election Commission	www.fec.gov	U.S. Census Bureau	www.census.gov
Project Vote Smart	www.vote-smart.org	Virginia General Assembly	legis.state.va.us
Switchboard	www.switchboard.com	For an update on this list, see http://web.syr.edu/~bcfought.	

To find the home page for a government body, try the standard formats listed below. They're used by many, but not all, governments. Substitute the name of the city or county for the capitalized term and substitute the state ZIP code abbreviation for XX:

city   www.CITYNAME.XX.us

county   www.co.COUNTYNAME.XX.us

state   www.state.XX.us

BASIC STORIES

Civic life reporters get used to sifting through a barrage of announcements, news releases and reports each day to select what's newsworthy. Their task is as much deciding what's not worth covering as it is to decide what is. Without news judgment, they'd never have time to step back and compare government performance to the promises of politicians or to show the impact of government action on people in the community. Still, much, if not most, government news is breaking news.

The city appoints a new parks commissioner. It announces receipt of a $90,000 technology grant from the state. It presents an award to five companies who have given employees incentives to volunteer. These announcements generally come in a **news release**, a document written in the form of a news story that gives the facts—all the facts, that is, that the city wants to share. Whether trying to make sense of a news release, a meeting agenda, a budget, an audit or bid procedures, reporters never assume they are being given the full story in the documents of government. Their job is to make sense of what they have and to figure out what more is needed. This thinking process is the basis of all reporting.

STORIES FROM NEWS RELEASES

Basic news gathering often begins with a news release, also called a press release. These handouts, whether from city hall or countless civic organizations, private businesses and individuals, generally provide the same basic information:

- The name of the organization sending the release
- A contact name
- A phone number, fax number and e-mail address
- A story that tries to inform your news organization and sell it on the value of that information

Good releases often are accompanied by photographs and other graphics that tell the story in different ways. But no self-respecting reporter rewrites a release and puts it on the air or in print without at least calling to verify its authenticity. And that is just the first step.

"What facts are missing?" the civic life reporter handed a news release asks. "Who might give me a perspective that is different from the city's? Who can best explain the city's point of view? What has already happened on this issue that would help me understand what's happening today?"

Take that new parks commissioner appointed by the city. The release, let's say, reads like this:

Marica Saunders has been appointed the new Parks Commissioner of Shelby.

Saunders, 42, brings a dozen years experience in the city's Parks Department, where she began as director of its Outdoor Education Program and, four years ago, accepted the position of Assistant Commissioner in charge of recreation and programming.

"I'm excited about my new position," she said. "I'll assemble a management team dedicated to keeping the parks as a vital outlet to Shelby residents of all ages."

Saunders said integrity in fiscal management would be another top priority of her administration. "We want the public's tax money to be spent on the taxpayers, not the administration of the parks."

Saunders replaced William Jewel, 48, who resigned last month as commissioner to return to the private sector.

What's missing in this story? Here are some questions you'd surely want to ask:

- What specifically has Saunders accomplished in the last 12 years?
- What do citizens groups and educators with an interest in the parks and their programs think of her record?
- What parks are there in Shelby and what kind of condition are they in? (Conversations with older folks and parents strolling kids through the park would help you here.)
- Does anyone in city hall, perhaps in the opposition party, have questions about her choice as commissioner?
- What will she be paid and how does that compare with Jewel?
- What is her department's budget and has it been going up or down?
- How many parks does Shelby have and how does that compare to other communities its size?
- What more does Saunders have to say about her priorities? Does her quote about a new management team suggest other people will be transferred or lose their jobs? Why? Does her quote about integrity of fiscal management suggest money has been misspent?
- And just where is Jewel headed and why? How long was he in the job and what did he accomplish? Was he given any incentives to leave?

The answers to all those questions might not fit in your story, regardless of the medium. You'd want to ask them, however, to be certain you are telling the right story, the right way.

For example, what if you discovered that Jewel was pushed out because he'd been using a city car for personal business these past seven years? What if parks department employees helped build the addition on his house? What if the city gave him a fat severance package? Might these facts change the nature of your story, starting with its first sentence, or lead? Of course they would. The story would be about Jewel, not Saunders. A story might begin like the one on the next page.

SUMMARY

NEWS RELEASE STORIES

1. Consider the news release a starting point for a story, not a story in itself.

2. Verify the authenticity of the release by calling the contact name at the top.

3. Ask who funded the organization putting out the release. The names atop releases can be deceptive.

4. Ask yourself what questions the release does not answer. Find the answers.

5. If you must quote from a release, make clear that you are quoting the release and not the person. The quotes of company presidents that appear in releases more than likely were made up by the company's director of public information.

6. Recognize that whatever organization puts out a release is trying not only to sell a story but also to sell a specific spin on that story. Ask yourself who holds a different viewpoint and call.

7. Translate all jargon. If you don't understand something, your audience won't either.

For seven years, William Jewel has toured Shelby's parks in a $43,000 Cadillac Seville. He likes the car so much he drove it to church on Sundays. He took it on weekend fishing trips. He even took it 6,700 miles on his family vacation to the Colorado Rockies.

Shelby's auditor says all this was at the taxpayers' expense. Jewel bought the car out of his department's budget.

Jewel was quietly forced out of his $63,000 job as Shelby parks commissioner this week. But not before negotiating a sweetheart severance package worth a half-year's pay.

Every story is slightly different from what happened before. It is the difference that makes news the most exciting. Handouts usually provide hints about what makes a story different or interesting. They are a starting point and no more.

MEETING STORIES

Meetings are the best glimpse the public gets of government in action. City councils generally meet at least twice monthly, once for a "work session," to which the public isn't invited but the press is. The other is for an open meeting to publicly deal with and debate issues raised at work sessions and, too often, out of the earshot of curious reporters.

City council meetings, however, usually are the last link in the chain of government decision making. Some issues—a proposal for a five-story medical center, for example—demand coverage a long time before they arrive at the council for a vote. So civic life reporters, who typically cover every city council meeting, also monitor, and sometimes attend, meetings of the planning board, the zoning board of appeals and a host of less visible committees run by appointees of the council. These might include the recreation board, the library board, the shade tree commission and the water commission, to name just a few. Some communities operate their own water and electric utilities, with boards that oversee operations and set rates. Others create special committees to draw up a master plan or vision for land use and development.

When a board meets publicly, the public has a chance to have its say as well. But few people spend their week tracking developments at city hall. That's why it can be even more important for reporters to preview the meeting's agenda than to cover the event itself. Often reporters do both.

MEETING PREVIEWS OR ADVANCES

Solvay Police Chief Rocco Femano wants the village to pay him for more than 200 unused vacation days, some dating back 20 years.

Femano will ask the village board Wednesday night to pay him more than $22,000 for 207 unused days.

The (Syracuse, N.Y.) Post-Standard

Generally, money talks. And when cities, villages and towns take up controversial subjects involving taxpayer dollars, the public shows up. That only happens, however, if alert reporters tip citizens to what's coming up and why it is important.

This is basic beat coverage. By law, public meeting agendas must be made available to the public well before the meeting takes place. This exact time frame varies but typically is three working days except in the case of emergency sessions.

OPEN MEETINGS

Government decisions should be made in the open—in the "sunshine." That's the logic behind the 50 state open meetings laws (sometimes called sunshine laws) and the federal government's Sunshine Act. These laws provide that the public, including reporters, have a right to attend official meetings of government bodies.

The key words are "official" and "government body." The law applies if a quorum of members are present and official business is discussed. That means a chance meeting or a social gathering usually doesn't count. Also the group must be a government body, such as the township trustees or the school board. The parents' Band Booster Club, a private organization, wouldn't have to follow the law.

Which public bodies come under the law varies in each state. Most state open meetings laws cover groups such as school boards, city councils and county commissioners.

Some laws apply to nongovernmental groups if they receive a large part of their funding from government. The federal Sunshine Act covers federal boards, commissions and agencies.

Reporters should know when meetings can be closed. Common reasons are real estate purchases, union negotiations or strategy sessions about lawsuits. In most states, the chairperson must state the reason for a closed session and take a vote to close the meeting.

Reporters who think a public body is going into a closed session illegally should object, remind the group of the law and ask that the objection be recorded in the minutes. Numerous news organizations have sued public bodies who meet in secret. Judges often fine governmental bodies for such illegal meetings and void any decisions made.

Civic life reporters seek out these agendas and the supporting documentation—reports, correspondence, figures—that goes into the packets of council or other committee members. When they don't understand an agenda item, reporters ask about it, sorting out what issues will be worthy of news and what won't. Then, after choosing the most important issue to be presented, reporters often file stories in advance, as Nina Kim did about Chief Femano. Kim notes that there's an important reason for writing advance stories of major meetings.

"The real thing that we're doing as reporters is telling people what's happening in their community so they can be an active part of it," she says. "If newspapers inform the community what's being considered before it's decided, [people] can be part of the process instead of hearing about the vote after it happens."

Good advance or preview stories do far more than announce that a meeting will take place. They examine the most important issue coming up at the meeting, getting a range of opinions. And they set the issue in context, explaining what happened before.

> Some village officials doubt whether Femano is owed those days.
>
> His former police officers say the chief instituted a "use or lose" policy for the rest of the department, meaning they could be paid for unused days.
>
> And the former village administration, under Mayor William Campagnoni, refused to pay Femano for unused days.
>
> *The (Syracuse, N.Y.) Post-Standard*

Finally, advance, or preview, stories tell the public when and where a meeting will be held:

> The village board will meet at 7 p.m. Wednesday in the high school cafeteria.

MEETING ACTIONS

Agendas aren't only important in previewing what's coming up at meetings. They are the way reporters prepare to cover them. Each Thursday night, Mike Shear logs onto his computer and clicks his way to the county government Web site of Prince William County, Va. There, he scans through the agenda packet of the county board to "see what doesn't make sense."

Shear writes for *The Washington Post,* a paper too big and broad in its readership to preview many local meetings. But he knows he will be writing on deadline following Tuesday's meeting, and he likes to be prepared. So on most Fridays, he is on the phone calling around to public officials, starting with the city's public information officer, who can explain items on the agenda. Sometimes the items don't amount to much.

"I noticed something the other day about an extension of the sewer system in a local community," he says. "I said, 'Gee, what's that? It sounds like they might have a big development proposed.' It turned out that three homes needed sewer connections. But at least it was clear I had nothing to worry about."

Sometimes Shear discovers the board has a vote planned. Then, he says, he tries "to count noses" ahead of time so that he can frame the skeleton of a story—called A or B matter by print reporters—and leave it in the computer system as the outline of the story he'll file. His goal is to control the agenda on deadline instead of letting the agenda control him.

"By the time I walk in there Tuesday there's little on the agenda that will surprise me," Shear says.

Even so, he stays alert for surprises. Good reporters know that the best stories in public meetings can happen extemporaneously and come from the audience instead of the podium. Sometimes these stories end up as the lead:

Nearly three dozen Fayetteville residents attended the Village Council meeting last night to complain about traffic rerouted down their street during bridge construction on nearby Genesee Street.

Sometimes action in the audience conveys a sense of the event:

The vote was greeted with a chorus of jeers and hoots.

Someone threw a wad of paper at the board.

"You're done, Billy," a spectator shouted at Trustee William DeSpirito as he cast his vote for the [police] merger with the city.

Syracuse (N.Y.) Herald-Journal

SUMMARY   MEETING STORIES

1. Get an agenda in advance, along with supporting documents.

2. Call sources on all sides of key issues before taking your seat in the audience.

3. Pick a dominant issue to be the focus of your story.

4. Carefully choose which items to report. Writing about too many merely muddies the story and confuses the audience.

5. Concentrate on the impact of the decision, not the process. Talk to those affected by the result.

6. Look to the audience for drama and sometimes for the news.

7. Include enough background to explain what came before.

8. Explain what comes next.

Television photographers typically cut away from the stage to show people in the audience. Radio reporters look for natural sound—the thud of a gavel, the scraping of chairs, the murmur or shouts after a vote. Whatever the medium, the best stories take the information from a meeting and tell it through the eyes of those affected (see Chapter 7).

Here is an example in which the reporter humanized the story of a planning board application by casting it as a spat between former friends. Notice that the story concentrates on a single issue considered by the board rather than trying to touch on the half-dozen or more issues that might be brought up during virtually any government meeting.

For over a decade, the two men attended St. Elias Eastern Orthodox Church together and maintained a cordial relationship.

But competition for customers who frequent the 3200 block of South Salina Street has put a wedge between Elias Sawalha and Emile Guindy.

Sawalha, who has operated a Mobil station at 3220 S. Salina St. since January, wants to convert an adjacent garage into a mini Mobil Mart. Gasoline alone isn't producing enough of a profit, he said.

Guindy, owner of Expressway Market at 3226 S. Salina St., says Sawalha is trying to take away his customers. Friday, he reapplied for a city permit to open a Sunoco station in protest of his neighbor's proposal.

Monday, the Syracuse Planning Commission heard Sawalha's proposal for a permit to sell groceries, but deferred its decision until Sept. 8. . . .

The (Syracuse, N.Y.) Post-Standard

BUDGET STORIES

Wonderful stories can be hidden in the dollars and cents of city budgets. All it takes is the patience to read the fine print.

Nearly every time that a city of Miami employee claims an injury, the taxpayers foot the bill.

Heart attacks off duty. Breaking a tooth eating a Snickers bar. Falling out of chairs at the office. A smack on the nose from a police horse. A bump on the head in a closet full of boxes. A bite petting the new firehouse dog. An injury putting on a weight belt. An allergic reaction to conch salad. Stepping on a rusty nail. Even kicking a body bag.

The workers' compensation claims, which cost $9.3 million last year, are a large factor in the city's $68 million budget shortfall.

Almost one of every three city workers files a claim every year. . . .

The Miami Herald

"Think about it," says Lisa Getter, who wrote that *Miami Herald* piece. "There's a document out there that details where millions, sometimes billions, of dollars goes every year, and no one pays attention to it. No wonder it's a gold mine."

A budget is a lot more than tables of figures. It lay outs a city's vision for the year ahead. It shows where and why expenses are going up and how they'll be paid for. It establishes a city's priorities and tells its residents which services will be getting better and which will be getting worse.

"No. 1 [is] what's going to happen to my taxes?" says Bob Crawford of Chicago's *WBBM News Radio 78*. "No. 2, what's the impact going to be on me? I try to keep in mind what I think most Chicagoans are interested in when they hear 'budget.' 'What about street repair? What about the alley lighting? What about trash pickup? What about recycling?' Another sensitive issue is, 'What's happening with wages?' People want to know, 'Are we paying people too much? And are there just plain too many people on the payroll?'"

Rena Singer of *The Philadelphia Inquirer* suggests reporters take several steps before poring over the latest budget:

■ Get five years of budgets to chart patterns of change.

■ Ask the city for its actual expenditures last year. Then see whether its actual expenditures came close to what it budgeted (the projected expenditures).

■ Don't settle for a budget summary. Get the full budget, complete with line-by-line expenditures for programs and departments and the accompanying narrative budget report. Together, these might run hundreds of pages. But they'll convey a big picture of both a government's expenditures and its philosophy.

"In the county I cover, the road department has grown something like 250 percent in the last decade," Singer says. "During that same time, the money for authorities—things like community college, the library, the drug and alcohol task force—went down 33 percent. This tells a story."

■ Look closely at such areas as engineering and legal services. They can serve as a tip-off to plans for development (if engineering expenses jump sharply) or to lawsuits filed by or against the city (check those solicitor fees).

■ Look at the **debt service**. This tells how much money the city is paying on bond issues—money borrowed to pay for construction. "The more debt your township has, the more it has to spend on something that's already been purchased," Singer says. "Just think of it as your credit card debt or the debt you are carrying from college."

■ Begin tracking the budget months before it is presented at a public hearing.

The best way to track the budget is to establish early what the budget process is. When do departments make their initial requests? Who acts on them? When is the draft budget released? Jot the answers down on a calendar, just as you do the dates of meetings for different boards.

Then, says Singer, "Talk to people the very first time the budget is proposed. Talk to the people who may be losing their jobs. Talk to people who may be losing services. Stuff like that."

At their most basic level, budgets are about expenditures and revenues. For a budget to balance, the revenues (the influx of money from taxes, user fees and grants from other levels of government) have to match the outflow of money on everything from salaries to new sand trucks.

Typically, taxes go up when the revenues don't keep up with increased demands to spend. People care about taxes. Unfortunately, the basic tax story is the one too many neophyte reporters, notoriously math-phobic folks, stumble through as the beginning and end of their budget coverage. It goes something like this:

Placertown residents will see a 3 percent hike in their property-tax bills next year. The money will cover salary increases for the town's police force and offset a slight drop in state funds.

For the owner of an average Placertown home, assessed at $80,000, taxes will go up $24. The total bill will climb to just over $800 a year.

Writing this story requires a series of questions and, yes, a few basic calculations.

■ What is the average assessed value of a home in my community? The **assessed value** of a property establishes the value at which it will be taxed. It is often different from the **market value**, or the expected selling price of the home.

■ How much overall will taxes go up or down?

■ How am I going to take this great big number, often in the hundreds of thousands of dollars, and express it so people will understand?

Often municipalities will lay out the tax implications of a budget on a summary page. They will calculate the percentage increase or decrease of taxes and explain how much the tax change will affect the owner of an "average" home in the community. Whether or not these numbers are provided, reporters should calculate them on their own. It's really not that hard (see the box, Working Out What Residents Will Pay).

WORKING OUT WHAT RESIDENTS WILL PAY

Taxes typically are described in terms of their rate per $1,000 assessed value. In this way, homeowners who know their assessed value can crank in the formula to determine actual taxes: Divide the assessed value by 1,000 and multiply the quotient by the tax rate.

$$\frac{\text{assessed value}}{1,000} \times \text{tax rate}$$

If, for example, the home is assessed at $80,000, and the tax rate is $15 per $1,000 assessed value, here's the computation:

$$\frac{\$80,000}{1,000} \times 15 = \$1,200$$

That means the homeowner will pay $1,200 a year in taxes.

It's just as easy to figure out by what percentage taxes have gone up or down. Start with the raw numbers: last year's tax rate and this year's.

$$\frac{\text{this year's rate} - \text{last year's rate}}{\text{last year's rate}}$$

$$\times 100 = \text{percentage change}$$

Let's say last year's tax was $14.50 per $1,000, and this year's is $15 per $1,000:

$$\frac{\$15 - \$14.50}{\$14.50} = \frac{\$.50}{\$14.50} = .034$$

$$\times 100 = 3.4 \text{ percent}$$

The increase is 3.4 percent.

OK. Hold it! Before you glaze over and skip the rest of this section, let's talk about why that basic boring budget story isn't by any means the whole story. Budgets are really about two things:

- What has changed in your community
- Who is going to be affected by those changes

The answer might be kids whose teen center will close because the city has decided it can't pay for a manager. It might be older folks already struggling to make ends meet when the city ends a program that sets a lower tax rate for homeowners over age 65. It may be families who benefit when a state grant helps pay for a new nature center at the community park. You tell these stories not with numbers but through experiences, with the voices and the faces of real people.

"Just because taxes aren't increasing or decreasing doesn't mean there isn't a story there," says Rena Singer of *The Philadelphia Inquirer.* "You can use the time you'd spend analyzing how angry people are about the tax increase to

SUMMARY

BUDGET STORIES

1. Look at the budget as the government agency's priorities and vision for the coming year.

2. Use current and previous budgets to get the big picture of what has changed, and then find out why.

3. Translate the numbers into topics about which the audience is most interested—a new immunization program for at-risk children, the opening of a community policing station, a scaling back of park maintenance.

4. Explain the impact of the budget in terms people can understand, such as the percentage tax increase or decrease for the owner of an average home.

5. Frame the stories around those outside city hall—the people who will be helped or hurt by the financial changes.

writing about how people are faring." (See her tips for working budget stories in the box, Learning From the Pros: Reading a Budget.)

Getter, of *The Miami Herald,* urges reporters to track down the original budget requests from departments. By comparing who gets more and who gets less than was asked for, reporters can measure both the priorities and power structure of the city or any other organization.

Ultimately, however, it is the average citizens, not those in power, who count. Never forget that budgets are for and about people. If you remember that, they won't prove so terrifying after all—to you or your audience.

AUDIT STORIES

Budgets tell the tale of how a city plans to spend its money. Audits review how well it's been spent and whether it has been spent the way it is supposed to be. Here is what the Detroit Auditor General's Office found when the staff examined how the city's recreation department was dispersing funds:

Funds from a Detroit Recreation Department bank account are supposed to be used for activities such as softball, tennis and festivals like the upcoming Downtown Hoedown.

But money from the account has also been used to pay for:

■ A luau for department employees.

■ A catered tent at the Grand Prix for department employees and vendors.

■ Temporarily covering one payroll.

Although such uses of the fund were not illegal, they do go against city procedure. For more than a decade, city auditors have been urging the department to change how it uses the fund.

Detroit Free Press

A thorough program or performance audit does more than look at how money is being spent. It evaluates whether an entire program has lived up to its billing. Such audits can be conducted by internal auditors; many larger cities have elected auditors to monitor the workings of government. Audits also are conducted by state or federal agencies that give money to cities. These, too, can be eye-opening.

When Herbert Lowe began covering the city of Camden for *The Philadelphia Inquirer,* he was greeted with a 168-page state audit of city performance.

"It was like the state had done all my work for me and handed me a report of everything that had gone wrong with the city," Lowe recalls.

The audit included a history of the city, an industrial power that had fallen on hard times. It discussed the issue of patronage in local politics, evaluated the performance of each department of government and laid out three pages of recommendations.

"There couldn't have been anything better," Lowe says. "I have often said that if I would only be assigned to the audits, I could write a [weekend story] every week."

Lowe started with the recommendations because these proposed solutions "were the heart of the story." They called, among other things, for the abolition of two departments, better monitoring of overtime expenses

Herbert Lowe of *The Philadelphia Inquirer* interviews a North Philadelphia community activist.

SUMMARY

AUDIT STORIES

1. Audits gauge whether a government agency is spending its money efficiently (and sometimes whether programs are performing as promised).

2. To find out what audits are undertaken each year, start by finding out whether the city has an internal auditor. Then check on what federal and state grants have been received and who keeps track of how that money is spent.

3. In reading an audit, pay special attention to the audit recommendations. They likely will provide the heart of your story.

4. In printing the findings, make sure to get a response from the audited agency. Like others in government, auditors can have political agendas.

5. Interview those who can flesh out the history behind the audit. Never hide behind the auditor's jargon. If you don't understand a reference, ask questions until you do.

and the need for a code of ethics. Even these, Lowe stressed, served as just a starting point for a story, not the whole thing.

"You have to talk to people," he says. "You have to walk up to people and say, 'What do you think?' And they'll tell you what's in between the lines that you wouldn't know. Just keep in mind that people are always going to promote their own agenda. But as long as you get all sides, that's context."

WRITING ABOUT BIDS AND CONTRACTS

All government work is not done by government workers. Some projects, from replacing the windows at city hall to repairing the sculpture fountain in the park, may be done by workers hired under government contract. Smaller contracts don't have to be put out for bid. They still deserve a close look, because this is a prime opportunity for elected officials to reward their friends or make an embarrassing choice.

Crawford of *WBBM News Radio 78* discovered that a $38,000 contract for paving in Chicago went to a company controlled by the city's top Mafioso. "When you check out contracts, that's the sort of thing you find out," he said.

Contracts over a stipulated dollar amount, which varies from place to place, must be put out to bid. Learn the bid procedures and limits in your municipality. Then pay close attention when the council awards contracts. This is often done without discussion or fanfare. It's a done deal by the time the council sits down to vote. So it's important to beware of certain things:

- Are the specifications of the contract written so narrowly that they favor a single contractor? "Sometimes when you look at the specifications, you realize only three or four companies can possibly meet them," Crawford says.

- Was the call for bids advertised prominently and in time for contractors to compete?

- Is the contract going to the lowest bidder? If not, why not?

- How strict are the terms of the contracts? How often do city contractors put through change orders—changes in the original bid—that drive up what they charge in the end? And do these changes regularly drive the cost of the work above the next lowest bidder? You can answer these questions by comparing the billed price to the bid price.

- Do the same contractors win city bids time and time again? Why?

SUMMARY
BIDS AND CONTRACT STORIES

1. Learn the system. Find out which contracts require bids and which can be awarded without them. Read bid procedures.

2. Make sure calls for bids are advertised prominently.

3. When bids are awarded, find out if the lowest bidder gets the contract. If not, find out why.

4. Always talk to the bidders who did not get the contract. Ask them if they think the bidding was fair. If they say no, ask why.

5. If few companies bid on a contract, find out if the bid specifications were written so narrowly that only one or two companies might qualify.

6. Find out whether contractors are coming in at bid or are consistently adding change orders that drive up the price of their contracts.

7. Periodically check the single-source contracts awarded without bid to see who holds them. Check whether these contractors contribute substantially to local politicians' election campaigns.

Tom Loftus and John Voskuhl were curious why the same people seemed to win the same road contracts in various parts of their state. So *The (Louisville, Ky.) Courier-Journal* reporters completed a computer analysis of state Transportation Cabinet bid records over a five-year period. Here is what they found:

FRANKFORT, Ky.—Buying out competitors and cultivating governors, an unabashed, street-smart road contractor named Leonard Lawson has quietly built over the last decade what may be the biggest blacktop monopoly in Kentucky history.

Lawson's main company, the Lexington-based Mountain Enterprises Inc., has rebounded from a federal bid-rigging conviction in the early 1980s to the point that in recent years it has received far more of the state's road-resurfacing business than any other contractor—the overwhelming amount of it without competition.

The (Louisville, Ky.) Courier-Journal

COVERING POLITICS

Doug Fox of *WFAA-TV* in Dallas has watched politicians at work for more than two decades. So when George W. Bush ran for governor of Texas, Fox knew early on he had a chance for an upset. Bush had an uphill battle. Polls showed his opponent, Gov. Ann Richards, to be very popular. And incumbents generally have an edge. But Fox knew something else: Bush was running a good race. Two things told him that. Surveys showed Bush was talking about the issues people said they wanted to hear. And Fox was taking his own pulse of the race. His conversations with the folks on Main Street told him the same thing the official pollsters were reporting.

"If you are going to cover politics, you've got to listen to people," Fox says. "The people are almost always ahead of the politicians."

Fox sometimes takes the questions of his viewers right to the politicians, a practice gaining increasing credence in print as well as broadcast media.

It certainly makes for good television to ask a question from "Joe Sixpack or Wanda Workingwoman," as Fox puts it. But savvy political coverage takes a lot more sophistication than that. Politicians are masters of image and symbolism. They'll tailor a stump speech so that it sounds just a bit more conservative and elitist in that affluent suburb and just a bit more egalitarian in the urban core. They're sometimes fond of selectively throwing around statistics to make a point, even if the statistic comes from a three-year-old report or is only half—the good half—of the story. And if you watch them closely, politicians sometimes say one thing when they've spent the last four years doing another. Fox knows this side of political reporting, too.

"If they say one thing publicly, the old grandstanding thing, but acted differently, you point that out. [Texas Sen.] Phil Gramm has done that for years."

It's all part of the art of campaigning. We'll touch on four basic aspects of political coverage: the horse race, the issues, the money and the vote.

The Horse Race

Who is going to win? That's the question bettors at American racetracks keep trying to get right. Journalists suffer from the same obsession.

"Horse-race" journalism—the constant barrage of reporting about the latest poll results—has come under plenty of criticism over the last few decades. And it should. But writing about who is winning will never disappear as an element of political coverage. The trick is to base such stories on solid information and, when the inevitable next poll gets released, to refer to it responsibly.

The first step is to know the rules of the race. How are candidates for the office you are covering selected? Will there be party primaries? If so, when? Can anyone run who submits a petition with a given number of voter signatures? When is the filing deadline? Who is expected to run? What are their backgrounds?

Reporters covering political campaigns will want to track what strategies the candidates are using, what issues they're talking about and whether they plan to debate face to face. Reporters will want to know whether voters are paying attention—they rarely do until a few weeks before an election. And reporters will look at how much money the candidates have amassed and how much attention they're drawing at campaign speeches or rallies.

With this information in hand, reporters will have the knowledge needed to evaluate the fluctuations of the polls and the background to make their stories more complete.

Fox says he's always skeptical about polls and uses them selectively. For one thing, he says, "I have banned from any copy I write the term front runner or leading candidate."

Polls, Fox points out, are a snapshot of the moment. They say who is leading on a given day and even then only within the **margin of error**—a range of percentage points that is as close as the pollster can ever get in a sample to capturing the views of a broader population.

When Fox uses polls, he likes to use them in the context of a broader analysis of the race. "When you have a polling result that shows a dramatic shift, then it becomes a little more significant," he says.

Finally, Fox always checks who has taken a poll and who is funding it.

First-time political reporters need to start by understanding what a poll is. Don't confuse it with a walk down Center Avenue, stopping to talk to every third voter. The proverbial man or woman in the street interview reflects nothing of a larger population. Pollsters sometimes err, but there's very clear methodology to their madness. **Random samples** are scientifically drawn to reflect a broad cross-section of the population. In comparison, interviews at an upscale mall would reflect nothing more nor less than the views of the upscale people who shop there—no matter how many people were interviewed.

TIPS ON UNDERSTANDING POLLS

Before deciding whether to use the results of a poll, reporters should get the answers to the following questions.

Who conducted it and who paid for it?

If candidate Lorraine Blair comes out with her own poll showing that she is dead even in the race for Turner County executive, it is going to carry less weight than a poll by respected organizations such as Gallup or Harris. "If polls come from politicians, be particularly suspicious," Fox says.

When was the poll conducted?

Public sentiment is a moving target. A candidate's standing might take a short-lived spike upward the day after he airs a 30-minute infomercial.

Who was polled?

As polling has grown more sophisticated, pollsters have begun to distinguish between polls of all possible voters, all registered voters and likely voters (those who regularly go to the polls). Those differences need to be spelled out in news reports.

How were the questions phrased, in what order and by whom?

Lorraine Blair's numbers in Turner County might look particularly good if her campaign workers start with the question: "Did you know that Lorraine Blair plans to give every taxpayer a 10 percent tax cut and her opponent wants to raise taxes?"

Expression, voice inflection, even a pollster's body language can influence the answers and outcome of a poll. That is why in national races reporters usually will look at a range of polls.

How many people were polled?

Polls require participation by a certain baseline number of people to be of significance. A poll of 45 means next to nothing. Conducted the right way, however, a poll of several hundred can reasonably reflect public opinion.

Two questions help determine the quality of a poll: What is the margin of error and at what level of confidence?

A poll showing a dead heat, but with a margin of error of plus or minus 5 percent means something other than a 50-50 race. That margin means that at the time of the poll either candidate might actually have had the support of as much as 55 percent of the electorate or as little as 45 percent. The level of confidence is an indicator of how often the poll's numbers are even further off the mark. A 95 percent level of confidence, for example, means that 5 percent of the time the distinction between the poll results and reality will be even greater than the range of that margin of error.

COVERING THE ISSUES

"Beware of the fax machine," says Fox. "Both campaigns daily will send you missiles directed at the other."

It doesn't always come to that. The race for council in a rural village may not amount to much more than door-to-door campaigning and fliers printed on the candidates' personal computers. Coverage in this kind of campaign often comes down to little more than interviewing candidates about their views and credentials and covering the debates sponsored by the local League of Women Voters. Clear issues can emerge—for example, whether or not to allow a superstore in the village's quiet downtown or to reinstate money in that budget for a teen center director. It's rare, however, for the sniping to get much worse than charges that one candidate or another tore down his opponent's campaign posters.

But when politics steps up to the arena of big-city, countywide, statewide and national office, reporters likely will run into their fair share of image meisters and mudslingers.

Fox and others who specialize in covering the arena of politics keep an ear open for the tips and tales of press secretaries and media consultants, campaign managers and campaign strategists, pollsters and think-tank pundits. Sometimes the dirt they shovel out proves to be a legitimate story. It is, for example, easy enough to check out a rumor that Candidate X hasn't voted in the last three elections; voter registration records hold the answer.

At least as often as not, however, the minions of big-time candidates spend their days "spinning" facts and events to cast their candidate in the best light and the opposing candidate in the worst. That's why, Fox adds, "I don't spend a lot of time on that sniping stuff."

Instead, Fox tries to keep pace with the issues, to follow not only what candidates say but also what they've done and how their positions have changed.

The Internet has helped. Fox will pull up newspaper accounts on web sites from around the state. He's used the **Congressional Quarterly** site to review a candidate's past votes and positions. And he's turned to **Project Vote Smart** for sources and additional background about candidates.

Reading helps Fox plan, and planning is particularly crucial to a reporter in a visual medium that tries to hold viewers' interest during a "talking heads" campaign.

"If you know the candidates are coming to town and you know what they are talking about, you can pick those issues you want to do a story on," Fox says.

During the Texas gubernatorial race, for example, juvenile crime emerged as an issue. "One of the things they talked about was boot camps. Well, what the heck is a boot camp? It's a detention facility in which they basically treat juveniles like they're at basic training in the Army. And we had one."

So when Fox aired a segment on juvenile crime, the script was wedded to pictures of youths at the camp. The script could draw on natural sound and interviews with those incarcerated at the boot camp as well as sound bites by the candidates. That's planning.

"We try to make it as visual as possible," says Fox. "We use a lot of graphics."

Graphics also have become a major element of print political coverage. As reporters try to hold candidates to the issues, a growing number of newspapers have turned to "truth boxes," which compare the candidates' claims in ads with the facts gleaned from voting records, reports and other sources that can be documented.

Print and television reporters also use graphics to compare different candidates' positions on the same issue. Increasingly, reporters for both media and their counterparts in radio are working together to survey voters about their concerns in an effort to force candidates to address those issues.

It was concern about voters' views that led the *San Jose (Calif.) Mercury News* in 1996 to establish its Listening Post, an interactive Internet site that led to a series of articles in the newspaper about the electorate.

"I think we were definitely on to something," says Holly Heyser, who for six months wrote stories based in part on her interviews with those who "chatted" with her newspaper online. "It was incredibly refreshing to talk to real people, people who haven't read every single story about a campaign."

FOLLOWING CAMPAIGN MONEY

People in glass houses on both sides of Congress started throwing stones after the 1996 presidential election as reports surfaced that foreign governments had tried to influence presidential politics by filtering money into Bill Clinton's campaign. Soon Democrats were leveling similar charges against their Republican counterparts.

No one can cover politics, from Podunk to the presidential race, without looking at who is footing the bill for everything from candidate mailers to flashy televised ads.

On a local level, reporters who track big contributors to the mayor's race are the same ones who just might see a familiar name when a developer is chosen to head the planning board. Money rarely is given simply out of a sense of largesse. By watching how it flows into a campaign, reporters may well get a preview of what issues and actions will eventually surface on a public official's agenda a year or so later.

Candidates for county sheriff to U.S. Senate are required by law to report how much money their campaign has raised. Beyond a dollar limit that varies from place to place, they also have to identify who is providing that money.

The first step is to find out where the money must be reported and at what point during the campaign. On a federal level, this information goes to the Federal Election Commission. On local and state levels, check with the town clerk or county election commission, and for good measure, read the law just to make sure. Tracking campaign contributions not only identifies the powerful behind-the-scenes players in politics and government but it also provides a pretty good sense of how a campaign is going and what kind of advertising endgame a candidate will be able to muster.

Jon Gordon of *Minnesota Public Radio* used FEC data to show radio listeners and Internet readers at the *MPR* Web site how out-of-state money was fueling a Minnesota race for U.S. senator. Gordon grabbed listeners' ears with a cut of Lyle Lovett singing, "That's uh, mmm-o-ney baby m-o-n-e-y" and then told them:

A notable 56 percent of Boschwitz's contributions of at least 200 dollars from individuals came from outside Minnesota.

For Wellstone, it's 47-percent from beyond the state borders. U-S Senate races always attract more money from national interests than House of Representatives contests because a Senate seat is seen as a bigger prize.

Minnesota Public Radio

By reviewing the data, Gordon was also able to tell his audience about two well-known Minnesota companies hedging their bets by contributing to both candidates. And he reported that the list of givers included Hollywood celebrities such as Steven Spielberg and Barbra Streisand.

ELECTION RESULTS

Plenty of stories on the campaign trail can be a complete surprise, but one story is etched in stone. Election night eventually arrives, and the public wants to know who won, how and why.

To do their best to answer that question under tight and competitive deadlines, reporters piece together as much information as possible ahead of time. They put together graphics and charts with the name, age and political affiliations of the candidates. They gather election-district maps and school themselves on which parts of town, the county or state tend to vote for which party's candidate. They find out where the candidates will be as the night unfolds and where their followers will gather to celebrate or console each other. Print reporters often write a good part of their story ahead of time, summarizing the chronology of the race.

Regardless of the media, reporters make sure the public is given the following information:

- Who won and by how much. Caution is advised here. Vote tallies can fluctuate wildly in some elections depending on which part of town reports first. Until it is mathematically impossible for the losing candidate to win, it's best to say the other candidate has a lead, a commanding lead or perhaps even "a virtually insurmountable lead."

- What percentage of the voters turned out and how that compares to past years.

- Election analysis. What did voters have to say about whom they voted for? What geographic areas of the district carried the day for the winning candidate?

During political campaigns reporters work many dawn-to-midnight days as they scramble to keep up with the candidates, emerging issues and the changing political landscape. Here Janet Wu of *NewsCenter 5* , Boston, does a stand-up at the Republican Convention in Massachusetts.

SUMMARY

COVERING POLITICS

1. Plan ahead. Planning provides context for stories, questions for the candidates and visuals for television.

2. Listen to the voters, not just the politicians. The voters can help shape issues to be covered.

3. Compare politicians' promises with their records.

4. Be wary of polls. When you must report them, make clear who the source is, what the margin of error is and how the poll was conducted.

5. Set your own agenda. Don't feel obligated to print every candidate's charge and countercharge. Check claims before you print them.

6. Regularly check campaign contributions. They can tell you not only who has a politician's ear but also whether the campaign is faltering.

7. On election night, don't declare the winner too early. Line up the candidates for comment ahead of time. And be sure to report the turnout, the results and the reasons why.

- Comments from both candidates or their campaign managers.
- Color. A sense of the scene in the winners' and losers' camps.
- Context. A quick synopsis of the race and how it played out.

Beyond the basics, there is room on big election nights for plenty of enterprise stories as well, from the scene at the polling booths, where the same folks work year after year, to stories about those people who stayed home and why.

ENTERPRISE STORIES

Cover the beat and not the building.

That phrase has become the mantra in a generation of newspaper newsrooms dedicated to deinstitutionalizing much more of their coverage. It's not really all that different from the example Doug Fox gave at the beginning of this chapter. When the council is talking about cutting midnight basketball, the good reporter in any medium wastes no time going to the courts to show what the program means and how the cuts will affect the players on the courts.

The best civic life reporting can't be found in a checklist on how to cover a budget or how to file on election night. It follows a path of thinking. That path leads reporters to the grass roots, to people who feel the impact of government and work outside of council chambers to change its direction. Civic life reporters have to understand the system of government and the process of forging policy to file intelligent stories. But if they don't look beyond that system to the people it serves, all that intelligence will be wasted.

Finding Stories at Street Level

Civic life enterprise starts with the bridge detour that makes it tough to get to city hall these days. Just what's going on here: Are neighbors concerned about the noise and pollution from the project? Are commuters fuming? Is the contractor staying on schedule? And what was wrong with the bridge anyway?

Practice some of the techniques outlined earlier in this chapter, and the world of civic life reporting gets a lot bigger than the confines of the council chambers. A plaque on a new park bench suggests it was dedicated to someone in the community. Who and why? The answer may be a touching story of a recently deceased older woman who fought to keep the area from being developed.

The planning board clerk you've talked with many times hands you a letter from a man who is furious about his neighbor's plans to build an 8-foot fence. This isn't a story to be covered in a meeting. You visit the neighborhood and tell about how two neighbors now wish they had never met.

After petitioning the council and negotiating a set of rules, a group of teen skateboarders has been granted permission to build a ramp near the village square. You tell the story of this early lesson in the politics of compromise and observe their construction efforts.

The list of civic life stories is as long as the streets winding through town. Walk them, talk to those who live on them and you'll see. Reporter Mike Cassidy came upon the story of a neighborhood turned ghost town simply by driving around the city of San Jose, Calif. Here is how it began:

Let's just say they don't have many block parties down on Anita Street where John Peña and his two children live.

See, the Peñas are the block. In fact, they're the whole neighborhood—or what's left of it.

Over the past 20 years, all the Peñas' neighbors in the southern half of the Coleman Loop have moved. Their homes have been summarily smashed to bits by wrecking crews clearing them out of San Jose International Airport's flight path and making way for the Guadalupe River Park.

All that's left is a ghost town.

San Jose (Calif.) Mercury News

LOOKING AT THE IMPACT OF GOVERNMENT ACTION

It began as a government decision—a city's plans to close one of its most blighted apartment buildings. In plenty of places, it would have ended right there: The poor, after all, rarely get much notice. But reporters for *The Spokesman-Review* in Spokane, Wash., scrambled over the following week to find out what this building was all about. "Desperate Days at the Merlin" was the result. It looked at the slow erosion of lower-income housing in their city. And it looked at the stories of those who would soon need new homes.

Orval Aldrich was cornered. Backed up against the rotting banister, his 82-year-old back rigid, his cane raised, he had finally had enough.

In 12 years at the Merlin Apartment in downtown Spokane, Aldrich had never been robbed. Two weeks ago, he was robbed twice.

Standing in the stripped, stained hallway of the 80-year-old hotel, he shook with fear and anger at the circle of strangers around him. He called for the manager. He called for the return of $95 of food stamps.

He couldn't call the police. The only public phone in the building was in pieces on the basement floor, coin box and quarters beaten out of it.

In four months, Aldrich's home had turned from a tired, old hotel into what officials say is a health threat, infested with cockroaches, overrun with drug users and steeping in raw sewage.

. . . This week, officials say they'll consider closing all or part of the 30-unit apartment building. . . . The closure would squeeze more people into an already tight market for low-income housing downtown.

The (Spokane, Wash.) Spokesman-Review

Stories about the reasoning behind government actions or their impact aren't always this dramatic. But they're invariably more dramatic, and more human, than nine people sitting around a conference table and voting. A city's decision to ban panhandling on its streets can be seen through the eyes of shop owners, shoppers and the indigents who will be forced to move elsewhere. A vote to install ramps for the disabled on sidewalks can be told through the eyes of those who need them. A decision to extend unemployment benefits can be seen from the vantage point of the unemployment office line. Looking at the actions of government through the eyes of those affected makes it harder to shrug off those actions.

Keeping Government Officials Accountable

As a computer-assisted reporting specialist for the *St. Paul (Minn.) Pioneer Press*, Dan Browning regularly applies new tools in checking out old-fashioned tips. That's what Browning did when sources told him that Lou McKenna, one of the most powerful politicians in Ramsey County, was spending a whole lot less time at work than he was being paid for.

Browning requested all the county phone records, time sheets and expense reports of McKenna, then county tax director. All of these, Browning knew, were public record. Using a computer spreadsheet, he keyed in the origin, duration and date of all the calls and compared them to days, according to McKenna's time sheet, that he was supposed to be at work.

"I knew if he was placing a call to the office from Key Largo on a day he reportedly was at work, there was a problem."

But that was just a start. Browning wanted to know whom McKenna was calling at county expense and precisely where he was calling from. He checked PhoneDisc Powerfinder, a set of CD/ROMs that matches names with most phone numbers in the country. He typed in the address for **Switchboard** on the Internet to look for numbers that might have changed since the CD/ROMs were issued. And he schmoozed with operators in small Minnesota towns that might have escaped the long arm of data compilers. The phone records showed a pattern that led Browning to check property records as well.

"He would go to Key Largo [Fla.], a rural cabin in Canada just north of Minnesota, and he liked to go to Vegas. I got him in Vegas through an expense report. I ended up saying that by the way he stole his time, he'd taken something like $25,000 from taxpayers."

Browning's story, which ran days before McKenna resigned, began like this:

For years, Ramsey County tax director Lou McKenna was logged as working or sick on days when he was lounging on a Florida beach, visiting Las Vegas casinos, relaxing at his Canadian cabin or taking long road trips, the Pioneer Press has learned.

The newspaper analyzed about 1,000 pages of time sheets, payroll stubs, court documents, property records, telephone bills, travel documents and expense vouchers in an effort to track McKenna's travels across the country.

Documents filed since Jan. 1, 1994, indicate McKenna collected sick pay or regular salary for at least:

- 31 days while on trips to southern Florida, where he has a 22-foot boat and a 12-by-50-foot trailer on Florida Bay in Key Largo.

- 23 days at or near his Canadian island cabin north of Voyageurs National Park, near Ash River, or on goose hunting trips to Montevideo, Minn.

- Five days on trips to Las Vegas, where he stayed at the Sand Casino & Hotel and the Flamingo Hilton.

St. Paul (Minn.) Pioneer Press

Reporters rarely fish indiscriminately for records that show how well, or poorly, government officials are doing their jobs. But they ask questions, and when a source hints something might be amiss, the paper trail—frequently computerized by now—is theirs to follow. In addition to expense reports and phone records, certain pieces of information often lead to interesting stories. They include:

- Overtime records
- Sick-time records
- Worker compensation claims
- Tax assessment records (Are certain city officials getting a break?)
- Parking tickets (Who is getting a break?)

CAR and Civic Life

Good reporters always have "followed the money trail." In the months before the 1870 New York City elections, for example, reporter John Foord reported the payroll-packing practices of the infamous Democratic boss William Marcy Tweed. City workers, Foord discovered, only painted its lampposts on rainy days, assuring the work would never be finished.

Reporters today who pore over records no longer have to use the hand calculations and long division that Foord did to find wrongdoing. Now, by setting up spreadsheets to evaluate financial tables, they can quickly calculate who, for example, is getting paid twice for the same job (although errors in data can make such calculations perilous without careful checking). It's called computer-assisted reporting (see Chapter 4). The massaging of data on the civic life beat can show how state and county road funds are dispersed, who has gotten the most overtime in the last decade and whether women in city government are commanding pay equal to that of men.

The results of CAR can be powerful, as Rena Singer of *The Philadelphia Inquirer* discovered when she used a spreadsheet to evaluate a string of city budgets in Norristown, Pa. The city, she found, was routinely cooking the books to come up with a balanced budget as required by law. Fact is, the budget was anything but balanced. Her story began like this:

> NORRISTOWN—If borough residents have become a bit skeptical about the meticulously balanced multimillion-dollar budgets they are presented around this time every year, it is with reason.
>
> . . . As the home rule charter demands, all of the inch-thick budgets adopted since 1992 have been balanced. But an examination of each shows that the borough has consistently under-budgeted some items, including salaries, insurance payments and debt repayment, by as much as $300,000 per line item per year. . . .
>
> . . . Every year since 1992 Norristown has had to spend about $1 million to repay its debt.
>
> *The Philadelphia Inquirer*

The computer was a tool that helped Singer. It was no more than a tool. The story grew out of her own curiosity and whisperings she had heard from sources. Good civic life reporting works like that: Curiosity and clear thinking comes first; fancy tools sometimes follow.

SUMMARY ENTERPRISE REPORTING

1. One definition of enterprise means "readiness to venture, initiative." On the civic life beat, enterprise starts with using your eyes and ears outside the office and away from city hall.

2. When government acts, tell the story through the effect those actions have on the people who either benefit or lose as a result. The tale of government price supports for farmers is a snooze unless it is told through the experience of a third-generation family whose farm is saved from extinction.

3. Reporters remain the best watchdogs of government. From overtime pay to worker compensation claims, the money trail traces whether taxpayer dollars are well or poorly spent.

4. Patterns make news. An increase in skunk sightings is worth noting in one community, but if the same is being reported by animal control officers throughout the county, the story may be worth the top of the news.

5. News in Washington, D.C., and at the state capital always affects those close to home in the end. When women's groups join for a march in Washington, tell the story from the perspective of a local contingent making the trip by bus.

Tracking Patterns

"When you start thinking in terms of watching patterns, you generate stories," Dan Browning says. "No one has to hand them to you."

Nina Kim, of *The (Syracuse, N.Y.) Post-Standard*, knows that. On several occasions over several months, Kim noticed that residents in the community she covered were presenting the council with petitions asking for lower speed limits on their streets. Her alertness led to a story about how speed limits are set and why they are hard to change. The answer: Some local roads are under the jurisdiction of the county, some of the town, some of the state. The story wasn't a big deal. But had Kim not been paying attention to the repetition of requests, it probably wouldn't have been told at all. She regularly "gathers string" on issues. Sometimes it pays off.

"Something that may not be big now may be huge in three months," Kim says.

Mike Shear knew the rate of growth was a contentious issue when he began covering Prince William County, Va., for *The Washington Post*.

"Supervisors for years had said, 'We want to slow the pace of residential growth.'"

But as Shear sat trying to sort through arcane meetings in which landowners sought approval for development plans, "I had a sense of [the supervisors] never turning one down."

The problem was proving it—a task Shear didn't even think of attempting until he took a one-week class on computer-assisted reporting. Excited about what for him was a new reporting tool, Shear asked the county planning department for its database of all cases involving property rezoning. Over the previous five years, he found some 300 votes. These he entered by hand into a computer spreadsheet.

"It was a nightmare," he said. First he learned that the data was messy; some zoning requests were entered multiple times. Then he realized a "yes" vote for rezoning didn't prove anything, since some "increased the number of houses and some decreased the number of houses."

Shear worked harder, sorting the data so that the spreadsheet showed how many homes could be built at each site before the supervisors voted and how many could be built afterwards.

"We were able to come up with a really good story that said flat-out that nine out of 10 times, supervisors gave zoning that could increase the number of homes that could be built."

Localizing

Ultimately, all the actions of government are local. When politicians in Washington, D.C., change welfare rules, people in your community pay the price. Local officials may find themselves scrambling to patch a tear in the safety net. Local volunteer agencies may suddenly see a rise in demand at their food banks. And local welfare recipients will have to scramble to find work. A decision forged hundreds if not thousands of miles away is being played out in your backyard.

By regularly perusing federal and state registers, which list new regulations, and tracking stories about new laws coming out of Washington, D.C., and the statehouse, reporters can find good local stories. Here is an example:

> One local affordable-housing agency has laid off staff members. Others are delaying renovation work.
>
> All are waiting—possibly in vain—for money they expected in the state budget, which is 81 days overdue today.
>
> *The (Syracuse, N.Y.) Post-Standard*

The story went on to show the real hurt being caused by squabbling politicians.

RECOMMENDED READING

AllPolitics. Atlanta, GA: Cable News Network. [Online]. Available: **http://www.allpolitics.com**.

When the campaigns go into action, this is the best overall site for searching politics. Although the focus is federal elections, the site includes helpful state resources. It's updated daily by *Cable News Network, Inc. (CNN)*.

DeSilva, B., & Mura, J. (1996). *The straight scoop: An expert guide to great community journalism*. Hartford, CT: The Hartford Courant.

This book, written by reporters at *The Hartford Courant,* includes seven chapters on covering municipal government that beginning reporters will find helpful. The chapters are short, well-written and packed with tips.

StateSearch. Lexington, KY: National Association of State Information Resource Executives. [Online]. Available: **http://www.nasire.org/ss**.

This is a great jumping-off place for anything about state government. From this site you can connect to any governor's office, state legislature or other agencies by topic.

Weinberg, S. (1996). *The reporters handbook* (3rd ed.). New York: St. Martin's.

If you're covering government, this book by investigative reporter Steve Weinberg is a must. Six of the 23 chapters focus on government alone. Also helpful are his many tips on where to go and how to track people and documents.

WWW Virtual Library: U.S. Government. Information Sources. Wheeling, WV: National Technology Transfer Center. [Online]. Available: **http://iridium.nttc.edu/gov_res.html**.

Here's where to begin when you want to find anything in the federal government. It has nearly 1,000 links to help beginning reporters track down federal information.

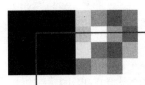

EXERCISES

A. RESEARCH

1. Using the Internet, find the following information. Include the location of the site you use.

   a. The population of your community according to the latest census data

   b. The name and phone number of your state's comptroller general

   c. The date of your congressional representative's last speech before Congress

   d. A description of what can be found on the Web site of your state, county and/or city

2. What document would you consult and whom would you contact to find the following information for a story? After discussing this, gather the information.

   a. The name and phone number of the village clerk

   b. City rules for accepting gifts

   c. The overall salary to be paid to the city manager's office this year

   d. Total overtime hours worked by the road department or its equivalent last year

   e. The telephone records of each council member

   f. The names of the tax assessor, his secretary and any other staff members

   g. The property holdings of the mayor

   h. The year city hall was built

   i. Which roads in your community are under local control and which are operated by the county

   j. How council members voted last month on issues that came before them

   k. The town's zoning laws for commercial property

l. The amount of money spent last year on pot-hole repair and/or snow removal

m. The schedule for trash pickup in your community

3. Define and translate the following terms.

a. ordinance

b. second reading

c. gridlock

d. certificate of occupancy

e. performance bond

f. R1 zoning

g. market value

h. power broker

i. debt service

j. annual report

k. glass ceiling

l. mill rate

m. ZBA

n. travel voucher

o. grandfather clause

B. FINDING ANGLES

1. Interview a member of the clergy. Ask a series of open-ended questions, such as how the congregation has changed, how the concerns of its members have changed, what are the greatest needs in the surrounding neighborhood, what mission work or social services the congregation provides. When you are done, jot down three possible story leads that have come from the interview.

2. Spend a half day with a city housing inspector or public health inspector. Write down three possible stories that you might pursue afterwards.

3. Visit a community center, charity or social service agency. Ask about not only the problems but also the successes of the organization. What are the most common requests or concerns staff members hear about? If people there could change three things about their community, what would they be? List five story leads that come from your inquiry.

4. Spend an afternoon in a commercial district talking to shop owners about what they think their local government could do to improve the climate for business. Did you find any common threads? Can you identify one or more possible stories?

5. Pick a committee in the community whose meetings are rarely covered. Read through the last six months of minutes. Can you find stories worth covering?

C. STORY DEVELOPMENT

1. First, write a memo that describes how you would report the following story. Then jot down how you might tell the story differently in print and broadcast media.

a. An enemy of the mayor tells you that the mayor has spent an inordinate amount of tax-payers' money on city travel in the last year. The source doesn't offer details.

b. Residents have complained about a bitter taste in local water supplies. You decide to look into the matter.

c. Rush-hour traffic has been particularly fierce this spring. You decide to map out how many local, county and state road projects are under way.

d. A source tells you that the city's fleet of garbage trucks is so old that the number of hours trucks are in for repair has increased sharply in the last three years.

e. You decide to compare local giving to the three largest charitable organizations in the community.

f. Residents in the poorest area of town say less money is being spent to keep up parks there than in more affluent neighborhoods.

D. BASIC STORIES

1. Write stories or memos based on the following assignments. Look for ways to tell the stories graphically and for ways to look at them in terms of their effect on members of your community. Discuss how you might approach the story differently for print, radio, television and the Internet.

a. Get the agenda and council packet for the next council meeting. Advance an issue to be taken up.

b. Get the last two years' budgets from your community. Write a news story that looks at one significant change between them.

c. Cover a planning board meeting in your community.

d. Ask for the last audit of a program in your community. Write an article about it.

e. Look up a competitive contract in your community. Write a story based either on cost overruns in delivering the contract or on the contract award itself. Did competitors consider the award fair? Was the low bidder selected? Why or why not?

E. ENTERPRISE STORIES

1. Put together stories for print, radio, television or the Internet based on the following assignments. Discuss how different media might approach your story differently and how graphics and pictures might be used to help tell the story effectively.

   a. Write a story about the contractor in your community who has held a noncompetitive contract for longer than anyone else.

   b. Explore how the city's debt has fluctuated over the last decade and why. Compare the debt to neighboring communities.

   c. Using a spreadsheet, compare how much money your community has paid for sick time in the last five years to the amount spent in two neighboring communities.

   d. Using the Internet, find a piece of legislation that recently passed either your state legislature or U.S. Congress. Develop a story about how it might affect people in your local community.

   e. Write a story based either on a local newsgroup discussion or on correspondence received at city hall.

   f. Write a story about local residents who are behind in their property taxes. You can focus on one person or look at the issue more broadly.

   g. What issue most concerns members of a neighborhood association in your community? Find out and develop a story about it.

   h. Stop by the local senior center and develop a story about an issue of concern to the elderly in your community.

   i. Develop a story off an item you read on a bulletin board in town.

   j. Read correspondence to the city and its planning board. See whether you can find the seeds of a story to tell by visiting a neighborhood. Then develop that story.

CHAPTER 11

Lifestyles

Wherever Tasneem Grace goes, she finds time to talk to teen-agers. She should: Covering teens is her job. It's a job she lobbied to create at *The (Syracuse, N.Y.) Post-Standard* in the late 1990s. She knew teens were rapidly becoming an endangered species as newspaper readers, and she thinks she knows why—papers pay little attention to what teen-agers have to say or to their lifestyles.

In Syracuse, that's changing. The paper has its own monthly tabloid, *HJ,* which is distributed to teens in the schools. And Grace has worked hard to bring the world of teens to a general audience as well, writing stories about everything from the debate in schools over ebonics (black English) to the art of body piercing. Her stories are filled with the words of teen-agers.

"Everyone has been a teen-ager, yet we develop selective amnesia," Grace says, explaining the need for her beat. "The utopian view is that every story should be inclusive [of kids' views]. But I don't think we think that way yet. I think we're a long way from thinking that way. And unless you are really conscious of efforts to diversify coverage in all kinds of ways, I think you'll fail."

At least in some quarters, signs are springing up of an increased consciousness of the need to broaden and diversify both the sources of news and the selection of stories. Reporting about how we live and who we are—our varied lifestyles—is bursting onto the front page of American newspapers and filling increasing time on television newscasts.

The trend reflects business concerns—newspapers, for example, are not attracting young readers. And readers, listeners and viewers across the media want different kinds of stories. They are clamoring for more about how they can best cope with a variety of so-called quality of life issues, such as caring for aging parents, juggling jobs and day care, understanding and building relationships, integrating issues of spirituality and values into their everyday lives.

As media work to meet these demands, they are making much more than a business decision. They are redefining the fundamental nature of news, putting more emphasis on enterprise reporting and less on the breaking news that comes over the transom.

More new beats are cropping up to reflect this change in emphasis than we can detail in a single chapter—beats on everything from personal computing to personal finance and from online communities to those that take shape over long hours of commuting. Like Tasneem Grace, reporters today are discovering that if they don't like the beat they are assigned, it doesn't hurt to invent and propose a new one.

"Two things are changing to make new beats possible," says Mike Antonucci, who created a "popular culture beat" at the *San Jose (Calif.) Mercury News.* "One is that society is *really* changing. It's not just our perception that life is more complex. It's truly a matter of life being more complex. The other factor is that complexity is changing what people care about."

This chapter will merely sample some of the emerging beats in the American media—five in all. It will:

- Introduce you to sources, resources and issues involved in covering two generational beats—teens and seniors, touching as well on the reporting of demographic population trends
- Explore some of the special challenges and special reporting skills needed to cover issues of cultural differences in America's increasingly diverse society
- Look at the burgeoning coverage of leisure, a wide-ranging beat that can take in everything from snowmobiling safety to a Saturday night concert
- Show how issues of relationships and family are emerging as serious topics of coverage
- Discuss the ways coverage of spirituality and ethics have become integrated into the fabric of news and feature coverage in print and broadcast

COVERING GENERATIONS

Walk into most newsrooms, particularly those in larger markets, and you'll see a preponderance of 30- and 40-somethings making decisions about what viewers, listeners and readers should get in their daily servings of news. Top newsroom managers have gradually come to realize that the makeup of a newsroom can and does affect coverage patterns. If news about teens too often gets short shrift, so does news of seniors. And in newsrooms that are predominantly white and male, the same can happen to coverage of issues about women and people of color. Changes in staffing take time. But changes in resource allocation and beats can help address gaps in coverage.

On the Teen Beat

It can be tough covering a beat with no mayor or city hall, no school principal or classroom, no judge or courtroom. Routine is harder to establish, sources are harder to find. Stepping outside the norm and thinking in new ways become more important than reportorial convention.

Michelle Guido learned that the hard way when she moved from education writer to become the *San Jose Mercury News'* teen writer. It's a beat she had sold her editors when an audit of news coverage came back with the surprising news that teens received the most negative coverage of any group in the paper.

"I spent a lot of time flailing around," Guido recalls of her early weeks on the beat. "It's 10 times harder when you start something that never existed before. There are no existing source lists or files that can be passed down between reporters. There's no central place to go. When you cover a beat that has no infrastructure, you don't know where to start."

PEOPLE TO SEEK OUT, THINGS TO READ

Guido couldn't wait around for handouts on her new beat; there were none. So she dove in. She dropped by community groups. At the teen center of the Mexican-American Community Services agency she found a former drug dealer who had traded his gang colors for work in gang outreach. She followed him as he scoured the streets looking for kids who wanted to get off of them and out of gangs.

Guido stopped by juvenile hall, talking to kids stuck in the system ("That's a story"). She met a kid who was going through a tattoo removal program ("That's a story, too"). She saw adults giving groups of teens a wide berth on street corners and in malls and started work on a story that ran on Page 1 under the headline: "Teenophobia." And she wrote about how savvy and comfortable many kids are in cyberspace.

As she turned her contacts into stories, Guido was doing something else. She was building a source base. Her sources included lots of adults whose professions brought them in contact with teens: juvenile court judges, church youth group leaders, psychologists who specialized in eating disorders, youth job coordinators, club

TIPS FOR TALKING WITH TEENS

Tasneem Grace of The (Syracuse, N.Y.) Post-Standard finds a little knowledge of teen culture and an open-minded attitude can go a long way toward opening up teens to being interviewed. She offers these tips:

- **Be patient.** "Hang out for a while. Kids don't like a barrage of questions."

- **Talk to kids on their turf and terms.** "You want to develop a comfort zone. Language is very important. So I pick up on their language and I never talk down. If they're talking about body piercing, I say, 'Wow. Can I see?'"

- **Converse, don't question.** "The art of conversation really works with teens because they want validation," she says. "Adults are happy to have me take notes while they talk. Teens want to converse."

- **Know their culture.**

- *Interview teens in groups.* Many reporters try to isolate teens to keep them focused. Grace prefers to talk to them in groups. The reason? "Their energy feeds off one another. Generally one person will start to talk and others jump in."

- **Present teens as they are.** Too many news stories present teens through the stereotypes or experiences of adults. Grace recalls an editor who kept pushing her to do a story on the return of the yo-yo. It was clear, she says, that the editor had loved yo-yos as a kid. "The trouble is, the yo-yo hadn't returned. You're talking about a generation gap."

- **Tread with care into sensitive issues.** Remember, teens are kids. Grace says she won't "leave them hanging out to dry." For example, she says, she'll write around kids who boast about being drug users. "With kids I'll say, 'How can we work with this so it doesn't get you in trouble?' I don't do that with adults."

On particularly sensitive stories Grace also checks with parents. She did that, for example, before writing a story on "objects of hate"—kids who because of their race or sexual preference were picked on by others. Some parents went along. Others were mortified. Says Grace: "A story is not as important as a family."

---

owners, members of advocacy groups for children and youth. But at the core of her list were teens themselves—kids she met in malls and schools, on the street and on school newspapers.

Of course, teens read, too. So teen writers try to keep tabs on teen publications. The reading list of Tasneem Grace of *The (Syracuse, N.Y.) Post-Standard* includes such magazines as *YM, Seventeen, Vibe* and *Rolling Stone.* She reads literature from local bands, skims school newspapers and scans the copy teen correspondents send to her paper's teen publication. After writing about kids in cyberspace, Guido added to her reading list: She began perusing the online chat groups to which kids gravitate.

The Syracuse Newspapers.

Tasneem Grace

PLACING TEEN COVERAGE IN CONTEXT

As she built her source and story list, Guido tried to think about teens differently—who they were, what affected their lives, what concerned them.

"Before we had a youth reporter, no one knew kids have a stake in all kinds of things—Supreme Court decisions involving abortion rights, Supreme Court decisions involving gay rights, city-imposed curfews, whatever. There was a segment of the population we pretty much ignored across the board."

Both Guido and Grace write for teens, not just about them. Both make sure voices of teens appear in all kinds of stories. Grace recalls a big story that ran in her paper about teen gangs. In the entire piece, there was a quote from only one kid.

SUMMARY

COVERING TEENS

1. Listen to teens. They have lots to say. Too many stories about them don't consult them.

2. Write for teens, not just about them. Teens have a stake in scores of serious issues, from pregnancy and abortion to school safety and the use of cyberspace.

3. In covering an unconventional beat like teens, use unconventional ways to build sources. Go where teens congregate, and think about who works with teens and can give context and insight into their views.

4. Read what teens read, watch the television shows they watch, listen to their music. All will teach you more about the culture in which they are growing up.

5. Encourage others in your news organization to incorporate teen views into stories about politics and social problems, leisure and learning.

"An awful lot of people in newsrooms look alike and come from the same experiences," she says. "If you changed newsrooms in terms of age, in terms of race, you'd see things more the way they are." Grace, herself just a few years out of college, tries to give the teen perspective of things. Here is how she started a piece on the growing number of rules to which teens are tethered:

> Rules can feel as stifling as a straightjacket.
>
> Curfews, dress codes, hall passes, permission slips, agenda books, "parental advisory" labels, television ratings, "no loitering" signs.
>
> Teens say such rules scream with stress-causing messages of distrust and low expectations. They resent the stereotypes that stamp them as rude, rowdy and rebellious. Gaining independence and self-determination, they say, seems unattainable . . .
>
> *HJ* magazine,
> *The (Syracuse, N.Y.) Post-Standard*

"There are a lot of ways teens can reenergize your paper," Grace says. "What other group in this country has as much chance to define itself? But no one even asks teens what they think. Adults are seriously afraid of them."

ON THE AGING BEAT

John Cutter covers elder affairs in St. Petersburg, Fla., a haven for retirees. His beat for the *St. Petersburg Times* has led him to stories about the reverse migration of some retired folks from Florida to the North, about the first of the baby boomers reaching 50 and about generational shouting matches online in the American Association of Retired Persons' forum. His beat, in short, is a lot broader than the stereotypical stories about the doddering folks in nursing homes that too often shape popular images of what covering the aging population means.

"The demographic profile in older people is the same as with other people," Cutter says. "They are rich and poor, they are healthy and sick. They are liberals and conservatives. And they're not all like your parents."

He might have added something else: There are lots of them, and their numbers are growing rapidly as more and more baby boomers spill into their 50s. Yet coverage of the economic, social, political and health issues of an aging America seems stalled in first gear.

"There is a need to get beyond the disease-of-the-month approach and to some extent the latest nursing home scandal," says Paul Kleyman, who produces a newsletter called "The Journalists Exchange on Aging" for beat reporters, general assignment reporters and free-lancers with an interest in covering the aging population.

Only about 10 news organizations assign a reporter full-time to issues about the aging, Kleyman says. Another few dozen cover the beat part-time. Kleyman expects to see those numbers change as the ranks of the elderly swell. In an article titled, "Beyond the Medical Model of Journalism on Aging," Kleyman notes: "Sometimes it is difficult to chisel away at calcified attitudes."

One of those who has gotten beyond narrowly stereotyping the aging beat as the feeble and infirm beat is John Cutter.

"I define the beat very broadly," says Cutter, who has completed most of the course work for a master's degree in gerontology. "My problem with a lot of coverage of aging is that it's often parked in the medical beat because the problems associated with age are often perceived as medical. At any time maybe 5 percent of the aged are in nursing homes. Well, we're not writing enough about the other 95 percent."

PEOPLE TO SEEK OUT

John Cutter has cast a wide net to find sources among the elderly, the people directly affected by what he writes. He visits senior centers as well as social service agencies, condo associations as well as senior citizens' political clubs. Cutter makes a point of accepting whenever he's invited to speak before organizations of seniors. And he listens when one of the many avid older readers of his paper calls him up.

A phone call gave him the idea of writing about older drivers and what keeping a license means to their sense of worth and independence. The piece began like this:

They drive slowly in the left-hand lane, right-turn signals blinking.

Their cars pull out suddenly in front of you, their white hair barely visible over the steering wheels.

They weave. They squint at signs.

Their bumper stickers read, "We're spending our children's inheritance," and you wish they would— on taxicabs instead of new Cadillacs.

Seniors who drive. Are these slight exaggerations or shameful stereotypes?

Younger Floridians love to hate older drivers. They are cursed on commutes and trips to the mall. They are characters in legendary stories about airport runways that are mistaken for interstates.

And they are the fastest-growing group of drivers on the road today.

For a teenager, a driver's license is confirmation of adulthood. When you are old, the loss of your license can seem like being given your last rites.

St. Petersburg (Fla.) Times

Trend stories about the aging make nice reading. But Cutter also has to keep a keen eye out for harder-edged news. This often comes from official sources, ranging from state and federal agencies to the directors of those centers where the elderly go to congregate. Here are some of his tips on how to build expertise on issues concerning the aging:

■ Contact the federal Agency on Aging near you. There are 500 regional offices nationally. The agency does everything from coordinating Meals on Wheels programs to funneling money to nonprofits and municipalities.

■ Go to senior centers and meet the people who run them. These often are where elderly residents go to talk, read and play games. It is a good place to sit and listen for ideas, Cutter says.

■ Discover which agency in your state oversees issues on aging. Federal law requires that some agency be designated for that role.

■ Find out about your state's "silver-haired legislature," the name given groups of elderly activists who get together annually to lobby state legislators. Cutter says the volunteer organization exists nationwide.

MAKING SENSE OF DEMOGRAPHICS

The next census, how it will be conducted and who fears being undercounted always makes for hot political copy. But you needn't wait for the changing decade to make use of the ever-changing snapshot the **U.S. Census Bureau** provides of the United States.

Paul Overberg, for example, makes a good piece of his living as a reporter for *USA Today* keeping tabs on the myriad numbers tracked by the U.S. Census Bureau on an ongoing basis. And as he told a gathering of reporters at the National Institute of Computer-Assisted Reporting, much less experienced reporters can do the same. All it takes is some work wandering through the massive online statistical files of the bureau and a little help setting up a spreadsheet to analyze them.

One reason you'll find interesting news is that the Census Bureau does a lot more than tell us who we are once a decade. It makes sense of these numbers, tracks economic data and estimates changes in population down to the county level even in noncensus years.

"Find out our nation's estimated population [at the time you ask] or how your local government spends its money or check out a . . . digital map file," states the agency's own brochure about its Web site. The site includes a census A-to-Z file that tells you state-by-state changes in interracial marriages, for example, or the percentage of the country's population living in rural areas (25 percent). The census Web site (**U.S. Census: County population**) provides extensive county population estimates that, if loaded into a spreadsheet, can measure such things as the migration in and out of your county or the change in its industrial base.

Here are some examples of the data Overberg says can help you draw a portrait of your county:

- Annual county-level population estimates: These estimates on the growth or decline in a county's population are released each March and are based on such data as births, deaths and net migration. Don't settle for the esti-

mates, Overberg says. Get raw information so you can do your own evaluations. "Net domestic migration is a sensitive barometer to your area's quality of life," he wrote in a handout called "Profiling Your Community With Census Data." So how can you tell if your own county is doing well or poorly? For a start, compare trends in the last five years to the five years before. You also should compare your county to neighboring counties and the state. Are more people coming or going?

- Annual county-level migration files: One agency that assists the Census Bureau in determining migration patterns is that much-maligned "tax man," the Internal Revenue Service. The IRS uses the Social Security number on each tax return, Overberg writes, to check where taxpayers live in consecutive years. And the agency correlates these migration patterns to household income. This means it's possible to see not only how many people are coming and going but also whether those coming are earning more or less than those going. You can also do stories about where newcomers come from and where those leaving are going.

- Annual county-level estimates for race, sex and age: These figures are about a year old by the time they're released, but they still can be a gold mine for tracking a variety of trends. Is your county filled with an aging baby boomer population, a boomlet of kids, both? Has the Asian-American population increased rapidly since a group of Cambodian refugees settled in the county's main city? These and other trend stories can be culled from the numbers.

- Annual county business patterns: This data, released about 15 months after it's compiled, shows how many people are working in what kinds of industries in your county. This information can help you determine which businesses and industries in your county are in demand and which are declining.

- Tap into the local chapter of the American Association of Retired Persons. It is the largest organization of senior citizens in the country.
- Go to your local university and find out what kind of research is being done there on aging and the economics of aging.

THINGS TO READ

At the outset of his five years on the beat, Cutter put together a reading list of books such as "You and Your Aging Parent," by Barbara Silverstone and Helen Kandel Hyman, and "The Economics of Aging," by James

Schulz, to background himself on the issues. He has built a small library of reference books, such as the "American Geriatrics Society's Complete Guide to Aging & Health." And he subscribes to magazines read by many senior citizens, such as *Aging Today, AARP Bulletin* and *Modern Maturity.*

Like all good reporters, Cutter also got his name on countless mailing lists, and he flips through the flood of press releases that come his way daily. A press release from a Michigan retirement community trying to lure Floridians north gave him the idea of writing about the reverse migration of Florida retirees to points north. The press release wasn't the story; it merely planted the seeds of an idea. Here is an excerpt:

Retirees say there are many reasons to go back. Some yield to the almost inevitable need for help from family in their final years or simply want to spend more time close to children and grandchildren.

Others return at the urging of adult children, who fear for their parents' health and safety because the families are divided by hundreds of miles.

Researchers call it reverse migration. They say the trend is fueled by increasing lifespans, the lack of government programs to help the frail elderly in their own homes, and a tight economy that makes regular visits harder for families that live far apart.

St. Petersburg (Fla.) Times

Such trend pieces make up much of the "news" on the elder affairs beat, Cutter says. The longer he is on the beat, the more he has realized that part of the specialist's job is to fend off the weary or overdone stories editors push.

"Editors often develop impressions from all the other media about the reality when you've spent five years trying to develop some knowledge independently. Sometimes you have to say, 'No.'"

To find fresh ideas, Cutter turns to the World Wide Web, as well as sources and the printed page. He finds himself online frequently, culling the Web sites of agencies such as the **National Institute on Aging** and the **National Science Foundation** for information, e-mailing researchers to set up interviews, and viewing bulletin boards and chat rooms, such as America Online's Seniornet, for sources and story threads.

Cutter's use of online resources has paid off in big ways and small. He developed an entire story off an angry generational exchange taking place on **AARP Online** and other cyberspace sites. Here is how the story began:

From: Kenny James

"ATTENTION MEMBERS OF AARP—HOW DOES IT FEEL TO BE ROBBING YOUR CHILDREN AND GRANDCHILDREN OF THEIR FUTURE? YOUR ORGANIZATION IS A CLEAR EXAMPLE OF THE 'ME FIRST' APPROACH TO LIFE—YOU SHOULD BE ASHAMED."

From: HUTCHCO

"Only in America could a blithering idiot be allowed to spew his dribble."

Those were the opening shots of a generational war in cyberspace, a place where when you scream, everyone with a computer and a modem

can hear. The first message truly was a screamer, because using all capital letters is computer-ese for yelling.

The messages were posted after the American Association of Retired Persons took its first step on the information superhighway in November with a service called AARP Online.

AARP's service and other bulletin boards on America Online, CompServe and Prodigy have become the most public place for generations to grouse about who gets what in this era of diminishing resources.

St. Petersburg (Fla.) Times

When Cutter was looking for a senior citizen in his area who refused to take a flu shot, he posted a note on the Seniornet health bulletin board on America Online. Sure enough, he soon had a source from within his own readership area. The Internet also can provide instant access to valuable factual data, Cutter says. He found

SUMMARY   COVERING AGING

1. Seniors are as diverse as any other group in society. Get beyond stereotypes of people in nursing homes.

2. Look for news and trends.

3. Draw together a list of agencies that serve the aging and introduce yourself to key people.

4. Go to places where older folks meet and spend time in their favorite online discussions.

5. Build a library of reference books that can help you understand issues of aging.

6. Older folks have time to chat online. Join them.

statistics for that story on the increase of older drivers on the *National Highway Traffic Safety Administration* site.

COVERING DIVERSE POPULATIONS

Ken McLaughlin returned from a Gannett Foundation Asian Fellowship in 1990 eager to apply what he'd learned to coverage of the 50,000-strong Vietnamese-American community in the readership area of his paper, the *San Jose (Calif.) Mercury News.* The reception was disheartening.

"I told [the city editor] I really wanted to cover the Vietnamese community as a sub-beat, and he said, 'Oh, we've already taken care of that: We hired a minority affairs reporter,'" McLaughlin recalls.

Eight years later, McLaughlin was one of a team of five reporters and an editor devoted full-time to coverage of race and demographics. The change in beat configuration has come rapidly to San Jose, in part because of the city's rich diversity. In one high school, administrators discovered students came from more than four dozen different national backgrounds. There are more nonwhite than white faces in the schools. Drive through the city, and it's not uncommon to hear conversations and read signs in Spanish or Japanese, Hindi or Mandarin. San Jose, in short, already looks like more and more of America will in the 21st century as the immigrant population grows and the numbers of nonwhites tilt into the majority.

To successfully capture and chronicle these remarkable changes in who we are—and the strains that accompany those changes—reporters of all backgrounds will have to broaden their horizons, wander into communities they haven't visited before, look for stories in places they haven't yet discovered. Some news organizations, such as the *Mercury News,* are changing the way they allocate resources to encourage more diverse reporting. All reporters will need to think differently.

THE LESSONS OF ONE PROJECT

Scott Maxwell knew he lived in one of the South's more conservative communities. And he knew he worked for one of the nation's whitest urban newspapers. But Maxwell still was confident of the *Winston-Salem (N.C.) Journal*'s plan to do a series on race relations. Then in late 1996 he took a week off to participate in a conference at The Poynter Institute in Florida on covering race. His confidence faded.

"The thing that became blatantly clear was that it would be impossible for an almost all-white newsroom to tell a compelling story about race relationships," he recalls.

Impossible, at least, without a lot more listening and self-examination. When Maxwell returned to North Carolina, he told his editors they'd have to rip up the project's plan and start over. The first step was listening, as his group had at Poynter, to separate citizens' panels, white and black. (The separate groups, he says, were formed to encourage more candor than would likely emerge in a mixed-race group.) The next step was for the newsroom's reporters to look at themselves, examine their own biases and listen to the experiences of colleagues.

"We did some exercises," he recalled. "One was, 'When has race been a factor in your life?' Blacks can rattle off countless answers, while whites have to think real hard about it."

The third was to get into the community and listen more—a lot more—before deciding on what stories the series should tackle.

"This was a case where we really wanted to start with a clean slate, to let people take us in the direction they wanted to go," Maxwell says. "When I cover the Board of Aldermen, I know most of the issues and can throw in some background. But when we are trying to have this truly open dialogue on race, which we really hadn't covered in Winston-Salem before, we don't really have anything to bring to the reporting."

When he arrived at Poynter, which trains journalists on a wide range of topics, Maxwell and his editors had planned to launch the series in February. They did—exactly one year later, a year devoted to some painful self-examination and some in-depth reporting. Among the 100-plus stories the paper ran was one examining the abysmal hiring and promotion record of the *Winston-Salem Journal*.

Maxwell's own first piece began like this:

> Buying gasoline is such a simple thing that many people take it for granted.
>
> Not Eddie McCarter. It makes him angry.
>
> When McCarter wants to fill up his Explorer, he faces a problem that many people in eastern Winston-Salem do. He is asked to pay before he pumps, night and day.
>
> . . . And so it goes throughout the eastern side of the city, where most residents are black. So many of the things that residents in other parts of town take for granted—often the smallest of things—add up to make life more difficult.
>
> There are no movie theaters east of 52. No nice sit-down restaurants, superstores, choices of supermarkets, large hardware stores.
>
> "If I want to get a single nail, I got to drive over to the west side," McCarter said.
>
> *Winston-Salem Journal*

USING RACIAL IDENTIFIERS

In 1994, when four groups of minority journalists met for the first time ever at Unity '94, the Center for Integration and Improvement of Journalism at San Francisco State University published *News Watch: A Critical Look at Coverage of People of Color*. Here is an excerpt of the guidelines it set for using race in stories:

- Apply consistent guidelines when identifying people by race. Are the terms considered offensive? Ask individual sources how they wish to be identified.

- When deciding whether to mention someone's race, ask yourself: Is ethnic/racial identification needed? Is it important to the context of the story? When it is, the identification needs to be sensitive.

- Consult a supervisor if you are unsure of the offensiveness or relevance of a racial or ethnic term.

- Use sensitivity in descriptions of sites and cultural events. Avoid inappropriate comparisons. For example, Kwanza is not "African-American Christmas."

- Be specific when using ethnic or racial identification of individuals. Referring to someone as Filipino-American is preferred to calling that person Asian.

Maxwell, who is white, says he has learned a lot working on the series and consulting with Keith Woods, the black former *(New Orleans) Times-Picayune* city editor who ran his Poynter workshop. They have kept in touch.

One lesson Maxwell learned was that code words fill the news—words that stereotype entire neighborhoods or groups for readers and viewers.

"We used the term East Winston almost every day, which meant 'black Winston,'" Maxwell said of his own paper. "We didn't even think about it."

Another thing he learned was that honest conversation about race takes patience and probing.

"The most important thing is listening, really listening, to what people are saying, past the sound bite, beneath the surface. Sometimes an interview can be conducted entirely with, 'What do you mean by that?'"

A third lesson he learned was how challenging and important it was to examine his own biases and feelings. "You have to turn yourself inside out a bit," is how Maxwell puts it. "That's hard to do. You've heard the debate that everyone is racist, and I don't know that we have to come down on one side of that or the other. But everyone has had [his or her] own life experiences and everyone has different perceptions of how the world operates. We have to understand that."

STEPPING OUTSIDE OUR COMFORT ZONES

Covering diversity is a much broader issue than crossing racial divides. Middle-class reporters know little about poor neighborhoods. Those who are straight find themselves uncertain about how to cover gay and lesbian issues. And those who speak English can struggle mightily in a community where the language of choice is Mandarin or Portuguese.

Regardless of the nature of the difference—the type of experiential gap between reporter and source—the first step in bridging it is the same: Reporters must step beyond their own comfort zones and beyond the stereotypes and stereotypical sources that dictate too much of the news.

Carolyn Mungo of *KPNX-TV* in Phoenix learned those lessons at the same Poynter seminar Maxwell attended.

"When I got back I put the issue of covering race and ethnicity on the front burner," she says. "I went into communities I was not familiar with. I took it upon myself to do my own research."

Mungo also made a point of including people of color in all kinds of stories. The paper had a "Rolodex of color, so to speak," Mungo says, but it often had gone unused. Now, when doing a story about the schools or medicine or any other place or profession, Mungo says she tries harder to "put someone other than a white doctor on TV."

Other changes in her routine took more courage. Television is a medium of action and conflict. And conveying race relations honestly is a matter of capturing grays, not black and white. One day Mungo came to work to learn that there'd been a racially motivated stabbing at one of the city's large urban schools. The assignment editor told her how to respond. "They said, 'Well, Carolyn, you go out and do the story. I'm sure other schools with similar populations are concerned. I'm sure they're adding security.' It was presented as a given when I left that meeting that [heightened security] was my story."

Mungo came back with something else. She found a school with similar demographics—a mix of students black, white, Asian and Hispanic. "I went there and asked the principal, 'How do you ask 3,000 kids of different colors to get along every day?' I got into a really cool conversation. She said, 'Look, for a lot of these kids we are their family. We had an incident on the bus where a kid was shot, and we had teachers going over to the hospital.'"

And then Mungo met Willy, a big security guard who kept order at the school and befriended many of its kids. There were no metal detectors. There were no plans to add any.

HOW TO REPORT ABOUT DIVERSE POPULATIONS

Keith Woods

As city editor of *The (New Orleans) Times-Picayune,* Keith Woods helped put out a comprehensive series examining race relations there. Today, as an associate in ethics at The Poynter Institute in St. Petersburg, Fla., he is training other journalists how to improve coverage of diversity.

Iván Román spent a dozen years covering undercovered groups from the gay and Puerto Rican communities of Rochester, N.Y., to the Haitian and Cuban communities of Miami. Today, in one of his roles as director of the Center for Integration and Improvement of Journalism at San Francisco State University, he monitors coverage of diversity, keeping a keen eye out for stereotyping and other shallow or biased depictions of minority groups.

In interviews, Román and Woods talked about how reporters can more effectively cover issues of cultural differences.

"Diversity," said Woods, "is a verb instead of a noun. It is a thing you are doing rather than a thing that you have. When you are dealing with diversity, it means you are working against a force that conspires to keep things monochro-

matic. It is everything from ignorance to isms. At a minimum [this force] takes some work on the part of journalists to overcome."

Cautions Román: "Cover [groups] from their point of view. Try to assume as much as possible the role of a member of that society. That way you won't cover them as exotic people or their food as exotic food."

Reporters, he adds, need to get beyond going into communities only to cover their holidays.

What follows is a checklist for covering diversity drawn from interviews with both men:

1. **Begin with yourself.** The first step, Woods says, is for reporters to inventory their own biases. Those can be as basic as the bias men bring to serious coverage of women's sports.

2. **Educate yourself.** "Unless you go through some serious immersion, you haven't really mastered a culture," Woods says. "I have a book here that says, 'Filipinos greet each other with their eyebrows.' If I meet someone who is Filipino and I raise both eyebrows, did I just say, 'Hello' or, 'I am shocked to see you?'"

Education is a lifetime process. Woods says when he meets people of different backgrounds, he'll typically ask them the names of five books they would recommend about their culture.

"There's no great resistance [by reporters] to learning about the school system when you cover schools. But there's a tremendous resistance to learning about things such as religion or sexual orientation."

(continued)

"I came back with what I thought was a cool story," Mungo said. "There was this big black guy and even though there were white kids and Hispanic kids and Asian kids [at the school] he got along with all of them. It wasn't utopia but I thought it was a balanced story."

Her producer had hoped for a story reflecting more tension, and Mungo says it took a battle to get her story on the air. But Mungo hasn't stopped fighting that battle. Sometime later she traveled to a largely black community to cover a dedication of the city's first memorial celebrating the civil rights movement. Across the park, away from the thousands of people attending the ceremony, a scuffle broke out between two guys over a girl. There were no arrests and no weapons. And there was no connection between the event and the ceremony in the park.

Mungo decided to ignore the fight but warned her producer that other reporters would not. "I said, 'You watch the promos [before news shows], and everywhere else it will be, Mayhem at a civil rights ceremony.'"

Mungo's prediction came true.

(continued)

3. **Evaluate how your news organization is perceived**. "I found many [minority] communities had no relationship with the media," Román says. "I found myself training people how to gain access."

Or, as Woods puts it, "There aren't any press releases coming out of the average poor community."

4. **Go to new communities**. Go to a different neighborhood to have lunch. Go into diverse communities without pad in hand and questions on your tongue. "The key is not to be obtrusive," Woods says. "Do the work off deadline as much as possible so you are building sources."

5. **Immerse yourself**. Try to find a listening post in an unfamiliar community. This, says Woods, is a place where people who live there congregate. Try to find guides—people who can introduce you to other people.

"If you cover cops and you find a cop who will take you to another cop, then you have made ground in an organization that historically does not trust you," Woods says. "That is what we are talking about when a white person goes into a black neighborhood or a black person goes into a Korean neighborhood. There may be a history of distrust . . . Your task is to try to find a way to truth, so getting someone who will be a guide helps."

6. **Read alternative newspapers and ethnic presses**. This allows you to track issues in communities new to you before you arrive.

7. **Watch body language**. It can show more than words and help gauge a person's reaction.

8. **Avoid stereotypes**. Don't use stereotypical and simplistic representations of large groups that have been drawn from one or two individuals. In short, look for cultural complexity and reflect it.

9. **Aggressively seek out the news**. "The idea that news comes to us, that we don't create it, is a lie on its face," Woods says.

Román says if he were reporting on underrepresented communities again he would be more aggressive in pitching stories. "I might work to educate editors that reporters pitching stories of communities they belong to should not be seen as advocating just because they belong to communities," he says. "Do you ask a business reporter if he or she has stocks? Obviously you know they have. I think a lot of the problem is the lack of recognition by media in general that we cover white corporate America. We wouldn't ask a white middle-class male whether he would be biased about covering white middle-class males. So why would you ask me [about covering minorities]?"

10. **Don't settle for the role of outsider**. "We are trained in journalism school to cover everything as an outsider because of the objectivity thing," Román says. "What I tried to do was place myself in [my sources'] situation as much as possible, whether I was covering a Salvadoran running from his country, or a gay man afraid he'd lose his job if he said he was gay, or the Asian who was one of the few in the community.

"Some of the best journalists I've seen covering the Cuban community in Miami were not Cubans but were Anglos who learned the language and learned to cover the Cuban community as a member of that community."

Using the Internet to Cover Diverse Populations

Covering news in a diverse area can require some crash education. When Ken McLaughlin was sent out to cover the Hindi New Year in San Jose, Calif., he knew little about Hinduism and nothing about the faith's New Year. He turned to the Net.

"It is very easy to find information about cultures on the Web using *Yahoo!*," he says, referring to one of the most widely used search engines. "I found a Web page out of an encyclopedia." As usual, McLaughlin was careful. He uses information on the Internet as a tip service, not as the gospel, he says. Too much false or defective information can be found there.

McLaughlin, who specializes in coverage of San Jose's Vietnamese community, also uses the Internet to monitor trends and find sources. For example, he said, he is on an Internet mailing list discussion for readers of *Vietnamese Insight Magazine*. And he has lurked on newsgroups that discuss issues of concern to the Vietnamese-American community to find sources.

COVERING DIVERSE POPULATIONS

"I send a Usenet posting," he said. "I describe who I am. I ask, 'Can you send me your thoughts as well as where I can reach you,'" he says. "It always works."

Language is the biggest barrier on his beat, McLaughlin says, not the reticence of would-be sources. "It might be a perception that it is hard to reach and to quote minorities," he says. "I haven't found that. [The Vietnamese-Americans] are dying to be a part of American culture."

McLaughlin cautions against overreliance on people you meet online. "Most of my stories I still find the old-fashioned way," he says. "By talking to people."

COVERING LEISURE

A story in *The Orange County (Calif.) Register* on fan fanaticism and support for a California Little League team that had reached the final round in Little League play began like this:

WILLIAMSPORT, Pa.—Luck comes in odd shapes and sizes.

But it did not come Tuesday in the new Little League World Series T-shirts worn by the parents of the Yorba Hills All Stars.

Moments after the team lost its first game of the series, 8-2, to Spring, Texas, last night, Mary Ann Shappi stood in the stands and yelled, "OK, we go back to our old shirts tomorrow."

The Orange County (Calif.) Register

Two things made the story extraordinary: The paper had sent a reporter to Pennsylvania to cover a recreational league sport. And it had run the story on Page 1.

Little League as front-page news.

Yet maybe *The Register* is onto something. Visit any suburban or rural town in America and there is little people care more about than the leisure activities of kids. Visit cities and places where something other than family life dominates conversation and the discussion is far more likely to turn to movies, books, fitness and leisure activities than it is to center around business, politics or crime. The world of leisure dominates much of our waking thoughts. Just witness the hoopla that surrounds a network's decision to end a favorite television series:

It's as if we've all tacitly agreed to go crazy. On Thursday night, the cable channel TV Land will stop regular programming for an hour and hang out a sign saying it'll be back after the "Seinfeld" finale. In tomorrow's episode of "Dharma and Greg," the couple decide to have sex in public and choose the perfect time: when the rest of the world is watching the last "Seinfeld." And that's just the hype NBC is not responsible for.

The New York Times

LEISURE IS BIG BUSINESS, BIG NEWS

Covering leisure means a lot more than following the world of television, although you might not think so after spending a few days in those American households where the tube reigns virtually nonstop. It also means more than reviewing films or concerts and covering sporting events, from the Boston Marathon to Alaska's dog-sled races.

Game stories, event coverage and reviews certainly are central parts of the leisure beat. They tell consumers what they might do with their spare time and whether it's worthwhile. But when they reach the top of the news, leisure stories are more likely to be about a contract dispute or a megamerger of two movie, cable or book companies than about even the final episode of "Seinfeld."

Certainly, leisure is often big news as we enter a new century. It may be news of the NBA headed toward a strike or the New York Yankees headed toward a new stadium. It may be news about the size of a movie star's latest contract or the television ratings for the top network shows of the year.

To report this news fully and accurately, leisure reporters must bring the same skepticism, sharp questioning and sense of what's come before to their work as reporters who cover more traditional hard-news beats. That can be particularly tough in an arena where hype too often prevails and criticism isn't commonplace.

As one veteran music reporter lamented in an e-mail post to a journalism discussion group: "Substitute 'Nashville' for 'Hollywood' and you have the same situation. I have steadfastly refused to write puff pieces and to sell out. I sleep well at night, but unquestionably my pocketbook has suffered."

If the leisure beat proves to be your passion, let your pocketbook suffer, too, rather than rolling over for the legion of agents who control the world of sports and entertainment. The spin they spit out, as in all quality reporting, must be filtered through the facts and tested against the perception of competitors, analysts and other outside experts.

Single-source celebrity interviews, to put it another way, are simply not news. Actors and athletes are no less self-promoting than politicians and business CEOs. In a world swirling with hype, the good leisure reporter retains a sense of proportion.

CHANGING TRENDS MAKE NEWS, TOO

Some news on this beat, as on others, breaks or is broken by enterprising reporters who discover information about a specific action—be it a sports trade or a star's decision to leave a show. Other news is more subtle. It comes from patiently talking to sources, reading brochures and reports, and asking questions of oneself that can lead to interesting answers. It requires a keen reportorial eye and ear for the story ever to "break" at all. Here is an example that landed on Page 1:

If numbers meant as much to art lovers as they do to sports fans, the following statistic would be quoted everywhere: In any given year, New York City art museums draw far larger crowds than all New York professional sports teams combined.

The New York Times

Art museums don't dominate the culture of most cities. Here is a story about a lower-brow trend that, once again, likely was observed rather than announced.

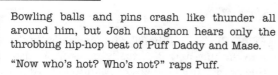

Bowling balls and pins crash like thunder all around him, but Josh Changnon hears only the throbbing hip-hop beat of Puff Daddy and Mase.

"Now who's hot? Who's not?" raps Puff.

Eyes shut, the 14-year-old Josh bobs to the music as clouds of fog swirl up the bowling lanes and arrows of laser light shoot down from the ceiling. Black lights set everything aglow, including Josh's white T-shirt.

. . . Halfway through the song, [Josh] grabs a ball and slings at the pins.

He pauses, watches his ball roll down the lane to make a spare, then starts dancing again.

"This is really fun," he says as the music lulls.

This is bowling with attitude.

Bowling alleys across the country call it "Cosmic Rock 'N' Bowl," "Extreme," or "Glow Bowling."

Teens call it "cool."

The (Syracuse, N.Y.) Post-Standard

THINGS TO READ, PEOPLE TO SEEK OUT

Mike Antonucci spends a lot of his time, both on the job and at home, doing things that might not be his first choice.

"If it were up to me I'd go to more hockey games, and watch 'Seinfeld' and go to movies I like. But doing my job means watching the TV show or going to the movie or restaurant or bar where I don't want to be but I know I need to go in order to keep track of what everyone else is doing."

His job is covering the popular culture beat at the *San Jose Mercury News*. It's a beat Antonucci, who covered sports, television and the cable industry before, invented. It's also a beat that has allowed him to write about everything from Princess Diana's death to the excitement generated by a traveling Smithsonian Institute show. And those are two of the more conventional stories.

Antonucci finds many ideas by keeping his ear cocked and his eyes open for something new to read every time he goes anywhere, from a pharmacy to fill a prescription to a store to buy his teen-age daughter new clothing.

Popular culture, after all, is vast.

"It is everything from the T-shirt you're wearing with the logo on it to the companies you work for that are cutting these licensing agreements . . . to the size, power and clout of entertainment in American culture," Antonucci says. "All of that adds up to popular culture.

"There are a lot of people who will tell you that America is about consumerism and consumerism is about entertainment," he adds. "If you step back and look at what's distinctive about America, it's what it exports in pop culture, isn't it."

Still, big as it is, popular culture is just one facet of leisure, a catch-all that could be used to describe drama critics and sports columnists, fashion writers and food writers, computing and car reporters. No single set of sources, no single set of readings fits all these beats. What we'd like to encourage is a mind-set that says whether your story appears in the food section of your paper or the entertainment block of your newscast, you'll take these steps to make sure your stories have integrity and are complete:

- **Double-check publicists' claims.** For example, ask the theater whether the upcoming new teen star concert really is sold out and what tickets will cost if it's not. Check with the editors of specialized music-industry publications on whether the performer's claim that "his latest album topped the charts longer than any album in three years" is true.

- **Cover all sides of a story.** One way to do that is to monitor fan clubs on the Internet, which often follow the ins and outs of their favorite stars better than anyone (see box, Genesis of a Story).

- **Ask for numbers and facts to support general statements.** "This show is the most successful we've had at the fairgrounds in years," makes for a nice quote. But giving the numbers for this year's main event at the State Fair and comparing those numbers to the last five years says a lot more.

In order to report in depth, leisure reporters, like those on other beats, develop strong sources in a variety of topics and learn where to look for new ones. They develop routines.

ONE LEISURE REPORTER'S SYSTEM AND SECRETS

"You want to know where I get story ideas?" Antonucci asks. "I listen. I eavesdrop. I try to get the most grass-roots tip I possibly can."

One day Antonucci was waiting in line at a discount sneaker store when he heard a conversation that pricked his imagination.

"A teen-ager walks up to one of the salespeople and says, 'Do you have the red Iverson's?' It's kind of a funny question and I had my head cocked when the salesman says, 'You can't buy them in a store. You've got to buy them in the street.' I said, 'Holy cow.'"

When he started asking around, Antonucci found that the remarkable, multimillion-dollar world of sneaker fashion had fragmented into so many specialized lines that some, indeed, are traded—sometimes between urban and suburban kids—online instead of in stores. He began a Page One story like this:

> The influential events at ground zero in U.S. fashion now include young men trading hard-to-find sneakers on Internet bulletin boards.
>
> They may be collectors. They may be gang-bangers. They may be guys watching too much MTV and BET.
>
> But whoever they are, they're fueling the buzz that, from New York City to Silicon Valley, translates street culture into routine style. They're part of an elusive, fickle process that shoe and apparel manufacturers are spending bundles trying to infiltrate.
>
> *San Jose (Calif.) Mercury News*

Antonucci looks as well as listens.

"You read until your eyes fall out," he counsels young reporters.

His own tastes? His favorite publication, he says, is called the *Comic Buyers Guide*. It's actually a group of publications—a series of magazines for collectors of everything from coins to comics.

But for Antonucci, that is just a start. He thumbs through magazines from the higher-gloss *Esquire* and *Vanity Fair* to the hipper *Rolling Stone* and *Details*. He devours *TV Guide*. He wanders the aisles of a huge Asian supermarket in San Jose that has English-language magazines covering the Pacific Rim and exports from Asia.

GENESIS OF A STORY

Reporters often can find the most interesting news tidbits by reading bulletin boards—in libraries, supermarkets and online. When he covered television for the *San Jose Mercury News,* Mike Antonucci regularly monitored Internet discussion groups. Antonucci would check the chatter about the television shows and stars he wrote about.

When *ABC-TV* canceled the popular television show, "My So-Called Life," his scrutiny paid off as Page One news. Many news reports told the sad tale of the show's talented teen-age star, Claire Danes, being put out of a job. But Antonucci knew better after finding an online post from the most active member of the show's fan club.

"He'd become so well connected during the campaign to save the show, that he had inside information about the negotiations with the lead actress," Antonucci recalls. "Because of her desire to pursue a movie career, she didn't want to come back to the show, which influenced *ABC*'s decision to cancel. I discovered that by reading a [fan club] message to other people online."

The result? "Instead of a story about *ABC* canceling this teen-age girl's vehicle, it was a story about this teen-age girl apparently betraying her fans by abandoning the show."

He taps into a Web site for the ***Sci-fi Channel*** and tracks an Internet mailing list that draws from technology-oriented publications of Ziff-Davis. He scans the newsletters of the Media Research Center, "right-of-center counterpoint to everything seen in the media," and visits another Web site, called the postfeminist ***Playground.***

And he reads newspapers: *The Wall Street Journal* ("Reporters there are smart enough to write some paragraphs of how the business thing has broader applications for culture"), his own and the one published at his daughter's high school. This he reads as much for the ads, fashions and concerns of the kids as for the stories. By covering his beat, Antonucci says, he is not only telling people what's hot and what's not but also learning about the heart of American life.

"Popular culture once was only important in terms of acknowledging that it had economic clout. I'm saying it is important in and of itself. In what it says about people's psyches, in what we imbue companies like Nike with. I am saying [popular culture] is socially and psychologically important in and of itself."

Mastering the Basic Story

Like his colleagues at *New England Cable News,* Scott Yount needs to be a jack-of-all-trades. Sometimes he covers fires, sometimes the weather. But Yount's first love is covering entertainment. And he brings a spirited and lively approach to these assignments that can be applied across all media. In covering entertainment, Yount says, he concentrates on getting beyond the facts to using storytelling skills built around what he sees, feels and senses to convey the excitement of the event.

"When you cover leisure, you don't have to prove it's true," Yount says. "A lot of your work is personal observation without being a critic. I can say, 'In the ballet tonight there were a lot of unsteady moments' without being a critic. I am making observations."

Yount's entertainment reporting covers a wide sweep. He's done pieces on a Picasso exhibit at the fine arts museum and about street performers at Harvard Square. And if one night finds him at the ballet, the next may find him at an Aerosmith concert. He offers the following advice to reporters covering the wide range of events included in popular culture, entertainment and leisure:

■ ***Remember the basics.*** Like any other piece of news, certain facts become second nature. Television viewers will want to know how many people showed up, how long the event runs, what it costs, where it is, what hours it's open and what they can expect to find. But that's not the whole story.

- **Look for a fresh angle.** The angle may be "a new album is out, they used all Boston people in the cast. Look for what's different," Yount says.

- **Capture the emotion of the event.** "On television, emotion is No. 1, right or wrong, good or bad," Yount says. "If you can capture people's emotions about the event, you've got a story. If you ask a bunch of college students, 'So what's great about Aerosmith,' they'll say, 'I don't know, ask her.' So I'll say, 'Wow. Do you believe that Aerosmith has been working on this album two years and they're opening the tour right here in Boston?' Then they'll say, 'Yeah, and blah, blah, blah' . . . With sound bites, I strive to get people's emotional viewpoints."

- **Be aware of the visual and sound images that can help convey the story.** This is essential not only in television, where the visual image can be seen, but also in radio, where sound creates visual images, and in print, where the descriptive writer can bring the reader to the scene. Yount tries to intersperse

Courtesy of New England Cable News.

In his reporting for *New England Cable News*, Scott Yount always tries to capture the emotion of the events he covers. To him, the tempo and cadence of a news story are as important as the tempo and cadence of the entertainment events he covers.

bits of the event throughout his piece. If it's a concert, he might start with a segment of sound. If it's any kind of performance, he works hard to get a strong close, or finish, to his piece from the end of a song, a dance, a line in a play. "I dog the shooter," he says, referring to the photographer who works with him.

- **Convey a sense of drama.** In covering the arts, Yount strives to give viewers a sense of the dramatic as well. This is not done by overwriting, which merely bogs down a piece with pretension. It's accomplished by thinking of the pacing and organization of the story.

"The timing and cadence [of a piece] is paramount," he says. "I try to build pieces so that each piece of track leaves you with a sense of suspense, a question and then an answer. I tell interns to look at all the pieces they have like inventorying an erector set. I've got natural sound. I've got video. I've got an interview. Only then do you put the words down and order what you've got."

All reporters in all media try to rough out an outline in their heads before writing. But Yount takes special pleasure in entertainment because it allows him, as the reporter, that much more freedom and creativity in approaching his craft.

SUMMARY   COVERING LEISURE

1. Help your audience sort out not only what events are coming up but also which ones are worth going to.

2. Look for the stories that reveal the underlying economics of leisure and how they affect consumers of leisure.

3. Be skeptical. Leisure writers should convey the excitement of sports, culture and entertainment without being mouthpieces for the agents and promoters whose job it is to make these events larger than life.

4. Try to find a fresh angle. If every entertainment story simply announces who is coming and what tickets will cost, your audience will quickly become bored.

5. Develop a wide range of sources so you can weigh the claims of actors, athletes and others looking for a glowing write-up against the reality of their actions and achievements.

COVERING RELATIONSHIPS

Some politicians, particularly of conservative bent, may still find it convenient from time to time to invoke a largely mythological image of the America of "Leave It to Beaver." You know: a simple place, where everyone married and had two kids, no one divorced, everyone lived in tidy houses with neatly trimmed shrubs, everyone was white, everyone went to a Protestant church on Sunday. But if some parts of America once looked and lived like that, odds are they don't today, even in the most bedrock, rural communities.

Our relationships and our communities are more complicated. We may have stepchildren or adopted children, share custody or visit four sets of grandparents. We may love someone of the same sex or a different race. We may define our family, in a loose sense, as a group of singles we share a house with, a group of fellow readers we chat with in a cyberspace book group or the co-workers with whom we share a long-distance commute.

Stories about the changing makeup of family and relationships in this country go well beyond trend stories and soft features. Often they are news that finds its way onto the front page, as was the case with this story:

> Mayor Rudolph W. Giuliani proposed legislation yesterday that would require the city's government to treat unmarried couples the same as those who are married, allowing them to continue as tenants in apartments leased to their partners and insuring their rights to be buried together in a city-owned cemetery . . .
>
> Mr. Giuliani's proposal, which fulfills a campaign promise he made to gay rights advocates last year, would give New York City one of the nation's broadest policies regarding domestic partnerships.
>
> *The New York Times*

Later in the story, the paper addressed an intriguing element of the mayor's proposal: He is a Republican, a member of the party that traditionally has worked the hardest to maintain the 1950s images of society.

> Several Republican leaders around the country said that they were baffled by [Giuliani's] proposal. . . .
>
> "You ask the average Republican on the street who would sponsor that kind of bill, and 99 per-
>
> cent would say a Democrat," said Chris Baker, the executive director of the Colorado Republican Party.
>
> *The New York Times*

The times, it seems, truly are a-changing.

One Beat, Varied Perspectives

Cheryl Lavin and Joel Dresang write in distant corners of what might be considered the same beat: relationships.

Lavin, a *Chicago Tribune* columnist, tells "Tales From the Front"—stories of adults seeking, recovering from or sorting through relationships. After a dozen years, her column has grown from the experiences of one divorced parent—Lavin—to encompass contributions from across the spectrum of love.

"We have letters from teen-agers, letters from people in their 70s and 80s. We hear from gays as well as straights. It's really anybody who has fallen into love and fallen out of love."

Dresang's title is family management reporter for *The Milwaukee Journal.* These days he finds himself writing a lot about the people affected by the huge upheaval in America's welfare system. But he's also written about relationships—not only of parents to kids but also of childless partners of the opposite or same sex and of families with intricate webs of relationships, from shared custody to stay-at-home dads.

"In my coverage I define families as any group of people living together with shared interests," Dresang says.

Coverage of "families," defined broadly in the way Dresang defines them, grew throughout the 1990s. When the University of Maryland's Casey Journalism Center for Children and Families conducted a survey in the middle of the decade, it found more than half of 62 newspapers and wire services had added beats devoted to coverage of families and children within three years. In broadcast, increased coverage was evident in specials but not on the nightly news.

Some stories simply tell of human foibles. Lavin, for example, told the tale of a woman who was a teacher and seamstress. Over the years she had made a lovely wardrobe for the man she dated. "He broke up with her suddenly and not very pleasantly," Lavin recalls. "She went over to his apartment with a scissors and a bottle of wine and over a couple of hours destroyed his entire wardrobe."

Some stories are sad and poignant. These stories bring to life dreary statistics, such as a sharp increase in reported child abuse in recent years, or the rise in HIV babies with no home or the lives of never-married single mothers, two-thirds of whom live in poverty.

LEARNING FROM THE PROS

INTERVIEWING VULNERABLE SUBJECTS

Joel Dresang of *The Milwaukee Journal* regularly interviews people who have no public relations representatives and aren't familiar with the ways of the media. He tries to deal with them honestly and to draw out their true thoughts and feelings, not the ones that fit a prescribed niche in his stories.

He suggests the following techniques in talking to those who don't talk with reporters every day.

- *Share something of yourself.* "Open yourself to the people you are interviewing," Dresang says. "It has to be more of a fair exchange. If they are being asked to answer intimate things about their lives, don't hesitate to answer some questions about yours."

- *Consciously try to explode stereotypes.* To grasp how many different ways people live and work means resisting the temptation to put people in boxes. One example? "The media haven't shown low-income people to be the working people that most are," Dresang says.

- *Leave your relationship open-ended.* In her years as a columnist for *The New York Times,* Anna Quindlen once referred to journalists as "hit-and-run drivers." The risk of some nasty glancing blows are high on the family and relationships beat. They can be minimized, Dresang says, by giving sources your phone numbers, making sure you keep theirs and following up regularly. Life doesn't end when your story about a family's crisis or success does. Check back. Follow up.

And some stories measure trends and changes in our culture. At *The Boston Globe,* reporter Lynda Gorov wrote about the ritual of parents and children getting reacquainted during summer months, when kids living with a divorced mom or dad visit their other parent. Her story began like this:

The whirlwind courtship lasted the entire long weekend: a baseball game, book browsing in Harvard Square, burgers on the beach in Boston, the new Batman movie, a cookout on the Cape and two sets of fireworks.

By Wednesday, Robert Mannino Jr. could say with certainty that he had won his son over again. He could tell because 9-year-old Michael was al-most begging for a few moments of father-son boredom. . . .

Like divorced parents everywhere, Mannino couldn't resist spoiling his son in the days after he arrived for an extended visit. That's part of a ritual that has become as American as outdoor barbecuing: the summer switch.

The Boston Globe

After about a year, one story came to dominate Joel Dresang's beat at *The Milwaukee Journal*: welfare reform. To Dresang, it was a human story and an economic one.

"In Wisconsin, the last welfare checks were cut last week," he said in spring 1998. "Basically we've ended welfare. What we've replaced it with is a work program that provides supports and benefits based on people's engagement in the workplace."

How well does it work? Dresang looked at the ripple effects—how could single mothers on welfare work and care for kids, how could they get to work, how did they balance work, kids and sleep? Suddenly the story resonated with many people other than the poor.

"I'm actually seeing increased support for low-income people, because now that they are working, people can relate to them," Dresang said.

The story, however, is far from a happy ending. Dresang spent 10 weeks following a welfare recipient and caseworker in the transition to the workplace. The story ended when the woman started her job. The follow-ups were less heartwarming. She's since lost the job and her kids.

"As far as trying to figure out the unintended consequences [of welfare] as they say, it's hard to say. I'm not sure push has come to shove."

THINGS TO READ, PEOPLE TO SEEK OUT

When Dresang was assigned the family management beat for *The Milwaukee Journal,* he shared the same problems of others on primarily noninstitutional beats: Where do you start to build a source list?

Dresang started by reading. First he wandered into a bookstore and leafed through magazines dealing with families. These included *Family Life, Parenting, Family PC* and *Money.* Next he considered how to build a source list. He looked through the calendars in his own newspaper and community weeklies, looking for family events to go to. He dropped by meetings of baby-sitting cooperatives and play groups, watching for a while and then approaching participants who looked as if they might talk.

"I just sort of invited myself to these things and talked about things [participants] wanted to talk about."

Dresang's research was anything but haphazard. Before long he was building his own database from the demographics of people he'd met. At one baby-sitting cooperative, for example, he handed out a questionnaire, asking the parents for names, addresses, income range, occupations and children's names and ages.

"With this database," he explains, "if an institute in New York does a study and I need to interview real people, I can just go to the files."

SUMMARY

COVERING RELATIONSHIPS

1. Keep in mind that today's "family" is a long way from the idealized version of "Leave It to Beaver." Look for stories touching on a wide range of relationships.

2. Learn the laws and regulations that affect relationships.

3. Look for sources in unconventional ways and places.

4. Treat sources unfamiliar with the media with particular sensitivity. Follow up on initial stories to see how things have changed.

5. Show something of yourself. Reporters can't expect people to reveal details of their intimate or personal lives if the reporters in turn disclose nothing about themselves.

Dresang also worked to educate himself. He attended experts' conferences, expanding his source list along the way. He got on mailing lists of local organizations dealing with issues of families. And he read the research—and introduced himself to the authors—coming out of such places as the Institute for Research on Poverty at the University of Wisconsin in Madison. Finally, he worked himself through the federal, state and local bureaucracies that apply to his beat, tapping into Web sites for those agencies that are online.

COVERING SPIRITUALITY AND ETHICS

Even as the 1990s came to a close, Michelle Bearden was poised to report in a new century. Bearden traveled to Cuba in 1998 for the pope's historic visit. She spent some of her time standing before a camera and some sitting before a keyboard. As usual, her stories appeared in print in the *Tampa (Fla.) Tribune*, on the air for *WFLA-TV* and across the country at *NBC* affiliates.

Bearden predicts a boom in religion reporting on television in the years ahead. And she loves working in two media.

"With the newspaper I get to tell the whole nuts and bolts," she says. "It lets me go in depth. But I can't imagine not doing TV now because the visual is so important and it brings the subject alive."

Taken broadly, the modern religion beat—which we call spirituality and ethics because its scope is greater than traditional religious institutions—"has so many stories it never ends," Bearden says.

"Every reporter in the newsroom should know a little bit about religion," she says.

What Bearden knows is this: To succeed on her beat she needs a curiosity that brings freshness to events that happen every year, a knowledge of history and a sensitivity to others' beliefs. Nothing means more to people and nothing is more personal and often private than issues of faith.

"Whether they are Bahais, Baptists or Buddhists, I will listen and learn what role faith plays in people's lives," she says. "You aren't only dealing with hard facts, you are dealing with heart. You have to be unbelievably neutral and objective."

Michelle Bearden

Beyond the Religion Page

Bearden finds plenty of news on the spirituality and ethics beat: international news such as the pope's historic visit to Cuba; regional and national news such as accusations that the head of the National Baptist Convention skimmed money from his church; local news, such as the Tampa Bay church without a congregation that turned over its facility to a congregation without a church.

She keeps an eye out for the unconventional. Here is how Bearden started a piece on an unusual, and spiritual, way to deal with bike theft:

TAMPA—When his stepson's bike was stolen not once, but twice, Russell Johnson couldn't help but get mad.

Instead of getting even, he got inspired.

That's how God's Pedal Power Ministries began.

"I had all this emotion bottled up and I wanted to put it into something good for the community," says Johnson, whose lanky 6-foot-7 frame fills a room. "Something that would make a difference for the better."

He makes it sound so simple: Do something good for the community. Focus on what can be done, instead of stewing about what doesn't happen. But few people are willing to make the commitment Johnson has.

Since July, Johnson and a loyal group of volunteers have sponsored a bike giveaway on Saturdays at University Baptist Church. Their target: kids and adults who have had their bikes stolen or can't afford one.

The Tampa Tribune

A Fresh Take on Tradition

Enterprise is one of Bearden's special skills. It takes originality and imagination to do stories on holidays that come up every year in a way that gives them fresh meaning. At Ramadan, for example, Bearden did a story on what it felt like to be a Muslim teen in a public high school. At Easter, a time of rebirth, she told the story of a former nun who had left her order in her 50s and changed her life by adopting children with medical problems. And at Rosh Hashana, she told the story of a local Jewish radio show.

"I think you lose it if you stick with theology and philosophy," says Bearden of her penchant to look for human stories that convey religious ideas. "I wouldn't want to read a story about Jewish theology unless maybe I'm Jewish. But if I can read about this great funny guy who has a Jewish radio show, I'm able to educate my readers a lot more. I'm able to break down barriers. To me that's important."

Breaking barriers. Educating. Understanding. Three concepts at the core of the spirituality and ethics beat.

Bringing Religion to the TV Screen

The image of a person in prayer or a pastor on a pulpit may seem static. It is hard to make people's beliefs visual. And it can be seen as intrusive to interfere with their religious observances. But neither is a deterrent to Bearden, who considers religion to be a colorful and visual beat.

"I have learned to be extremely creative," she says. "Showing a church steeple is not going to fill up a minute and a half. You have to be bold and go where cameras have not always gone."

That has included taping a bris—the circumcision ceremony common in the Jewish religion. It has included recording women's sacred circles—the chants, prayers and candles that are part of the rituals of this New Age spirituality movement.

When she journeyed to Cuba, Bearden, who was raised a Roman Catholic, knew the story encompassed more than the people of one faith. She looked at broader issues of freedom of religion in Cuba and discovered the country's Jewish population was nearly extinct. And there she found a visual story.

"We went to the one synagogue still in operation and my [videographer] got some great shots of it falling apart. I was able to do a voice-over and say, 'Times have been tough.' I don't say that the paint is peeling because you can see that. Then there was a prayer service, and they let us go in and hear the sound of the chanting and I say, 'But they still hang together. They're not extinct.' Then there were kids who do Israeli folk dancing, and the kids did some dancing and I say, 'Now things are coming alive. Youth are bringing it back.'"

An oversimplified recounting? Sure, but Bearden says she has learned that strong visuals and sound are central components of a strong television story. Accompanied by succinct, clear writing and selective details that expand on the visuals, the pictures can take viewers to the scene in ways her newspaper stories cannot.

TOMORROW'S REPORTER

The way Michelle Bearden sees it, hers is almost the perfect job. Her stories for television, she says, improve her writing for print. Her stories for the newspaper enable her to go into depth she's not able to on television. And her beat—spirituality and ethics—allows her to write stories for all sections of the newspaper and all segments of the newscast.

Bearden gives us a taste of how much fun reporting will be in the new century: The boundaries of departments peel away just as the boundaries of a single medium do. Bearden delights in talking about the different stories she has written. There was the business cover on business executives who credit faith for their success. There was the sports story on a Christian coach. And the Page One story, which ran on the National Day of Prayer, of a little convent where the nuns said prayers for people who were too busy to say them for themselves. That story ran nationwide.

"Most religion writers will tell you we think we've got the best beat in the world. We can go into all areas: Education, politics, social issues."

SETTING A NEW STANDARD

Joan Connell would agree with Bearden. She came to the spirituality and ethics beat at the *San Jose (Calif.) Mercury News* in the mid-1980s when it still was considered the "boneyard beat" on many newspapers. ("That's where they sent the burned-out reporters and punished them by having them do obits and God," she jokes.)

Connell instead saw religion and ethics as an integral part of news and a beat that afforded her the chance to define her work as "local, global and cosmic." It's a mind-set she later carried to the *Newhouse News Service,* where she was a national correspondent covering the moral dimension of public culture, and to the *Religion News Service,* where she was editor. Today she is opinion editor at *MSNBC* in Seattle.

When she started covering spirituality and ethics, the models Connell saw in other papers were this: "People had done a good job of religion, but it was basically keeping track of institutions."

Connell broke from convention. She wrote about the ethics of surrogate mothering and in vitro fertilization. She wrote about business ethics. When the Gulf War started, she wrote a piece called "Bombing the Cradle."

"Our missiles were bombing and destroying the artifacts of civilization," she recalls. "It was a religion story, a morality story and an ethics story all in one. And completely off the news. That's the way you've got to do it. [Good spirituality and ethics reporting] gives depth and dimension to the news."

But depth and dimension, Connell warns, must be grounded in education. She urges those interested in writing about spirituality and ethics to seek a broad-based educational foundation.

"You have to come to journalism not with an idea of what an inverted pyramid lead is but with an idea of not just Western civilization but world culture," she says.

That learning process continues throughout a career. Connell has had a fellowship at Yale University to study ethics and another fellowship at the University of Hawaii, where she studied Eastern religion and culture.

Not everyone approaching a religion story has Connell's grounding. She offers four tips for getting things right:

- Have a reason for the story.
- Check your biases at the door, "so you can hear and see and understand what the people you are writing about believe."
- Treat subjects with the utmost respect. "When you are writing about somebody's spiritual life, it's not like you are asking them their age and address and what they do for a living. It's what a person holds most dear."
- Avoid simple characterization. "How would you feel if somebody was to carelessly say in two sentences what you believe? You really have to be careful with characterization."

She might have added a fifth: Know the unique language of religion. Even the God beat has its jargon and it's awfully embarrassing to flub it. See the box, Tips on Terms for the Spirituality and Ethics Beat.

PEOPLE TO SEEK OUT

OK, you've visited local churches, synagogues and mosques. You've introduced yourself to the clergy, connected with the youth group leaders, contacted the social action committees and the congregation's lay leaders. But where as an outsider do you find the experts on this beat if you're assigned a story, for example, about an argument among different branches of the same faith?

For the quick-hit story, Connell recommends contacting **Profnet** (see Chapter 4), the central clearinghouse of public information officers at universities, think tanks and corporations around the world. But that's just a start. To build a list of experts, she suggests contacting the **American Academy of Religion**, in Atlanta, or going to universities and asking what experts are on the faculty in the areas of interest.

TIPS ON TERMS FOR THE SPIRITUALITY AND ETHICS BEAT

No reporter writing about sports would make the mistake of referring to the Dallas Giants. Talking about a Baptist priest is just as bad. Here are a few tips to keep you from becoming red in the face when you're writing about spirituality:

1. **Call them by the right name**. The Jewish faith doesn't have ministers. It has rabbis. The spiritual leaders for Muslims are called imams. Only the Roman Catholic, Episcopal and (Christian) Orthodox churches use the term "priest." If you want a term for all, the best one to use is "clergy."

2. **There's no such thing as a Reverend**. Don't use Reverend as a noun. So you wouldn't write, "the reverend says . . ." It's a title, such as "the Honorable." The correct term to use is "The Reverend Edward Jones," not "Reverend Edward Jones."

3. **Only Roman Catholics celebrate Mass**. The proper term for other Christian groups is "worship." For Jews,

it's "services," and Muslims gather for "congregational prayer." Houses of worship vary from being called mosques (Muslim) to churches (Christian) to synagogues or temples (Jewish). You can call them all "congregations."

4. **Ecumenical is not interfaith**. Christian congregations, such as United Methodists and Presbyterians, might run a soup kitchen together in an ecumenical alliance, a term used among Christians. But if those same Presbyterians are joining with Muslims to sponsor after-school tutoring, it's called interfaith because two religions are involved.

5. **Crack a history book**. It helps to know that Islam, Judaism and Christianity all trace their roots to the same person: Abraham. It also helps to know that all congregations of the same faith tradition are not alike. Sort out the differences among conservative, mainline and liberal branches. Southern Baptists, for example, are conservative. American Baptists are more liberal.

VERIFYING LINKS

Since moving to *MSNBC,* veteran journalist Joan Connell has learned that being an ethical journalist involves more than what you put in your story. In the world of online news, she discovered the hard way, the links a story makes to other stories say something about the quality of the producer's own work. Connell was writing a piece about the right to die tied to the death of author James Michener.

"I was writing about a guy who lucidly chose to die," she says. "He was dying on his own, said I'm tired of this dialysis and pulled the plug. A lot if it was being talked about on the Internet. I just decided to write about the end of life."

As is standard practice at the online news organization, Connell, after finishing her piece, looked for Internet sites to which she could link, or connect, readers. Up popped a Web site for something called the Open Society Foundation.

"I said, this looks interesting," she recalls and thought little more of it. Later she learned the site was backed by an advocate of physician-assisted suicide. This disturbed Connell, who didn't want to proselytize for anyone's viewpoint under the veil of journalistic objectivity.

"On *MSNBC* we have a little caveat that says we are not responsible for a link's content," Connell says. "Well, I disagree. We are responsible for giving readers an intelligent set of choices to link to."

In this case, she added, "I felt bad. I didn't really understand what was behind what I had set up. You have to balance your links and explain what they stand for."

Other sources include

- The ***Religion Newswriters Association***, a group of reporters covering religion.
- The Internet. "Every denomination from the Vatican to Zoroastrians have Web sites," Connell says, "which can really help in covering an international story." During the Rwandan genocide, she says, a group called ***InterAction*** provided better field reports over the Web from disaster workers in that country than those the wire services could get out.
- Ethicists.

As a reporter who has written about everything from the culture of lying in Washington to the ethics of environmental preservation, Connell taps a wide range of sources. She has two warnings. The first is to know the funding behind fancy names. Some supposedly objective ethicists have an ax to grind. The other is to approach any story on ethics by looking at three things: a person's intent (or motive), that person's means, or methods, and the outcome of an action. These tools help a reporter frame an issue, she says.

"What did Terry Nichols intend to do?" she asks about the lesser of the Oklahoma City bombing defendants, a man who escaped a first-degree murder conviction. "What are the ethics of that verdict? How did he do it and what was the outcome? The jury said he didn't intend to kill those people. God knows what his intent was. They couldn't figure it out. What were his means? He carried the fertilizer around. What was the outcome . . . 168 people died and a nation was terrorized. It helps you frame the question."

THINGS TO READ

It takes scholarship, curiosity and a hunger to read and learn to educate yourself about all the world's religions. This, in short, is not a beat for the nonreader. A good Bible or two undoubtedly will come in handy. So will the Koran. But covering this beat takes far more than reading the words of faith. It means understanding history, tradition, evolving belief and scholarship.

Two magazines, *Christian Century* and *Christianity Today,* follow issues in the dominant religions in the United States. Wander through the religion section of a large bookstore and look for comparable publications for religions that interest you or are the subject of your research. Odds are you'll find some.

COVERING SPIRITUALITY AND ETHICS

1. Think of the stories on this beat as ones that belong anywhere in the newspaper and anywhere on the newscast. Cover spirituality and ethics as they influence people's daily lives.

2. Read, then read some more. Religion is rich in history and filled with scholarship.

3. Look for new ways to cover the traditions and holidays that return like clockwork each year. Teach your audience about other people's beliefs by telling stories that show spirituality through the practices and experiences of people.

4. Be sensitive to and knowledgeable of people's beliefs. Nothing is more personal than faith. Do your homework beforehand.

5. Go beyond the clergy when developing sources. Talk to ethicists and scholars, to religious activists and agnostics. Recognize the divisions that exist within as well as between congregations. And look as hard for cooperation and conciliation as for division.

Books that help with understanding, sources and context should find their way onto the shelves of any reporter planning to devote much time to what Connell calls her "local, global and cosmic" beat. Here are some key books Connell recommends:

- Yearbook of American and Canadian Churches—Published annually by the National Council of Churches, this book contains information about every denomination and its membership, religious associations and religious periodicals. An indispensable source of contact names and numbers.

- HarperCollins Dictionary of Religion—This is a basic encyclopedia of religion written with the assistance of scholars from the American Academy of Religion.

- "How to be a Perfect Stranger: a Guide to Etiquette in Other People's Religious Ceremonies," by Arthur J. Magida.

- "With God on Our Side: The Rise of the Religious Right in America," by William Martin.

- "A Generation of Seekers," by Wade Clark Roof—This book chronicles the spiritual journeys of the baby-boom generation.

RECOMMENDED READING

Biagi, S., & Kern-Foxworth, M. (1997). *Facing difference: Race, gender, and mass media.* Thousand Oaks, CA: Pine Forge Press.

This anthology of articles from both the popular press and academic sources covers a wide range of topics such as power and the media, words as weapons, and how the media reflect who we are. Edited by two master teachers of courses on race, gender and the media.

Dart, J. (1998). *Deities & deadlines: A primer on religion news coverage* (2nd ed.). Nashville, TN: Freedom Forum First Amendment Center. [Online]. Available: **http://www.freedomforum. org/newsstand**.

From reading references to religious sources, this 20-page report tells you how to find your way around the religion beat. Need to find the Council on Islamic Education? Look here. Want a good source for the nonreligious? Try Freedom From Religion in Madison, Wis. A good practical guide.

Funabiki, J. (project director). (1995). *News watch: A critical look at coverage of people of color, Unity '94.* San Francisco: Center for the Integration and Improvement of Journalism.

This 55-page report, compiled for the first joint convention of four minority journalism organizations, takes a hard look at some of the stereotypes still prevalent in mainstream media. It also suggests ways to teach diversity effectively in the classroom.

Harrington, W. (1997). *Intimate journalism: The art and craft of reporting everyday life.* Thousand Oaks, CA: Sage Publications.

This book, filled with marvelous narrative tales, celebrates the art of telling stories about everyday life. It is filled with annotated, award-winning stories about everything from a man who could not read to a girls' high school basketball team. "What's so baffling to me," writes Harrington in his prologue, "is why we can't include in our reports more of the everyday worlds in which we and all our readers live."

EXERCISES

A. RESEARCH

1. Visit a place that caters to members of a community in which you don't spend much time. It could be a community of seniors or teens, young mothers at a play group, or gay or lesbian couples, racial or ethnic minorities or a religious group unfamiliar to you. Ask people there how the media are covering their community. Do they read about their concerns in print, see those concerns addressed on television, hear stories about their issues on radio? Ask them what stories they think are severely undercovered and what stories about their community are covered too much.

2. Visit a religious, ethnic or racial community with which you have had no experience.

   a. Before going, write down any biases or preconceptions you hold about this community. Be honest with yourself. It is often necessary to recognize bias or stereotypes before we can report effectively on areas with which we are unfamiliar.

   b. Carry a notebook in your back pocket, but don't go with any story in mind. Read bulletin boards, listen to conversations, observe. Note anything that you find unusual and possibly worth following in a story.

   c. Without checking your notes, write down what surprised you when you return home. Has anything made you reevaluate preconceived ideas?

3. Identify an organization in an unfamiliar cultural, racial, religious or ethnic community. Set up an appointment with its director, and after reading background information about the organization, interview that individual. Ask what the organization's goals are, what obstacles it has faced in achieving those goals and what solutions it is now trying. Ask how the community or organization it is in has changed over the last five years. Ask where people in the community go and whom they talk to when they need assistance or advice.

4. Take a guided tour of an unfamiliar community, relying on a new source from your organizational interview or on someone else recommended by that organization's leader. When you return, write down everything that surprised you. Then write down any stories that you think the tour has identified.

5. Go out and gather reading materials from a religious, racial or ethnic community with which you are unfamiliar. These should include community newspapers, organizational newsletters and fliers posted on bulletin boards. You should also use a search engine to find information about the group online, including relevant mailing lists, newsgroups or forums (see Chapter 4). After gathering this material, brainstorm possible story ideas with classmates.

6. Spend an afternoon at a senior center. Ask the residents there what their concerns are and how those concerns have changed over the last five years.

7. Spend an afternoon hanging out with a group of teens. You might observe an academic or sports club at a school, chat with a group at the mall or find a teen center. Ask teens how their parents can do a better job of letting them grow up. Ask them what they think about the way teens are treated in school and in the media. Ask them how things should be changed so that they'd be taken more seriously.

8. Go to the library or a large magazine stand and read through a half-dozen leisure or popular culture magazines for an age group or on a topic you know little about. Jot down at least five story ideas that you'd like to follow up for your student newspaper.

B. BASIC STORIES

1. Write either stories or memos based on the following assignments.

a. Attend an event such as a concert, a play or a show of some kind. Look for some element that makes this event different from others. Try to find a story around that difference. Be sure to include basic information such as the location, cost, time and audience size. Capture the emotion of the event by interviewing at least three people who attended.

b. In advance of a religious holiday you know little about, look for a fresh way of approaching the story, perhaps by looking at changes in how it's celebrated or at the story of one individual or family. Include sufficient background so that readers, listeners or viewers unfamiliar with the holiday will learn something from your story.

c. Visit the U.S. Census Bureau's Web site (see box, Clipboard). Read the bureau's recent press releases under "news." Using information from the site as a starting point, develop a story idea about a census-related announcement or trend.

d. Set up an interview with the director of a food bank that provides services to poor families. Ask the director how things have changed over the last five years. Ask if donations are up or down and why. Ask if the nature of those seeking free meals has changed. Ask if the number of people has changed. Use your interview to build information for a story on how food services for the poor are changing.

e. Find out whether your campus has a multicultural center. Explore how the center came about, who funds it and how well it's serving the community, or look into efforts to bring such a center to the campus.

f. Talk to college students about what they do for fun. Look for a story angle about a place that's a hot spot on campus or a trend story about a form of leisure—from bowling to ultimate frisbee—that's growing in popularity on your campus.

C. ENTERPRISE STORIES

1. Arrange to spend a full day observing and following a religious leader in your community. Concentrate on how that individual found her faith and how she tries to instill that faith in others. Ask the individual about the greatest challenge she ever faced and how she overcame it. Then write a profile based on a day in the life of that religious leader. Bring in observations, dialogue and discussion with others you meet during the day.

2. Use the Census Bureau's Web page (see box, Clipboard) to track changes in the number of interracial couples in the United States. After tracking the changes over the last decade, interview interracial couples in your community and ask them about their experiences. Do they face prejudice? From their own families or within their communities? Are things better today than they were when the couple first got together? What unique challenges do they face as parents?

3. Write a feature story about the workplace benefits at different employers for unwed partners of the same or different genders. Is the number of employers extending such benefits increasing or decreasing? What efforts are being made to provide those benefits? What is the reaction of political and religious leaders in your community?

4. Write a feature story on the availability of day care for infants in your community. Does your campus provide such facilities for working parents there? What problems do working mothers and fathers with primary responsibility for infants and toddlers face? How do they overcome them?

What pressures are being placed on the university to expand its own services?

5. Spend an afternoon at a senior center. Use the time as a starting point for writing a story about the stereotypes older people are subjected to.

6. Develop a project that looks into your university's rhetoric and performance in issues of diversity. Does the university have any written policy or statement encouraging diversity on campus? In what way? Does the curriculum have any requirements that teach students about people of different racial, religious or ethnic backgrounds? How do the numbers of tenured minority administrators and faculty compare to those at comparable campuses? What efforts does the university make to recruit and retain nonwhite students?

CHAPTER 12

Learning

Working the education beat once meant little more than skimming stories off the school board agenda and setting up systematic chats with the school superintendent and school principals. Those stories, pressed on newsprint or broadcast from car radios, usually covered the party line and tended to be institutional and often superficial in approach.

The more savvy education reporters gradually began spending less time in the district's boardrooms and more in its myriad classrooms. They began capturing the voices of teachers and students to tell stories of how learning was (or wasn't) taking place.

Today the learning beat is continuing to evolve, not so much in how it's covered but in who and what are covered. In an age of downsizing and new technologies, more frequent career changes and waves of new immigrants, even formal learning no longer stops at age 18 or 22. It's a lifelong process. That's why we're calling this chapter "Learning" rather than "Education." The topic has broadened far beyond what's happening inside a school or on a college campus.

What's happening in children's classrooms remains the meat and potatoes of this beat. But reporters earning their marks in the new century will be mingling with single parents in required work-for-welfare programs, too. They'll be chatting with displaced homemakers picking up computer skills at a job center and watching as a volunteer helps an adult refugee sound out strange syllables in a new language.

The Syracuse Newspapers, photo by David Lassman.

Even kindergarteners get their day to graduate at Frazer Elementary School in Syracuse, N.Y.

In this chapter you will:

- Meet reporters in print, radio and TV who share their best tips for writing stories about the core of this beat—covering grades K-12 and higher education

- Expand your concept of how to cover education by looking at how learning is going on in the workplace

- Learn about how to construct four of the basic stories most reporters cover on the learning beat

- Hear about how some of the best reporters in the country go in depth with enterprise stories about learning at all age levels

PEOPLE TO SEEK OUT

As we've told you elsewhere, people bring ideas to life. That's why Zenaida Gonzalez of the *Marin (Calif.) Independent Journal* spends a lot of time talking to people whenever she visits a school. The experiences of these people fill stories with examples. But by just wandering around, Gonzalez also finds great stories about people themselves.

One day while visiting a San Rafael, Calif., school, Gonzalez followed her ears to some scratchy violin music wafting out of a fourth-grade classroom. As she talked to students and teachers there, she found herself in the midst of a wonderful human interest story. A local musician, who had heard the school had no money for music, had rounded up his musician buddies to come in and teach for free. It turned out someone had done the same thing when he was an elementary student in Mexico. He was just giving back.

Gonzalez and other K-12 reporters make it a practice to get into schools regularly. "I drop by a school just to chat and observe," she explains—and, sometimes, to be surprised by the sounds of something like music. But if some of the best stories are found in students' conversations and school corridors, others still start in those boardrooms the old-fashioned education reporters never left.

Zenaida Gonzalez of the Marin Independent Journal (Calif.) advises reporters new on the learning beat to always ask when they don't understand, "Be honest and say, 'hey, I'm new, tell me a little about what this issue is about.'"

GOVERNING BOARDS

In public school systems, the policy makers are elected and sit on a board of education. At the college level, these people are known as trustees or regents. Private colleges are governed by trustees as well, but they aren't selected through the political process. Don't be surprised to hear political as well as educational agendas when you meet with these folks. Reporter Brian Cofer made a point of sitting down individually with every board member when he started covering education for the Beaumont (Texas) Enterprise. He asked them their concerns.

"It was interesting how many different things seven people could tell you," Cofer recalls. "I learned a lot real fast."

The African-American board members were concerned about the quality of education in the majority black schools. The white board members worried that the predominately white schools would get less money amid efforts to address decades of historic injustice. One member told Cofer he was fighting for the school in his neighborhood; another fretted about busing.

Self-interest doesn't surface in only K-12 education. Corporate training programs serve the agendas of higher-ups too. Anne Lewis, a free-lancer in the Baltimore area, says young reporters should be skeptical when business sources portray their companies as altruistic in funding workplace learning.

"Reporters need to go beyond rhetoric and beyond the 'we're doing this because it's for the good of the community' and look at whether there's a tight labor market and that's why businesses are getting involved in programs such as this," Lewis says.

Those covering adult learning and workplace training should expand their source files to include such people as human resource managers, private industry councils and business coalitions that manage federal dollars earmarked for training. For Robin Farmer, veteran education reporter at the Richmond (Va.) Times-Dispatch, the policy makers who matter still sit on school boards. That is why she spends more time than she'd like to admit at their meetings. Although these meetings can drone on for hours, Farmer says she often gets exclusive stories because other media don't bother to come.

"I broke this story about a principal at a predominantly black school assigning every white child to the same classroom," says Farmer. "She said it was for their social and emotional comfort."

The story made the front page and was picked up by the wires. How did she find it? Merely by perking up her ears during the public comment section of the board meeting. Here's part of her story:

An outraged parent has accused Bellevue Model Elementary School's principal of segregating black and white pupils, and he wants the Richmond School Board to investigate.

. . . His wife Valerie said that all white pupils in the same grade have been placed in one class—

with a white teacher—during the three years their son has attended the school.

Richmond Times-Dispatch

The parents' complaints led to a federal civil rights investigation. The school board changed the policy and reassigned the students at midyear.

STAFF AND TEACHERS

While Farmer's story about a flap inside a school came from a meeting of the district's top elected officials, Zenaida Gonzalez got much of her fodder for a story involving a district's top officials by tapping those toward the bottom of the sourcing ladder. Reporting works that way.

Gonzalez had heard a rumor that a much beloved teacher at one school was being forced out by the administration. She called two sources with whom she'd exchanged numbers on a visit to the school: the school secretary and janitor. The calls paid off. They tipped her to a memo that had circulated, so when she called the district superintendent, she could say, "I know there was a memo issued, tell me what's going on."

In addition to staff, other must-have sources on this beat are teachers, trainers and professors. And to really understand what they are doing, says Jody Becker of *WBEZ-FM,* Chicago, observing in a classroom is essential.

"Go into the classroom and see how un-black-and-white it is," she says.

Becker spent a whole morning in an elementary classroom before interviewing the teacher at lunch for a story on bilingual education, often a controversial issue. She found she could ask better questions after having seen the students learning up close. Becker says she's covered several beats and finds that teachers are among the most accessible of sources.

"Even when you are profiling the school that's the worst in the city, these teachers have dedicated their careers to trying to change a school like that," Becker says. "They're doing work that is noble and tend to be more open than you might expect."

In the workplace, the teachers may have different titles. For example, in an article on what skills workers need to learn to keep jobs in the 21st century, *Chicago Tribune* jobs columnist Carol Kleiman quoted a sociology professor, two futurists, a labor economist, the director of an employment center, an author and the head of the trade association of trainers.

Reporters watching workplace learning might want to attend the monthly get-together of corporate trainers or human resource managers. In like manner, those covering higher education ring up members of the faculty council (a representative body of the faculty) or officials with the union to help them generate stories.

PARENTS

Quick: What is the largest and most passionate group of readers about learning? You've got it—parents.

Because of their interest and their involvement in schools and their kids' lives, parents also can be key sources. Parents will know if students continue to learn by rote despite the district's boast that it will "emphasize writing in all classes." Parents hear about the good teachers and the bad. Parents hear about it if the school has suspended kids for drinking on a Model United Nations trip, even though it's not the kind of information administrators put out in a press release.

So where do you meet them? Gonzalez makes a point of going to parents night and other social functions at school.

"Parents feel more comfortable talking to me in those kinds of settings," she explains, "And by being more visible in the community, people tend to be more comfortable with you and will call you."

She takes down parents' phone numbers so when something happens related to a school, she knows whom to call.

Most schools have active **PTAs** or **PTOs**, parent-teacher associations or organizations. Get to know their leaders and get on the mailing list for their newsletters. These can tell you about everything from fund drives for saving the band to letter-writing campaigns for reinstituting driver's education as part of the school curriculum.

One other tip: When you start the learning beat, ask about ways in which parents are active in the schools. Districts and teachers that attract parents as volunteers and make good use of them tend to be healthier than districts that keep parents at arm's length. An early feature on a particularly effective parental volunteer program can help develop sources to tap the next time a crisis comes up that the district office isn't anxious to talk about.

COMMUNITY SOURCES

When Anne Lewis wrote a story on the basic learning skills needed by workers reentering the workplace, she, too, went beyond their classroom. She called on personnel managers at local companies to see what these workers needed to know before they could be hired. Lewis, a free-lancer who specializes in workplace learning, regularly branches into the community. For a story on adult reading levels, for example, she would call the local literacy council. For a piece on teaching non-English speakers, she found a business whose sole purpose was to help hotels learn how to work with employees who had difficulty reading things such as labels on cleaning fluids.

 **ETHICS** ## TRUSTING SOURCES

Education reporter Brian Cofer, now with the *Arkansas Democrat Gazette,* once developed a background source, a person he could go to for explanation, but whose name never appeared in his stories.

"This guy was a local businessperson who knew everybody and everything going on in this town," says Cofer.

The source proved very helpful many times. But then came the exception. Cofer heard people gossiping that the president of the local college was about to be fired. His background source confirmed it, and even the college president told Cofer he thought he was about to be canned. So Cofer wrote a story saying the board of regents (the governing body for the college) was going to fire the president that day.

It never happened.

"Part of me thinks I was on the right track and got used," says Cofer. "I felt kind of stupid, frankly."

He thinks he might have been a pawn of those who wanted to keep the president and tried to preempt board action by getting the story in the paper. Or the regents might have been floating a trial balloon to gauge public reaction. Whatever the reason, Cofer ended up embarrassed.

"You've just got to be so careful to look for hidden agendas," warns Cofer.

When reporters rely on anonymous sources, they make it easier for sources to plant those hidden agendas without any repercussions for the source. And even when sources are on the record, predictions are a dangerous business in the news, as Cofer learned.

Community sources also fill the phone lists of mainstream education reporters. In his first months at the *Beaumont (Texas) Enterprise,* Brian Cofer sought out people and groups interested in education, such as the Black Ministerial Alliance and the Chamber of Commerce, which had organized an education committee.

"They said, 'This is our work force,' and they were trying to stem the white flight from the schools," Cofer explains.

Community activists such as taxpayer groups and special interest organizations should be in the source file as well. Organizations such as a council for children with special needs will be tuned to needs of disabled children and adults, while a local Latino organization may be working on teaching English and job skills to immigrants. Be sure to connect with local nonprofit organizations, such as Girls Inc. or Big Brothers/Big Sisters, that run after-school programs for kids.

STUDENTS

Most of you reading this text haven't been out of high school all that long. You can remember being "in the know" about what was really going on in the school's corridors and cafeteria. You probably have ideas for some good stories on your current campus, too. Students, after all, see the daily reality of any learning environment. They are the consumers. They can separate the pronouncements of those in charge from the performance of those in the classroom. And that, says Robin Farmer of the *Richmond (Va.) Times-Dispatch* is why they are great sources.

"Kids will tell you everything they know," she says. "And that's crucial when you find out someone brought a gun to school and it's 6 p.m."

As you read and listen to news coverage, do you see the youth viewpoint? Probably not enough. That is because reporters don't do a good enough job of seeking it out. So when the education team at *The (Syracuse, N.Y.) Post-Standard* sat down to develop goals for beat reporters, high on the list was a commitment to including students' comments in as many stories as possible.

Like any other sources, students need to be cultivated. Spend time hanging around the schools and talking to kids after school and off deadline. Volunteer to talk to classes and clubs. Be sure to give them a number where they can call you, and get home numbers, cellular phone numbers and beeper numbers where you can call them. And as with other sources, ask them what students they most respect and think you should add to your source list.

Schools are no more homogenous than any other part of society. Yet reporters too often gravitate to student leaders, great students, great athletes and "bad kids." Look for a broader range. Some students are into art, others into voluntarism. Some visit from foreign countries or have visited them. Some struggle but work extra hard to make it. Some have a gift for math, others for rebuilding cars. They come from a range of racial, ethnic and economic backgrounds. Don't, in short, just look for the kids who seek out reporters or are comfortable talking with them.

But don't ignore this group either. No sources in schools are better than the kids who work for the student paper. That is why Jayne Noble Suhler of *The Dallas Morning News* seeks them out in covering higher education.

"The editor and reporters at the student newspaper really know what is going on," she explains. "They understand the business. They are great resources."

One day she heard Southern Methodist University reporters were working on a story about an uprising among the SMU journalism faculty. She rang them up.

INTERVIEWING STUDENTS

Sharon Stevens

A school superintendent once banned Sharon Stevens of *KSDK-TV,* St. Louis, from school property for several weeks after she aired a story on a brewing controversy over the use of a prayer at graduation. The superintendent refused to talk to her about it and became incensed when she did the story anyway.

"The superintendent hears I'm talking to kids outside and he's just furious," she says. "He said, 'How dare you; you didn't tell me you were going to talk to students.' I said that I don't think I have to tell you."

Legally, Stevens was most likely on firm ground as long as she was interviewing students on public streets or sidewalks. But ethically, reporters must think about which topics are appropriate for interviewing students of various ages.

Few if any reporters would have a problem talking to seniors about the graduation day prayer. But when young children opened fire in a middle school, as happened in Jonesboro, Ark., reporters debated whether they should camp out on school grounds the following week to get student reaction.

Here are some guidelines on talking with schoolchildren:

1. **Ask questions you know the child has the knowledge to answer.**

   After the Jonesboro shooting, a "Today" show anchor asked students in a live interview why they thought the two boys opened fire. That isn't a question they could possibly answer.

2. **Allow a lot of time for the interviews.**

   Kids like to converse. They expect you to tell them something about yourself as well as pull information from them. It takes time to build trust.

   "Sometimes I see colleagues who really don't give kids a chance to answer," Stevens says. "You have to be very patient with children. I think it's important that you look encouraging, not threatening, and get down at their eye level."

3. **Don't print or air everything kids blurt out.**

   "Children will tend to tell you a lot more than they should," says Bill Graves of *The (Portland) Oregonian.* "You can't hold them responsible; you have to be responsible. Our standard is not to put anything in the paper that would hurt the child."

4. **Get parental permission for controversial interviews.**

   This is a judgment call. Reporters needn't call parents before interviewing a 10-year-old participating in a Saturday crafts program. The parents likely will be thrilled to see her picture in the paper or on the air. But that same child shouldn't be put live on the air and asked if she was scared when a disgruntled employee threatened her teacher in front of the class. The answer, of course, is yes. The question is exploitive and could make the child feel worse.

   When Graves wrote a series of stories about one classroom over the course of a year, he needed to tell the story of a child who was failing reading. He got the parent's permission to use the name.

5. **Avoid asking leading questions.**

   Because children often want to please adults, they will agree when asked such questions as, "You'd like to be an astronaut when you grow up, wouldn't you?"

6. **Ask the school staff to get clearances for photographs and interviews of children on noncontroversial topics.**

   Stevens says many schools send a standard form home at the beginning of the year asking parents whether they want their child in media shots.

   "If Johnny isn't supposed to be photographed and is in a classroom we're going to, we try to go to another classroom or shoot around him," Stevens explains.

   Once she and a videographer carefully worked around a child who wasn't to be seen. He soon ran to the office and called home begging to be on TV. The mother relented.

"I said, 'I'm interested and would love to follow your story.' They gave me everything the night before their story came out. I made some phone calls [the next day to confirm and add information] and had the story done by noon."

As we said at the start of this chapter, the definition of "student" is outdated. Look, too, for the 50-year-old graduate student started on a third career and for the 35-year-old divorced mother finishing an undergraduate degree so she can start on her first career.

Look for the rapidly growing international community on campus and for students in all kinds of new "campuses" nowhere near a traditional school. Brokers, bankers and financial analysts keep up in their fields by reading course work and taking tests at Financial Services University via the Internet or a corporate intranet (a networked computer system within a company). In other places, company trainers are downloading continuing education materials from their in-house intranet to digital audible players, which managers hook into their car stereos for learning while commuting.

MISCELLANEOUS SOURCES

When Jane Noble Suhler of *The Dallas Morning News* was writing a story about remedial classes for first-year college students, she called Rep. Irma Rangel, chair of the state's House Higher Education Committee, who'd been outspoken on the issue. Such state legislators have a say about the money public schools and colleges receive, as well as about funds for welfare-to-work training programs and retraining incentive grants. In addition, experts in the county and state education departments should be on the source list. Here are some others:

- Educational research organizations or think tanks such as the Brookings Institute
- Trade and professional organizations such as the National School Boards Association or the American Association of University Professors
- Accrediting bodies that make sure schools meet set standards, such as the Accrediting Commission for the National Association of Trade and Technical Schools of the Career College Association

THINGS TO READ

Education Week, the weekly magazine covering K-12 education, is a must-read for anyone covering children and youth. Its twin at the college level is the weekly *Chronicle of Higher Education.*

"The *Chronicle* does a wonderful job covering not only national trends and issues important to the country, but it covers stories on a state-by-state basis," Suhler says.

Suhler knows that her editors like trend stories, so she keeps an eye out for national issues she can localize. She read one intriguing *Chronicle* story telling how liberal arts colleges in the Northeast found themselves so short of men that they had to gear up special recruitment campaigns for guys. Suhler made a few phone calls and discovered the same thing was happening at a small Catholic university in her area. The editors ran her story on the front page.

PUBLICATIONS

Radio reporter Jody Becker makes sure she leafs through educational journals, such as *Rethinking Education.* "They did a fantastic issue on ebonics, the smartest thing I've read about that," she says.

She also uses other media, such as *The New York Times,* as a touchstone. The paper, she says, helps her feel confident that "I am doing the right kind of stories." For example, she carefully reads *Times* stories about bilingual education and mainstreaming of disabled children into conventional classrooms.

"The issues in New York are fairly similar to Chicago, which is the third largest school district in the nation," she adds, noting that her stories for Chicago radio listeners often put local events in a national context.

Even though she finds personal sources are best for tips, Sharon Stevens, education reporter at *KSDK-TV*, St. Louis, will occasionally skim through community newspapers for leads on what's happening in schools, especially the private schools, which sometimes don't seek or get the attention of publicly funded ones.

Stevens' reading list includes a variety of specialized media, including *Emerge*, a monthly focusing on issues of interest to the African-American community. "Sometimes I get the grain of an idea just from reading it," she says. For example, an article on school desegregation prompted her to write a day-in-the-life story about the impact of desegregation on one family. She showed the children as they got up, ate breakfast, took a cross-town bus ride and studied in their morning classes.

Reporters also look out for institutional brochures and studies by nonprofits and think tanks that look at a specific educational issue. Such information sent to students' homes or to newsrooms by the schools is in a sense public relations. But it often gives good history and other background material.

NEWSLETTERS

Reporters covering learning also want to be on the subscribers list of a number of newsletters, such as the one for the teachers' union.

"When teachers gripe about stuff, they do it in their newsletter because they're comfortable sharing amongst themselves," says Robin Farmer of the *Richmond (Va.) Times-Dispatch*.

After reading in one newsletter that the top job in human resources for the schools wasn't filled, Farmer set out to investigate. She confirmed that the post had been vacant for three months but found an even better story—the school board couldn't agree on whether to hire from within the school system or not. Here's how she laid out both sides:

> ...With training, several employees could be groomed to manage the department, the board members said. Not promoting from within, they said, sends a troubling signal that no one in the school system is qualified.

> But some board members say the position is too crucial for on-the-job-training and doesn't require an educator or a school system incumbent.
>
> *Richmond Times-Dispatch*

Other subscriptions that tip reporters to good stories include college and high school newspapers, newsletters from school boards and PTAs, and pamphlets from citizens or taxpayer groups.

MINUTES AND OTHER DOCUMENTS

A good ready reference, especially if you are a beat newcomer, is a year's worth of minutes from the school board or college trustees. You might want to look back to see the details of that school discipline policy or find out when the trustees first learned that the college biology lab was woefully out of date. For the new reporter, such documents give a sense of history.

Reporters often find gems of information tucked into grant proposals for training programs. Other helpful resources are annual reports—those made by school superintendents, college presidents, local companies and organizations that have nabbed government training grants.

Whenever you meet sources, ask them the timetable of their regular reports, and note these dates on a calendar so you know when to ask for the latest information. Also find out what federal and state programs local officials are administering. Such programs are subject to regular performance **audits**—reviews by independent evaluators to measure how well the program is being run. Reports released after these audits are completed are public information.

INTERNET RESOURCES

When Zenaida Gonzalez needs information to feed into her stories, she often starts on the Internet. A common rest stop on her Internet travels: the *U.S. Department of Education*. There she finds an index, with topics from A to Z, where she can research subjects from early childhood education to family literacy and vocational education.

This government home page also features information on topical issues. One day it linked to a new "idea book" profiling 20 schools doing a great job involving the whole family in education. There, Gonzalez could read about a model program, the Parent Resource Center, in a California school in Stockton.

Reporters covering adult learning should stop at the Department of Education's site, too. On one occasion they would have discovered a link off the home page to information about $6 million in new federal money being dispersed to employers with school-to-work programs in information technology.

Sometimes Gonzalez researches off directories, such as those at *Yahoo!*, which lists the topic "education." From there, she can click on whatever subject comes closest to what she's working on. She also finds specific school sites helpful. For example, she went to the Web site of the *Los Angeles Unified School District* to download statistics about that city's need for teachers in a story about teacher shortages:

> The Los Angeles Unified School District has estimated it will need 2,200 to 2,600 new teachers by September. And officials are still working with different schools to determine the final number.
>
> *Marin (Calif.) Independent Journal*

Nearly all schools and colleges have Web sites where reporters can find background information, course listings, news releases or links to the student newspaper. Bill Graves of *The (Portland) Oregonian* finds e-mail helpful in tracking stories—especially those off the beaten path. One day he was working on a story about the new trend in *unschooling,* a type of home-schooling that allows children to learn on their own by exploring what interests them rather than using a set curriculum. One of his sources led him to an online community of parents involved in unschooling.

"She had a network on e-mail and sent out a query for me. About four or five e-mailed me back and I ended up talking to them by phone," says Graves. He probably never would have found them using traditional reporting methods.

Graves is one of several reporters active on the *Education Writers Association* mailing list, another online community on the Net. Each week, the association invites an expert to join the mailing list discussion and answer questions. One week it might be the author of the latest national study on public schools, the next week

CLIPBOARD   INTERNET SITES MENTIONED IN THIS CHAPTER

Education Writers Association	www.ewa.org	U.S. Department of Education	www.ed.gov
Los Angeles Unified School District	www.lausd.k12.ca.us	Yahoo!	www.yahoo.com/Education

For an update to this list, see http://web.syr.edu/~bcfought.

a reading expert. Graves says even if he's not working on the "topic of the week," he often prints out the responses and tosses them in a file for future use.

REFERENCE WORKS

Jayne Noble Suhler of *The Dallas Morning News* says every reporter on the learning beat should have a stash of college phone books, directories and experts lists. She gets lists of faculty experts for Dallas-area universities as well as big-name schools such as Harvard and University of California at Berkeley.

Another standard is a guidebook to colleges such as Barron's or Peterson's. Suhler also recommends the Higher Education Directory.

"It's an index of every school and college with general stats by state, phone numbers and the names of everyone from the president to the librarian," Suhler says.

BASIC STORIES

A late-1990s study, commissioned by the Education Writers Association, showed that the public has a great thirst for news about learning. Forty percent of respondents said they were particularly interested in public schools, compared to 36 percent interested in crime and 22 percent curious about the local economy.

But the study showed people complained that they saw too many stories about conflict and not enough about content. What topics did they want to hear more about? Academic standards, curriculum, school safety, innovative programs and the quality of teachers. Stories on these topics help make up the bulk of basic stories written by learning reporters. In the sections ahead, you'll learn of four standards on the beat: stories about performance (test scores and the like), money, new teaching methods and safety.

PERFORMANCE STORIES

It may be a story about test score results or graduation rates, the numbers of students reading at grade level or mastering advanced placement tests. There's always an article or script to write about how well people are learning or how favorably one group of students stacks up against another group. Such is the category of stories we'll label "performance stories." Here's how Bill Graves started one:

> Students attending urban schools learn more in Oregon than in most parts of the country, according to a national study to be released today.
>
> The study gives Oregon a B+ for setting clear and rigorous academic standards, a C for teacher qual-ity and a D- for school climate, partly because of Oregon schools' large and growing class sizes.
>
> *The (Portland) Oregonian*

Here, the results come in the form of letter grades, which most people can understand. But many times test scores are reported as raw numbers or percentages that, by themselves, don't mean much. There are several ways reporters can make sense of those numbers.

One way is to put the numbers in context. Are those results better or worse than previous years for similar students? Looking at scores over a continuum of five years gives a better picture than comparing only the previous year. Another way, Graves advises, is to look at how many students are getting to grade level or above. Most state education departments set standards as to where students should be academically in a certain grade. Even though students are doing better than in previous years, the students still might not be learning what they should be learning.

Here's how Graves compared those Oregon students' performance to a set standard:

Reporter Bill Graves in *The (Portland) Oregonian* newsroom.

> In non-urban schools, 67 percent of Oregon eighth-graders scored at basic levels or better . . .

Similarly, for workplace learning it might be more helpful to show how many of the workers taking a retraining program are hired within two months rather than how many passed the course.

You can also compare one set of students to another group. Graves, for example, compared the performance of Oregon students in high-poverty urban schools to those in other urban schools:

> About half of eighth-graders in high-poverty urban schools in Oregon reach basic levels in science and math, but more than 80 percent of their peers in other urban schools perform at basic levels or better.
>
> *The (Portland) Oregonian*

Always be sure the comparisons are fair. Different districts, for example, may use different tests. Or their scores can be skewed because a higher or lower percentage of students take anything from advanced placement tests to college boards. Socioeconomic differences also should be noted.

"There's a tendency to want to compare Richmond [Va.], which is an urban district, to the suburbs," says Robin Farmer, who covers Richmond schools. "Then it's easy to say the Richmond test scores are atrocious, but that's comparing apples to oranges. It's unfair."

ETHICS   HOW TO SPIN NUMBERS

Even if you have verified the numbers you're using in a performance story, you can use them to give different impressions about how well people are learning. Take a look at these two leads from competing newspapers on the same day:

> Average Scholastic Aptitude Test (SAT) scores are down for the third-straight year and the major decline is in students' verbal skills.
>
> *The Detroit News*

> For the sixth consecutive year, Michigan students scored higher than the national average in the Scholastic Aptitude Test, which is used widely for college admissions.
>
> *Detroit Free Press*

At first read, it might seem that one of the stories is incorrect. But they are both accurate. Take a look again and see if you can figure out what's different.

It's a case of whether the glass is half empty or half full. One reporter led with the fact that the national average is down, while the other reporter stressed that the local numbers went up. The first, however, gives a more negative impression.

Discuss in small groups what you would do if you had the same situation: Local students' scores are improving, but nationwide the scores are going down. If you could only write one story, which would you emphasize and why? What additional information would help you make a better decision?

PERFORMANCE STORIES

1. Focus the story around people. They best convey the main plot; numbers are the supporting actors.

2. Probe behind the numbers to find out why students' performance is better or worse.

3. Get a reaction to the performance figures and press those being interviewed for what will and won't change in the future.

4. Review a variety of ways to show performance, remembering that test scores are just one criterion.

5. In using numbers, report fairly and accurately, making sure you understand them and who came up with them.

6. Add context and comparison to the story so people can see trends or understand the bigger picture.

A better idea, says Farmer, would be to compare Richmond to a similar city, say Norfolk.

Test scores aren't the be-all and end-all of whether students are learning. In fact, a lot of teachers say test scores don't show much of anything about students' creativity or abilities to think through problems. So reporters such as Graves look for other indicators of performance. In a recent profile of a Portland high school, Graves checked enrollment trends, attendance figures, the percentage of students who took the SAT test as well as a test with questions such as whether students had read a novel recently. All those helped him better show just how well students were learning.

A final tip: Check out potential bias of the group that publishes any performance report you use, as well as the validity of the numbers. Many of you are familiar with college guidebooks, published to help prospective students whittle down their college choices. Reporter Steve Stecklow of *The Wall Street Journal* found that the guidebook authors often took the college's word for the statistics on graduation rates, acceptance rates and SAT scores. In checking the numbers, he found that some colleges inflated the numbers to make themselves look more desirable.

Enough about numbers. Performance stories must go far beyond regurgitating them. Reporters want to probe for the reasons why. Was there a new program or increased emphasis that helped the third-graders score better each of the last three years? Is the reason first-year students aren't doing so well in algebra linked at all to the fact that the college tutoring program was dropped due to budget constraints?

Reporters also look for reaction and follow-up. Now that the results are out, what will the trainers do to help their students perform better in the future? Does the school have continued funding for the special program that helped boost student learning?

Even if the story measures change, show it through people and their experiences. In the end, readers and viewers are interested in the human experience, not the statistical one. The best reporters show people learning or chronicle students' struggles and successes.

MONEY STORIES

It might be a story about an increase in teachers' pay, or one that chronicles five years of steady cuts in funding for music and arts. Or maybe it's a story on the audit showing that the state grant to build a better bilingual education program didn't go to those who should have benefited.

In this era where every dollar counts, how much money goes to learning, and how well it is spent, is an important story. The same is true whether you're writing about a university or a nonprofit association teaching adults, says Jayne Noble Suhler of *The Dallas Morning News*. The first step in writing a money story is to understand how the money flows. That requires a good understanding of the budget. It shows where money is to be spent and serves as a blueprint of priorities.

As discussed in Chapter 10, budget stories trace the flow of funds into and out of organizations and thus are the most fundamental of all money stories. Suhler has written dozens. Here's one:

The budget for the 15 universities and health science centers in the University of Texas System will rise more than 6 percent for the 1998 fiscal year, mostly to pay for faculty salary increases and rising utility bills.

The Board of Regents unanimously approved a $4.76-billion system operating budget for 1998 at its meeting Thursday at the University of Texas at Dallas.

The Dallas Morning News

Suhler says the essentials to include in the basic budget story are these:

- The total budget figure as well as the percentage increase or decrease. It helps to have several years' budgets to look for patterns.
- The major items being added or cut. In the case of the University of Texas story, rising utility rates and faculty salaries accounted for the increase.
- The source(s) of any new money in the budget. For public colleges, it's often the state legislature. For a workplace learning program, it might be a new government grant. In public schools, taxes provide most of the revenue. Look also for new money from earnings on investments or carry-overs from the previous year.
- The impact on students, whether they are middle-schoolers or mid-lifers. Measuring impact, of course, means talking to "real people," not just budget analysts or school trustees. Sometimes interviews with those affected can reveal surprises. Tuition might stay the same, for example, but hidden costs might get passed on in sharply higher lab or technology fees.

For tips on reading a budget, turn to page 144 in Chapter 10. Substitute the word "school" or "university" for "city," and the advice is just as good.

"Always write a budget story from the standpoint of how it is going to affect the reader's pocketbook—that's a good philosophy," Suhler says.

That philosophy carries over to other money stories. If it's a story about tuition hikes or changes in financial aid, good reporters humanize the story with miniprofiles of students. Stories about prepaid tuition plans—trade-offs by which universities guarantee the amount of tuition for four years in return for upfront payment—should be written with working parents in mind. Even stories about fund-raising or how colleges invest their money should have a different kind of bottom line—what it means to the audience reading or hearing the story.

If money stories scare you or you need help in deciphering the figures, Steve Carter of *The (Portland) Oregonian* suggests you look for help from:

- The company that audits the books for the institution or organization.
- Financial experts at the state education department.
- A budget review committee, either within or outside the institution. "Portland schools have a citizens outside review committee that includes one or more accountants," he notes.
- Associations such as state school board associations. Some publish explanatory materials for laypeople.
- Applications for bond ratings (documents that schools or colleges submit in order to borrow money) or grant applications from companies doing worker training.

Another tip from Carter is this: Go beyond the administrator.

"What happens a lot is a reporter will quote school people saying, 'We need this much money to operate or the sky will fall,'" says Carter, "and if you just write stories with that as your parameter, you don't get the viewpoint of people who have to fund the schools and may have some other things to say."

SUMMARY

MONEY STORIES

1. Make the story relate to readers, viewers or listeners by putting it in terms of their pocketbook or what it means to them. Spice the story with comments from those most affected.

2. "Follow the money trail" was good advice at the time of Watergate and is still good advice today. Be sure you understand the numbers.

3. Boil down all the dollar figures to three or four key points of change (increase or decrease), and focus on the when and why of those. Money stories crammed with too many numbers become mind-numbing. Be selective.

4. Give the readers and viewers a comparison of what's happening now with what's gone before. Perspective is essential.

5. Check out all claims that "the sky is falling" to make sure it's really so.

Bounce the "company line" off a taxpayers group, parents or the teachers union head. If it's workplace learning, check with those in a similar program or the people auditing the grant that pays for the program.

Carter got caught once. He believed an administrator who predicted massive pink slips if a certain proposal passed. It did. No pink slips were issued.

"When you hear things like, 'We're going to have massive layoffs,' don't believe it," says Carter. "Ask where, how, when and who?"

STORIES ABOUT TEACHING METHODS

One public school announces it's now including character education as part of its curriculum. Another is branching out to full-day kindergarten to give children a better start. The local university now allows students half a world away to take its courses off the Web. And the adult education program is doing away with lectures and textbooks, saying that adults who couldn't learn by this method as children shouldn't be forced to endure it again.

Do these "innovations" work? That is a key question asked by students, parents and taxpayers. The way we learn, and by implication how we teach, is a prime topic on the learning beat.

In California, Zenaida Gonzalez began to hear from parents and teachers in the Larkspur (Calif.) School District about a "fantastic new program" called MathLand. It was more about math than arithmetic, more about letting children explore until they grasped the big concepts than about drilling for rote memorization. Gonzalez made it a point to get the opinions of students into her story. She purposefully sought out students who'd taken math the old way and thus could make comparisons between the two methods. Here's what she found:

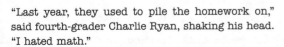

"Last year, they used to pile the homework on," said fourth-grader Charlie Ryan, shaking his head. "I hated math."

He said he would race through the sheets of equations but didn't think much about them afterwards. Now his mind keeps calculating even after the homework is done. . . . "I used to hate math," said fourth-grader Joy Kim. "Now we're doing this neat stuff like surveys. I love it, because it means more than numbers. You can get conclusions out of it."

Marin (Calif.) Independent Journal

Parents were upbeat about it as well. Gonzalez quoted parent Sandra Huyser:

> "... my daughter Jessica goes around converting everything into equations. We baked brownies the other day and she was even converting that with her friends. I guess it's working."

Gonzalez asked parents how they'd learned math and whether they liked it. The answers didn't end up in her story, but they did help shape it. She thinks it's important to give readers a measuring rod for comparing the new method to some standard criteria. She told them MathLand was based on national teacher standards and met state guidelines for what children should learn at each grade level.

New approaches are often controversial. Gonzalez was quick to point this out in her story:

> The program was born out of the mathematics reform movement, which has drawn fire from critics because of its unorthodox approach.
>
> *Marin (Calif.) Independent Journal*

Here are some other tips on teaching-method stories:

- Get opinions from a variety of sources. Gonzalez talked with local education experts who understood the method and could set it in a bigger frame of reference. She tracked down college math professors to find out whether their students had missed basic concepts somewhere along the way and what trends they saw in how well or poorly the schools were preparing students for math at the college level.

- Estimate comparative cost, where possible. Figure out what *isn't* being done.

- Watch out for biases. "Remember that everyone has an agenda," Gonzalez says. "Nothing is ever black and white. It's always gray." Obviously the people who've worked hard to make the new program succeed will tend to think it's worthwhile.

- When it's hard to figure out who's "right," summarize the positions and let the audience decide. "Give people enough information to draw their own conclusions," says Jody Becker of *WBEZ-FM,* Chicago.

  She thinks she has an advantage in broadcast because people can infer a lot from hearing a speaker's voice. "To hear the way someone says something can give it meaning," she explains.

- Look at the impact of the program. If it's being copied in other school districts or universities, let readers and listeners know.

- Remind readers that success is hard to prove. Often, results on whether the new method works or doesn't aren't available for years.

SUMMARY

TEACHING-METHODS STORIES

1. Explain the new method or curriculum clearly, using examples, anecdotes, dialogue or sound bites. Show as well as tell.

2. Compare the new method to other techniques or programs. Show how it stacks up based on an independent standard such as a state guideline.

3. Make sure to work student voices into the story.

4. Assess the cost in time, talent and money.

5. Let the audience know that results and impact aren't always quantifiable.

Gonzalez says she avoids running with grandiose statements. The only fair assessment she could make:

> The results of the program may not be known for a while, but it's off to a good start with some parents.

STORIES ABOUT SAFETY

Cheryl Lu-Lien Tan, in her first job out of Northwestern University, had been at *The (Baltimore) Sun* just a year when her beeper chirped at 3:15 one afternoon. Here's the lead to the story she rushed after:

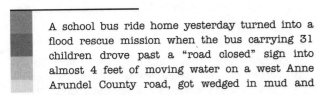

> A school bus ride home yesterday turned into a flood rescue mission when the bus carrying 31 children drove past a "road closed" sign into almost 4 feet of moving water on a west Anne Arundel County road, got wedged in mud and teetered on its left side, fire officials said. The children were removed safely before a tow truck pulled the bus out of the water . . .
>
> *The (Baltimore) Sun*

"In a safety story, especially one with kids, everybody wants to know the details and everybody is scared," Tan says. "These are the stories that sometimes have the most impact."

Safety stories do have impact: not only stories about school bus safety but also articles about dogs sniffing lockers for drugs, school security guards using metal detectors on high school teens or inspectors testing the safety of cafeteria food. In the workplace, employees want to make sure they stay safe both on the job and coming to and going from it. So you'll see stories about one company's plans to offer self-defense classes at lunch time or a new state mandate requiring refresher training about safety on the factory floor.

In writing a spot news safety story, Cheryl Tan knew what basics to include. That's why she put the why in her lead and quickly followed it with the essentials of who, what, when and where. You'll find more on how to cover breaking news in Chapter 13. If you want to peek ahead, see page 225.

Tan quickly followed that summary information with reaction from a student. A quote high up helps take readers to the scene:

> "It was way tilted," he said. "[The bus driver] told us to all get on one side."

"I always want to get a lot of color and get a lot of quotes," Tan says. "Because it was a school bus, a lot of people would say, 'That could have been my kid on the bus,' and they also wanted detail about the sequence of events, what did the bus drivers do, what did the firefighters tell the children."

She quoted neighbors, a county road official and a school supervisor as well. She told her readers of the dramatic rescue effort by passersby and firefighters. To be fair, she gave the perspective of the driver, who said he misread the sign to mean only one lane was closed and his side was open.

Her story had four other elements that made for good reporting:

- Impact
- Context
- Expert opinion
- Follow-up

The accident's impact was covered in a few different ways. No one was injured but authorities told them to shower immediately because the river is polluted. Tan also told readers that officials hadn't charged the driver. Tan put the story in context by telling readers this wasn't a new problem. She quoted a man whose horses and wagons got stuck there back in 1926, and she gave some up-to-date context:

> But [the school bus driver] wasn't the only one who ignored the 'road closed' sign, said a 30-year-old resident who would not give his name. He said he often sees drivers swerve around the signs and keep going . . .

Tan says it's important to get an outside authority to evaluate the situation. She called the National Highway Traffic Safety Administration because she remembered reading a bus safety story in *The Washington Post* a few days earlier that mentioned the federal agency. Here's how she used this information:

> Residents and parents expressed relief that no children were hurt—which Tim Hurd, a spokesman for the National Highway Traffic Safety Administration, said often can be attributed to how school buses are built for children's safety. . . .
>
> "Twenty-two million children ride in school buses every day and the number of incidents (that cause injuries) are extremely low," Hurd said. "Those buses are safer than any means of transportation, whether it's walking or riding in a passenger car."

Tan gave readers a sense that the story wasn't over by telling them a county official said the county would install new signs that are automatically activated by high water. But residents complained that wasn't enough.

Tan says most safety stories demand additional coverage. In this case, another reporter followed up the next day, telling readers that the driver was suspended.

"It's really important to follow through," Tan says. "People want to know what happened afterwards. You have to keep giving them information until the story is dead."

The best reporters don't wait for an accident or a safety scare. They're proactive. Robin Farmer of the *Richmond (Va.) Times-Dispatch* suggests reporters walk around with school personnel as they check out systems or equipment. It's also wise, she says, for reporters to take a look at the school's safety plan, a blueprint for what the school would do in case of violence or disaster. And if it doesn't have one, that's a story in itself.

SUMMARY

SAFETY STORIES

1. If it's a story about one incident or crime, give the basic who, what, where, when, how and why. Get reactions from all parties involved.

2. Avoid sensationalizing. Give the audience context so they can judge how serious the safety issue is.

3. Remember to tell the audience about the impact. The immediate impact is who, if anyone, was hurt or what was damaged. The longer-term impact may mean disciplinary action or changes in policies, procedures or design.

4. Always check to see whether safety guidelines were followed and whether those involved in an accident had a history of trouble before.

5. Look for success stories as well as failures. Sometimes schools take actions to prevent accidents or harm—for example, by stockpiling food and supplies in earthquake country.

ENTERPRISE STORIES

Even the best writer of basic stories tends to feel, after a while, that there's something more. Robin Farmer of the *Richmond Times-Dispatch* puts it well: "We do our readers a disservice when we do one story and walk away from it and don't probe what's underneath."

That is what enterprise is all about—taking time to do stories in depth, to follow trends, to chronicle change.

GETTING INSIDE THE STORY

Farmer had been working the education beat for nine years when another in a series of new superintendents came on board in Richmond. It seemed as good a time as any to propose an idea that had been brewing in her brain. Suppose she went inside the schools and taught?

The superintendent gave the OK, and Farmer set out on one of the most unusual experiences in her reporting life. She spent eight weeks teaching writing at Thomas H. Henderson Model Middle School in Richmond. She then chronicled her experiences in a series entitled "Trading Places: From the Newsroom to the Classroom." It ran in both paper and online versions. The stories included anecdotes of a crazy day of teaching, profiles of four challenging students and ideas about reforming the system.

Farmer says her goal was to be a teacher first. The reporting came later. She knows that some reporters might frown on this much reporter involvement in a story (see box, Ethics: Reporter Involvement). But for her, it paid off in many ways. Primarily, the teaching experience opened her eyes to a view of learning she couldn't get from mere observation:

> The backgrounds and experiences of my pupils ran the gamut. Some had visited Disney World, others never had been to a zoo.
>
> I taught children from stable homes with supportive families who shielded them from harsher realities their classmates knew in detail. Several pupils in one of my classes described how, when smoking crack, the plastic tube darkens and turns black. They knew, they said, because someone had smoked it in their presence.
>
> . . . Some of my kids had a firm grasp on the basics of writing. Others wrote with no attention to grammar and punctuation. Their papers, even down to the handwriting, resembled a third-grader's weak effort.
>
> *Richmond Times-Dispatch*

ETHICS REPORTER INVOLVEMENT

Think about the ethical issues reporters face when they become involved in their stories. In this chapter you read about Robin Farmer, a *Richmond Times-Dispatch* reporter who taught in a classroom for eight weeks. In Chapter 17 you'll read about reporter Jane Stevens, who worked on a research ship in the Antarctic, toiling out on the ice gathering samples (see page 303).

Discuss in small groups or write out your answers to these questions:

1. What's the difference between observing the story and being a part of it?

2. What guidelines would you set for how much involvement, if any, reporters should have with their subjects?

3. What potential conflicts does a reporter like Farmer risk creating by walking into a classroom as a teacher?

4. What do reporters do when they uncover a big story while they are involved in the story?

5. Are there nuances that reporters might find by participating that they wouldn't understand by observing from afar?

6. Does the type of media outlet the story will appear in make a difference as to whether a reporter should be involved in the story?

"This experience also helped me understand how difficult it is to teach, especially in an urban situation," Farmer says. She'd heard teachers say it for years, but once she got involved in the students' everyday lives, she too agonized about how to best help them.

Farmer's example reminds readers that today's educator is a far cry from the schoolmarm of the 1950s. Today's teacher, especially in urban schools or those with large immigrant populations, is a social worker, counselor, translator and coach, all rolled into one.

Here's a portion of one of her stories about a student she calls "Ghost," because she wandered in and out of classrooms:

> As I worked with my kids, I saw Ghost writing furiously.
>
> Suddenly, she crumpled her loose-leaf paper and threw it in the trash can.
>
> "Go get that," I told her.
>
> "You don't want to read it," she said defiantly.
>
> "Yes, I do."
>
> "Oh, no, you don't. Trust me."
>
> "Trust me. Yes, I do."
>
> She handed me the balled-up paper. I unrolled it and nearly had a heart attack. She had written the same sentence over and over again: I need to die.
>
> *Richmond Times-Dispatch*

Although students such as Ghost are atypical, the vignette shows the drama that teachers sometimes confront.

Besides learning a lot about teaching, Farmer found her sabbatical at school netted her a bounty of good contacts for the long run.

"This really opened the doors for me to talk to many other educators," she says. People return her phone calls more quickly and call her up with ideas.

"Folks may still not like me, but they respect me because they've told me they learned something about me and they learned I really cared about the children," she explains.

USING NUMBERS TO FIND HIDDEN STORIES

Anne Lindberg of the *St. Petersburg (Fla.) Times* found another way of getting an inside story. She used a computer spreadsheet to input school budget figures and compute which principals were hoarding money from year to year rather than spending it on classroom basics. Here's some of what she found:

> . . . Parents are out slogging away at fundraising. Teachers are buying basic supplies out of their salaries. Students go door to door selling candy, wrapping paper and sausages. All because parents are told the schools don't have money.
>
> Yet Pinellas schools had more than $1-million in discretionary money left at the end of the 1994–
>
> 95 fiscal year—a quarter of last year's total discretionary budget for the schools.
>
> And that doesn't include the additional $3-million schools will get this year for discretionary spending.
>
> *St. Petersburg (Fla.) Times*

Lindberg found the top savers and big spenders; those getting windfalls and those going without.

"The computer lets you get at different levels and layers of stories because it does so much organization work for you," says Lindberg, who's now a convert to computer-assisted reporting. "It's such a wonderful way to take a lot of information from a lot of sources and stick it all together and see if there's any relationship."

These are some of the ways she says the computer analysis helped her in this story:

- Typing in the numbers forced her to know and understand the figures much better than if she just read over them a few times.
- Results gave her comparative statistics between schools to use in her interviewing and questioning of parents and principals.
- Once she set the format, she could easily input figures from previous years to confirm that the practice had been going on for a long time.

Lindberg's story generated so much discussion that one parent told her the principal spent a whole evening explaining why he had a surplus and how he'd spend it all right away on his elementary school, only carrying $100 into the next year.

TRACKING TRENDS

While computer-assisted reporting may be a stretch for some student reporters, taking on an enterprise story shouldn't be. Here is an excerpt from an intriguing story about a new type of college student. It was written by a Syracuse University graduate student on an internship at the *Newhouse News Service*:

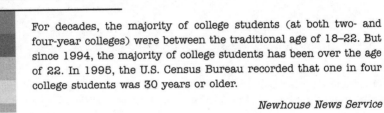

For decades, the majority of college students (at both two- and four-year colleges) were between the traditional age of 18–22. But since 1994, the majority of college students has been over the age of 22. In 1995, the U.S. Census Bureau recorded that one in four college students was 30 years or older.

Newhouse News Service

Nkiru Asika read something about older women being an increasingly large part of the college population. "I thought it was an interesting idea," she said.

An interesting change, a new development—that's a trend story. Readers, listeners and viewers look to reporters to help them chronicle history and to interpret what's up, what's down and what's coming around the corner.

Asika had the luxury of spending 10 days researching newspaper databases, thinking about new angles, talking to experts and finding women to profile. She told her readers that while women of the 1970s studied art history or literature, they now sought credentials to advance professionally. The most common majors? Education, health and social work.

She examined why the numbers of older women were up—because fewer women than men got college degrees right out of high school and because of economic necessity in today's competitive market. She also probed the impact on colleges, finding that older students made fewer demands for health services and housing but more demands for evening classes and accelerated programs. Here's what else she found:

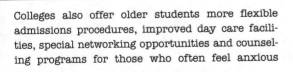

Colleges also offer older students more flexible admissions procedures, improved day care facilities, special networking opportunities and counseling programs for those who often feel anxious about taking exams, writing papers and keeping up with the course load after a long absence from school.

Newhouse News Service

The story was Asika's first on the learning beat. She said she found it fascinating—so much so that she wanted to keep researching and expanding the story (a common tendency with trend stories). Some avenues she didn't have time to explore:

SUMMARY	ENTERPRISE STORIES

1. Look for the untold success stories of learning at all stages of life, especially preschool and adult learning, topics often not covered enough.

2. Compare and contrast new teaching methods or programs to find out what is working and what isn't. Do follow-ups on programs touted five years before to see if they are still in effect.

3. Monitor other media outlets and specialized publications to identify trends worth examining in your area.

4. Take a computer-assisted reporting course or a computer science course where you learn spreadsheets and databases. Use that knowledge to analyze test scores, school expenditures and other statistics to find stories others don't report.

"I wanted to look at different groups, to what extent Asian-Americans and African-Americans were returning to college. And how much the women's lives do improve after they've gotten their degrees and whether it's worth it."

Sharon Stevens, education reporter at *KSDK-TV*, St. Louis, produced a three-part series that examined the trend toward putting computers in every classroom. She found out that too often the students were teaching the teachers.

"The more important issue was that teachers weren't trained," Stevens said. "The kids were surfing the Net at home and augmenting what they already knew, where teachers weren't up to speed."

She reported on the need for teacher training—which meant more money and time out of the classroom.

RECOMMENDED READING

Education Week [Online]. **Available: http://www. edweek.org.**

This is the Internet presence for this well-known publication. It covers hundreds of subjects within education. One section, "The Daily News," allows reporters to read some of the best education stories of the week from various online publications.

Education Writers Association. (1993). *Covering the education beat.* Washington, DC: Education Writers Association.

A handbook written just for reporters. This three-ring binder (with Internet updates) contains backgrounders on 50 topics in secondary and higher education ranging from business/school partnerships to state governance to college athletics. It includes excellent references and contacts.

ERIC. Educational Resources Information Center. [Online]. Available: **http://www.aspensys. com/eric/index.html.**

This site can connect you with experts in all areas of learning and provide backgrounders on innumerable subjects. It has a whole section on adult career vocational education, which is helpful for reporters covering workplace learning.

U.S. Department of Education. [Online]. Available: **http://www.ed.gov.**

The official site of this federal agency with links to federal data, other agencies and many helpful resources.

The Virtual Library: Education. [Online]. Available: **http://www.csu.edu.au/education/library. html.**

A megasite with numerous links. Here you can search by topic, educational level and even by country. You could spend all day linking off this site.

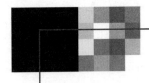

EXERCISES

A. RESEARCH

1. Define these terms as you'd explain them in a script or story:

   a. academic freedom

   b. ESL

   c. Federal Educational Rights and Privacy Act (also known as FERPA)

   d. Head Start

   e. learning disabilities

   f. magnet schools

   g. multipoint videoconferencing

   h. retention rates

   i. service learning

   j. Title I

   k. Title IX

   l. vouchers

B. BASIC STORIES

1. Write either stories or memos based on the following assignments.

   a. Interview six students at a local high school about their best idea to improve learning at their school. Then talk to administrators, parents and the school board to see how likely it is that idea could be implemented.

   b. Get copies of the last three years' budgets for a local school district or public university in your area. Pick out two or three key changes or differences worth writing about.

   c. Look for an innovative teaching method being used on your college campus. Talk to the professor and to current and former students in the course. If the same course is being taught by another method, talk to the professor and students there and do a comparison.

   d. Check campus police and local police records to find out the most common safety issue at your college, and talk to students and administrators about what they are doing to turn it around.

   e. Talk to the security head at a local school district to see what emergency plan he has for a weather disaster or crime in the schools. Find out how often the plan is updated and whether dry runs or mock drills are held. Talk to students, parents, administrators, counselors and the head of the teachers union.

C. ENTERPRISE STORIES

1. Trace a local worker training program funded by a state or federal grant. Get a copy of the grant application, reports and audits. Interview employers who hire or promote these workers, as well as the workers, their teachers and legislators who funded the program. Write a story either from the perspective of taxpayers or students. Examine whether the program has helped or hurt adult learners and whether it will be continued.

2. Peruse the *Education Week* Web site or leaf through the magazine at the library looking for trends in K–12 education. Select one and explore how this trend is affecting learning in your area. Are schools ahead or behind the curve?

3. Check the graduation rates at your college over the past 10 years, and write a story about what you find. If possible, use computer-assisted reporting. Are more or fewer students being graduated in four years? How about five years? What about persons of color? Athletes? Interview students, admissions staff, administrators, minority affairs administrators and state education officials.

4. Compare the information and statistics in one of the college guidebooks with statistics your college publishes in public relations materials and in required government reports. Write a story about what you find.

5. Spend a day in a preschool or Head Start program carefully noting or tape recording vignettes through the day and the dialogue and interactions between teachers and students. Write a day-in-the life story, using care to show, more than tell, what happened.

6. Get the payroll list for a nearby state university or school district. It's available under the state's open records law. See what interesting story you can find about who has the highest salary and the lowest salary, or what female coaches make compared to male coaches.

CHAPTER **13** Crime and Safety

About every 13 seconds in this country somebody's house is burglarized. Some 1,600 people are murdered each month. And 41,000 people die on U.S. roadways in a year. Individually, many of these stories draw bold headlines in newspapers, sensationalized teases on TV news and splashy graphics on news Web sites.

Yet every day millions of people drive safely about their business, millions of children walk to and from school without harm and families return home from vacation to find the house untouched. We don't hear about those things. For news, by definition, long has been considered to be something out of the ordinary.

When applied to what's long been called "the cops beat," that definition falls short today. Oh sure, lots of people have a fascination with crime. They want to read about it, hear about it and see it.

But perhaps in part because of the drumbeat of crime coverage, society's fear of crime is escalating even as violent crime, according to the statistics, is going down. And that's a story, too.

More and more people are moving to walled communities, installing home security systems and hooking up Caller ID devices. Sometimes they're doing something else as well: They're blaming the media for spreading fear by reporting too much crime. Reporters will always make somebody mad; this is not a call to ignore what hurts and makes people unhappy. It is a call, however, for better, more intelligent context in covering what we'll call the crime and safety beat.

Those who cover crime these days must do much more than the easy whodunit, which doesn't leave the audience with much more than a heightened sense of fear. Reporters need to get beyond the latest horror story to consider why it happened, whether it's part of a broader trend, and what both police and ordinary people are doing and can do to care for their homes and communities. They need to look at the effect of crime on how people live and the renewed emphasis in police work on preventing it before it happens.

Ultimately, reporters covering crime and safety face the challenge of alerting their audiences to the reality of crime without sensationalizing it in a way that distorts society's perceptions or proposed solutions. Some news organizations are now setting guidelines

Reporters covering crime and safety work not only to bring timely and accurate stories about fires, accidents and disasters but also to help their audiences understand how to prevent such tragedies and stay safe.

for crime coverage. For example, one television news shop tells tape editors not to use shots of blood. Others, such as *KVUE-TV,* Austin, Texas, match each crime story against a news department checklist to see if it fits their criteria of impact and significance (see box, Ethics: News Judgment and Crime).

This chapter will help you frame your news judgment and ethical position on crime coverage. It will also:

- Introduce you to the myriad sources you'll need to be an effective reporter on the crime and safety beat
- Tell you the resources, both print and online, to make your job easier
- Give you checklists for what should be in basic stories on a crime, accident and fire
- Teach you how to think beyond the basics to come up with enterprise stories

ETHICS   NEWS JUDGMENT AND CRIME

The hows and whys of crime news often need to be discussed a lot more in news departments. They're doing that at *KVUE-TV* (Austin, Texas) with this five-point checklist for whether a story will air:

- Does action need to be taken?
- Is there an immediate threat to safety?
- Is there a threat to children?
- Does the crime have significant community impact?
- Does the story lend itself to a crime-prevention effort?

"Before, we used to talk about *how* do we get it to air. Now we talk about *why*," said news director Carole Kneeland when she began the policy. "We have many more thoughtful discussions every day."

Kneeland acknowledged the decisions aren't easy and sometimes the station makes the wrong call. But it's better to make a thoughtful mistake than a thoughtless one, she suggested. It's better to have the discussion about stories than to automatically air them just because a crime occurs.

Here's one way this policy played out. One afternoon a police swat team surrounded the home of an 82-year-old man who had earlier stabbed his elderly wife. She escaped and was not hurt badly. After four hours of negotiations, the man finally came out, looking frightened. He was so frail police had to help him out to the police car. It all ended just before the top of the 5 o'clock show.

KVUE-TV hadn't gone live from the scene but had a crew there and could have. Should it have gone live? Should it even air the story?

Kneeland said reporters were working the story intently and had traced the names and address through police records. They'd found no previous domestic violence reported, and the couple's children and grandchildren told them this was unusual behavior for the man.

"It was an isolated personal situation that was a one-time-only deal," said Kneeland. "It was very uncharacteristic for that man and didn't affect anybody but that family."

The station didn't run a thing. Its competition led with it.

Opinions differ, and other news directors might argue that policies such as *KVUE-TV*'s are mere marketing ploys or, at worst, self-censorship. In this case, the unusual nature of the crime, given the couple's age and the fact that the standoff took place in public and must have raised the interest and concern of the entire neighborhood, also might have been raised as arguments to air the story.

These are legitimate concerns. So, however, are the arguments of media critics and consumers who complain that the news media, especially TV, hype crime. A group of former reporters and producers now teaching journalism surveyed eight television markets on four random days. The group, called the Consortium for Local Television Surveys, found that crime dominated TV news with 29 percent of the stories. Compare this to the time devoted to health (7 percent), education (1 percent) and race relations (1 percent). And this was during a time when reported crime was on the decrease.

Work together in small groups to discuss these questions:

1. What are the pros and cons of a policy such as *KVUE-TV* uses?

2. Would such a policy work in your community?

3. Why would or wouldn't you like to work for a news organization with such a policy?

4. Does one news operation in your town give a higher priority to crime news than the others? Why?

5. How would you respond to an angry reader or viewer who says your news organization overplays crime?

6. Compare how crime is covered on local TV and the local newspaper. Note whether crime gets higher play on the weekends—why or why not?

PEOPLE TO SEEK OUT

Reporters covering crime and safety need a variety of sources, from police who give an official version, to the witness who describes the drama, to the emergency medical worker who leaks what the police aren't ready to reveal.

POLICE

No one revels in making routine cop checks.

"Making beat calls was one of my least favorite jobs," says Michelle Williams, about her internship at *WMUR-TV* in Manchester, N.H. "I had to call every police and fire department in the state and ask them if they had anything going on or if they had any press releases."

But, she learned, such calls can pay off. During one such check, police told her they had arrested a man on charges of indecent exposure and that a *WMUR-TV* viewer had helped nab the suspect. The viewer had recognized the man from a story the station ran the day before and called the police.

"It's not a glamorous job, but it is a vital one," says Williams. "After that I looked forward to doing the calls in hopes of stumbling onto something big."

Something big is what every reporter pines for and what many police try to keep under wraps. Although police are the most traditional sources for a crime story, they also are often the most reluctant to talk. They're suspicious of reporters, who, from their perspective, make solving crimes more difficult. Police are unlikely to spill much of anything to the unknown reporter at the other end of a phone line. But reporters who spend time with cops on the beat and at the precinct can get a jump on the competition.

That's why Gary Baumgarten, a reporter at all-news radio *WWJ-AM* in Detroit, passed out his business card like candy.

"Make sure you give the cops your pager number and home phone," says Baumgarten. "They don't like calling newsrooms and going through editors to get to reporters."

After 25 years covering news in metro Detroit, Baumgarten would get at least one call a day from a source. Many gave him confidential information that helped him stay on track even when he couldn't use it in the story.

"Police will always say, 'Look I'm going to tell you what the real deal is, but you can't use it,'" says Baumgarten. "If you can't live with that agreement, walk away."

Reluctant though they may be as sources, police are essential. They're the ones who provide the authoritative version of what happened, whereas witnesses and victims give the color and drama.

If reporters get to a crime scene quickly enough, they get their basic information from the ranking officer on the scene. Many police departments have policies about who is authorized to talk to reporters—it's often the captain in charge on the scene. If not, reporters likely will have to wait for the public information officer or watch commander—the ranking officer on the shift—to get back to them. From top down, the common hierarchy in departments is chief, captain, lieutenant, sergeant, detective and officer.

Just who handles a case—local police, state police, highway patrol or the FBI—usually depends on the type of crime and where the crime was committed (see box, Whom Do I Call? in the next section). Sometimes cases are coordinated among several of these agencies.

Other law enforcement sources to tap, depending on the story, are the jail guards, sheriff's deputies, state police, FBI agents, Drug Enforcement Administration officers, probation officers and police union officials.

Whatever the crime or crisis, good reporters don't stop with police. They may not even start with them.

ETHICS   ESTABLISHING TRUST WITH POLICE

Reporters' relationships with police officials often are tense, sometimes tumultuous. Building trust is essential.

"They're not your adversaries. They are valuable news sources," says Patrick Bradley of the *Niagara Gazette,* Niagara Falls, N.Y. "Once they accept you and trust you, you'll get more stories out of them than you know what to do with."

Bradley has earned respect and almost unlimited access to local police because he follows a set of ethical guidelines he set down with police from the start. Here are his rules:

1. If we agree something is off the record, it will remain off the record—forever.

2. I will not publish the names of suspects until charges are filed or a grand jury hands up indictments against them. Our paper occasionally modifies this, on a case-by-case basis, when an arrest warrant has been issued but the suspect is not yet in custody.

3. I will not publish the names of victims of sex crimes (such as rape, sodomy, sexual abuse) unless the victim comes to me and says she (or he) wants the story published.

4. I will not print information that interferes with or impedes the progress of an ongoing investigation. Police sometimes have very valid reasons for not wanting details of crimes released.

5. I normally print victims' names. But if a victim requests no publicity, I will consider the case on its merits. Basically, the rare exceptions I make involve cases in which the victims are either very old or very young and fear reprisal from their assailants. I then write the item but fudge on the name ("An 84-year-old North End woman told police Wednesday . . . ").

6. If a cop screws up—gets arrested, for example—I have to write the story. I will always give that cop and his or her lawyer a chance to comment. That is my job.

7. If I commit a crime, I expect a cop to arrest me. That is her or his job. I expect no special treatment.

8. If any employee of our newspaper is charged with a crime, that arrest goes in the newspaper. We do not play favorites with our own employees and will not play favorites with others.

OTHER OFFICIAL SOURCES

At an accident scene, emergency medical technicians may give you basic information about injuries, but their first responsibility is saving lives. EMTs may be firefighters, they may work for a private ambulance company or be part of a volunteer squad. After hours, they can be valuable resources for information about the 911 dispatching system or the drama of a particular rescue.

When covering a fire, check with the ranking officer on the scene. Often it's the person wearing the white cap. As with the police, firefighters have their own protocol and often the fire chief or deputy chief are the only ones to speak on the record to reporters. Later, in following up a suspicious fire, the reporter might stop by the fire company and have a soft drink with the firefighters or call up that arson investigator who was tromping around the scene the morning after.

Hospital public relations practitioners provide basic information about accident victims. Reporters keep the home phone numbers and pager numbers of these sources in their black books. It also helps to stop by and meet the nursing supervisors. They're the ones who come to the phone when reporters call late to get an update on patients' conditions.

When an accident or crime victim dies, it's the medical examiner or coroner (and some states have both) who usually certifies the cause of death and decides whether an autopsy or other investigation is needed. MEs are usually physicians and are appointed to their jobs, whereas coroners are usually elected and often aren't doctors. They might not tell you the exact cause of death right away if it depends on test results that take time. But reporters who have taken time to develop sources in these offices sometimes get details about a murder or accidental death that police are not yet releasing.

Funeral home directors are also a good source for background on the deceased, and sometimes they'll serve as an intermediary to contact the family.

WHOM DO I CALL?

Most crimes (assault, burglary, drugs, homicide, robbery, theft)	Local or state police, sheriff
Auto accident	Police, sheriff, highway patrol
Bank robbery	Police or FBI
Boating accident	Police, sheriff, Coast Guard
Bombs and explosives	U.S. Alcohol, Tobacco and Firearms
Civil rights violations	Police or FBI
Credit card fraud	U.S. Secret Service
Drugs	Police, U.S. Drug Enforcement Administration
Federal prisoners	U.S. Marshal's Service
Fires/arson	Fire department
Gambling	Police or FBI
Gas leaks, explosions	Gas company, police
Illegal immigrants	U.S. Naturalization and Immigration Service, border patrol
Income tax violations	Internal Revenue Service
Kidnapping	Local or state police, FBI
Weapons (illegal)	Police, U.S. Alcohol, Tobacco and Firearms

VICTIMS AND WITNESSES

Police and firefighters deal with crime and accidents every day; average citizens don't. So that makes events all the more dramatic and traumatic for them. Their reactions are far from the straight recitation of a cop. The stories of victims and witnesses are full of emotion, color and immediacy.

"There was a loud roar and everything was shaking. It was beginning to tilt and then everything just shook and stopped," Matthews said.

Associated Press

That is an eyewitness account from a passenger on an Amtrak train that police said someone sabotaged in the Arizona desert. Weaving powerful quotes or sound bites through a story makes it memorable. So, too, do the details of what people at the scene saw, heard and smelled (see Chapter 7). They're details that a witness likely will recount much more vividly than a cop—details that bring the reader or viewer to a scene that cameras didn't capture.

But witnesses provide more than color and detail. They may corroborate or contradict official accounts. If police got rough making an arrest, the watch commander won't volunteer it. Witnesses may well tell you. By going to the crime scene or fire scene, reporters often get information about what happened before police are willing to discuss it.

Those familiar with a suspect or victim—family, friends, co-workers, teachers, pastors and neighbors, for example—also can build a picture that looks beyond an isolated crime. Their stories may lead to a poignant tale of why a particular victim was in a particular place on a particular night. Or they may help give insight into why something happened rather than merely what happened.

RIGHTS OF VICTIMS AND SURVIVORS

Interviewing crime victims and disaster survivors can be unsettling for reporters, especially when they know that talking about an assault or event can trigger traumatic flashbacks for those involved. Such interviews must be handled with care. Some survivors are eager to talk and share; others aren't.

The **National Victim Center**, Arlington, Va., endorses the following media code of ethics drawn up by participants in a 1985 symposium in Seattle. The center says the code recognizes the demands journalists face, yet encourages them to treat victims with dignity and respect—especially early on. Here are the guidelines (printed with the permission of the National Victim Center):

I shall:

- Provide the public with factual, objective information about crime stories concerning the type of crime that has occurred; the community where the crime occurred; the name or description of the alleged offender if appropriate under existing state law; and significant facts that may prevent other crimes.

- Present a balanced view of crime by ensuring that the victim and the criminal perspective are given equal coverage when possible.

- Advise victim and survivors that they may be interviewed "off the record" or "on the record" if they desire such an interview, and advise them that they have a right not to be interviewed at all.

- Quote victims, families and friends fairly and in context.

- Avoid photographing or taping crime scene details or follow-up activities such as remains of bodies or brutality, instruments of torture, disposal of bodies, etc.

- Notify and ask permission from victims and their families before using pictures or photographs for documentaries or other news features.

I shall not:

- Photograph, tape or print for publication, photographs of victims, graphic crime scenes or victims in the courtroom without permission.

- Print or broadcast unverified or ambiguous facts about the victim, his or her demeanor, background or relationship to the offender.

- Print facts about the crime, the victim or the criminal act that might embarrass, humiliate, hurt or upset the victim unless there is a need to publish such details for public safety reasons.

- Print, broadcast or photograph lurid or graphic details of the crime.

- Promote sensationalism in reporting crime or criminal court cases in any way.

If time allows in talking to victims, witnesses or families, there is no substitute for a face-to-face interview. Working with people who've been traumatized or are in shock takes special care and consideration. They shouldn't be browbeaten. But often they want to share their thoughts, the memories of a loved one, the horror of what they've seen. When they won't talk, it's often because of their emotional struggle.

DEFENDANTS

The other people who often won't talk about crimes are suspects and defendants. Their attorneys have told them to keep their mouths shut. However, sometimes reporters find they can set ground rules to interview defendants by making the request through defendants' attorneys.

"I've been successful in getting some very interesting interviews with people through their attorney," says Tom Flannery of the *(Lancaster, Pa.) Intelligencer Journal.* Among them: an interview with the head of an outlaw motorcycle gang who eventually was convicted for his role in a one-night rampage that left several people dead.

OTHER SOURCES

Whatever the crime or incident, the best reporters push beyond the badges and suits in the justice system. Other experts, with a different perspective or broader view, are all around:

WATCHWORDS

■ **Criminal/defendant/suspect**: Police may be looking for a **suspect** or have a person they call a suspect in custody for questioning. But remember, our legal system is based on the presumption of innocence: Someone is "innocent until proven guilty." You can't call a person a **defendant** until he is formally charged in court. A person is not a **criminal** until the person has pled guilty or been convicted of a crime.

■ **Felony/misdemeanor**: A **felony** is a serious crime such as homicide, assault, burglary, drug dealing, manslaughter, rape or robbery. State law often defines each crime in levels of severity, such as first-degree or second-degree (less serious). A felony usually carries a sentence of more than one year in prison and/or a fine. **Misdemeanors**, or lesser crimes, cover offenses such as shoplifting or smoking marijuana. For those crimes, people usually get less than a year in jail and/or a fine.

■ **Murder/manslaughter**: These are general terms referring to a **homicide**—the killing of one person by another. Each state will have its own list of charges, such as first-degree murder, second-degree murder, voluntary manslaughter and so forth. **Murder** means the killing was done intentionally or after premeditation, so it's not correct to say a person was murdered in a car accident. That is **manslaughter**, which means the person who committed the homicide didn't intend to kill anyone.

■ **Burglary/larceny/robbery**: When a person breaks into a building, that is **burglary**, and if the person takes something from the building, it results in a second charge called **larceny** or theft. Taking something from a person through force or the threat of force is **robbery**.

■ Advocacy groups such as the American Civil Liberties Union, the NAACP or Parents of Murdered Children
■ Neighborhood Watch groups
■ Citizens' police review boards
■ Social service agencies and caseworkers
■ Bail bondsmen
■ Pawnbrokers
■ Businesspeople who sell crime-prevention equipment
■ Insurance adjusters
■ Researchers or criminologists

SUMMARY
CRIME SOURCES

1. Make routine police checks religiously—they're boring, but sometimes you hit pay dirt.

2. Develop police sources to feed you information when a story breaks.

3. Whenever possible, go to the crime scene. Look for the ranking officer who's authorized to talk.

4. Interview victims and witnesses. They'll give you firsthand dramatic accounts and sometimes provide details that dry police reports or accounts omit.

5. If you're not at the scene, get the public information officer to connect you to somebody in the know—the ranking officer who was there or the detective heading up the investigation.

6. Look beyond the usual sources. Talk to emergency medical workers, probation officers, funeral home directors, arson investigators, neighbors and advocacy groups.

THINGS TO READ

While reporters sometimes discover their stories by being alert to the crackle of a police radio, more often they find them by methodically checking police records. The paper trail, and now the cyberspace path, can corroborate the sources' accounts, offer intriguing details for the story or provide new angles to search out.

POLICE REPORTS

A great tip sheet for reporters is the daily list of situations to which police have responded, called a **blotter** or desk log. It's usually available at the police station. The best details are found in **incident reports** written by officers on the scene. They describe the scene and what witnesses recounted (see sample in Appendix C). The **arrest log** (also called booking log) tells the name, address, age and charges for each person arrested, while the **investigative files** detail follow-up work and the current status of the investigation (see box, Where Can I Go? What Can I Get?). When police deflect a reporter's request for these with, "Sorry, that investigation is in progress," reporters need good contacts inside.

Some law enforcement agencies, however, are making reporters' work easier. Reporters from *The Orlando (Fla.) Sentinel* dial in by computer to the Lake County sheriff's computer when they hear an interesting police call on

WHERE CAN I GO? WHAT CAN I GET?

Laws in each state differ, so be sure to check your state law or ask your news organization's attorney. Get a copy of the media policies of each law enforcement department you cover. Here are some general guidelines:

Accident/disaster scene	Reporters and photographers get access but can't interfere with investigators. Being on a first-name basis with police and fire officials helps.
Accident report	Available from police. See sample in Appendix C.
Arrest (or booking) log	Available at police station: name, age, address and occupation of the accused; charges; circumstances of the arrest; next court date and who's investigating.
Autopsy report (coroner's)	Availability depends on state law. Includes nature of the accident, the time and cause of death, evidence of struggle and next of kin.
Blotter	Available at police station: lists brief information about police calls including time, location and type of request for all calls to police.
Grand jury deliberations	Closed. Once an indictment has been handed up, it's available from the prosecutor or court clerk.
Hospital patient information	Most hospitals will release the patient's name, age, occupation, nature of injuries, treatment and condition.
Incident report	Available at police station: location and circumstances of the crime; charges pending; name, age, residence, occupations of those arrested. Exceptions in some states are sex crime victims and juveniles.
Investigative files	Sometimes available from police. Filled with witness statements, follow-up reports, probation information and lists of evidence.
Jail logs	Available at the jail: brief information on who is incarcerated.
Search warrants	The request, the warrant and the return (which tells what was found) are usually available at the court once the search is completed. See sample return in Appendix C.

the scanner. They scroll through the dispatcher's log to read what's been typed in about 911 calls and where officers are being sent. They also read the Orange County sheriff's daily Watch Commander Report, which comes to them on e-mail.

"One day I had called the cops and they said nothing was happening," says Christopher Quinn, police beat reporter. "But I looked at the commander's report and saw that a bunch of vandals took 12 golf carts from a golf course, went joy riding on the greens and put the carts in a couple of lakes on the course."

The popular course was closed for a few days for greens repair. That is the kind of **talk-about story** or **brite** that the police often don't think to tell a reporter.

But don't count on easy access. Most police shops aren't as open as the one in Florida. Working inside sources and paging through the records the old-fashioned way are the only ways for many reporters to get their stories.

OTHER CRIME-RELATED REPORTS

When police aren't cooperative, reporters have to look elsewhere. In the case of a homicide or accidental death, reporters check the coroner's or medical examiner's report, sometimes called an **autopsy report**. In some states, with no more than a name or a vehicle license plate, reporters can trace the name, address, description and previous infractions of a vehicle's owner. Some media organizations buy this list annually and keep it in-house, although in recent years some states have cut off access on privacy grounds.

Fire reports are usually available at the fire station. In disaster stories or in cases where police or fire department performance is questioned, 911 tapes can provide a dramatic rendition of a victim's pleas for help. Often reporters can get a copy of the tape or a transcript (see box on page 222, Where Can I Go? What Can I Get?).

Let us emphasize again: What your own eyes see at the scene of a crime or fire may prove more valuable than any report. Seeing the destruction firsthand or pacing off the distance of the skid marks may make your words come alive in a way the most clearly written official report cannot.

DIGITAL CONNECTIONS

When the FBI arrested two men in connection with an attempted bombing of the Reno, Nev., IRS office, reporters at the *Reno Gazette-Journal* learned just how valuable database resources can be on the crime beat. Their electronic connections put them ahead on the story—even ahead, at one juncture, of the FBI.

While a reporter and photographer jumped in a car headed to the hometown of the suspects, 50 miles away, others on the staff jumped onto their computers hunting for addresses in the Gardnerville area.

CLIPBOARD INTERNET SITES MENTIONED IN THIS CHAPTER

Arlington County (Va.) Police Department	www.co.arlington.va.us/ arlcty/pol/index.htm	N.Y. Division of Criminal Justice Services	criminaljustice.state.ny.us
Landings	www.landings.com	Switchboard	www.switchboard.com
MapQuest	www.mapquest.com	Yahoo!Maps	www.yahoo.com
National Victim Center	www.nvc.org	For an update to this list, see http://web.syr.edu/~bcfought.	
NBC13 Interactive Neighborhood	www.nbc13.com		

CRIME AND SAFETY REPORTING ONLINE

Todd Mazza is among a small but growing new breed of reporters—those working online. As Internet producer at *WVTM-TV*, Birmingham, Ala., he's responsible for the content and look of the station's Web site, **NBC13 Interactive Neighborhood**. He selects the stories and their order and rewrites them from the broadcast scripts, adding details, history and useful links.

When a tornado ravaged the area and phone lines dangled on the ground, the station's Web site became a prime source of information for worried family members from around the country who couldn't get through by phone to find out where the tornado touched down, details on storm damage, and the progress of the search and recovery.

Another day, a bus loaded with students crashed on the highway from Birmingham to Montgomery. As the station broke into programming with details on the accident, Mazza quickly loaded the story at the top of his Web news page. He told Internet readers the details of the accident, the location, the school involved and where injured students were being treated.

"Many parents sent e-mails saying they were at work when they heard about the accident and found it difficult to find information," says Mazza. "But once they found our Web site, they had most, if not all, the information they needed."

He kept them updated through the day, adding information as it streamed into the newsroom.

On the day of a large warehouse fire, Mazza put images from the dramatic fire on the Web site's Ham-Cam, which updated the picture every two minutes.

"This allowed people to actually see the fire from *NBC13* even though they didn't have a television in front of them," says Mazza.

Knowing that hundreds of his readers were online from work, he uploaded detailed traffic information so they could find the fastest way home.

The search of the suspects' drivers licenses showed only post office boxes—a situation not uncommon in rural Nevada. But assistant city editor Linda Dono thought to see if, by chance, anybody else shared a box with the suspects. Sure enough, she found another name. She then used a CD/ROM phone book to bring up all the listings under that name and parceled out the numbers to various reporters who started dialing.

A woman answered one of those calls and said yes, she knew one of the suspects: He was her son-in-law. As she continued telling the reporter what a terrific guy he was, she heard a knock on her door. It was the FBI, wanting to look at her gasoline and oil cans.

This is just one example of how reporters are learning that computer resources are a valuable complement to traditional gumshoe reporting when the big story breaks. The other helpful digital aid is the Internet. As with other beats, crime reporters use the Net to make connections, background themselves on topics or find statistics. Some law enforcement agencies provide a precinct of sorts online. A reporter new to the crime beat in Arlington County, Va., could spend an hour at the online **Arlington County Police Department** to read up on department history, find out which officer is assigned to each neighborhood group and learn how the beat system works.

Crime stats abound on the Web, from the federal government on down to the states. For example, a reporter in Oswego, N.Y., could connect with the **N.Y. Division of Criminal Justice Services** to track the county's conviction rate on rape.

Wayne Harrison, assignment manager at *KMGH-TV*, Denver, finds the Internet indispensable when news breaks.

"We had a plane go down on the Continental Divide and sent our chopper up to get pictures," says Harrison, noting it was a two-hour flight one way. "Our pilot flew over the crash site and managed to get the tail number of the plane."

The only other information available was that three or four people were believed to be on board and were dead. But no one was saying who they were.

CRIME REPORTS

1. Use the blotter or desk log as a tip sheet, but get details of the crime or fire from the incident report.

2. Whenever possible, look through the investigative file, arson report or other internal documents that lay out more details about the crime or incident.

3. Look in the indictment for the police's theory on how the crime occurred.

4. See the coroner's report or autopsy report for the cause of death, as well as other information about the crime—evidence, for example, of bruising or of alcohol or drug use.

5. Remember that the Internet and databases can help track records and locate sources on deadline.

Using the tail number, Harrison first turned to an aviation Web site, **Landings**, to find out who owned the plane, what kind it was and where it was registered. When the owner turned out to be an obscure corporation identified by three letters, Harrison checked a Web phone book, **Switchboard**, in hopes of finding out more. The company wasn't listed, but that didn't stop Harrison. Using two Internet mapping pages, **MapQuest** and **Yahoo!Maps**, he found the airfields nearest the company's address and used Switchboard to find numbers for aircraft service companies nearby. This time, his Internet search paid off. A person at one company had serviced the aircraft, knew the owner and knew when the plane had taken off.

"I found out the owner was a dentist who was flying with his wife and two friends on a cross-country trip," says Harrison.

But he didn't use that information on the 10 p.m. news. The reason? He hadn't been able to second-source it yet. Harrison's aggressiveness and caution both make interesting points. Reporters don't give up when they're blocked at one turn. They try another route. Neither do they rush to air or print everything they learn. First they look for verification.

BASIC STORIES

The most common stories reporters write on the crime and safety beat are the crime story, the accident story and the fire story. The checklists in this chapter will help you remember which questions these stories need to answer. But these questions are just a start. Keep in mind that reporting from a checklist has its dangers. Reporters don't want to rely on a formula for stories. Each one is different.

THE CRIME STORY

People who follow the news are usually most interested in *what* crime occurred and *where* it happened (was it in their neighborhood?). In gathering

While reported crime is on the decrease, media reports on crime stories are on the increase. Critics argue that managers slot a lot of crime stories because they're easy to cover. What's needed, they say, is fewer stories on random crime and more stories with context and perspective.

CAPTURING THE DRAMATIC MOMENT

The crime and safety beat is filled with drama—flames, crumpled cars, barricaded gunners, heroic firefighters. On no other beat can the observant or the persistent reporter bring so much drama to her audience (see Chapter 7). The following dramatic description, re-creating the moments before the Oklahoma City bombing, couldn't have been written if it had not been coaxed from the subject through aggressive reporting.

OKLAHOMA CITY—At precisely two minutes past nine on Wednesday morning, April 19, Priscilla Salyers, an investigator for the U.S. Customs Service, was reading a file at her desk on the fifth floor of the Alfred P. Murrah Federal Building when agent Paul Ice approached her cubicle and asked a question.

Salyers looked up and said, "What?"

Joe Mitchell was on the first floor, applying for retirement checks in the Social Security office. He'd left his wife in the waiting room and he'd forgotten her birthdate, which he needed to fill out a form. He got up and stepped into a hallway to find her.

U.S. Agriculture Department veterinarian Brian Espy was in a conference room checking slides he planned to use for a lecture the following week.

At that same moment, Oklahoma City Police Sgt. John Avera was taking a breather from moving heavy equipment in his office 10 blocks from the federal building. He eased into a chair with a cup of hot coffee.

And then the bomb went off.

Knight-Ridder News Service

Radio and TV reporters often have an edge because they can capture live sound and pictures. But they don't always get there in time to tape the most dramatic action. In such cases, they're on the same footing as print reporters, and they have to recapture the drama from those who saw it. The point: All reporters have to push those they interview for description, no matter which medium. That's the start of good writing.

---

information for a crime story, as any other, the reporter must answer the fundamental questions: who, what, when, where, why and how.

The following is a list of the top 10 pieces of information to get for a basic crime story. Not all of it may be available by deadline, but the point is to *try* to get everything.

CHECKLIST FOR A CRIME STORY

___ Location and time

___ Nature of the crime and how it occurred

___ Status of the investigation; name and phone of the officer in charge

___ Arrests, arraignment and bail information

___ Description (or name) of suspect

___ Name, age, address of victim(s) and witness(es)

___ Relationship between criminal and victim

___ Crime and safety factors (unlocked door, high crime neighborhood, unique property, alarm system, etc.)

___ Deaths, injuries, or property loss or damages

___ Weapons or materials used in crime

Here's one example of a basic crime story. See how it stacks up to the checklist.

Several people playing cards were robbed early Sunday by a pair of assailants, one wielding a sawed-off gun, according to Syracuse police reports.

A 65-year-old man, who lives in the 1500 block of South Salina Street, told police a man and a woman stormed inside his home about 2 a.m. Sunday. The male robber aimed a pump shotgun at the homeowner and five of his guests as they played cards, police reports said.

The robbers lined the people against a wall and forced them to give up their money, police reports said.

The victims, three men and three women, weren't injured. The robbers then fled with an undetermined amount of money in a gray Toyota, police reports said. No suspects had been caught as of Sunday night.

The (Syracuse, N.Y.) Post-Standard

This reporter asked questions and carefully noted details to make this story much more than a routine report. Note the type of gun (sawed off), scene of the crime (1500 block of South Salina Street), the time (2 a.m.) and the number and gender of the victims (three men and three women).

When a reporter's story lacks intriguing details, it doesn't necessarily mean that the reporter is a poor writer. It may be that he didn't press for details in the first place. A reporter may have to pare some details away from the final story because of time or space constraints. But it is better to leave out a fact by choice than to simply forget to gather it.

A story with details captures attention. In crime stories, perhaps more than any other, those details must be exact. Reporters must tell their audience not only *what* they know but also *how* they know it. Reporters will stay out of legal trouble if they carefully write down the information, as well as the source (see box, The Legal Line: Libel and Privacy). Did you notice how many times the reporter above attributed the information? Five.

THE ACCIDENT STORY

A fender bender probably won't make news in the smallest of weekly papers or neighborhood cable news stations. But when accidents cause injuries or death, when the traffic backs up for an hour, or when the tanker leaks toxic chemicals, accidents make news. Reporters sent to an accident must think quickly and logically. Here are some of the basics for an accident story.

CHECKLIST FOR A TRAFFIC ACCIDENT

____ The names, ages and addresses of the dead or injured, the nature of injuries and where the injured were taken

____ The number and type of vehicles involved; the nature of damages to cars and property

____ How the accident occurred

____ The location

____ The time of the accident and how long it took to clean up

____ Contributing factors such as road conditions, hazards, speeding, alcohol or equipment malfunction

____ The number and identity of police and emergency vehicles responding and their response time *(continued)*

Breaking news stories, such as a flash flood, call forth the best in reporters, who often work 18-hour shifts to help readers, listeners and viewers know the status of relief efforts, how to stay safe and where to go for help.

Courtesy of *The (Cleveland) Plain Dealer.*

____ The lead investigator: name, rank, organization, phone number

____ Arrests or citations issued

____ Traffic tie-up, rerouting or road closures that result from the accident

Why and *how* are the questions most people want answered in press reports of an accident. A *Chicago Tribune* reporter led this story of a traffic accident with a possible answer:

A local woman, whom police described as mentally disabled, was struck and killed Tuesday afternoon as she tried to cross a busy intersection.

Cathy Bishop, 37, of 9652 S. 78th Ave., was in the middle of 95th Street at 78th Avenue when she tried to walk south against oncoming traffic at 5:07 p.m. Tuesday, according to Hickory Hills Police Detective Michael Tardi.

Bishop was struck by an eastbound pickup truck and thrown into the westbound lanes of 95th Street, where she was struck by a car.

Chicago Tribune

The reporter completed the story with other basics from the checklist, including where the woman was treated and details from witnesses. The reporter also made an extra effort to put perspective into the story—telling readers this was the second traffic fatality in that suburb in the last month.

THE FIRE STORY

In a story about a fire, most readers and listeners want the answer to the question *how:* How did the fire happen? It's a self-protective mind-set—they want to make sure the same thing can't happen to them. After answering the basic questions, starting with who was killed or hurt, reporters look for what makes each fire unique. The answer may be in the courage of neighbors who led the victims from the burning house. It may be in the fire department's quick response. Or it may be that a gas can, found in the alley nearby, suggests **arson**—a fire deliberately set.

Always look for what is different. One reporter who didn't probe for details about a fire on a hot summer day missed a key angle. It turned out that children had opened the nearby water hydrants to play in the cool water, weakening water pressure and hampering the efforts of firefighters. Here are other key questions to ask when covering a fire:

CHECKLIST FOR A FIRE STORY

____ The names, ages, addresses of the dead and injured (get either the nature of injuries, current condition or cause of death)

____ The type of structure and the owner's name

____ A damage estimate and information about insurance

____ The time and source of the first call; the number of alarms

____ The origin of the fire, how it spread, and when it was brought under control

____ The number of firefighters and equipment involved

____ Contributing factors such as poor water pressure, code violations, no smoke alarms or sprinklers, combustibles or wind

____ Rescue stories/heroes

____ The status of the investigation; information about any arrests

____ Area evacuations, traffic rerouting or other dislocation

LIBEL AND PRIVACY

LIBEL

WKBW-TV, Buffalo, N.Y., reported that a local restaurateur, John Prozeralik, had been abducted in an incident related to organized crime. But the station was wrong—it was another restaurant owner. The anchor said she believed the FBI confirmed the name for her, but the federal officers denied it. Prozeralik sued the station for **libel**—damage to his reputation. After 11 years, numerous appeals and two jury trials, Prozeralik won $11 million, the largest libel verdict to date in New York.

Reporters and editors work in fear of such suits. The Libel Defense Resource Center reports the average judgment against media defendants in the 1990s totaled more than $5.8 million. And even when the media win, they spend a lot of money and time fighting the suit.

Libel law differs state to state, so it's very important to know the rules in the state in which you are working. This is merely a quick overview with generalities, so check with your news organization or a statewide press association to learn the specific rules in your state.

Defamation, the legal term for injuring someone's reputation, includes both libel (written) and **slander** (verbal). To win a defamation case, plaintiffs must prove not only that something defamatory was said but also that the defamation was about them, hurt them, was false and was reported due to negligence or recklessness.

Elected government officials and people working in high public policy positions have to prove more than a private person does to win a libel case. That is based on the belief that political speech is so important that some errors in criticism of government officials must be tolerated. So public officials, and now, well-known public figures as well, have to prove a national standard derived from the legal case *New York Times v. Sullivan.* This standard is known as **actual malice**. Those attempting to prove actual malice must demonstrate that the media defendant knew the information was wrong and printed it anyway, or recklessly disregarded information that the story was false. It's a difficult standard to prove.

The standards for private people vary. But in most states private individuals only have to prove that a reporter was **negligent**, meaning the reporter didn't use the care that an ordinary reporter would use.

The best protection against libel is truth.

Dawn Phillips, general counsel for the Michigan Press Association, says she tells reporters covering crime, "The first rule is to lay your hands on every government document you can. I jokingly tell reporters that's rule 1,3, 5, 7 and 9—get the document.

"You want that hard piece of paper," adds Phillips. "You don't want the police's oral recollection—people don't remember."

Phillips says reporters shouldn't think they're off the hook by using the term, "allegedly." "It doesn't give you any protection," she advises.

Another rule on Phillips' list: Sex, she says, is seldom safe.

"When you're talking about sexual misconduct, you are in dangerous territory," says Phillips. "Be exceedingly careful."

Media law attorneys remind reporters to be equally careful in getting criminal charges correct, getting the name of suspects exactly right and giving an official source for allegations.

If the information reported is clearly an opinion (not fact couched as an opinion), can be proved true, or is reported accurately from official documents that turned out to be wrong, the media will usually win a libel case.

PRIVACY

A kissing cousin to libel law is privacy law, which concerns people's right to be left alone. These laws vary greatly among states. Reporting sensitive personal information such as medical test results or intimate sexual information can be the basis for a suit for **publication of private facts**. To win such a suit, a person has to prove the media published private information that is highly offensive and not newsworthy.

Shooting a picture with a long telephoto lens and invading someone's privacy could be grounds for a suit for **intrusion**, whether or not the photograph or video was published. But photographing something anyone can see from a public street isn't considered intrusion.

If an online producer uses a file photo for a Web site or a TV editor selects generic video to illustrate a story, that news outlet could be subject to a suit for **false light** if a person in the photograph or video is portrayed in a way that is untruthful. For example, a producer wouldn't want to use video of gun owners practicing shooting at a gun range in conjunction with copy that talks about criminals illegally using guns.

ENTERPRISE STORIES

Basic stories look at single events—the sexual assault of a jogger or the drug raid that netted 14 arrests. In an enterprise story, the reporter digs deeper to look for links between events, to explain why they happened or to probe what is and isn't being done to keep the community safer.

BUILDING FROM BASIC STORIES

Beth Willon of *KNTV-TV,* San Jose, Calif., used a basic crime story as the beginning point for two enterprise stories. Soon after her breaking news story about a high-tech heist of computer chips in the Silicon Valley, she learned that this was one of a series of nasty robberies.

As she worked the broader story, she found out the robbers often got inside information by pressuring people who had run up enormous gambling debts at legal casinos in the area. She also learned that the thieves were changing their patterns, holding up truck drivers rather than hitting the companies where they delivered.

"I got two good stories spun off a simple high-tech heist," Willon said. "You had your gambling debt, you had your truck jackings."

Enterprise stories built off of basic crime stories contain these additional elements:

- More information about the who, what, where, when and why. This may not be available at the time the basic story is written.
- Context that explains how one crime relates to others.
- Insight into how the crime has affected people or businesses.

It's not that reporters don't try to make their stories complete the first time around. But crime often breaks late, and the details can be sketchy in initial reports. Follow-up is critical.

Enterprise follow-ups often allow more room for storytelling and narrative writing. Sometimes they reconstruct events from start to finish, weaving in new detail and, in broadcast, new sound and video. Sometimes efforts to reconstruct events turn the spotlight away from the crime or fire itself toward how well officials responded.

Such was the case in the in-depth story "The Pang Fire: What Went Wrong," written by two *Seattle Times* reporters. They told about an arson at a warehouse in which four firefighters ended up dead. After opening the story with a quote from the fire chief who said that all safety procedures had been followed, the reporters wrote

> But a Seattle Times investigation—based on the review of Fire Department records and scores of interviews with firefighters, witnesses and other experts—points to a different conclusion:
>
> Everything did not go as it was supposed to. In fact there is a good reason to wonder whether James Brown, Walter Kilgore, Gregory Shoemaker and Randy Terlicker would be alive today if not for human error, official disregard, malfunctioning systems and misguided policy.
>
> *The Seattle Times*

One of the hallmarks of such enterprise reporting is to answer the question *why* and look at lessons learned from the event. *The Seattle Times'* reporters showed, among other things, how those in charge didn't know the warehouse had a basement, that they misjudged the origin of the fire and that the firefighters' personal alert pagers (to help find them when they're down) frequently didn't work properly.

FINDING NEW VIEWPOINTS

Crime and safety reporters also find original enterprise by looking at their beats from a different viewpoint. When Raoul Mowatt took over the public safety beat at the *San Jose (Calif.) Mercury News,* he set out to bring new voices into his stories.

Mike Wendland

"We wanted to open the door to groups we haven't been covering, such as Neighborhood Watch groups and other parts of government that aren't police agencies but do play a role in fighting crime," he said.

Mowatt's new approach has led him to stories about the preventive efforts of community policing, about ATM machines with 911 panic buttons and about how to make neighborhoods safer. Such stories go far beyond the whodunit and offer readers new ideas and sometimes new hope.

Mowatt is one of a new breed of crime and safety reporters who try to understand and explain crime through the eyes of many more people than those who enforce the law. Mike Wendland, I-Team reporter for *WDIV-TV*, Detroit, is another. For an investigative series on car theft, Wendland decided to seek the perspective of one particularly knowledgeable group—those who steal the cars.

"It's the criminals who really know the story," said Wendland, noting that too often reporters settle for what the cops-think-the-criminals-think.

He pulled the names and prison addresses of car thieves off his in-house database of state criminals and mailed them a survey asking them about their car-stealing techniques. More than 100 convicts sent back completed forms (what else do they have to do in prison?).

Wendland's methods wouldn't win praise in a research class: It wasn't a random sample. But it gave considerable insight into a world we usually only hear about through the filter of law enforcement. When he coded their answers and analyzed them by computer, he found:

- The thieves had stolen 28 cars on average.
- The most popular location to steal from was a driveway or garage.
- Fifty-three percent stole at random, 28 percent stole for an order and 19 percent said they did both.
- The average money made per car was $938.
- The best protection against theft was a car alarm.

Enterprise reports don't end with the numbers, however. Since he works in television, Wendland needed pictures. He spent hours on surveillance and recorded dramatic video of a theft in progress. He interviewed victims, police, criminals and insurance investigators. Then he presented the story in layers: a taped piece, followed by an on-the-scene live shot and a second-day taped story again followed with a live shot. In one of these segments, a former car thief demonstrated how quickly he could break into a car and drive it off—22 seconds.

SUMMARY   ENTERPRISE STORIES

1. Good enterprise can start with follow-up stories that look for connections between events.

2. Details missed in initial accounts can lead to compelling stories that reconstruct from start to finish what happened at major crimes, fires or accidents. Such stories are built on telling detail, a time line of events and in-depth interviews that take the audience to the scene through the memories of those who were there. In broadcast, they also need new sound and video.

3. Some enterprise stories document a problem that needs solving, a policy that isn't working or a system that appears broken. In the course of reporting, consult experts about what can be done to get things back on track.

4. The crime and safety beat is more than the police beat. Hunt down people in the community with different viewpoints, and give readers, viewers and listeners different perspectives on crime and efforts to combat it.

The world of computer conversation also opens up avenues to find new perspectives. Free-lancer Bill Clede, who often writes for *Law and Order* magazine, regularly wanders through discussion forums on CompuServe, an online information service. One day he saw a message from a police officer questioning whether cops obey seat belt laws any better than other motorists. Besides finding a different take on a story, Clede had a ready pool of interviewees in the online discussion forum.

RECOMMENDED READING

Access to places. (1997). *Photographers' guide to privacy.* (1994). *Police records: A guide to effective access in the 50 states & D.C.* (1997). Arlington, VA: Reporters Committee for Freedom of the Press.

These booklets provide reporters and photographers with simple guides on access issues—where they can go on public and private property and how to get police records. They make good, inexpensive primers before that first job.

Access to campus crime reports (3rd ed.). (1996). Arlington, VA: Student Press Law Center.

Students covering campus crime will find this a helpful guide as they work with police in finding out about campus crime.

Bureau of Justice Statistics, U.S. Department of Justice. *Bureau of Justice statistics.* [Online]. Available: **http://www.ojp.usdoj.gov/bjs**.

This federal government site is the best jumping-off place for crime statistics.

Deppa, J. (1994). *The media and disasters.* Washington Square, NY: New York University Press.

Although this book focuses on one disaster, the crash of PanAm 103 over Lockerbie, Scotland, its lessons apply for all disaster coverage. Particu-

larly insightful is the section on how reporters experience post-traumatic stress disorder.

FireSafe. [Online]. Available: **http://www.firesafe. com**.

An excellent directory of resources and organizations on safety with links to hundreds of sites.

Law of the Student Press. (2nd ed.). (1994). Arlington, VA: Student Press Law Center.

This 270-page paperback is written for student reporters and covers all the basic legal fronts—First Amendment, access, privacy, defamation, copyright and more. It's highly recommended for every campus newsroom.

Meredith, J. *Police officer's Internet directory.* [Online]. Available: **http://www.officer.com**.

A Boston police officer runs this site—the best we've found for networking with people, organizations and resources in law enforcement.

Sanford, B. (1991). *Sanford's synopsis of libel and privacy.* New York: Pharos Books.

Professionals make a run for this when it's available at a conference. It's a handy 35-page guide giving the basics of both libel and privacy, written by well-known media attorney Bruce Sanford.

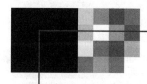

EXERCISES

A. RESEARCH

1. Research the following terms using people, print and online sources. Then write explanations that could be used in an article or script.

   a. controlled substance
   b. DUI and/or DWI
   c. department pre-fire plans
   d. five-alarm fire

e. jaws of life

f. service difficulty report, SDR

g. uniform crime report, UCR

2. You've arrived at the scene of an apartment house fire that firefighters have just brought under control. Whom do you talk with first? What pictures do you suggest your photographer or videographer get? Who might describe what the scene is like? How do you get a damage estimate? Who might tell you the cause of the fire? How would you find out the owner of the building? Where will you go tomorrow to get the official report on the fire?

3. You get a tip that a local electronics store was broken into overnight. Where would you go in your community to get the police report? Whom would you want to interview? What would you look for at the scene? What are five questions you'd ask the store manager?

4. You hear about a five-car pile-up on an icy freeway. As reporters are heading out to the scene, whom do you call? What six questions do you need answered?

5. You get a tip from a source that local and federal law enforcement officials, working together, have raided a house on the outskirts of town believed to be a factory for manufacturing methamphetamine. Police are close-mouthed. How might you go about reporting the story?

B. BASIC STORIES

1. Write either stories or memos based on the following assignments.

a. Get the police report from a recent crime. Interview the investigating officer and victim or witness, if possible. Find out the court date or next step in the investigation.

b. Get a recent accident report on a collision with injury or property damage. Interview the investigating officer and victims or witnesses, if possible. Find out the latest on the injured, the property damage, pending charges or the status of the investigation and the cause of the accident.

c. Find out how frequently fire officials inspect the fire detection systems or extinguishers in hotels in your town. Has anyone been fined

for defective equipment? What, if anything, is the penalty? Is the program adequate, according to fire officials? What do tourism officials say? How does it compare to a neighboring community?

d. Find out what plans your community has for managing a disaster by talking with the emergency management staff, police, transportation officials and the Red Cross. Based on those interviews, write a media plan for how a local news outlet should work with those agencies to cover a disaster.

e. Suppose you are the producer of a cable news show airing at 5 p.m. Write a philosophical statement about how that show will cover crime news, remembering that the audience includes children. Now assume you're the editor of a morning newspaper. What are your standards for front-page photos that might end up on the breakfast table next to the children?

C. ENTERPRISE STORIES

1. Compare perceptions of crime in one neighborhood of your community with actual reported crime. Get the crime statistics compiled for a specific precinct. Then talk to people who live in the neighborhood. What are they most concerned about? Do they think crime is getting better or worse? Why? Do the numbers surprise them?

2. See if local police have begun a community policing program—a current trend in law enforcement. In such programs, officers walk or bike their beats, regularly visit businesses and schools, set up police ministations in neighborhoods and work with youth in crime prevention programs. What kind of balance does the department try to keep between preventing crimes and investigating crimes?

3. Find out whether new technology in the justice system, such as computerized or online records, digital fingerprinting and DNA testing, is making it easier or harder for police to do their job. Are defense attorneys concerned that improvements in computer and biomedical technology are jeopardizing citizens' rights? Do advances in technology require police to seek more and more education?

4. Check out whether arson is on the increase in your community. Talk with insurance adjusters,

fire department arson investigators and neighborhood groups. Analyze fire statistics for trends in the location, types of buildings or methods used.

5. Chronicle what's happening on the teen drug scene in your area. Are arrests up or down? How are police working to stop the flow of drugs into the area? What's the current drug of choice? What prevention and education programs are under way to combat its use? Is there enough treatment available to help users overcome their addictions?

CHAPTER 14 | Justice

Reporter Mike TeSelle packed his gear into the *KFBB-TV* news car outside the Cascade County, Mont., courthouse and watched as his TV competitor sped away. Now he had a few extra minutes. He didn't need to head back to the station to edit the story for an hour. The story script was already jotted down in his notebook. He'd scribbled it there while the pretrial hearing was going on. So he sauntered back inside to chat with court employees in the hope of digging out one more nugget of news.

"I don't usually leave a scene of anything [too soon] for fear that I might miss something," TeSelle says.

And had he left on this day, he would have missed something.

Since his arrest on murder charges a year before, Carlos Ambriz had denied he'd shaken his crying, month-old son to death. TeSelle first learned about Ambriz's arrest during his routine morning checks of police incident reports. He'd stayed with the case ever since.

Now, as he worked the courthouse corridors, two sources he'd developed tipped him that Ambriz was considering a guilty plea.

"Through the door, I glimpsed the defendant [Ambriz] crying," TeSelle explained. "So I said to the bailiff, 'So how's life?' And he said, 'It's getting a lot better because this episode's about to end. I think he just signed a plea agreement.'"

TeSelle grabbed his gear and set it up again. Within five minutes the judge climbed back on the bench and the defendant took the stand.

"He started to break down as each question got harder and harder," said TeSelle, "and then I got some great SOT [sound on tape] when he said, 'I didn't mean to kill my child . . . it wasn't deliberate.'"

TeSelle's story led the newscast at 5:30 p.m.: "The man accused of murdering his 36-day old son is now pleading guilty . . ."

The competition, television and print, had nothing on Ambriz's plea.

The best reporters have a basic understanding of the justice system, because when a big story breaks on their beat, they'd rather cover it than hand it over to the court reporter. So whether you cover science or sports, labor or lifestyles, it's to your advantage to bone up on the legal beat.

TeSelle's work illustrates several important points we'll elaborate on in this chapter. These include the need to:

- Make calls and check records daily. Such checks are boring and routine, but they deliver interesting stories. That's how TeSelle first found the Ambriz story.
- Develop good rapport with people who work in the criminal justice system—not only judges and prosecutors, but secretaries and bailiffs, court clerks and defense attorneys.
- Go where the story is happening, or might happen. Reporting by phone just doesn't supply the same detail and drama. And you might miss "the big one."
- Arrive early, stay late. "Don't set your agenda according to someone else," says TeSelle. "The other reporter left because he thought I was leaving."
- Think and plan as the story evolves. TeSelle revised his script several times during the afternoon.

PEOPLE TO SEEK OUT

On the justice beat, one suspect's journey through the legal system can take months, sometimes years. No reporter can keep track of each case's progress toward justice without developing good sources and keeping good files.

ATTORNEYS

Despite the dozens of impromptu interviews on the courthouse steps you've seen on TV news, many attorneys never talk to the media. And sometimes they have legitimate reasons, because their ethical guidelines (yes, they have them) prevent them from saying anything that might prejudice the case.

"Almost everybody you talk to by law has sworn to somebody that they aren't going to tell you anything, " *The Boston Globe*'s Judy Rakowsky says. "You can't demand anything because they aren't supposed to tell you."

She's right. Many won't tell you much more than the mere basics of the case: the defendant's name, address and employment; circumstances of the arrest; the charge and the status of the investigation. But Rakowsky has picked up a few techniques in her years covering the attorneys at the Boston federal courthouse.

Judy Rakowsky of *The Boston Globe* knows the importance of developing good sources on the justice beat. When a case is filed late in the day or the prosecutor isn't talking, Rakowsky has a thick card file of sources who can steer her in the right direction.

"I just try not to insult their intelligence," she says, explaining that she knows attorneys won't tip their hand on their inside witness or a key piece of evidence. "I might say, 'I know you can't talk about that but I need some flavor of what's happening' or, 'is there any place you can point me to—a document, a person?'"

Most crimes are violations of state law, so technically it's the state that is prosecuting the person. Representing that state are prosecutors (sometimes called district attorneys or state's attorneys). They're valuable sources because they set the pace for the court schedule and have great discretion in dropping or reducing charges and in **plea bargaining**—negotiating with the defendant to lower the charge if the person will plead guilty.

Keep in mind, however, that you are hearing about the case through the prism of the attorney's role in it. All attorneys are trained to be advocates, not impartial observers. So the prosecutor will make it sound as if there's hardly a need for a trial, the evidence is so compelling. Conversely, the defense attorney will often discount the evidence, blame sloppy police work and make the defendant sound saintly. Your job is to find the truth, usually somewhere in between.

Many attorneys don't handle criminal cases; they work on what's known as the civil side of the court system. **Civil cases** are those in which one party or company sues another over some wrong, not necessarily a crime. For example, a minority employee sues the company for racial discrimination or a landlord sues a tenant for back rent. Attorneys often specialize in certain areas such as labor law or real estate law. In civil cases, as in criminal matters, make sure you interview the attorneys for both parties.

JUDGES

Judges are attorneys too, but now that they're on the bench they're supposed to be impartial decision makers. So they can't comment, on the record, on a case before them. Some will be helpful off the record in explaining the issues in the case. Often, however, reporters find it easier to get information from those who work at the courthouse.

COURT EMPLOYEES

As Mike TeSelle of *KFBB-TV* found when covering the shaken baby case, the best sources are often those who don't star in the courtroom but play out their roles in the courthouse offices. His were two secretaries.

Reporters on the justice beat always try to develop a good rapport with the people who work in the court clerk's office. They control all the case files, which means they're a key conduit or roadblock in the information flow. They're also the ones who are first to see a civil suit being filed and, with nurturing, might tip off a reporter.

Law clerks, usually law students working for judges, handle the files and exhibits while the case is being heard. Count on them, as well as the judge's secretary, for answers about the court **docket**, or schedule. In addition, bailiffs, jury clerks and court administrators should never be overlooked.

OTHER SOURCES

Besides those who work at the courthouse, look for sources with broader and different perspectives:

- Victim assistance workers
- Families of victims and suspects
- Probation officers and those working in alternative sentencing projects
- Court watchers—people who monitor hearings for a justice group or out of personal interest
- Bar association staff
- Social service agencies and caseworkers
- Justice committees of religious organizations
- Researchers or criminologists
- Law professors

Colleagues are also helpful sources—well, if they're not your competitors. Court reporters in other cities can be helpful when the tentacles of your story expand widely. The ***Cops & Court Reporters List*** on the Internet is one way of making connections.

"I often use it to reach a colleague in a city where I need information or clips quickly," says Mark Rollenhagen, a reporter from *The (Cleveland) Plain Dealer* who runs the discussion group.

In addition to making connections via e-mail, the group publishes its directory on the Web.

WATCHWORDS

- **Arraignment/indictment**: An **arraignment** (sometimes called a first appearance) is an initial court proceeding at which a judge tells the defendant the charges and sets bail. An **indictment** (or true bill) is a document listing the charge(s) against the person. It is "returned" by a **grand jury**—a citizens' panel that reviews the evidence brought by the prosecutor and votes whether the case should continue. If it votes to continue, the grand jury "hands up" the indictment. Otherwise, the grand jury offers a **no bill**, which means there's no reason to continue, and the case ends. Grand juries and indictments are used in the federal system and some states.

- **Guilty/not guilty/acquitted**: A judge or jury finds a person either guilty or not guilty. Even when a person is found not guilty beyond a reasonable doubt, it does not mean the person is innocent, so the term "innocent" is not technically accurate. You will find reporters, however, using it to eliminate confusion when "not guilty" can sound like "guilty." **Acquitted** is another term for being found not guilty.

- **Jail/prison**: Before and during trial, defendants who aren't out on bail live in the **jail**. Sometimes persons convicted of lesser crimes serve short sentences here also. The **prison** (or penitentiary) is the place where persons already convicted are serving their time. Jails are often run by the city or county, whereas the state usually runs the prisons. Persons convicted of federal crimes serve their time in a federal prison.

- **Parole/probation**: A criminal released from prison may be put on **parole**, a conditional release under which the person has to follow certain rules and is supervised by a parole officer. Persons who violate parole can be sent back to prison. **Probation** is usually an alternative to incarceration for persons convicted of lesser offenses who agree to follow guidelines to stay out of jail.

THINGS TO READ

When the police won't divulge much, the record at the courthouse might tell a lot. For most cases, the records are kept at the county courthouse. They may be categorized in several divisions—criminal (crimes), civil (one person or company suing another), probate (wills and trusts) or juvenile (for defendants 16 and under).

But that county courthouse won't have the records for persons charged with federal crimes, such as large-scale drug prosecutions or bankruptcies. For those, reporters go to the nearest federal courthouse. Justice reporters also wander the Internet to read the law, track pending legislation or gather statistics. The best reporters are sleuths in cyberspace and efficient record checkers at the courthouse.

CRIMINAL COURT RECORDS

At either the federal or county courthouse, the court clerk keeps the case files with the basic information. If you're researching a crime, such as burglary, assault or manslaughter, check with the clerk who keeps track of **criminal cases**. You can usually tell a criminal case by its citation, in the form "State v. John Doe" or "People v. Jane Doe," which means the prosecutor, on behalf of the state, is bringing the charges against a defendant named John Doe.

Valuable documents in criminal cases are:

- **Search warrants** and **warrant returns** that tell where the police searched and what they found. These must be made available to the public within a specified time period after they are issued.
- **Indictments,** returned by a citizens' grand jury, listing the charges against the defendant.
- **Arraignment files** or **case files** that might include statements from the suspect, witnesses and victims, or **rap sheets**, which list previous criminal records. (See box, Where Can I Go? What Can I Get?)

All the documents will make a lot more sense if you have spent some time walking around the crime scene. That'll help you also when you hear witnesses' testimony in court.

CRIMINAL CASE RECORDS

In criminal cases, the prosecutor believes some-one has violated a state criminal law and brings charges in the name of the state against that person.

1. Review the case file at the clerk's office or judge's office.

2. Look in the case file for the indictment (or prosecutor's information form), search warrant returns, witnesses' statements, the defendant's prior criminal record and the next court date.

CIVIL COURT RECORDS

Not all wrongs are "crimes" under the law. Such things as payments for accident injuries, differences over business contracts or property damage from toxic waste also end up in court, but as civil cases. In these cases, one person or company is suing another, for example, "Jane Doe v. John Roe." In civil cases, the losing defendant doesn't get jail time but has to pay out money.

Civil court records are also kept with the clerk at the courthouse. Reading these records is essential because there's little action in the courtroom to write about. Civil cases drag on for years, and about 95 percent never go to trial. That's because judges force the parties to settle so they can use more of their courtroom time for criminal cases.

The process by which each side finds out the other's information in a civil case is called **discovery**—the sharing of documents back and forth. Although reporters can't always get all documents from discovery, often the key ones they can get are:

- The **complaint**, which outlines the wrongs done to the plaintiff—the person bringing the case
- The **answer**, which gives the defendant's version of events
- **Interrogatories**, which are answers from a witness (typed and sworn to) based on questions from a party in the suit
- **Depositions**, which are transcripts of testimony, under oath, by parties or witnesses, in answer to an attorney's questions before the trial

Sometimes one incident can end up as both a criminal case and a civil case. For example, in a criminal case O. J. Simpson was found not guilty in the homicides of Nicole Brown Simpson and Ronald Goldman, but he was found liable in a civil case for wrongful death after the Goldman family sued him for compensation for the loss of their son.

CIVIL CASE RECORDS

In civil cases one person or company is suing another person or company over some wrong, which may not technically be a crime.

1. Get the case file at the clerk's or judge's office.

2. Look inside for the complaint, answer, interrogatories or depositions and the notation of the next action in the case.

3. The files are the key to your stories, as there will be little action in court on which to report.

Although it is very rare, a person can be tried by both state and federal government for actions during the same incident. The state of California tried Los Angeles police officers for beating Rodney King, and then the federal government tried the same officers for violating King's civil rights, a federal charge.

Despite all the juicy details in the court records, remember, records are just the starting point for justice stories. Many lawsuits are frivolous. Angry people exaggerate their claims. Attorneys write documents favoring their clients. The motives are often revenge or publicity more than righting wrongs. The good reporter checks and double-checks and always interviews all parties or their attorneys before writing the story.

ELECTRONIC CONNECTIONS

When Mark Rollenhagen wants a quick overview of a topic, he'll often use his electronic connections first. On his beat covering federal courts for *The (Cleveland) Plain Dealer,* Rollenhagen says the Internet has become a familiar and daily resource. One day he was working on a story about a case involving child pornography being distributed on the Internet. Rollenhagen needed to find out quickly what types of computer porn cases prosecutors pursue and what courts have said about possessing pornography that did not involve children.

"I needed a quick review of obscenity laws," says Rollenhagen. "I also knew that while federal prosecutors in Cleveland and many other districts had not prosecuted an obscenity since the 1970s, prosecutors in Memphis had."

So Rollenhagen went to one of his favorite sites, the **Cyber Space Law Center: Cybercrime** to search for

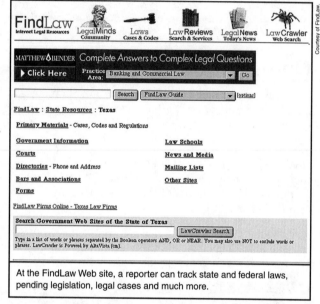

At the FindLaw Web site, a reporter can track state and federal laws, pending legislation, legal cases and much more.

appeals court decisions on obscenity. There he found a recent case from Memphis and within it just what he needed—a quick history of obscenity cases as well as a section on the distribution of porn on computer bulletin boards.

Another day he was working on a story about a flight attendant being assaulted by a passenger. He traveled the Web to the **U.S. Department of Justice** and used its search engine to scan the press releases of the U.S. Attorney's offices. His search terms, "assault" and "airline personnel" helped him find a similar case, which he included in his story.

CLIPBOARD   INTERNET SITES MENTIONED IN THIS CHAPTER

Cops & Court Reporters List	www.reporters.net/ccr	TRAC	trac.syr.edu
Cyber Space Law Center: Cybercrime	www.cybersquirrel.com	U.S. Department of Justice (press releases)	www.usdoj.gov/press.html
Superior Court, San Diego Co.	www.sandiego.courts.ca.gov/ superior	For an update to this list, see http://web.syr.edu/~bcfought.	

WHERE CAN I GO? WHAT CAN I GET?

Laws in each state differ, so be sure to check your state law or with your news organization's attorney. Here are some general guidelines:

Cameras/recorders in court	Most states allow, but check state law. Not allowed in federal court.
Court calendar/schedule	Available from court clerk.
Court file	Available under court rules or state open records law. Usually found in the court clerk's office; sometimes in the judge's office.
Depositions	Available if in court file. Or ask an attorney for a copy.
Grand jury deliberations	Closed.
Indictments	Once an indictment has been "handed up" by the grand jury, it's available from the prosecutor or court clerk. Later a copy will be in the case file.
Jurors' names	Usually available—check state law.
Jury selection	Open.
Juvenile court	Often closed—check state law.
Juvenile files	Varies state to state. When a juvenile is tried as an adult, the files are usually open.
Pretrial hearings	Usually open.
Trial	Open. Judges can only close a trial after stating on the record an overriding governmental interest that requires closure.

The Net provides reporters like Rollenhagen not only background information but also access to journals, articles, organizations and statistics to use in stories, sidebars or hyperlinks for Net publications.

Increasingly, courts are putting their calendars and filings online. Reporters in San Diego have it made—with a few clicks on the **Superior Court** Web site, they can check the docket and review the latest filing in cases they are tracking.

BASIC STORIES

The basic diet for justice reporters centers around criminal and civil court stories. There are many ways to flavor such stories as they move through the court process so that readers and listeners stay enticed. Read on for tips.

CRIMINAL COURT STORIES

If you've taken a course in theater or attended a stage play, you'll find yourself in familiar surroundings when you go to court: There is plenty of drama inside a courtroom. The players know their roles. Much of what's said is scripted. The storyline ebbs and flows and leads to a culmination, with the attorneys playing to the emotions of the jury.

Reporters can use that drama in writing interesting stories. They can bring their audience to the scene, describing the events through the eyes of key witnesses, capturing the maneuvering of the defense and prosecution teams and, ultimately, bringing readers, viewers and listeners the climax of a verdict.

PREJUDICIAL REPORTING

"Innocent until proven guilty." Defense attorneys frequently fault the media for convicting their clients before or during a trial.

In some states reporters and judges have set forth guidelines for both the media and the courts during criminal trials. The guidelines from the New York Fair Trial Free Press Conference, for example, caution reporters to think carefully before printing or airing information that could prejudice a case, such as:

■ A confession

■ Test results

■ Prospective testimony

■ A potential guilty plea

The guidelines also impose a responsibility on judges to do their part in ensuring a fair trial (see box, The Legal Line: Free Press, Fair Trial, later in the chapter).

Monitor local TV and radio newscasts for a week and take notes about court stories. Compare those stories to similar ones in two local newspapers. Discuss in groups of three to five how the media in your area cover trials and whether you see any of these guidelines being followed. Would you agree to them? Why or why not?

Also discuss whether there is any gruesome evidence or personal information that comes out at a trial that you would not include in a story. Does the type of medium or the audience affect your decision?

Here's part of the script from Mike TeSelle's story in the shaken baby case:

(TeSelle narration) Carlos Ambriz wanted to have his say in court for so long. Thursday, he got it. Ambriz wasn't planning on admitting that he killed his infant son Taylor. Instead—today was supposed to be the final hearing before this trial next week. But after more than an hour of attorneys sifting through photographs of his son, Carlos Ambriz took the stand—and accepted the state's plea agreement.

(Attorney during hearing) You took your son by the jaw and squeezed it. (Video shows Ambriz breaks down). That's one of the acts you did that night.

(Ambriz) Yes.

KFBB-TV (Great Falls, Mont.)

Note that TeSelle's story shows he'd mastered the legal process—he understood the original charge, the type of hearing he was covering and the impact of the plea. While in the courtroom, he knew to keep the tape rolling all the time the defendant was on the stand, not knowing whether he would get anything usable or not. And he remembered, amidst the hubbub at the end, to get reaction from the attorney and to find out the next court date. Those details appeared later in the script. With all those elements, he had lots of material from which to write.

This dramatic confession surprised everyone during a routine hearing some media outlets didn't even cover. That isn't unusual. Few reporters follow every action in a case, as TeSelle did in this high-profile one. It wouldn't be possible. Dozens of cases can go on simultaneously in a single courthouse, most of them not particularly newsworthy. Usually, reporters follow the most important cases, writing stories at key times.

Often, the first story comes at the indictment or preliminary hearing. Here's how *The Sacramento (Calif.) Bee* began its story about the indictment of Theodore Kaczynski for the so-called Unabomb explosions:

A federal grand jury in Sacramento on Tuesday indicted Theodore Kaczynski, a reclusive former mathematics professor, on charges related to four

Unabomber explosions that killed two people and injured two others.

(continued)

The jury issued a 10-count indictment in connection with the bombings that killed Sacramentans Hugh Scrutton in 1986 and Gilbert Murray in 1995, and seriously injured researchers Charles Epstein of the University of California, San Francisco, and David Gelernter of Yale University in June 1993.

The Sacramento Bee

The first few paragraphs here cover the basic information readers need to know: who took action against whom (a federal grand jury against Theodore Kaczynski), what was done (he was indicted), when (Tuesday) and where (Sacramento).

Another essential element in indictment stories is to get the charges correct and in detail. That's the way to avoid legal hassles. The charges, summarized in the lead here, were later carefully explained by the reporters. The story included other topics important in an indictment story: the status of the defendant (jailed in Montana), his potential punishment (life imprisonment or death penalty), details of each bombing, reaction from those injured and the next steps in the judicial process.

When a newsworthy case goes to trial, reporters may write some or all of the following types of stories:

- Advancer, a few days before the trial begins, recapping the history of the case and the key issues in the trial.
- Trial opening story, highlighting the opening arguments when the attorneys tell the judge and jury what they're going to prove.
- Trial highlights, with key testimony recapping the drama and describing the evidence of the most important witnesses.
- Closing arguments, comparing the attorneys' differing versions of what happened.
- The verdict, giving the decision, the reaction of those involved and, when possible, a sense of what led to the jury's decision.
- Sentencing, if the defendant was found guilty. These stories explain the sentence and where and how it will be served.

THE CRIMINAL PROCESS

The following is a general outline of the steps a criminal defendant goes through, but since the terminology differs among states, be sure to know the process used in the state where you are working.

- *Arrest:* The police physically restrain the person and explain the charges.
- *Booking at the police station:* Mug shots and fingerprints are taken. The arrest is noted in a booking file.
- *Initial appearance:* In this court proceeding, the judge tells the defendant the charges against him and explains his rights. The defendant enters a plea, usually "not guilty." Then the judge sets bail, and if the defendant can post the bail, he is released.
- *Grand jury indictment or prosecutor's information:* Both these steps are designed to be a check on the police and prosecutor.

In states that don't use a grand jury system, the prosecutor files a document called an information that lists the charges against the defendant. Within a specified number of days a judge will hold a preliminary hearing to make sure there is probable cause to continue holding the person. Witnesses may testify at a preliminary hearing, and the defendant and her attorney attend.

In some states if the prosecutor doesn't get the case to a grand jury within a certain number of days, a judge will hold a preliminary hearing to make sure the case should continue. If the judge believes there isn't probable cause, the defendant is released and the process stops.

CRIMINAL COURT STORIES

1. Work the naturally occurring drama of the case into your stories.

2. Know the process and how the system works to better tell the story and fit the day's events into the overall time line.

3. Get down descriptive details and listen for the quotes or sound bites that characterize the story.

4. Be exact about names, dates, charges and testimony. Libel suits start with careless errors.

5. Develop a system to monitor the case as it progresses so you can write stories at the key junctures.

- ***Arraignment in trial court:*** The initial appearance may have been in a lower court, but this proceeding is held in a trial court. Here the judge tells the defendant of the charges and reviews the bail.

- ***Pretrial hearings:*** The judge may schedule several court dates to deal with preliminary matters such as admitting evidence, allowing testimony or determining sanity. Plea bargaining is possible at this stage.

- ***Trial:*** Either a jury or a judge hears the evidence and determines the verdict.

- ***Sentencing:*** The judge usually determines the sentence. It may be incarceration and/or a fine.

- ***Appeal:*** If the defendant is convicted, she has one automatic right to appeal the verdict to a higher court.

WHAT HAPPENS AT A CRIMINAL TRIAL

Reporters covering a criminal trial should know it usually follows these steps:

- ***Voir dire:*** A process of screening jurors to eliminate those with bias.

- ***Opening arguments:*** The prosecution goes first. The defense attorney has the option of giving an opening statement.

- ***Prosecution's case:*** The prosecutor calls witnesses and presents evidence to prove each element of the case. After the prosecutor questions witnesses, the defense attorney may query them, and then the prosecutor has another chance.

- ***Motion for directed verdict or dismissal:*** This is a usual maneuver by the defense to ask the judge to end the case because prosecution hasn't proved the crime. It is rarely granted.

- ***Defense's case:*** Since the burden is on the prosecutor, the defense doesn't have to present a case at all but can call witnesses and present evidence. The defendant does not have to take the stand.

- ***Closing arguments:*** The order is prosecutor, defense attorney, then prosecutor again.

- ***Jury instructions:*** The judge explains the law the jury must use in deliberations.

- ***Deliberations:*** The jury meets in secret to determine the verdict. The verdict must be unanimous: guilty or not guilty. If the jury can't agree, it's a mistrial, and the defendant can be tried again.

CIVIL COURT STORIES

Following civil court stories is often more perspiration than inspiration. Here's one place where dogged diligence and good organizational skills help out. Reporters spend hours sorting through legalese and repetitious documents. Files stand idle and lonely for months. But it's the hard-working, file-checking, source-calling tenacious reporters who break stories on the civil side.

The civil stories that often grab front-page space or lead the newscast are lawsuits against a big employer in town, allegations of discrimination or a divorce contest involving a local celebrity.

Let us interject a cautionary note here: People allege things they end up being unable to prove. They often ask for far more money than juries believe they deserve. Be skeptical, check out the allegations and get the versions of the other party or parties before writing the first story.

That first story usually appears once a suit has been filed. Here's one example:

> Family members are suing Mercy Hospital in Cadillac over the death of a 48-year-old Manton woman after a doctor used the wrong dye in a spinal X-ray procedure.
>
> Kay Lynn Musselman suffered spasms, seizures and cardiac arrest as the "proximate result," alleges a civil complaint in Wexford County Circuit Court.
>
> Musselman died in the hospital nine days after undergoing a Feb. 15 myelogram—a relatively routine procedure in which a dye is injected into the membrane around the spinal cord prior to X-rays.
>
> *The Detroit News*

The story continues with other important elements that can be a checklist for what to include:

- Legal grounds for the suit. In *The Detroit News'* story it was negligence.
- Response from the defendant or the attorney.
- Damages sought.
- How the harm occurred.
- Details on the product, service or contract in dispute. In this story the reporter explained the drug and how it was used.
- Background of all the parties.
- Subsequent actions. This story told readers that neither the doctor nor technician involved were now working at the hospital.

After the initial flurry of paperwork, civil suits seem to languish. They may take two, four, even seven years to be resolved. Delay is often a strategic tactic of attorneys.

The most important tip from reporters on the court beat is this: Develop a calendar system or a computer "tickler" file to remind you of deadline dates to check so you don't miss other key stories. These include:

- Disclosure of key documents, such as the contract in a dispute or financial documents in a bankruptcy.
- Depositions (sworn testimony) or interrogatories (written answers) from the parties and important witnesses.
- **Injunctions**—orders from the judge requiring or preventing a certain act, such as picketing or selling off assets.

Another tip: Keep in close touch with the attorneys and court staff the week before the trial—a common time for the parties to settle. Settlement often happens the morning the trial is scheduled to begin.

If the settlement agreement is outlined in the file, there's a ready-made story—as long as you get to the file first. But too frequently, the parties ask the judge to seal the file, which means nothing is made public. That's where good sourcing pays off.

CIVIL COURT STORIES

1. Keep contact with sources and review the files regularly to find stories and monitor the status of cases.

2. Be skeptical of allegations and damage claims. Push the sources for verification of every allegation.

3. Write up a time line or case history to refer to when writing stories.

4. Determine the two or three key points in contention. These will be the centerpieces for your stories.

5. Although the parties may be reluctant to talk, be sure to fairly represent both sides in all stories.

As with criminal cases, reporters file advancers or previews when cases are about to begin. Here's an example from the *San Jose (Calif.) Mercury News:*

The biggest, nastiest publicly fought celebrity spat since Jose Canseco rammed his Porsche into wife Esther's BMW three years ago gets under way Monday in a Redwood City courtroom.

Attorneys for the respective parties will argue whether Sun soon-to-be Bonds, a newly arrived Swedish bartender in Montreal when soon-to-be San Francisco Giants superstar Barry Bonds locked eyes on her, understood the prenuptial agreement she signed on the way to their Las Vegas wedding in 1988. Can she be held to a document that deprived her of any interest in her husband's substantial income?

San Jose Mercury News

The important factor in an advancer, as in any court story, is to simplify the legalese of the court documents to focus on the parties' main gripes. Here the focus is a common one: money. An advancer also includes a summary of the history of the case, key theories of all parties and an explanation of the law on which the decision will be based.

Civil cases that do get to trial are sometimes followed with the same interest as criminal cases. It doesn't hurt to have a celebrity involved. Here's the verdict story in the Bonds case:

Baseball superstar Barry Bonds won big in his long-running, very public divorce case, as a San Mateo County judge ruled that he could keep sole ownership of his houses and slash by half alimony payments to his former wife.

"I'm psyched," Barry Bonds told reporters in the dugout at Scottsdale Stadium in Arizona after learning he'd won the court case that has raged on publicly for more than a year. "The truth came out, the truth prevailed."

San Jose Mercury News

This story continues with several segments that form the framework of common verdict stories: the decision, the judge or jury's reasoning, reaction quotes, a summary of the case history and the next step in the process.

ENTERPRISE STORIES

While the basic stories on the justice beat are often driven by the court calendar, enterprise stories are driven by the reporter's curiosity about what's going on behind the scenes. News on the justice beat involves more than peeking into a world of tragedy and pain recited from the witness stand. It also can unveil for the public how and where justice *isn't* being served—where flooded dockets or inept attorneys lead the system to breakdown and where the concept of fairness too often turns out to be a myth.

DOES THE SYSTEM WORK?

Some enterprise stories delve into the "why" behind all those case files—helping the reader, viewer or listener understand where the justice system is running amok.

After *WINK-TV*, Ft. Myers, Fla., reported that two elderly Floridians were injured in a teen's robbery and shooting spree, assignment editor Jim Walrod sent reporter Matt Callinan to get the story behind the story.

"Police blotter stories have absolutely no impact on the viewer or reader," says Walrod, "They don't tell them what they need to know to adapt and live in society today."

What Callinan found was a hard-core criminal in the body of a 16-year-old. The young man committed 13 felonies over four years, served time in prison and went back to robbing folks soon after he got out. Callinan told viewers it was but one example of a much-troubled juvenile justice system:

At the age of 14 . . . [he] was arrested four times in just three months. His grandmother tried everything . . . church groups . . . school counseling . . . parole intervention. But the lure of the neighborhood was just too much. She told us [he] would say his "friends" here on these streets would protect him. Police say [he] is a symptom of a juvenile justice system that cannot handle today's "hard-core" offenders.

WINK-TV (Fort Myers, Fla.)

Callinan's story told viewers that the system, ostensibly designed to rehabilitate, was outmoded and ineffective.

In a remarkable example of student reporting, three Northwestern University students dug into the case of four men convicted of the abduction and murder of two young adults in Illinois many years before. What started out as a project in an investigative reporting class ended up with the men's release after 18 years in jail for crimes they maintained from the start they didn't commit.

The three students, with help from a private investigator and a team of lawyers, unearthed a recantation from the prime witness against the men and dug up police notes that pointed to the real killers, two of whom soon confessed.

The students passed their discoveries on to print and electronic reporters in the Chicago market, and the reporters published them. One, Eric Zorn of the *Chicago Tribune* pointed out after DNA tests exonerated the men that the tragic screw-up leaves the public wondering how often it's happened before:

Why did officials turn a blind eye to the inconsistencies and absurdities in their evidence? Why did they not pursue other leads? Why did they argue falsehoods to the jury in an effort to put innocent men to death? Why should we trust that this doesn't happen often? Why did authorities have to rely on a pesky pack of journalists and volunteer lawyers to push them toward the truth?

Chicago Tribune

Other enterprise stories show that even if the system does work, it doesn't work the same for all.

IS THE SYSTEM FAIR?

Using computer analysis, reporters can go beyond a handful of cases and anecdotes and examine how fairly the system is meting out its sanctions: Are some judges tougher on minorities; how much of a sentence does a prisoner really serve; is justice really blind to gender and geography?

FREE PRESS, FAIR TRIAL

Picture an old-fashioned weighing scale, a type of seesaw with a plate on each side. On one plate is the First Amendment, the media's right to publish. On the other, the Sixth Amendment, the defendant's right to a fair trial. Which plate weighs more? It's a tough call for judges, and one that defense attorneys in particular fuss a lot about. They maintain that pretrial publicity about evidence or confessions can skew the opinions of potential jurors.

Few verdicts have been overturned because of excessive pretrial publicity. Judges find several ways to protect jurors from prejudicial media influence: screen jurors carefully, move the trial to another location, order attorneys and witnesses not to talk with reporters and admonish the jurors not to read or listen to media during the trial.

In extreme cases, the judge may **sequester** the jury, which means they're holed up in a hotel, away from the media as well as from family and friends.

Where you live turns out to be a big factor in whether people are prosecuted for tax fraud. That is what *The New York Times* told readers one April:

If you happen to live in New Mexico, Idaho or South Dakota, you can relax, more or less. But if you're thinking of playing games with Uncle Sam in Roanoke, Va., Pittsburgh or Tulsa, Okla., you may have something to worry about.

A trove of Justice Department data now being made available on the Internet shows that your chances of being recommended for prosecution on tax fraud charges in 1994 were 57 times greater if you lived in the Roanoke area than if you lived in New Mexico. They were 29 times greater in the Pittsburgh area than in Idaho, and 17 times greater around Tulsa than in South Dakota.

The New York Times

The Times, and more than 30 other news outlets, used data developed on the Web by the ***Transactional Records Access Clearinghouse (TRAC)*** at Syracuse University to show the wide gaps in how U.S. Attorneys and IRS agents tackle tax cases. Reporters then talked with government officials, tax attorneys and defendants to try to explain the reasons for the discrepancies.

Fairness was also one of the subjects in a major series, "Cash Register Justice," by Michael Berens of *The Columbus (Ohio) Dispatch.* Berens found that some drunken drivers in Franklin County were paying $1,500 to avoid both jail and a notation on their drivers' licenses, a practice unheard of in other Ohio counties.

County municipal judges and city prosecutors justify the deal under a legal practice called "bond forfeiture."

They interpret a vague section of the Ohio Revised Code that defines bond forfeiture, in part, as any "agreement with the court and prosecutor in the case." Court officials call it a plea bargaining tool.

The law, however, does not say defendants can pay money to have a clean record or bypass mandatory jail sentences. Franklin County decided to interpret the law this way more than 20 years ago, court officials said.

The Columbus Dispatch

The prosecutors claimed the practice was only used for out-of-state drivers without a prior record. But the *Dispatch*'s computer analysis showed otherwise, pointing out cases where prosecutors allowed forfeitures for drivers with previous convictions and local ties.

Another example of how the system seemingly plays favorites with some comes from *The (Syracuse, N.Y.) Post-Standard.* A team of reporters analyzed unpaid parking tickets and found that many of the delinquents were, of all people, those sworn to uphold the law—lawyers. What made the story even better was that they found attorneys got their tickets excused at a far greater rate than the average citizen.

RECOMMENDED READING

American Bar Association. (1995). *Law and the courts.* Chicago: ABA Press.

This 80-page booklet covers the court systems, dispute resolution and the roles of attorneys and judges. Especially helpful is the glossary of terms.

Denniston, L. W. (1992). *The reporter and the law: Techniques of covering the courts.* New York: Columbia University Press.

Lyle Denniston gives helpful tips on how to cover trials based on his years of experience at the *Baltimore Sun.* He tells how to prepare, outlines the steps in both criminal and civil cases, discusses ethics, and gives tips on how to construct stories.

FindLaw. [Online]. Available: **http://www.find-law.com**.

One of the best one-stop shopping sites we've found for legal resources, from lawyers to cases to courts to codes.

Indiana University School of Law Library. *WWW virtual library: law.* [Online]. Available: **http://www.law.indiana.edu/law/v-lib/lawindex.html**.

This is part of the WWW Virtual Library, and it links to everything related to the law. You can conduct open-ended searches or use the topical directory

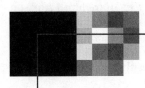

EXERCISES

A. RESEARCH

1. Research the following terms using people, print and online sources. Then write explanations that could be used in an article or script.

   a. appellant

   b. brief

   c. common law

   d. contempt

   e. dissenting opinion

   f. nolo contendere

   g. preemptory challenge

   h. restraining order

   i. stay

   j. summary judgment

2. A well-known athlete in town is accused of assaulting his girlfriend. The preliminary hearing is set for tomorrow. Where would you go to get the background on this case? Whom should you interview? How would you find out where the hearing will be held? If the athlete won't talk, how do you get his version of the story?

3. A former student is to be sentenced by a county judge after being found guilty of raping a woman on campus. Find out the name of the most severe sexual assault charge in your state and the range of options the judge has in sentencing a person for that crime.

4. Outline the process of getting a divorce in your state, as well as the average cost.

5. Find out the judicial process your college uses to discipline students who've violated school rules, and write a memo comparing it to the legal system.

B. BASIC STORIES

1. Write either stories or memos based on these assignments:

   a. Attend the opening or closing arguments of a criminal trial. In preparation, find all the background you can from police and court files.

Also read previous news stories about the crime. After you write or produce your story or memo, compare radio, television and print accounts to your own.

b. Read a civil case file in which a local business is being sued and summarize the issues of both sides as they near settlement or trial.

c. Spend a half day with a judge who is a woman, minority or disabled person and prepare a profile story or memo.

d. Explain how indigent defendants get an attorney and who pays for their defense.

e. Write about the house arrest program or another alternative sentencing program in your area. Include an interview with a defendant in the program.

C. ENTERPRISE STORIES

1. Write either stories or memos based on the following assignments:

a. Look up the last 10 civil cases filed against your college or university. Pick one of the cases. In addition to reading the case file, talk to attorneys for the plaintiff and the university and anyone else you think should be interviewed for a complete story.

b. Analyze what the justice system does to help victims of crime as their cases progress through the system. Talk with victims, prosecutors, social workers and the advocates who attend court hearings with victims. Include online resources for victims of crime.

c. Investigate whether personal bankruptcies are up or down in your area and why. Talk to people who've declared bankruptcy, attorneys and court administrators and explain how easy or hard it is to erase debts. Profile several cases.

d. Find out whether a new technology such as computerized or online records, digital fingerprinting or DNA testing is making an impact on local cases. Are defense attorneys concerned that improvements in computer and biomedical technology are jeopardizing citizens' rights?

e. Talk to members of the minority community, legal aid workers, the bar association, attorneys and judges and write an in-depth story on where racism or discrimination is surfacing in the court system and what is being done about it. If anyone has done a computer analysis of cases, include those results.

CHAPTER 15

Consumers

Reporter Susan Wornick was getting nowhere. The mattress company spokesperson wouldn't explain why the company wouldn't honor its $50-off coupon for a consumer. In fact, he seemed rather amused that she'd even think the company was doing something wrong.

So Wornick, a nobody-pushes-me-around consumer reporter at *NewsCenter 5* (*WCVB-TV,* Boston) told the company official she was going with the story whether or not he responded. She asked again for an on-the-record comment.

"Well, you just go *do* your little story," the corporate executive finally huffed.

So Wornick did. After her three-part series, an attorney general's investigation and a fine of $100,000, the company finally answered Wornick's question. It apologized to the customer and donated mattresses to the homeless.

Consumer stories like Wornick's can make things happen. They can help people make their lives safer, easier or less costly. That's why stories off the consumer beat often capture so much attention in lunchroom and dinner table conversations. People love to see the little guy duke it out with the big business, the used car dealer or the scam artist. Or they relish being the know-it-all who can quote the latest reports on why gas prices are so high or Brand X is better than Brand Y.

Some consumer reporters work as troubleshooters, helping consumers solve their problems. For example, Jeanie Blake at *The (New Orleans) Times -Picayune* often devotes her daily column to helping a reader out of a jam. Other consumer reporters, however, shy away from such an advocacy role.

The list of topics on the consumer beat is nearly limitless, promises Elizabeth Crenshaw of *WRC-TV* in Washington, D.C. In one month, she wrote pieces on stolen credit cards, lead in water, credit ratings, adult nutrition drinks, a federal telecommunications bill, interest rates, tax tips, a car seat recall, parking fees, house problems caused by snow, four-wheel drive sales and auto accident liability.

"I never get bored," she says, "The nice thing is it doesn't get old."

In addition to sampling from the variety of stories that come under the consumer umbrella, this chapter will help you:

- Learn where to go for consumer information and how to contact key agencies that monitor consumer products
- Use the Internet as a resource in researching consumer issues
- Adapt the tips of award-winning consumer reporters on how they organize and write their stories
- Learn how to develop in-depth consumer stories

PEOPLE TO SEEK OUT

The consumer reporter's contact list encompasses people working for trade groups, government and consumer organizations. Perhaps more importantly, it should include numbers for those without position or title—the consumers. Some of them can be cultivated, but most of them come calling.

TIPSTERS

It's not unusual for consumer writers to publicize how they can be reached—by phone, by e-mail, by fax. This isn't altruism. On the consumer beat, more than any other, news often comes from tips called in out of the blue by someone with an angry tale and a thirst for revenge.

That's why the first tip we can give you in consumer coverage is to encourage, rather than cut off, those callers who always seem to reach you about five minutes before deadline. At the least, get a name, a phone number and a time to call back. Tipsters can be great sources, because not only do they give you the story, but they're also willing to star in it.

"They are angry and frustrated because they can't get any help and they feel totally cheated," says Wornick at *NewsCenter 5* (*WCVB-TV*, Boston). "You can't help but empathize with them, and your inclination is, 'I can't wait to get this on the air and blow the bad guys out of the water.'"

But keep that reporter's healthy skepticism about you, she advises. Wornick says there are at least three sides to every story: the consumer's, the business' and the truth. She says once she talks to someone at the company, she might find out the consumer was remiss or misunderstood.

"I can't begin to tell you how many times I get calls from people who say, 'You know, I got a suit and I didn't like it and I went right back and I saved my receipt and they won't let me exchange it,'" says Wornick. "And I ask them, 'What's the store's exchange policy,' and they say, 'What do you mean?'"

Wornick repeats the line she so often includes in her scripts—find out the policy before you purchase.

But even if some tips don't end as a story, a few will end up being worth all the other phone calls—such as the mattress company coupon story.

Some news organizations even set up a special phone line just for tips. *The (Louisville, Ky.) Courier-Journal* runs a short blurb saying "call if you know about this," with "this" being a story on which reporters are already working.

Courier-Journal reporter Bill Wolfe says more than 30 readers called in when the paper asked them to share secrets on how to make your car last forever. Everyone he talked with told him to change the oil every 3,000 miles despite what the manufacturer says. Several suggested, "Find one mechanic you like and stick with that person."

Wolfe says their information added to what he got from more traditional sources "You can go talk to mechanics, but talking to a dozen people who've run up 100,000 miles on their cars is a different perspective," he said.

Student reporters aren't on the receiving end of a lot of tips. But once you're in the business, you'll attract them. Asking for information or establishing yourself through your byline or on-air presence is the best way. Other sources are nurtured in the more traditional ways.

CONSUMER ORGANIZATIONS

Steve Everly of *The Kansas City Star* has developed relationships with sources at the major consumer organizations that test various products. So when he began researching a story on smoke detectors, he made a round of calls.

NAMES TO KNOW

Here are six of the best-known consumer and public interest groups that reporters often consult. For an update to this list, check http://web.syr.edu/~bcfought.

1. Consumers Union of U.S., Inc., New York City.

A consumer testing organization and the publisher of *Consumer Reports.* Contact: (914) 378-2000; www.ConsumerReports.org.

Working on a vacation feature and need some information about single-use cameras? Get the results of recent tests by Consumers Union.

2. Consumer Federation of America, Washington, D.C.

An association of 240 consumer groups. It pushes pro-consumer policy before Congress and federal agencies and publishes educational materials. Contact: (202) 387-6121.

The *St. Petersburg (Fla.) Times* called this agency for analysis of how a new federal telecommunications law would affect consumers.

3. Council of Better Business Bureaus, Inc., Arlington, Va.

The umbrella group for Better Business Bureaus. Contact: (800) 955-5100; (703) 276-0100; www.bbb.org.

The BBB staff can explain how business is supposed to operate. For example, staff members can sort out just what happens during arbitration of car complaints and will know which local BBBs do arbitration.

4. National Consumer's League, Washington, D.C.

Covers issues such as food and drug safety, child labor, the environment and telecommunications. Contact: (202) 835-3323; http://www.natlconsumersleague.org.

National Public Radio's Jim Zarroli interviewed a spokesperson from here to find out whether consumers would come out ahead when Post Cereal lowered its prices but cut back on cereal coupons.

5. National Fraud Information Center, Washington, D.C.

Channels fraud complaints from consumers to a National Electronic Fraud Database run by the Federal Trade Commission and the National Association of Attorneys General. Contact: (800) 876-7060; http://www.fraud.org.

If you want the lowdown on the latest scam sweeping the country, these are the folks in the know. They'll also have ideas on what people can do so they don't get taken.

6. U.S. Public Interest Research Group, Washington, D.C.

A watchdog and lobbying group for consumer issues. Contact: (202) 546-9707; http:// www.pirg.org/uspirg/index.htm.

The *(Fort Lauderdale, Fla.) Sun-Sentinel* used a U.S. PIRG study in a story on banking costs. The study showed that the average Floridian paid over $215 a year to keep a regular checking account.

"I go through a series of checks," he explains, "Underwriters Laboratory, Consumers Union, the National Safety Alliance—I call them regularly."

Dozens of other national public interest groups speak out on the consumer's behalf, publish educational brochures, test products and monitor legislation (see box, Names to Know). In addition, several of the national organizations have local affiliates. Better Business Bureaus, for example, operate in more than 130 cities. Consumers can check up on a business with the BBB or ask the staff there to help resolve a dispute. But BBBs are funded by businesses. They collect complaints rather than initiate investigations. So reporters don't use them as the only source for whether a company is on the up and up. Reporters find them most useful in locating victims and confirming trends: "Yeah, we've had 23 calls about that scam."

Elizabeth Crenshaw of *WRC-TV,* Washington, D.C., says she always checks out a group's funding before she uses them in a story, to make sure it's not a smoke screen for industry. Lots of business groups create organizations with gussied-up names that make them sound like consumer groups.

"I look for ones that don't get money from corporations or industry so I know these people don't have a bone to pick with anybody," she says.

GOVERNMENT EMPLOYEES

Other people with their fingers on the pulse of consumer issues can be found at city hall or the state office building in agencies that investigate consumer problems. Nearly every city, county and state government has an office of consumer affairs that handles complaints and investigates suspected fraud. For example, Detroit reporters often call the city-run Detroit Consumer Affairs Department for information or comments on stories ranging from taxi cab licenses to sweepstakes mailings. Other government agencies set standards or license professionals in a host of fields, ranging from asbestos removal contractor to chiropractor.

To find the right office, don't stop with agencies with "consumer" in the title. If you open the phone book to a myriad of government agencies and have no clue as to which one deals with the subject of your story, here's your first step. Think: Who is in charge of regulating this business or this individual?

The local health department, for example, typically carries out restaurant inspections. The county office on aging tracks scams on the elderly. Licensing boards keep tabs on which contractors are registered (and which aren't). And code enforcement officers know who the slumlords are.

At the state level, the key source is the attorney general, who usually enforces state consumer laws and investigates fraud. On the federal scene, the staff at the Consumer Information Center's media hotline can cut through the bureaucracy for you and tell you whom to call (see box, Where Do I Go?).

After reporters find out who's in charge, the next questions they need to ask are:

- What standards exist, and are they adequate?
- Are the existing standards enforced?

Remember those tips on building a beat in Chapter 9? By learning how the system is supposed to work, reporters take a giant step toward understanding when it doesn't and why. Sometimes the answer lies with the agencies themselves, with lax licensing standards or spotty enforcement.

There also are plenty of dedicated public officials and stores of records that can establish whether, for example, that mattress company has had complaints filed against it before.

TRADE AND PROFESSIONAL ORGANIZATIONS

No matter what the product or service, no doubt there's a national association of members who manufacture it or provide it—from the Aerospace Industries Association of America to the Water Quality Association. Since these groups want to promote their industry or profession, they're glad to give you their expert to explain their views.

The key words are *their* experts and *their* views. Don't expect unbiased analysis here. Expect information from a trade association perspective that may help your understanding of an issue or at least clarify your understanding of how industry views it. For example, reporters working on stories comparing drug prices at local pharmacies versus mail-order drug businesses might call the National Association of Retail Druggists. The spokesperson for that group, however, is not likely to make a strong case for mail-order purchases.

Industry groups or professional associations are best at providing reports supporting their viewpoint and offering a local representative for an interview. When you're investigating a problem with a service or product, they can tell you the industry standards or guidelines, explain what they're doing to police their own or perhaps offer an industry explanation.

When, for example, a computer snafu at First National Bank of Chicago made 800 depositors instant millionaires, a *Chicago Tribune* reporter wanted to know just how big a goof this was. He called the American Banking Association for perspective and used their information in this way:

WHERE DO I GO?

Here are several common consumer issues and the federal agency that oversees them. Check to see if there's an office in your area.

Auto safety	National Highway Traffic Safety Administration	(800) 424-9393
Consumer price index	Bureau of Labor Statistics	(202) 606-7000
Dangerous products	Consumer Product Safety Commission	(800) 638-2772
Drugs	Food and Drug Administration	(301) 827-4420
False advertising	Federal Trade Commission	(202) 326-3131
Food content or labeling	USDA Meat and Poultry Hotline (see FDA above)	(800) 535-4555
Mail-order scams	U.S. Postal Service	(202) 268-3207
Other issues	Consumer Information Center's media hotline	(202) 501-1794

And it's the largest error in the history of U.S. banking, according to officials of the American Bankers Association, who said deposits are occasionally credited to wrong accounts but not quite in this magnitude.

Chicago Tribune

Caution: When you're dealing with such groups for the first time, find out who they are, who pays their bills and how long they've been doing what they do. You don't want a wanna-be trying to gain credibility; you want a valid and respected organization.

THINGS TO READ

Consumer reporters are always watching to see what's the latest scam, what's the new trend. One way to keep up is to read what specialized media are reporting about consumer trends.

Herb Weisbaum, consumer correspondent with *CBS News,* says the magazines *Consumer Reports* and *Kiplinger's* are on his required reading list along with a variety of newsletters put out by trade associations and consumer watchdog groups.

"Sometimes you read one of these little teeny, tiny, four-paragraph articles and say, 'Boy that would be a good story,'" Weisbaum says.

Reporters can also follow trends by seeing what's airing on "Steals and Deals," a *CNBC* cable TV program that showcases consumer stories from TV stations around the country. What's happening in Dallas might be on its way to Duluth.

Herb Weisbaum

GOVERNMENT PUBLICATIONS

"If there's one thing you had to get, this is it," Weisbaum says. He's talking about the "Consumer's Resource Handbook," published by the federal government.

"It's one guide that will steer you to a million places, it's updated every year and it's free," he adds.

The book is jampacked with hundreds of phone numbers for consumer groups, state attorneys general offices and major corporations. Plus it lists "red flags" for fraud, tips on avoiding scams and ideas on how to write a complaint letter to a manufacturer (see Recommended Reading at the chapter's end for how to get a copy).

You've probably seen another publication from this federal office advertised on TV public service announcements. It's the "Consumer Information Catalog." Inside you'll find descriptions of more than 200 consumer booklets—everything from how to buy a home to how to read a food label.

The feds aren't alone in knowing consumers will check online for help. States are also adding consumer tips and hints to the World Wide Web. The *Florida attorney general* and police run a site that explains the state's lemon law, among other topics.

Some government agencies are slow at getting onto the Net, so you'll have to settle for the old-fashioned method—books. Check your news organization's library or the public library for government manuals that describe state and federal agencies and what they cover.

ELECTRONIC AND PRINT RESOURCES

A quick trip into cyberspace to the *National Fraud Information Center* site tells a reporter of three potential scams: vacation rip-offs, a college scholarship "finder" service and investments in Internet-related companies. Likewise, the Web site of the *Better Business Bureau* has included articles on how to get refunds for 900 calls, tips on purchasing jewelry and warnings about office con artists. These two online sources provide not only ideas but also content for consumer stories. And they're listed, along with 1,100 other sites, at *Consumer World*, one of the best master directories for consumer sites on the Internet.

Bill Wolfe of *The (Louisville, Ky.) Courier-Journal* says he uses the Net regularly in his research. He usually starts his hunt with *Lycos*, one of the many Internet search engines. For a story on hearing aids, he typed in *hearing aids* and got a list of 30 sites with those terms. He quickly clicked through them all. At one of the sites he found tips he could use in a story—how people can tell whether they need hearing aids.

You can't find all your resources on a trip through cyberspace, however. And just because it's on the computer screen doesn't mean it's accurate; enough material on the Web is flawed that reporters should double-check factual information found there.

The Net is a quick source of vast stores of knowledge; nonetheless, some things still are found the more traditional ways. A valuable publication for finding contacts in industry and consumer groups is the Encyclopedia of Associations. It contains names and phone numbers for 23,000 organizations in the country. For example, if you needed the pilot's perspective for a story on airline safety, you'd check it for the location and phone for the Airline Pilots Association.

In addition, consumer groups, trade associations, businesses and universities are pumping out dozens of newsletters and magazines on consumer issues. Many are free to reporters. Take, for example, the "Tufts University Diet and Nutrition Letter." Herb Weisbaum used one of its articles detailing health scams on the Internet as a starting point for a piece that aired on "This Morning" on *CBS*.

"It's a good resource because they're very good at debunking myths and trends," he explains.

As with the Net, all publications aren't equal. So Weisbaum advises checking out who funds a publication and what its bias is. And, he says, even if the publication seems respectable, good reporters verify the veracity of information by going to its source, not accepting a secondhand version filtered through a publication.

"The trend in this business, because everybody is working so fast, is that if you attribute something, you're legally safe and morally clean," he says. "That's not good enough for me. The person you're attributing it to may be wrong. The goal is to get it right."

BASIC STORIES

Most day-to-day consumer stories fall into three categories: stories that compare products, stories about scams and stories that offer advice on everything from building a twister-proof storm cellar to baby-proofing your living room.

PRODUCT COMPARISONS

When you go shopping, you probably look for the best product at the best price. So do the people you write for. Consumer reporters know, however, that all products are not of equal interest to readers. A story on the potential hazards of certain kids' water guns likely will draw better than one comparing the strength of various garbage bags. The biggest draws are something on cars, for kids or about safety.

Steve Everly of *The Kansas City (Mo.) Star* decided to do a story on smoke detectors but didn't want to write the "same-old, same-old" story that scared people into buying detectors and merely reminded them to change the batteries once a year. So he set out on a telephone hunt, calling testing labs to see what was new. He discovered that Consumers Union had just tested home smoke detectors.

What intrigued him was that CU recommended that people install two different types of detectors—ionization ones as well as photoelectric detectors. Everly didn't even know there *were* two different types. He figured his readers didn't either, so now he had the new angle he'd been seeking. Here's how his story began:

The smoke-detector test was simple and to the point: Consumers Union, the publisher of Consumer Reports, put some detectors in a room and gradually filled the space with smoke to find out how quickly the alarms sounded.

As it turned out, one type of detector responded quickly. Another type still hadn't let out a beep when the room was so full of smoke you could hardly see across it.

The Kansas City Star

Everly found that homeowners needed both: ionization detectors (the most common) to catch smoke from flames and the photoelectric ones to catch smoldering fires, such as upholstery fires.

Everly could have told the results, listed the CU recommendations and gone home early. But to him, test results are only the beginning of a story.

"I've found that it's dangerous to just reprint the recommendations," he says. "As much as I like a lot of the stuff they do, the product listings and some of the things are out of date."

Plus, the models tested aren't always on store shelves in Kansas City. Everly says it does no good to tell people about something they can't get. Sure enough, when he went shopping, he found out local stores didn't have the photoelectric detectors, but managers said they'd get them if customers wanted them.

Further checks showed fire department officials knew the second type of detector was useful but weren't promoting it, saying they were glad if people had any kind of smoke detector. There was another twist for his story.

CONFLICT OF INTEREST

A television reporter was fired after station management learned that for several months he had been driving a car that was loaned to him by a major automaker. The company supposedly sent the car so the reporter could test it out for a story on new car models.

In teams of three to five people, develop a news organization policy about reporters' uses of products sent free of charge by companies seeking publicity.

Everly says product-testing stories take special care because not all tests are valid. Here are some of his tips:

- Find out whether the testing is done by the manufacturer or an independent lab.
- Learn what and how much was tested. "They'll tell you what things were checked—just what they were looking for—and it's often not as extensive as you might think," he explains.
- Tell how the tests were conducted.

When he probed why three child car seats passed one test but flunked another, Everly found the difference: three miles an hour.

"The testing of these child seats can vary from 27 mph to 30 mph," he explains. "Three mph seems insignificant, but the force involved is 20 percent more."

Usually Everly doesn't recommend brands. Consumer writers, he says, have to take special care not to promote products in their reporting. But in the case of the smoke detectors, "There were only a few types and they were hard to get, so it was worth mentioning."

Everly reported on somebody else's test results, but sometimes consumer reporters pay to have testing done just for them. Wornick at Boston's *WCVB-TV* asked a certified laboratory to test tap water for a series on bottled water. And for a lighter touch to the story, she also arranged for a less scientific test: She asked the chefs of two of Boston's top restaurants to see if they could distinguish between bottled water, tap water and filtered tap water. They could.

There's one essential final step before a product comparison story runs. Fairness dictates that before reporters slam a product or service, they give officials of the company being criticized a chance to respond in detail.

SUMMARY
PRODUCT COMPARISONS

1. Find a local angle when reporting somebody else's tests.

2. Know the reputation of the testing organization and the validity of its results before you use them.

3. Explain how the tests were conducted so the audience has a basis on which to judge the results.

4. Be wary of promoting certain products or brands.

5. Think carefully about how involved the reporter should be in the testing.

6. Get a reaction from a spokesperson for the product or service being evaluated.

"When I confront somebody, I say very clearly that we were told by the testing lab, 'Let me read you, quote . . . ,'" explains Herb Weisbaum of *CBS News*. "The more concrete info you can give, the more valuable the response will be and the more fair you will be."

Sometimes companies have a legitimate explanation or offer a different perspective. At other times, they want to let the public know they've changed their ways. At all times, they're due a fair hearing.

SCAMS

You've heard the line before: If it sounds too good to be true, it probably is. Yet the lure of a quick buck or a free vacation cruise often hooks consumers who willingly open their pocketbooks and come away empty handed. *Los Angeles Times* reporter and syndicated columnist Kathy Kristof has seen it time and again. She finds the scams go in cycles.

"They rise during a recession," she notes. "The con artists are pretty intelligent people who read the newspaper, and they figure out people are getting laid off and running out of benefits so they're probably looking for some opportunity."

In one of her stories, Kristof started with an anecdote of an English immigrant who received a letter announcing he'd received a valuable prize. When he called about it, the operator said he had to buy a $400 product. Here's how Kristof continues the story:

Tom was torn. He didn't want the product but the prizes appeared so valuable it seemed foolish to refuse. Tom rattled off his credit card number.

"Being so new in the country, I didn't even think to be skeptical," he says. "I know it sounds stupid, but I agreed. And I wanted to get my huge prize."

Los Angeles Times

Both the prize and product were worthless. Tom couldn't get his money back.

Kristof profiled another victim, Harold. When he called to claim his prize, he punched through a series of automated responses, not realizing he'd been charged $40 for his 20-minute phone call. Both were victims of telemarketing fraud.

Putting victims in the scam story is essential, says Kristof.

"They are incredibly important," she explains. "It makes the story much more personal."

Both men contacted her—one by e-mail, one by letter. Before she got so popular as a personal finance writer, Kristof says she sought out stories at the courthouse by looking at lists of cases recently filed.

"You can just whip through these or look for particular companies that you suspect," she says. "I would pick up trends and sometimes a story that is funky and fun."

One was about a drive-through church that went bankrupt after a member scammed the pastor and constituents out of thousands of dollars.

Kristof advises reporters, once they've found a possible scam, to check it out first with the state attorney general, Better Business Bureau or a government regulatory agency. The first step is to verify the scam. The second is to check whether it's an isolated case or part of a trend.

"The challenge as a reporter is to evaluate when this person is indicative of a trend and when it's just one sad case," she says. "It's usually a story when this scam is one of a whole series."

Kristof researches the law and industry practices so she knows what's supposed to happen and what the consumer can do when it doesn't.

SUMMARY

CHECKLIST FOR A SCAM STORY

1. Seek out victims' stories.

2. Find how the scam works.

3. Measure its impact: How many people were hurt, how much money was lost.

4. Learn laws or industry practices violated.

5. Get quotes or sound bites from experts.

6. Identify the recourse for consumers.

"Until you develop a certain expertise, it is just a matter of hard work," she says. "You make twice as many phone calls at the beginning as you make five years down the road."

Consumers always want to know what they can do. In this case, Tom and Harold had options:

> ...the federal Truth in Lending Act says that if you have a problem with the quality of property or services purchased with a credit card and you have tried in good faith to correct the problem with the merchant, you may have the right not to pay the remaining amount due. There are two caveats: You must have made the purchase in your home state, or if not in your home state, within 100 miles of your home. And the purchase price must have been for more than $50.
>
> In addition, both Tom and Harold are covered under California law, which bars as illegal "lotteries" that require you to make a purchase to claim a prize...
>
> *Los Angeles Times*

HOW-TO STORIES

Some stories come in the mail. An editor at *The (Allentown, Pa.) Morning Call* dumped a pile of news releases on the table.

"Anybody interested?" she asked, holding up two from rental truck companies.

Rosemary Jones was. She knew the releases themselves weren't news, but they triggered an idea. The summer moving season was fast approaching. Jones began thinking of how to layer stories together: a main story about saving money by moving yourself, a second story that profiled one local family on the move and a sidebar on driving a rental truck.

Such how-to stories are another staple in the larder of consumer stories. Readers and listeners like these "news you can use" stories. After all, everybody wants to know tricks for making life run easier or ways to do something well.

For the sidebar on driving a rental car, Jones flipped through the information from Hertz and found a list of driving tips. Tucked in the packet from U-Haul she came across a factoid that intrigued her: The accident rate of U-Haul drivers was lower than that of professional drivers competing in an annual safety contest. After 28 years in the business, she figures if she's still interested, her readers will be, too.

With those two nuggets, she had a start. She set out to find a local angle.

"A news release is so generic—who cares," she says. "You have to remember your audience and localize a story as much as you can. Make it pertinent to your readers."

A few phone calls later, she discovered Pennsylvania drivers have a very low accident rate with rental trucks. Here's how her story began:

> Its size alone makes driving a truck very differ-
> ent from driving a car. Add to that unfamiliarity
> with the vehicle and there's the potential for an
> accident.
>
> But surprisingly, statistics indicate that rental
> trucks are involved in relatively few accidents.
>
> *The (Allentown, Pa.) Morning Call*

Jones interviewed a safety engineer and verified the U-Haul figures with a spokesperson for the company. The tips, which she rewrote, closed out her story. Among them: Know whether the truck can clear canopies at gas stations, downshift when descending hills and check the mirrors before you make a move.

Lists of tips are common in how-to stories. Bill Wolfe of *The (Louisville, Ky.) Courier-Journal* says he likes to gather tips from many sources.

"Some tips will be way out," says Wolfe, "but if you get four people giving you the same tip, then it's probably good."

For a story about how to teach your children about money, Wolfe solicited tips from several elementary school teachers, a university professor, a national consumer education group and a local author who'd written a book on the subject.

It's one thing to simply run a list of tips. It's another to build the tips into a story about someone's real experience. Wolfe started the story with an incident that happened to him—helping his 5-year-old daughter decide whether to spend or save a $5 bill sent by Aunt Nellie.

The body of the story offered hands-on advice. Here's one segment:

> Participate. Do things with your children that help
> them learn the basics of personal finance. When
> you visit the library to check out books, that may
> be a good opportunity to talk about borrowing—
> and what happens if you don't repay a debt . . .
>
> When you're making small purchases—at a fast-
> food restaurant, for example—let the youngster
> pay the bill. This teaches assertiveness, gives con-
> fidence and helps a child learn how to transact
> business.
>
> *The (Louisville, Ky.) Courier-Journal*

Veteran reporters suggest running tips past several experts. This can lead to an interesting give-and-take and can identify which suggestions are more controversial. Wolfe says tips should be as concrete as possible.

"Don't just tell them to check with authorities," says Wolfe, "provide the numbers and addresses."

SUMMARY HOW-TO STORIES

1. Remember your audience. Find a local angle.

2. Random lists of suggestions or lectures on what to do don't make interesting stories. Find a human interest story that illustrates the problem, concern or success.

3. Tips in press releases, on the Internet or from companies are a starting point, not an ending point.

4. Find tips from more than one source and check them out with several experts before including them in the story. Make them specific.

5. Without being too promotional, give the audience names and numbers of where to go for more information.

Lists of names and addresses are easier for print reporters such as Wolfe to provide than for reporters in radio and TV. Most people aren't sitting still while listening and watching. Nor do they have a pen handy. But radio and TV reporters can still offer "where to go" advice—they just air the numbers and addresses more than once, emphasize them with graphics or provide them on a call-in phone line.

ENTERPRISE STORIES

The difference is one of degree. That's what sets an enterprise story apart from one of the basic consumer stories: more details, more probing, more work. Enterprise stories on the consumer beat are often investigative stories. As such, they take time.

Herb Weisbaum's story on lemon laundering—how car dealers resell lemons to unsuspecting customers—simmered for five months before airing on CBS' "This Morning."

"Anytime you're at a station that says you have to have three investigations on a week, you're in trouble," he says.

Weisbaum produced two pieces that documented how lemons were being resold without notice of their problems. He traced a car with bad brakes from a Fresno woman back to the original owner in Nevada City, Calif. The previous owner had so much trouble with the brakes that she convinced the manufacturer to buy the car back and trash it. Or so she thought.

Carmakers told Weisbaum the examples he found were isolated problems, but a consumer group told him it was "business as usual." His piece included an update on the latest lawsuits against carmakers and offered viewers tips on how to protect themselves from defective cars. Among them:

- Find out the previous owner.
- Avoid so-called executive cars or program cars, because you don't know what you are buying.
- Take the car to an independent mechanic before buying it.

"I'm a big one on research," says consumer reporter Susan Wornick, *NewsCenter 5*, Boston. "I don't want to be just briefed. I want to know everything."

Susan Wornick at *NewsCenter 5* in Boston was playing, not working, when she stumbled on a racket in the furniture business. Traipsing around to estate sales, she began noticing similar furniture at different sales. She'd seen enough to pay attention, when another shopper recognized her, nudged up beside her and said, "This stuff is all a fraud . . . I'll call you."

The man's tip: The antique treasures at this particular estate sale were actually reproductions, straight off of a New York City showroom floor. Wornick and crew took a hidden camera to several estate sales and auctions and then matched the supposedly old furniture to that on the New York showroom floor.

Wornick's story made clear it wasn't the furniture makers who were in the wrong, it was the auctioneers. She says it's important in consumer stories to point the finger at the right culprit.

"What is illegal and immoral is that two different auctioneers sold it as if it was old furniture," Wornick explains.

Wornick only uses hidden cameras, as she did here, as a last resort.

ETHICS | HIDDEN CAMERAS

Producers at *ABC News* worked undercover and used hidden cameras to try to uncover unsafe food-handling practices at a major grocery chain. The story wound up the subject of a multimillion-dollar lawsuit and spawned discussions in newsrooms across the country as to when it is ethical to use hidden cameras.

Work in groups of three to five and discuss these questions:

■ Are there some stories that cannot be documented unless hidden cameras are used?

■ Are there ways to show the impact of the story without hidden cameras?

■ What are the pros and cons of asking people inside the operation to take the video?

■ Is it ever appropriate to lie to get the pictures?

■ What checklist would you go through before allowing hidden cameras?

Come up with a policy on use of hidden cameras for a local television news outlet. Compare and discuss your policy with other small groups.

"My rule of thumb is that you don't use the hidden camera unless there is absolutely no other way to document the wrongdoing," she says.

Most stations have similar policies. The best bet before launching an undercover investigation is to make sure you've talked out all the legal and ethical issues with management and media lawyers (see box, Ethics: Hidden Cameras). Lately the courts haven't been siding with the media when such stories end up the subject of lawsuits.

Wornick of *NewsCenter 5* (*WCVB-TV*, Boston) and *CBS'* Weisbaum offer several tips on investigative stories:

■ ***Don't rush.*** Time isn't a luxury in investigative pieces; it's a necessity.

■ ***Develop good note-taking skills.*** You should be able to fact-check every line in your story with your notes. A well-organized and detailed notebook is good evidence when you're in the midst of a lawsuit five years down the road. Weisbaum jots down *every* phone call he makes—date, time, phone number, who answered the phone and what was said.

■ ***Run down all the angles.*** Thorough research is the heart of an investigative story.

SUMMARY | ENTERPRISE REPORTING

1. Enterprise stories can cover the same topics as basic stories—scams, how-tos or product comparisons—but with more research, context, examples and depth.

2. Reporters must convince management to allow them the time to do investigative stories properly.

3. Reporters should personalize the problem by telling the stories of real people with whom the audience can empathize.

4. In today's litigious society, reporters should cross-check the script or article with their notes to make sure each statement has solid backup.

5. A comment from the target or subject of the investigation or enterprise story must be included, even when it means delaying the story.

- *Do everything you can—then more—to get a comment from the target of the investigation.* The line "so-and-so was unavailable" or "he didn't return our calls" won't cut it. Fairness demands you wait and try harder, the two pros say.

   "Most people work for days on a story, and two hours before they're going on with it they call for a reaction," Weisbaum says. "We contact them as soon as humanly possible without screwing up the story."

   He started tracking down the carmakers and dealers in his lemon laundering piece three months before he aired it.

- *Report fairly.* If you ever wonder whether you've done enough on an investigation, answer these two questions: If I was treated this way, would I think it was fair? And, how is the jury going to react when I explain what I've done?

RECOMMENDED READING

Consumer Information Center. (1998). *Consumer resource handbook.* Washington, DC: General Services Administration.

This "buying smart" guide is put out by the federal government for consumers. Reporters can get a free copy. Besides the consumer tips and story ideas, the best section is the 40-page directory for consumer groups and government agencies.

Consumer Information Center, U.S. General Services Administration. *Consumer information catalog.* [Online]. Available: **http://www.pueblo.gsa.gov**.

Here you'll find more than 100 pamphlets on consumer topics and a wealth of other helpful consumer advice from the federal government.

Dworsky, E. *Consumer world.* [Online]. Available: **http://consumerworld.org**.

Edgar Dworsky is a former TV consumer reporter as well as a lawyer and keeps current a great directory with over 1,700 links to all types of consumer issues.

National Institute for Consumer Education. *NICE.* [Online]. Available: **http://www.emich.edu/public/coe/nice/nice.html**.

This is the information center for NICE, located at Eastern Michigan University. It's written to educate consumers, so reporters will find it helpful in getting up to speed on various consumer topics. Most helpful here are the investment guide, resource lists and the "Jump$tart" search function.

Roper, B. (1998). *Covering the market: The essential guide for personal finance journalists.* Arlington, VA: The Investor Protection Trust [Online]. Available: **http://www.investorprotection.org**.

This guide is a terrific primer for reporters who cover personal finance. It includes information on securities laws, how brokers and companies are regulated, what types of information readers and viewers want, and what questions they most frequently ask.

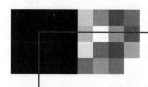

EXERCISES

A. RESEARCH

1. The state legislature has just passed a law requiring all children under 16 to wear a bicycle helmet. To whom do you make your first three calls, and what will you ask?

2. The wires report that four-wheel-drive vehicles of a certain model and year are being recalled for brake defects. What do you need for a story? What natural sound, videotape, still photos or descriptive detail would you get for your story?

3. A tipster calls and tells you she was the victim of a bait and switch—the local health club offered a great membership deal for six months, but she's just realized she signed a two-year contract. Whom do you call to see if there's a story here? What do you ask?

4. You get an e-mail message from a reader, listener or viewer that says he's received a postcard claiming he's won a free trip to a Caribbean paradise. How would you check out this offer?

5. You hear on the radio that the Consumer Product Safety Commission has just released a warning about a child car seat that is defective. How would you get the report, and whom would you interview locally about it?

B. BASIC STORIES

1. Write a story or memo on these topics:

   a. Find the results of a recent test by Consumers Union (or by a lab at your university) and localize it for a product evaluation story.

   b. Use the contacts listed in this chapter to find one of the latest scams making the rounds in your area. Make sure your story or memo includes information from an expert and a victim, and tips on how to avoid such scams.

   c. Using the Internet, find a tip sheet online. If you do not have access to the Web, get a tip sheet from a consumer organization. Relying on techniques from this chapter and Chapter 2, select an approach, then interview people locally.

   d. Check the calendar and think seasonally. What's coming up in the next month that people need to know how to do? Winterize their car? Select holiday toys that are safe? Buy a car for a new graduate? Research the story on the consumer Web sites (see box, Names to Know), through government agencies or a trade associ-

ation. Make sure you've got at least three local sources for your how-to story.

C. ENTERPRISE STORIES

1. How safe is restaurant food? Review local restaurant inspections for the past year and find a story. Some possibilities: the most frequently cited restaurants in town, the most common problems for which restaurants are cited or the adequacy of the local inspection system.

2. Compare and contrast the mortgage rates offered by the area banks and credit unions and explain the differences and options.

3. Find out if there's an arbitration process for consumer problems in your area. If so, write about how it works, interviewing people who've used it. Evaluate its effectiveness. If there isn't arbitration in your area, find out why not and if anybody is doing something to start such a service.

4. Review the latest state and federal laws about dietary supplements. Then check the advertising from local health food stores and check out what these products promise on their labels. Are they misleading? What type of information and training do health food store employees get? Seek out interviews from customers, physicians, naturopaths, nutritionists, the state attorney general, the diet supplement industry and health food stores.

5. Talk to preschool educators, pediatricians and emergency room nurses to find out their concerns about safety for infants and toddlers. Review the latest safety recalls on products for children. See if you can develop a "news you can use" piece for parents about purchasing equipment and furnishings, how to select toys correctly or ways to avoid common accidents with little ones.

CHAPTER 16 Working

Numbers, calculations, confusion. Economic jargon, bar graphs, delusion. Being assigned to cover the world of business sounds to many like a fate worse than comprehensive exams.

The workplace is about money, all right. But it's also full of the drama, tension, plotting and intrigue of those vying to come in first: to build a better widget, to buy the competitor before the competitor buys them, to win the race to fill the boss's chair. It is more like watching a soap opera than figuring out formulas. New megastores push out the mom and pops. The whiz-kid entrepreneur makes her first million at age 19. A new drug company promises a vaccine for AIDS, only to declare bankruptcy six months later.

Workplace reporters track the technological revolution and try to sort out how it will affect people's lives. They make sense of how changes in the workplace, from widespread downsizing to the shift toward more flex-time jobs, affect the places where most adults spend 40, 50 and 60 hours a week. They monitor small businesses and the consultants and entrepreneurs who have opened their doors to serve leaner industry and the public itself. And they keep a watchful eye on nonprofit organizations, which often dish out as many dollars as local industry and have a great influence on the quality of community life.

The world of working has changed a great deal since the heyday of steel plants. Today those covering "working" are more likely to tour a high-tech clean room or visit a consulting firm than to track events behind factory doors.

We've called this beat "working" rather than "business"—a change that is more than just semantics. The reporters of the 21st century will continue to chronicle the comings and goings of the major businesses in town, but not just by covering the financial moves of those at the top. Increasingly, reporters are developing news from the perspective of customers, of clients and of the workers who make business go.

Still not interested in business? That's all right. But don't ignore this chapter even if you think you'd never cover business. Because sooner or later money becomes a key issue on every beat, counsels Diana Henriques of *The New York Times*. And at that point, the reporter who shrugs and simply says, "I'm no good with figures," will fall short on the job.

"Whether you cover government and politics or arts and culture, you'll deal with corporate donors and corporate contractors," says Henriques, who covers finance. "Education is big business; so are prisons and health care and environmental cleanup. Bankruptcy courts are a fixture on the music beat, and if you cover sports, the new arena will probably be financed with municipal bonds on terms that will affect your teams and your taxpayers."

When it comes to work and money, people tend to make claims that don't hold up. A sure-bet investment can swallow up a couple's nest egg. The mayor's grandiose plans for a new development never leave the drawing board. The old promise of a job for life becomes one more promise unkept.

In this chapter, you'll learn that a healthy skepticism is essential on this beat. You'll also learn that:

- Sources on the working beat run the gamut from the assembly line to the corporate office.
- Online and paper records, from a company's annual reports to those it files with the government, are significant sources of information.
- Writing the most common stories on the workplace beat—new businesses, company changes, negotiations and profiles—becomes easier if you follow certain tips.
- Reporters covering working issues can easily get trapped by conflicts of interest or other ethical dilemmas.

PEOPLE TO SEEK OUT

When you cover the workplace, you'll need to talk to the boss and other top company officers, of course. But you'll want to keep tabs on what workers are saying, too, as well as the buzz at the unemployment office. And you'll want to check in regularly with government offices that monitor companies' finances and safety records, with competitors and with the financial wizards who make sense of what's happening downtown, at the industrial park and out in cyberspace.

WORKERS AND FORMER WORKERS

Often, people who will give the most honest account of what's going on aren't the corporate executives or the public relations staff. Start instead with those closest to the work—the hourly workers who'll tell you whether those "improvements" in quality control really have improved anything or whether having a woman as production supervisor has changed the way sexual harassment is looked at in the workplace.

To find workers and supervisors means camping out at the plant gates, swinging by the union hall or stopping at the downtown deli about lunch time.

Many skilled workers, such as plumbers, electricians and flight attendants, are unionized. **Unions** are workers associations that represent the workers in negotiations for wages, hours and working conditions and in resolving grievances. Knowing the union president or shop steward is a helpful entry for labor issues or stories on contract negotiations. Don't stop, however, with the official spokesperson for the workers, whether the company is unionized or not.

"Former employees are the world's greatest source of information," says Steve Stecklow of *The Wall Street Journal*.

They'll often open up more than the folks still on the inside, and if they've only recently departed, they'll still have plenty of insight into how a company works. That insight might be colored with a biased filter, of course.

Others on the outside who deal regularly with those inside:

- Career counselors
- Staff with outplacement companies, whose job it is to help employees laid off or bought out find jobs
- Teachers in retraining programs
- Unemployment counselors
- Laid-off worker support groups

MANAGEMENT

Top managers likely will toe the company line. But it's a line reporters will always need to know, if for no other reason than to compare image to reality. Just don't expect the picture painted by those on top to be complete.

It's still wise to talk to top executives directly. Many companies have policies that all media calls or permission for taping must go through the public relations staff. Make PR a starting point, not an ending point, however.

"If you happen to hit them on a subject that they want to talk about, corporate PR people can be very helpful," says Maria Shao of *The Boston Globe*.

But sometimes Shao finds they're more of a roadblock than a gateway.

"The worst thing is that they can totally stonewall, they might not give you access or sometimes they totally puff," adds Shao.

After 17 years in reporting, Maria Shao became an assistant business editor at *The Boston Globe*. She tells business reporters to keep an eye on what happens at the statehouse and on Capitol Hill—it often has a dramatic effect on business.

She finds PR people most helpful when you can say, "Hey, I'm doing a story on this and this, and I need some examples from corporate America."

Small businesses usually don't have a PR person, so you'll try to get to the president or owner. Some middle-size companies will hire an independent PR firm. Business sources, whether the PR practitioner or the small-business owner, take nurturing. Many are suspicious of reporters.

"A lot of reporters have a tendency to make an initial contact and then not talk to a source until something's wrong," says Heather Newman of the *Detroit Free Press*. "And that's when they least want to talk. You have to keep up with folks."

Some PR firms offer a so-called experts service, suggesting names of clients who have expertise in the area the reporter is researching (see Chapter 4). One service, BznetUSA, operates on the Net. It's run by Gehrung Associates, a New Hampshire public relations firm that specializes in higher education and represents colleges and research universities. A reporter types out a request, e-mails it to Bznet and gets back an e-mail message or phone call with suggestions of business professors who might fit the bill.

Michael Barrier of *Nation's Business* used Bznet to find sources for a cover story on what small-business owners should look for in hiring employees. Bznet led him to experts at the University of Maryland and the University of North Carolina—people he probably wouldn't have talked with otherwise.

BUSINESS-RELATED GROUPS

Promoting business—that's the number one goal of the local chamber of commerce, an organization to which most local businesses will belong. Even though members of the chamber's staff are probusiness, you'll find them helpful in figuring out who's doing what and in identifying the latest local trends.

Reporters also keep contacts among:

- Neighborhood business associations, such as a Westside Business District Association. The association's director will explain struggles and successes in luring people to the area and in battling zoning decisions at city hall.

Suppose Juanita Collazo's husband works in management for the largest company in town. Should she be allowed to report on that company? It's an issue with which reporters and their families, as well as editors and news directors, wrestle.

Write a policy for your news organization about reporters' conflicts of interest. Include a statement about which business stories reporters should not cover because they are too closely involved with a company. Consider family ties, spouse's occupation and types of financial investments.

- Trade organizations to which local companies belong. For example, a reporter in a city with a large chemical plant would keep handy the phone number of the media office of the Chemical Manufacturers Association.

- Real estate developers. They'll know about plans for new buildings, shopping centers and apartment complexes.

- Suppliers or subcontractors to the biggest businesses in town. When a big beer plant announced it was leaving Fulton, N.Y., reporters checked in with the company down the road that made the cans for the beer.

CUSTOMERS

Like workers, those who use the business's products or services often have a unique outlook that helps in workplace stories. Reporter Heather Newman regularly lurks on the Internet, looking for sources and story ideas. When she worked at *The (Nashville) Tennessean,* she regularly checked in with an Internet discussion group of Saturn owners, since Saturn's auto plant was located just outside the city.

"Mixed in with all the people who are shooting off their mouths, occasionally something will come along that's a good story," Newman said.

On one of those occasions, she read messages from emergency medical technicians writing that the plastic panels on Saturns proved tricky when rescuing crash victims. Newman queried the writers online and found a similar discussion thread (messages on the same topic) in an online group for EMTs. That led her to more sources and interviews.

Reporters may often find themselves on the receiving end of gifts from PR practitioners or companies: from cold cuts in the convention pressroom to a bountiful thank-you bouquet of flowers from the hospital featured in a recent story.

One old codger was heard to say, "It's OK if you can eat it, smoke it or use it in a day." Some newsroom policies set a monetary limit, such as $25, on gifts that can be accepted.

Discuss in small groups:

- Is the old codger's standard a good one?
- If you set a monetary limit, what would it be?
- Does the gift's value matter? What about the giver?
- Even if you know a gift wouldn't affect your reporting, does it have the appearance of impropriety? Would it diminish your credibility if readers or listeners knew about it?
- Should it be returned? Given to charity?

Here's the lead of her story, which landed on the front page of the Sunday business section.

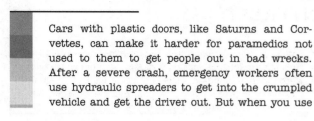

Cars with plastic doors, like Saturns and Corvettes, can make it harder for paramedics not used to them to get people out in bad wrecks. After a severe crash, emergency workers often use hydraulic spreaders to get into the crumpled vehicle and get the driver out. But when you use the Jaws of Life on a car with plastic panels, the doors just tear, shatter or spring back into place, according to emergency workers in Tennessee and throughout the country.

The Tennessean

COMPETITORS

The auto dealer on one side of town knows a whole lot about the auto dealer on the other side of town. And that Ford dealer probably has a good idea the Toyota dealer's promotional scheme is or isn't working and who turns over used cars the fastest. Competitors are great sources to let you know if somebody else isn't playing by the rules.

So whether it's the mom-and-pop bookstore casting a wary eye at the new megabookstore opening at the mall or the local bakery protesting to the zoning board about caterers working out of their homes, be sure to talk with others in the same line of work.

Just remember the usual caution: They'll have their own agenda to push in the process.

GOVERNMENT SOURCES

A variety of government sources can help a workplace writer understand the many issues that come up on this beat. Among these sources are regulators, statisticians and economic development officials.

The cheerleaders who encourage businesses to stay, expand or move to town are found in a city or county economic development office. They work as liaisons between business and government to assist companies in getting tax breaks, loans and city services. It's the economic development folks who know who's about to open, close or relocate.

The regulators—at the city, county or state level—are the ones charged with making sure the businesses do what they're supposed to do. For example, if you're checking out a tip that a local garment manufacturer is cheating employees out of overtime, you'd talk with investigators from the state labor department.

Workplace reporting often involves analyzing numbers so that the audience can measure what's changed. Statisticians not only provide the numbers but also help interpret what the numbers mean. So to get a sense of why the unemployment numbers are starting to creep up, a reporter might call a statistician at the state labor office.

FINANCIAL EXPERTS

Since many of us picked journalism because we're math-phobic, we need more than just government statisticians to help us sort out the economic jargon and get a fix on what the numbers mean. Reporters turn to a variety of money experts, recognizing that they, too, may have a vested interest behind their expertise. "Sell-side" analysts, for example, work for companies that sell stocks to the public. These analysts' bonuses or compensation might be pegged to the volume of stock their company sells. Beware.

"Buy-side" analysts work for institutions such as mutual funds or pensions that invest their own and clients' money. They're more independent but also more media-shy. No matter which expert is chosen, the first thing reporters must learn is not to be intimidated by all the terms, says Jennifer Moore, the longtime business reporter at *WDIV-TV,* Detroit. The workplace beat is like any other—it takes lots of hard work, but reporters can develop expertise.

"Most people who are medical reporters are not doctors," Moore says. "You learn by asking a zillion questions, by reading books and following stories."

Reporters seek out a variety of experts:

- Local economists at a bank or university can give a perspective on the financial health of the region.
- Credit union managers or bankers are knowledgeable about the housing and loan industries.
- Retail analysts can help interpret sales figures. For example, the International Council of Shopping Centers in New York City lends its expertise each December to reporters covering holiday shopping trends.
- Market analysts explain investing trends and the volatility of the stock market.
- Labor consultants or university professors can explain key issues in negotiations. For example, Don Gonyea of *National Public Radio* often uses David Cole, head of the Center for the Study of Automotive Transportation at the University of Michigan, for analysis on auto industry labor talks. Cole, the son of a former General Motors president, worked as an auto executive and now studies the industry, so he has a wide-ranging perspective from which to comment.

THINGS TO READ

While people sources are most helpful, don't overlook the wealth of information online, in media, books and government documents.

MEDIA

The Wall Street Journal, along with *Money, Fortune* or *Forbes* (paper or online versions) are must-reads for everyone covering the business side of money. Radio and TV business shows, such as "Bloomberg Business News" or "Moneyline" on *CNN,* can often trigger story ideas or tip you off to trends and issues.

There are also lots of specialty publications covering certain industries. For example, Gonyea, who covers automotive issues for *National Public Radio,* says *Automotive News* is his assigned reading.

COMPANY PUBLICATIONS

Companies publish a lot of information about themselves in sales brochures, annual reports and on the Internet. Even small businesses probably have a marketing brochure. Reporters skim these to background themselves on the company and find names, office locations and the like.

But remember, the company's putting its best foot forward in these publications, and that's not always news. Diana Henriques, a *New York Times* reporter, told her readers what was *not* in the slick annual report of the Culbro Corporation, the maker of premium cigars:

. . . But forget the graceful annual report. The really juicy news cannot be found there this year—it is all tucked away in the frumpy Form 10-K filed with the Securities and Exchange Commission last month.

There you can read about the 3,000 pounds of marijuana seized by Customs agents at a company plant in Alabama last spring; about the internal investigation that stumbled across a crooked invoicing scheme that defrauded the company of about $1 million over four to five years; about a senior executive, dismissed last year, who has filed a lawsuit accusing the company of bribing foreign officials and cheating on federal campaign laws.

The New York Times

SLEUTHING THROUGH BUSINESS REPORTS

Here are four types of reports that businesses file with government. Check them for story ideas or background.

- **DBA listings:** County offices keep names and addresses of people who run businesses. Ask for the listing of "DBAs" (doing business as) or "fictitious names"—names under which businesses operate.

- **Business registrations:** State governments register businesses, so they'll have documents with basic information about a company, its officers, address and whether or not its stock is publicly traded. Be careful, however, so you aren't fooled as one reporter was. The "incorporator" on those documents isn't necessarily the owner. It might be the attorney who drew up the papers.

- **Layoff listings:** Heather Newman of the *Detroit Free Press* recommends checking with the state labor department for a list of companies that are laying off employees.

Federal law requires companies downsizing by more than 50 employees to file their plans two months ahead of time.

- **990s:** Some of the biggest dollars in town are not being spent by businesses but by nonprofits such as hospitals, charities or cultural institutions. The IRS 990 form, required of all nonprofits, is packed with information on property, salaries and fund-raising costs.

Cincinnati Magazine used 990s to track 200 nonprofits in its area and told readers interesting tidbits such as which arts organization spent the most on travel (Cincinnati Symphony) and which local festival hauled in the most dollars (St. Rita School for the Deaf).

You'll find 990s at the nonprofits' offices, attorney general's office or the regional IRS center.

This information about who is suing a company is just one tidbit that companies must report to the government in an annual 10-K report. It can make news. So good reporters dig deeper than company PR packets.

BUSINESS REPORTS TO GOVERNMENT

When Amber Smith, a *Syracuse (N.Y.) Herald American* reporter, got tipped that a new health maintenance organization was elbowing its way into the area, she set out to find out everything she could about the new HMO. Here's part of her story:

Its president is Leonard Abramson. His annual salary—including bonus and fringe benefits—at the end of 1994 totaled $3.87 million, according to documents from the U.S. Securities and Exchange Commission. That doesn't count $1.8 million worth of stock options.

. . . One daughter directs health education; she made $267,000 in salary and bonuses in 1994. A son-in-law oversees the pharmacy and dental operations; his salary and bonuses were $300,000 the same year. Another daughter got a $510,000 contribution from U.S. Healthcare plus a $10 million line of credit to start a communications company.

Syracuse (N.Y.) Herald American

You might guess that it took Smith days of searching through paper files and hours of knocking on doors to compile all that. Not so. It took only a couple hours of downloading off a computer.

All the information in her story, including the salary figures, was in reports the HMO is required to send to the federal government because its stock is traded publicly. Smith asked the news librarian to download the reports from an online database, Lexis-Nexis. They're now available online free via the SEC's *Edgar* Web site. For clues on what to look for in these reports, see the box, Learning From the Pros: Understanding SEC Documents.

For other insights on where to find the scoop on businesses, see the box, Learning From the Pros: Sleuthing Through Business Reports.

Government Reports

So far, we've only talked about government documents sent in by businesses or nonprofits. But government agencies that deal with businesses pile up paper and fill up hard drives on their own. Government documents to help you on the workplace beat come in at least three forms:

- *Annual or summary reports:* They summarize office operations in order to justify their existence to the legislators who set budgets.

  A county economic development report brags about how well it's done in luring new businesses. The county welfare office reports that its job skills program took dozens of people off welfare and helped them enter the job market.

- *Trend reports:* They track trends, provide statistics and explain processes. The (federal) Office of Thrift Supervision publishes reports about the money held in savings and loans, and the **Bureau of Labor Statistics** Web site explains how it measures unemployment.

- *Regulatory reports:* They're audits or summaries of how businesses are complying with the law.

Kathy Kristof, a newspaper columnist with the *Los Angeles Times Syndicate,* says a good reporter never overlooks the regulatory role of government. When she started covering banks and savings and loans, she sat herself down and read through all the banking rules. It's not the most exciting reading, but the discipline paid off.

"I was breaking stories about banks on the precipice of failure that the daily [newspaper] didn't have," says Kristof, who was then working for a weekly. "It's like playing Monopoly. If you don't know the rules, you get really lucky sometimes and you'll win, but if you know the rules you can strategically win a lot of the time."

Winning means knowing where to look in the documents and how to interpret the columns of numbers there. To find the documents, think who would be regulating the industry you're covering. Leafing through a government manual (a state or city directory on how government is organized), or even the phone book, can tip you off to which office handles what. For example, the city licensing department probably keeps licenses of downtown sidewalk vendors, and the state occupational safety and health office collects complaints of worker injuries.

If any government money has gone to a business—for example, it's part of an urban redevelopment project or it got a small business loan—there will be a paper trail to follow. Following that trail online at the federal level can be done by starting at a master index for federal sites on the Net called **FedWorld.** Here reporters can search for any federal agency or read recently released government reports. If you're not on the Net yet, check for a federal government manual at the library.

Remember, also, that court files are full of information on businesses. If you're tracking a business that went belly up, you might find out why in the federal court bankruptcy files.

Books, Databases and Internet Resources

For financial details on a company, check the public or university library for company reports published by Standard & Poor's, Moody's or Dun & Bradstreet—companies that monitor corporations. Or surf over to **Hoovers Online** on the Internet. Reporters searching for an analyst often refer to the book known as Nelson's Directory. Business Information Sources, also at the library, gives reporters ideas on where to go when they're at a dead end.

UNDERSTANDING SEC DOCUMENTS

If a company's stock is traded on a national stock exchange, it has to file periodic reports with the Federal Securities and Exchange Commission—the watchdog agency over stocks, bonds and public corporations.

Here's a guide to the most important of those documents from *New York Times* reporter Diana Henriques:

■ A registration statement (or S-1) contains all the essential information about a company.

"This tells you the background of the founders, competitors, who the underwriters are and anything imaginable about the company," says Henriques. "This is the mothership."

If a company is new, this statement will include a **prospectus** that the company must issue to raise money. In addition to detailed financial information, it tells the risks the company is facing, whether from competitors or lawsuits, and what it plans to do with the money it raises. Another tip: Check later to see how the company is meeting the goals it sets out in the prospectus.

Diana Henriques

■ 10-Ks and 10-Qs explain the business operations, parent or subsidiary companies, property owned, finances and pending lawsuits of public companies as well as the backgrounds of major officers. The 10-Ks are filed annually, the 10-Qs quarterly.

Henriques says to be sure to check the headings she calls "the good parts": Litigation, Certain Transactions and Related Party Transactions.

■ A proxy statement is a notice to stockholders about the annual meeting and the issues to be voted on there. Perhaps more importantly, here's where you find out how much dough the top executives are pulling in.

■ 13-Ds are filed by investors when they buy more than 5 percent of the company's stock. Henriques calls these "lucky 13s" because she finds great tidbits, such as the background of the buyer, where the buyer got the money to make the purchase and descriptions of the corporate structure of the investor (even if it's a privately held company).

■ 8-Ks tip reporters off to significant changes in the company's ownership or finances, such as the sale of assets, new management, a lawsuit, a court judgment or an SEC fine. They must be filed within 15 days of the activity.

"If some PR guy is saying this is the hottest story down the pike and it should go on Page 1, ask him if they've filed an 8-K," says Henriques. "If not, ask him why not."

Photo by Fred Conrad.

If you thought there'd be no more homework after you graduated, think again. Many reporters teach themselves the trade, starting with materials produced by brokerage houses, such as "How to Read a Financial Report," from Merrill Lynch (see Recommended Reading at chapter's end), or online primers, such as the frequently asked questions (FAQs) page on the **Dow Jones** Web site.

Large news organizations can afford to buy into specialized business databases. One is *Bloomberg Business News,* a news service that transmits hundreds of business stories, stock prices and securities analyses each week.

It doesn't cost nearly as much to surf the Internet for workplace stories. And you can even get some of that Bloomberg information, for example, online. Many companies use a standard address format: www.company-name.com. Substitute the name of the company or an abbreviation for "companyname." Reporters use online phone books to find a company address as well.

Internet search engines are the best choice for starting research on a company or topic. First, check what the business says about itself on its home page. Then plug the company name into a search engine to find other sites where the company is mentioned. If you were in Sacramento, Calif., and wanted to track the trend in advertising homes online, a good place to start might be with the **HotBot** search engine where you'd type in *'real estate' and Sacramento* and get a long list of sites to surf.

CLIPBOARD   INTERNET SITES MENTIONED IN THIS CHAPTER

Bureau of Labor Statistics	stats.bls.gov	Financial Data Finder	www.cob.ohio-state.edu/dept/fin
Dow Jones FAQs	averages.dowjones.com/faqs.html	Hoovers Online	www.hoovers.com
Edgar (SEC)	www.sec.gov/edgarhp.htm	HotBot	www.hotbot.com
FedWorld	www.fedworld.gov		

For an update to this list, see http://web.syr.edu/~bcfought.

Reporters also use indexes of business sites as a springboard for research. Warren Cohen of *U.S. News and World Report* recommends that rookie cyber-reporters start with Ohio State's **Financial Data Finder.**

BASIC STORIES

Watch the next business segment in a TV newscast or pick up a newspaper business section. You're sure to see one of these five basic types of workplace stories:

- Tape measure story: what's up, down or coming around in business
- Change story: a merger, acquisition, layoff or shutdown
- New business story: who's opening up or moving in
- Negotiations story: bargaining between management and workers
- The profile: an inside look at a business person or company

Let's look at each and get a few tips on how to handle them.

THE TAPE MEASURE STORY

Reporters on the workplace beat write hundreds of what we'll call tape measure stories: stories measuring activity, such as whether sales are up or down, the economy is growing or stagnating, the stock market has jumped or fallen, interest rates are up or down.

Numbers are at the core of such stories—numbers that reporters should use selectively and accurately. Following are some tips and examples.

- **Put the numbers in context.** Notice any problem with this story?

> Early-August sales of domestically built trucks soared 32 percent, powered by incentives. But passenger car sales slid 1 percent, according to figures released Thursday.
>
> *Associated Press*

What's missing? The time period. The reporter forgot to write whether sales are "soaring" in the past month, past quarter or past year.

- **Use numbers that relate to the audience.** As *NewsCenter 5* (Boston) TV reporter Mark Mills designed the graphics for a story on the increase in home heating oil costs, he realized the statistics he'd gotten through research from an online service were for oil futures—the commodity market price for future sales.

"Oil futures are not as relevant to the homeowner as the actual cost of what they pay the oil guy," says Mills, who then set out to get numbers that meant something to his viewers. Here's what he found:

> A year ago the average price per gallon of heating oil in Massachusetts was 90 cents. Today it's about $1.05 and will probably go higher.
>
> *NewsCenter 5* (Boston)

- **Check the accuracy of the numbers.** Just because another media organization reports numbers does not mean you can borrow them. Good reporters always go to the original source.

To get those oil prices, Mills called an oil dealer, a consumer group and a state official. But the numbers didn't match. Two out of three is good enough, right? Not for Mills, who checked back until he found the error.

"I was concentrating very hard on making sure I had good accurate numbers for averages for last year and this year," he says, "because that's the heart of the story—how much is it up."

- **Use numbers sparingly.** A few numbers add weight to a story; a lot of numbers just weigh it down. Numbers should illustrate the point, not obscure it. This is especially true in TV and radio scripts because hearing numbers is harder than reading them in print.

- **Use the numbers, graphics and charts that are right for the story.** Sometimes the form of numbers is important.

"I try not to use percentages," says *WRC-TV* (Washington, D.C.) reporter Elizabeth Crenshaw. "Tell them this bowl of cereal costs this much and that bowl costs that much, rather than saying one is 16 percent more expensive."

But sometimes the percentage, particularly when used with the actual numeric change, makes more sense. A chart pointing out that the median sales price of a home in the county last year was $82,000 and is now $88,900 may not mean as much as a graphic with the headline "up 8.4 percent."

The day when reporters—even print reporters—were expected to think only in words is a thing of the past. All reporters should ask themselves, "How can I illustrate the story? What graphic or chart can tell the information simply?" This is not true only of working stories, but such stories tend to involve data that often can best be explained graphically.

- **Give the numbers a human face.** Just because we left this tip until the end, doesn't mean it's less important. People want to read about people. That's essential.

Even when numbers are a basic ingredient in the recipe, those numbers will quickly lose meaning unless spiced up with real people's stories. For example, a story about the expansion of health-care services in the community might be accompanied by a chart showing job growth and another showing the relative strength of several competing HMOs.

SUMMARY

TAPE MEASURE STORY

Using numbers appropriately is the most important consideration in a tape measure story:

1. Put the numbers in context—make sure they make sense.

2. Use numbers that relate to the audience.

3. Make sure your numbers are good.

4. Use numbers sparingly.

5. Think visually—think about what graphics will tell the story.

6. Put people in the stories to humanize the numbers.

But, particularly in broadcast, it should start with a person: perhaps a doctor preparing for surgery in the city's first open-heart surgery unit. A story on corporate downsizing in your community might have a chart comparing the number of white-collar management jobs five years ago and now. But its power will come from the story of a now-unemployed long-term manager discussing his plight with others in a support group.

THE COMPANY CHANGE STORY

While the tape measure story ranks as the most common workplace story, a close second is the story about company change—shutdowns, layoffs, buyouts, mergers or acquisitions. AT&T announced a company reorganization and 40,000 fewer jobs this way:

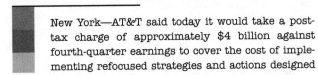

New York—AT&T said today it would take a post-tax charge of approximately $4 billion against fourth-quarter earnings to cover the cost of implementing refocused strategies and actions designed to increase its competitiveness and efficiency as it restructures into three independent companies.

AT&T

The Wall Streeters might get it, but most folks won't.

By now you've figured out tip number one for a change story: Make it understandable. That means decoding the jargon pervasive in business and substituting language the person on the street can comprehend.

See if this version from *National Public Radio* makes more sense:

AT&T said today that it would eliminate 40,000 jobs, or about 13 percent of its overall work force, as part of its plan to split into three separate companies.

National Public Radio

Besides being simpler, the *NPR* story provides the essential element—perspective. How many jobs are 40,000? Thirteen percent of the workforce. Later in the story the reporter added perspective again by telling listeners this was the largest corporate cut since 1993.

What such decisions mean locally is also important for a change story. As a national network, *NPR* can't do that. But the hometown paper of many of AT&T's executives, the *(Morristown, N.J.) Daily Record,* did:

. . . Morris County is home to 12,000 of New Jersey's 480,000 AT&T jobs. Spokesmen said that 5,000 to 7,000 workers would lose their jobs in the state but refused to speculate on how many workers would be fired from each division of Morris County's largest private employer.

(Morristown, N.J.) Daily Record

Reporter Ray Day continued by weaving in quotes on the impact from a local economist and a real estate agent.

The change story should also give readers or viewers a sense of why the change is taking place. Here's one way to do that, from a *New York Times* series, "The Downsizing of America."

At the Newport News, Va., shipyard of Tenneco Inc., a diversified manufacturer, 11,000 of 29,000 workers have been shed since 1990, largely because of technological efficiencies like automated welding.

The New York Times

COMPANY CHANGE STORY

1. Make what happened understandable: not "involuntary reductions" but "layoffs."

2. Tell what the numbers mean—40,000 is 13 percent.

3. Localize the story with information and interviews in your area.

4. Explain why the change is taking place.

5. Work to be fair. Tell why the company believes it has to make this change.

6. Explain the impact on the audience. What will this mean in people's daily lives?

Times reporters in the same series resisted doing what too many reporters do—portraying the company only as the big, bad bully. They strove to find balance in a series of powerful stories on the impact of downsizing on workers.

See how these quotes from corporate executives humanize and explain their role in laying off workers from a different company:

"I felt lousy about it," Arthur C. Martinez, Sears's Chairman, said, "But I was trying to balance that with the other 300,000 employees left, and balance it with the thousands of workers in our supplier community and with 125,000 retirees who look to Sears for their pensions, and with the needs of our shareholders."

[another CEO] . . . "I knew that she was the best in the department," he said. "But she had not networked. And I had to inform her that she was terminated. And she looked at me with tears in her eyes and said, 'But Charlie, you know better.' I will never forget what she said and how she looked that day."

The New York Times

Such segments bring balance as well as perspective to a story.

A final tip for reporting on a company layoff or expansion—get to the bottom line.

"Break it down and get past the jargon and say here's what's going to happen to you in your daily life," Heather Newman says.

Here's how she did that in a story about the impact of a new telecommunications law:

Result: You're going to get a lot more phone calls. If you thought the competition between long-distance companies was bad, wait until there are a dozen local phone companies vying for your dollars. The good news could be the number of dollars you have to shell out.

The (Nashville) Tennessean

THE NEW BUSINESS STORY

While the county's large employers might be going through their midlife crises, down the road, entrepreneurs are giving birth to new companies. Every workplace reporter keeps tabs on the upstarts, so the "new business" story is a standard.

When *Post-Standard* reporter Charlie Hannagan got a tip that a new airline was starting in Syracuse, NY, she didn't have a clue as to what it took for an airline start-up. But she did know what's essential for a story on a new business. Here's the checklist she's developed for approaching such stories and how that information appeared in her story:

- Explain the product or the service: "Northern plans to serve six northeastern cities from Syracuse, offering fares as low as $39 to $49 each way. As part of that, it expects to offer nonstop jet service to some markets that either currently do not have jet service from Syracuse or do not have direct service."

- Identify who's behind this venture and their track record: "Northern Airlines officials say they are studying a 'short list' of candidates for president and chief executive officer. Its current top managers have held executive positions at major and regional airlines."

- Find the source of the money: "Northern is seeking $15 million from private investors. . . . The city has kicked in $90,000 in the form of a 7 percent loan from the Syracuse Economic Development Corp. The loan comes from a revolving loan fund paid for by federal grants and loan repayments."

- Tell the number of jobs created and when.

- Include first-year goals as well as long-range plans.

- Tell readers the effect on them. In Hannagan's story, it was lower fares.

In addition to this checklist, make sure you keep that essential trait on the money beat—your skepticism. New businesses hand out slick promotional brochures, trot out the mayor to pump the project and brag about how they're helping a community desperate for more jobs. But look beyond the glitter and lights. Amidst the hoopla about the new airline, Hannagan pointed out the downsides:

> Yet the airline doesn't have federal government permission to fly, a plane to take off in or the money to lease one.
>
> . . . Of the 48 airlines that applied for operating approval to the Department of Transportation since 1990, only 26 got the go-ahead to begin flying. Of those 26, 15 continue to operate, five ceased operations and six never got off the ground.
>
> *The (Syracuse, N.Y.) Post-Standard*

Such qualifiers help the reader get the big picture and evaluate the odds of whether the business will get off the ground.

Writing the basic new business story isn't as easy if the company isn't a public one. Veterans of the workplace beat suggest good old shoe-leather reporting: talking to everybody, checking court files (lawsuits, real estate records, divorces) as well as building permits, zoning changes, regulatory reports and online databases. Many reporters will use a paid service that provides business profiles. They also recommend talking with business consultants and venture capitalists.

SUMMARY — NEW BUSINESS STORY

1. Explain the product or the service.

2. Find out who's bankrolling the venture.

3. Tell the projected impact on the job market.

4. Include the goals of the business.

5. Tell the readers the effect on them.

6. Explain the hurdles this business must overcome before it can succeed.

7. Maintain a healthy skepticism.

THE PROFILE STORY

Another standard recipe when you're cooking up stories on the workplace beat is the profile story. It might focus either on a person (the scientist and her new patent) or a company (the 20th anniversary of the downtown deli).

The main stumbling block for beginning reporters writing profile stories is keeping them from being so glowing that they look like they came off the public relations office printer.

Here are five tips for a profile story:

1. Seek out anecdotes about the person or company.

Talk to family members, friends, competitors and independent analysts to fill out your perspective. These add depth, lightness or humor to the basic who, what, when, where, how and why.

In a small-business profile of the first day of a candy store, *Wall Street Journal* reporter Stephanie Mehta noticed the owner's nervousness. When she probed, she found out the panic-stricken entrepreneur was afraid she wouldn't know how to ring up the first sale on the new cash register. That gave Mehta a lead for the story.

2. Show, as well as tell, about the subject.

"Sometimes you read a story and the [business] owner is boiled down to a one-sentence description," Mehta says.

In her story Mehta included information about the woman's children, who did homework at the store after school, and the fact that she cared enough about her community to have the store sponsor a Little League team in the summer.

This vignette shows the woman's sense of humor:

When she opens the shop at 9 a.m., there is very little traffic on Main Street except for two young boys with shovels slung over their shoulders. They peer eagerly into the store. "Maybe my first customers," Ms. Graziano says brightly. "Or maybe they want me to be their customer."

The Wall Street Journal

3. Get details and descriptions in your notebook or on tape.

Again, *The Wall Street Journal* story:

At about 10 a.m. the boys with shovels return. After a few minutes of careful deliberation, they select several packets of Airheads, a popular taffy-like candy. Ms. Graziano carefully punches her first sales—totaling $2.12—into the register.

Note that Mehta tells what the first customers bought (Airheads), explains what they are (a popular taffy-like candy) and what they cost ($2.12—"about $2" would not do). Specific details bring a profile to life.

4. Include the business strategy or niche—what makes this different and why it will or has succeeded.

5. Discuss the challenges or roadblocks. Put the person or company into the big picture.

THE NEGOTIATIONS STORY

All reporters, at least once or twice in their careers, draw the red-eye stakeout at the site of contract negotiations or get sent to work the picket lines for quotes and sound bites. Stories about labor negotiations are another of the basic stories all reporters should know how to write.

SUMMARY

THE PROFILE STORY

1. Find a theme or story line to hold the story together.

2. Show as well as tell through anecdotes, pictures, natural sound and descriptive detail.

3. Expand your interviews beyond the subject or company to competitors, suppliers, friends, family.

4. Set the story in context of the big picture.

5. Retain a sense of balance in reporting. Don't produce puffery.

Too often reporters don't cover negotiations until the issues reach a boiling point—the union conducts an informational picket, the negotiating team leaves the bargaining table, or a strike ensues. But the best reporters will monitor the steps along the way and be ready with stories.

Although we're covering this story type in the context of business, contract issues also top the newscast and play on Page 1 when the picketers are teachers, nurses or county bus drivers—people usually covered by reporters on other beats.

Because he's based in Detroit, the fulcrum of the labor movement, Don Gonyea of *National Public Radio* has covered more stories on labor negotiations than he can count. Early on, says Gonyea, the reporter needs to sort out the main stumbling blocks.

"Usually it boils down to one or two issues that are really the things that prompt people to walk out," says Gonyea.

Don Gonyea

These days, he says, they're often not money, but health care and job security. Here's how he set out the main points during a United Auto Workers strike against General Motors:

> The union's position is that it wants to hang on to as many parts-making jobs at GM as possible—and any time an outside company is awarded a contract by GM—then that's lost work for UAW-represented workers.
>
> General Motors—meanwhile—is being pushed to take a hard line with the UAW in this dispute by its board of directors—and by Wall Street. Analysts say the reality is that GM's per-car manufacturing costs are much higher than those at Chrysler and Ford because GM produces a bigger percentage of its parts at in-house, unionized plants.
>
> *National Public Radio*

It sounds simpler than it is to select those key points. Both company and union spokespersons usually give reporters meaningless statements about how dedicated they are to working through the issues, but they won't give much detail.

Even when he includes those obligatory statements from both sides, Gonyea turns to inside contacts to get the guts of the story.

"Talk to people who aren't directly involved in the negotiations because they can be a little less guarded," Gonyea suggests.

SUMMARY
NEGOTIATIONS STORY

1. Outline the key issues simply so the audience can understand.

2. Make sure you've got all the viewpoints covered—management, workers and any other.

3. Use experts to explain the impact and what's really going on.

4. Use personal anecdotes in the story; find them on the picket line or where the workers hang out.

5. Watch the jargon—translate terms into understandable language, but make sure you understand subtle differences in the technical language.

For example, his key source for a strike at one of the Big Three automakers was the union president at one of the larger plants. The source got frequent calls from the negotiators and was able to tip Gonyea when the tentative settlement had been reached.

Once there is a settlement, Gonyea goes for the reaction comments from both sides. Of course, both labor and management are going to claim they "won." So he uses independent experts as the umpires: Wall Street investment analysts, business consultants with expertise in the industry he's covering and university professors who double as industry watchers.

All that can be informative, but dull. So Gonyea suggests adding the human dimension by going to the site of the negotiations or the picket line.

"There's where you can really get the feel of the strike, how long it will be or how a victory by one side or another will affect the workers," he explains. "It's only there that you get a sense of the potential sacrifice that individual workers may be making."

It was at the strike site that Gonyea captured the struggle of a well-known columnist who broke ranks and crossed the line in a newspaper strike:

[Gonyea] "Hardest thing you've had to do for this paper?"

[Columnist] "I think the only thing that would be harder would be not to . . ."

[Gonyea] As he entered the building's back entrance, McDermott turned briefly to his colleagues, still picketing and said, "Good luck to you guys."

The reply—cries of "shame on you" and "scab." [natural sound, strikers shouting angrily]

National Public Radio

ENTERPRISE STORIES

While all reporters on the workplace beat do their share of the routine stories, most say the real fun comes in the enterprise stories. That's when they can delve into a topic, live and breathe it for days—sometimes even weeks—and come out with a creative story or series that gets people talking.

"With business journalism, you're always learning something about the way the world works, compared to fires and crimes where you might not learn much after you've done it a few times," says Maria Shao of *The Boston Globe.* "I just find it's intellectually more stimulating."

One type of enterprise story is the dramatic behind-the-scenes account of how that labor settlement was reached in the 11th hour, for example, or how management pulled together to fend off a hostile takeover. Other enterprise stories cover trends, track business performance with the help of computer-assisted reporting or analyze the impact of unions on the workplace.

TREND STORIES

The best reporters keep their ears open to catch the distant drumbeats of new workstyles, hear the latest gurus on good management or pick up on the gadgets to make work more fun, if not more functional.

Melissa Preddy caught on, before many, to how work was changing for some white-collar types. Here's the lead for her Sunday feature in *The Detroit News*:

> Checking in at the office means more for Joan Cartter than making a telephone call. It means reserving herself a desk. Cartter and about 100 other employees at Andersen Consulting in Detroit no longer have a designated place to sit at the corporate suite.
>
> Instead, each morning they call a coordinator who registers them in one of 25 offices for the day. It's called "hotelling"—the latest slant for corporations with an increasingly mobile workforce equipped with portable computer equipment.
>
> *The Detroit News*

Her story discussed virtual offices and "work from anywhere" programs at several businesses. A sidebar story focused on a Michigan furniture maker that's refitting a van into a mobile office complete with desk, computer, printer, fax and phone.

The key with trend stories is to identify common threads, and then weave them with interviews and anecdotes into good storytelling.

PERFORMANCE STORIES

Other enterprise stories are born of an analysis of massive business or government records. That whizzing hard drive can tabulate numbers faster and easier than paper and pencil ever could. At *The (Nashville) Tennessean,* reporter Heather Newman checked up on airline performance. She found plane arrivals missed the mark 22 percent of the time, though in her area, the numbers ranged from 13 percent to 18 percent.

Newman used a federal database for her analysis. She regularly thumbs through the Directory of Transportation Data Sources to find all types of databases that she can analyze. In this case she compared all airlines for three summer months, contrasting Nashville figures with nationwide averages. Two intriguing numbers that popped out: the best and worst times to fly.

> In Nashville, the worst time of day for arriving planes is 6–7 p.m.; and carriers are most likely to get to the target city late if they leave here from 7–9 p.m.
>
> But those are not the busiest times of day. For arriving flights, the busiest hour also has the best-
>
> on-time record: 7–8 a.m. The best hour to depart from here is 8–9 a.m.
>
> *The Tennessean*

Newman prefers massaging the numbers herself to taking an analysis from somebody else.

"You can break [the numbers] down much better than the federal agencies can or would have reason to do," she says. "This is a way to give your audience a more useful grasp of the information."

SUMMARY
ENTERPRISE STORIES

1. Look beyond the day's news to pick out trends and changes in the workplace.

2. Build a story's foundation on timely, expert information, but use poignant anecdotes and strong pictures or sound to engage your audience.

3. Learn computer-assisted reporting skills to help you find the stories in the numbers.

4. Monitor performance and tell why a program, company or product is or isn't working.

5. Weave a sense of history into stories to give context and perspective.

ANALYSIS AND HISTORY

Sometimes we can only understand what's happening now by taking a look in the rearview mirror to see who and what have come this way before. Through the experience of his beat reporting, Don Gonyea of *National Public Radio* knew the labor movement was changing even as its numbers declined. He used the news peg of Labor Day to examine the changing role of labor unions and their effect on people's lives. He interviewed current strikers, union officials and analysts and reported that although union ranks are slimming, a new crop of leaders is taking over, vowing to have an impact on politics and bring back the union's clout. Here's how he sums up the piece at the close:

> Union leaders say they'll work to better inform union members about which political candidates best represent their interests. And over time—they say—they'll reverse Republican gains in Congress.
>
> They also promise aggressive organizing drives in manufacturing facilities—including Japanese-owned auto plants in the U.S.—and in an area where they've enjoyed some success in recent years—the service sector—where new jobs are being created—but at low wages.
>
> Labor analysts say part of the challenge is figuring out how to organize people who don't want to rock the boat and who often feel lucky just to have a job.
>
> *National Public Radio*

A look back might also come at the time of the opening of the 10th store in a home-grown pizza parlor chain or the 50th anniversary of that well-known product first designed right there in your hometown. Historical footage, old photographs and old-timers' reminiscing add flavor and intrigue to such stories. But more importantly they give context to what's going on now and add perspective.

RECOMMENDED READING

Financial Data Finder. [Online]. Available: **http://www.cob.ohio-state.edu/dept/fin**.

This directory, located at Ohio State University, is a great master list of links to more financial data than you could ever use.

Gentry, J. K. *Covering business*. Los Angeles, CA: Foundation for American Communications [Online]. Available: **http://www.facsnet.org**.

Click onto "Reporting Tools" and you'll find articles written by James K. Gentry, dean of the School of Journalism at the University of Kansas. There's an excellent overview of business reporting with tips on finding stories and how to approach them. You'll also find helpful articles on reading financial statements and analyzing businesses. Access requires registration but is free.

Hoovers Online. [Online]. Available: **http://www.hoovers.com**.

For a quick summary of a company, this is the place to check. Hoover's Company Capsules gives a brief background on nearly all companies traded on the stock markets and more than 1,000 private companies and nonprofits.

How to read a financial report. (1993). New York: Merrill Lynch, Pierce, Fenner & Smith.

This is just what it says—a simple, readable guide to understanding financial reports, something all reporters covering businesses should know. It's usually available from a local broker.

Thomas Register. [Online]. Available: **http://www.thomasregister.com**.

Use this site to find the name or phone for a company or to find out who produces a certain product (more than 120,000 items listed). You can search by company, product/service or brand name.

U.S. Securities and Exchange Commission. Edgar. [Online]. Available: **http://www.sec.gov/edgarhp.htm**.

The search function at this government site allows you to put in the name of any public company and get all the SEC reports it must file with the federal government. Those documents are full of interesting background and detail about the company, its staff, locations and operations.

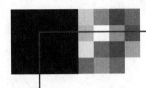

EXERCISES

A. RESEARCH

1. Explain the difference in these terms:

   a. stock, bond

   b. income statement, balance sheet

   c. closely held corporation, partnership

   d. realtor, real estate agent

   e. bank, credit union, savings and loan

2. Start a business contacts list. Find out the top 10 businesses in your city based on the number of employees. Also list who handles media calls at each and how to reach them.

3. Review the annual reports for three of the largest publicly held corporations in your area and suggest three story ideas and five contacts.

4. Compare a company's annual report to its 10-K filing with the SEC. List three possible stories suggested by the 10-K that are not in the annual report.

5. A wire service reports that small businesses are growing nationally at a rate of 20 percent. What five people would you contact for interviews about what's happening in your region?

6. A news release from the state labor department shows the unemployment is up 2.5 percent in the past quarter in your county. How would you find an unemployed worker to interview? If assigned this story, where would you look for natural sound, what pictures would you shoot, what descriptive details should you note?

B. BASIC STORIES

1. Write a story or memo on these topics:

   a. Find a new business that is just about to open or has opened in the past two weeks.

   b. Track the trend in unemployment in your area. Start with the latest monthly figures for your county's unemployment, but look at what's happened over the past year. Personalize the numbers by interviewing at least one person who's seeking work and an unemployment counselor.

   c. Find a union that will be negotiating a new contract in the next six months and write about the key bargaining issues. Be sure to interview persons from the union and the company.

d. Search the wires or a national newspaper for a recent statistical report or a numerical study about business or the economy. Get a copy of the study and build a story from it. Be careful how you use the numbers and be sure to humanize the story.

e. Write a profile of someone who's recently won a business award or been named the small business entrepreneur of the year.

C. ENTERPRISE STORIES

1. Look at the retail clothing industry in your area. Through interviews and a review of new business filings, determine whether discount stores have begun to push out higher-priced chains.

2. Find out what training opportunities exist for displaced homemakers, disabled persons or downsized employees. How do their approaches differ?

What is the waiting list? Are there enough? You may choose to key on one program and write a profile.

3. Find out where the most contentious labor dispute has been in your area in the past three years. Do a follow-up story on how workers and the company are faring now.

4. Studies show fewer of us are working 9 to 5. Look at those working overnights, the afternoon shift crew, the weekend warriors and others on nontraditional schedules. Show how they are coping and the impact this has on the workplace, the community, the home.

5. Write an in-depth piece on one of the top three publicly held companies in your area, its future challenges and the stability of its work force. Use SEC documents to help track how the company is changing nationally and examine how this might affect your area.

CHAPTER 17

New Frontiers: Science, Health and the Environment

The whooping, cheering and high-fives looked like the euphoria that erupts after the final out of the World Series. But these weren't sports maniacs. They were scientists cheering the first panoramas of the Martian landscape sent back 119 million miles from a feisty little 3-foot-long spacecraft named Pathfinder. The wave of euphoria even splashed over some of the reporters watching from the press center. Magazine reporter Andrew Chaikin put it this way: "It was the feeling you get when you know you're seeing things no one in history has ever seen before."

Having a front-row seat to discoveries is part of the excitement of covering new frontiers—science, health and the environment. It also is the delight that came over *Fresno (Calif.) Bee* reporter Russell Clemings when he came upon the fragile white blossoms of the Carpenteria californica, an endangered species found in only six places in California. Or it is the deep sense of satisfaction that Rhonda Mann, medical unit producer at *News-Center 5* (*WCVB-TV,* Boston), gets when she realizes that one of her stories might make life a little better or easier for some of her viewers.

"You really get a sense that what you are doing is helping them, by educating them about new things or showing them that other people out there have similar ailments or problems," Mann says.

But even though a sense of wonder draws many reporters to the new frontiers beats, they, too, must temper their wonder with worldly reminders of reality. Even the best science is little more than baby steps in a remarkably vast universe. Sometimes scientists reach the wrong conclusion simply because their knowledge is incomplete. A few cut corners or ignore conflicting evidence because their research promises vast financial gain. And sometimes science can have nasty side effects: Marvelous chemicals for everything from taking the grease off metal parts to killing weeds have polluted the underground water supplies of more than one community.

So reporters in science, health and the environment learn not to take everything at face value. They sweat to temper the words and images they use to make clear information people rely on greatly but understand little. They know theirs is a beat with impact. Readership

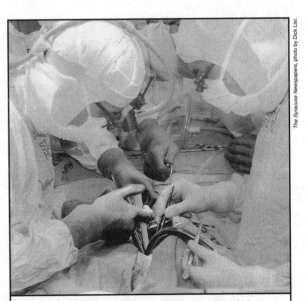

The procedures of open-heart surgery have extended life for thousands of people whose arteries have become clogged. It is one of countless advances in medical treatment tracked by those covering the new frontiers.

surveys and focus groups alike show that consumers want more depth and context in stories about body and earth. As baby boomers age, they are growing more concerned about their waistlines and their lifelines. They want to leave a safe planet for their grandchildren.

This chapter looks at science reporting broadly. In bigger news organizations, the beats included here—science, health, the environment—are parceled out among several specialists. Students will learn these points:

- The best science writers share scientists' wonder in discovery and in the perennial search for new advances. But they also share the healthy skepticism of journalists who know life's solutions are rarely all that simple.

- The disciplines of science, like those in other fields, are overseen by professional and governmental groups. It is crucial to seek the perspective of regulators as well as that of those affected by scientists' actions.

- Covering science often takes two levels of reporting. First reporters work to understand the science and its implications themselves. Next, they work to make both clear to general audiences without sacrificing accuracy. Often reporters achieve this by using analogies to compare the unfamiliar to things people know about.

- Science generally advances in incremental steps. Science writers, like scientists themselves, learn to temper what they write and say with qualifying phrases such as "the study suggests" or "the study provides further evidence" rather than absolutes such as "the study proves." As hard as scientists work to control variables in their research, the world is a complicated place.

PEOPLE TO SEEK OUT

Reporters covering the new frontiers might be reporting on smokestack emissions one day and smokeless tobacco the next. The topics are diverse and filled with jargon and statistics. That's all the more reason that a reporter's card file must be bulging with a variety of contacts.

GETTING STARTED

Whether the story is the environment, health or science, reporters often turn to those who can provide background and context before turning to the experts. A good place to start is local colleges and universities.

A radio reporter set to do a live interview with the Canadian astronomers who just discovered a new asteroid might first talk with a local astronomy professor about what asteroids are. An online reporter writing about the illnesses of local Gulf War veterans might call up a chemistry professor to learn more about the chemicals to which those vets were exposed. On background, these professors can arm reporters with the context of what's happened before and with a basic vocabulary to take the next step. They can also point reporters to good background reading and sources or Internet sites.

Reporters also seek help from public relations practitioners, who often serve as a bridge between reporters and scientists, medical researchers or doctors who are wary of the press. The best public relations practitioners know a lot about what's going on in their institutions, put together extensive background material for reporters and set them up for interviews with the right people. But remember: The PR folks haven't done the research. Reporters should use them mostly for background information and to open doors.

SCIENTIFIC AND MEDICAL EXPERTS

The "feel" of the story, as well as the facts, is best found from the experts. But inexperienced reporters are often hesitant about picking up the phone and calling them. No question—the approach of a reporter differs from that of a scientist. The meticulous researcher works for years to test a hypothesis before announcing it, while the reporter wants fresh discoveries every day.

Don't let the scientists' expertise intimidate you, says Adam Rogers, who works the science and technology beat at *Newsweek*. He often uses e-mail to ease his way in. Or he double-teams sources with e-mail and a voice mail message.

"Ninety percent of them check their e-mail obsessively, and they answer it," he says.

Many scientists read online at home—a bonus when it's after hours and you're on deadline. When the big story is brewing, Rogers says e-mail is a secret weapon. "If every other journalist in the country is covering the story, they're calling them by phone. If they've got 35 voice mail messages and two e-mail, they're answering the e-mail first."

Finding the right people is no easy job. It takes planning and persistence.

"Doctors and scientists do not drop everything because a reporter wants to talk to them," Cara Birrittieri of *New England Cable News* says. "It's not like a politician."

She often has to set up shoots several times—a frustration for a reporter who needs to produce every day.

A cautionary note here: Not all experts are equal. New reporters tend to get so excited when they finally find a person who knows something about their topic that they often go with the first person who will talk to them. Experienced reporters work a little harder. They screen experts both to find out who does cutting-edge work in the field and who can talk about it in plain English, not formulese (see box, Learning From the Pros: Getting Good Quotes).

When science reporters need a specialty source who can't be found locally, they often turn to the **Media Resource Service**—a nonprofit group whose sole purpose is to link journalists with scientists. It lists over 25,000 of them. And it's a free call.

Remember that scientists honestly disagree. Bounce the research claims of one off another. See whom they've cited in their research articles and call those people for comment. Ask who heads the professional organization in their field. Find out who in their field is familiar with their work but not necessarily in agreement with it. Good scientists won't mind telling you.

One way reporters expand their lists of contacts is to attend scientific conferences.

LEARNING FROM THE PROS **GETTING GOOD QUOTES**

Scientists and health-care experts have a lingo all their own. And often they don't even realize that most people don't understand their alphabet soup abbreviations.

Dr. Tom Linden, who has reported for California print, broadcast and online publications, says reporters shouldn't settle for the person who can't talk straight.

"There's always another person who's equally informed who can communicate well," he advises.

Linden coaches his interview subjects. "I tell doctors, look, if I'm going to use anything that you're going to say on the air, you've got to speak in plain English. Don't talk about M-I, myocardial infarcts, talk about heart attacks . . . don't talk about the basketball player's meniscus, talk about his cartilage."

Russell Clemings, an environment reporter at *The Fresno (Calif.) Bee,* offers another tip: "Ask them to pretend that they are speaking to an audience of bright eighth-graders and not to me. Most of them have children or have spoken to groups of children or young teenagers."

Young reporters are often embarrassed to admit they don't understand. But if they don't get it, the audience won't either. The confused reporter needs to press the scientist to explain it again, more simply.

A final tip from veterans: At the end of an interview, summarize the main points the expert has told you to make sure you've understood.

PATIENT CONDITIONS

When a hospital gives out a patient's condition, here's what it means:

Good: Vital signs are stable and within normal limits. Patient is conscious and comfortable. Indicators are excellent.

Fair: Vital signs are stable and within normal limits. Patient is conscious but may be uncomfortable. Indicators are favorable.

Serious: Vital signs may be unstable and not within normal limits. Patient is acutely ill. Indicators are questionable.

Critical: Vital signs are unstable and not within normal limits. Patient may be unconscious. Indicators are unfavorable.

(Reprinted with permission from the American Hospital Association.)

PEOPLE IN THE FIELD AND ON THE FLOOR

Some of the most exciting stories take place in the field—capturing the stories of the heart surgeon who saves a life with the help of a new procedure, the naturalist who finds a species thought to be extinct, the archaeologist who finds signs of an ancient civilization. The "field" includes the farmland where geologists trace the source of that polluted well and the homes of patients discharged from the hospital within hours of serious surgery.

Those living the story are often the best interview subjects. And in medicine, they're often the hardest to get.

"On a daily basis, it's difficult to find patients who are sick," says Birrittieri, a medical reporter for *New England Cable News*. "They don't want to be on TV."

But they're essential to the story. For one story Birrittieri profiled a group of pilots who volunteered to fly patients long distances to get specialized medical treatment. Since she knew the story would only work by showing a patient and a flight, Birrittieri searched until she found a patient who would agree to be interviewed and photographed—a woman with advanced breast cancer. Birrittieri had to set up the shoot three different times before the woman was well enough to take the flight. Birrittieri's story, however, wouldn't have been the same without her.

GOVERNMENT WORKERS

Reporters new to the health, science or environment beat might not think of making stops at city hall or the state office tower. After all, this isn't the government beat. But it is a beat government keeps an eye on. The much-maligned bean counters in government can often provide a revealing glimpse of what's happening in the health of the community. One *Omaha (Neb.) World-Herald* reporter checked with the staff at the county health department about lead levels among children, knowing that lead contamination can lead to developmental problems and low IQs. Here's a segment of that story:

. . . reports from the first three quarters of testing in Omaha said that 51 of the 482 children tested, or about 10.6 percent, had elevated lead levels in their blood. That is higher than the 4.4 percent nationwide average of elevated blood-lead levels for preschool children in a February report by the U.S. Centers for Disease Control and Prevention in Atlanta.

Omaha World-Herald

By comparing the local figures to the national ones, the reporter helped readers make sense of them. It's a good reporting technique. Reporters have hundreds of federal agencies to tap for national stats and contacts (see box, Where Do I Go?).

Beyond compiling numbers, government officials can help journalists trace the money trail in health-care funding or tell them who's following environmental laws and who's not (see box, Regulatory Sources).

Theoretically, pure science takes place outside the arena of politics.But discovery leads to application and here scientific advance is at the heart of public-policy formulation. So reporters also need contacts in state legislatures and Congress. An *(Albany, N.Y.) Times Union* reporter used sources in state and federal government in reporting how political pressure led to renewed testing of the air quality near New York's Adirondacks Park:

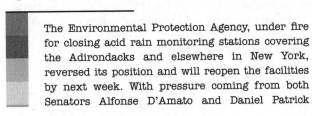

The Environmental Protection Agency, under fire for closing acid rain monitoring stations covering the Adirondacks and elsewhere in New York, reversed its position and will reopen the facilities by next week. With pressure coming from both Senators Alfonse D'Amato and Daniel Patrick Moynihan, as well as groups such as the Adirondack Council, the EPA reversed field and reopened 38 acid rain stations that were closed at the beginning of the year due to funding cuts.

(Albany, N.Y.) Times Union

TRADE GROUPS AND ORGANIZATIONS

Suppose you're writing about the shortage of nurses at the local hospital and you want to put the story in context. Is this happening elsewhere? The American Nurses Association, the professional organization representing the nation's 2.2 million registered nurses might help. More than 2,000 such medical and scientific associations exist. They are ready resources for reporters.

Some of the groups focus on professions, such as the nurses group. Others focus on topics or diseases—the Sleep Research Society or the American Cancer Society, for example. Most have Web pages and can be found

REGULATORY SOURCES

Regulators and the documents they use fall into four broad areas. Here's a quick overview:

- **Licensing and permits:** Professionals must hold a license to work and businesses often need a permit to operate or do certain work. A TV producer tracking a medical scam would know to call the state licensing board to make sure the man claiming to be a doctor truly is one. States monitor a vast number of professionals, from barbers to radiology technicians. Likewise, local or regional governments monitor everything from a sidewalk food stand to the new organic vegetable store.

- **Inspections:** Government workers regularly check up on certain people and businesses to find out if they are following the regulations or rules that apply. So reporters would call a state environmental official to find out if the water quality tests at the county beach show it's safe for swimming. Or they might verify a tip from a neighborhood group concerned about improper emissions from the nearby tire-burning plant by leafing through recent inspection reports at the facility.

- **Audits:** Audits are another type of inspection, an inspection of the books. Is money being spent where and how it should? The first to know the answer are the government auditors who routinely check up on various government programs and contracts. Auditors never seek the limelight, and too often their reports don't see the light of day. But these reports expose much.

An *Austin (Texas) American-Statesman* reporter found a state audit showing $1 million in questionable expenses by nursing homes, including the purchase of a fancy car, baseball tickets and salaries for people who never worked.

- **Laws/regulations:** Politicians set the policies, but the ones who flesh out the details are usually the staff of various agencies. It's in the minutia of regulations that reporters find the who, what, when, where and how of the laws. That's why staff members are the ones reporters want to talk to as regulations are being proposed, debated and enacted.

A *St. Petersburg (Fla.) Times* reporter kept track of the last day on which the public could give its views on a proposed regulation to protect manatee by banning swimmers and boaters from parts of Kings Bay. The next day she called a staffer at the U.S. Fish and Wildlife Service to find out what he'd heard. Eighty-three people had written in, most in opposition.

using search engines such as **Altavista** or **InfoSeek** (see Chapter 4). All of them are listed in paper form in the voluminous Encyclopedia of American Associations. Many have local chapters, so there may be an affiliate right in your hometown.

Every reporter's card file should also list contacts at public interest groups—the citizens groups that serve as watchdogs in many areas where science and public policy overlap, such as genetic research, air pollution or toxic waste.

One such group is the **Center for Science in the Public Interest,** which follows food safety issues. The center has criticized the government for its piecemeal approach to screening food, saying all food safety efforts should be coordinated under one federal agency. *National Public Radio*'s Ray Suarez called the center's staff for a live interview when more than 150 Michigan children came down with hepatitis after eating tainted strawberries at school.

In looking for sources, always be aware of an organization's biases. While the nurses group may give you accurate numbers for the growth of emergency-care nursing, its interpretation of those numbers may be colored by the group's own particular interests. In addition, reporters need to know who is funding a group. The Council for Responsible Nutrition might sound like an independent organization, but when you talk to people there for a story on melatonin, you'd better know this is the trade group for the nutritional supplement industry. Science writers who've been around a while know when they get a news release from the American Crop Protection Association that it's from a pesticide makers group. So they'll call the National Coalition Against the Misuse of Pesticides for another perspective.

ETHICISTS

Reporters would be remiss if they didn't include among their contacts those who measure with an ethical scale and a moral compass. Such persons can temper the wonder of science with commentary on whether society should venture into all the frontiers to which science leads.

WHERE DO I GO?

Agriculture	County cooperative extension service, Farm Bureau, state department of agriculture, U.S. Department of Agriculture
Biomedical research	Local university, National Institutes of Health (Bethesda, Md.)
Environmental issues	State environmental agency, U.S. Environmental Protection Agency, advocacy groups
Diseases, virus outbreaks	Local and state health departments, U.S. Centers for Disease Control and Prevention (Atlanta)
Health statistics	County and state health departments, U.S. Centers for Disease Control and Prevention, hospitals
Hospital accreditation	Joint Commission on Accreditation of Healthcare Organizations Association (Chicago)
Worker injuries	State occupational and safety agency, U.S. Occupational Safety and Health Administration, National Institute for Occupational Safety and Health
Medicaid/Medicare	County and state health agencies, U.S. Department of Health and Human Services
Science research	Local research company, universities, National Science Foundation (Arlington, Va.)
Space	Local planetarium, National Aeronautics and Space Administration
Weather	Regional office of National Weather Service

NEWS JUDGMENT

You get a call in the newsroom about a spaghetti supper fund-raising event for a local 3-year-old who has cancer and needs a bone-marrow transplant. You're about to propose this as a story when another reporter says, "Yeah, I've gotten two calls about other kids in the last few months, but I told them we don't do stories like that because we don't want to be promoting one kid over the other."

Write out a policy for how your news organization will handle cases such as fund-raising for transplants, organ donations and rare medical procedures.

Such perspectives can be found locally at a nearby college, the hospital chaplain's office or among the local clergy. National centers such as The Hastings Center, Westchester County, N.Y., include specialists on bioethics—the study of ethics and science.

After the issue of human cloning took center stage with the advent of a cloned sheep, *Christian Science Monitor* reporter Peter Spotts looked at the role of ethical and legal experts in the national discussion. This is how the story opened:

The first clue that Alta Charo's world was about to change came on an aluminum-gray day in February. As the University of Wisconsin law professor scanned a copy of the Sunday paper, a sheep named Dolly stared out at her from the front page. The headline proclaimed simply: "With Cloning of a Sheep, the Ethical Ground Shifts."

"I knew in an instant that my life had just changed," she recalls.

She wasn't alone. For the next 97 days, Dr. Charo and 17 other members of a federal advisory panel would wrestle with the ethical pros and cons of a technological feat potentially as profound as the first controlled nuclear chain reaction.

The Christian Science Monitor

THINGS TO READ

Behind the "Star Wars" figures lining Adam Rogers' bookshelves at *Newsweek* are rows of reference books, magazines, and even dog-eared copies of his old college chemistry and biology textbooks.

"I still refer back to them—how does this thing work," says Rogers, who landed a coveted spot on *Newsweek*'s science team just a year after graduating from Boston University's science writing program.

Rogers uses the old standby books for reference, but he's also added Net surfing skills to his research repertoire.

"We're information machines," he explains, referring to journalists. "You've got to have the information."

Writing for the new frontiers beat takes you to new frontiers. Here's Adam Rogers, reporting a story from Antarctica.

BOOKS

The information Rogers needed one day centered on how the heart works. His editor assigned him to write about the heart bypass operation of Russian leader Boris Yeltsin.

"I called a bunch of famous cardiac surgeons, but after I'd signed off on the story for the last time, I realized I wasn't sure I'd gotten my atria and ventricles right," he says. "I ran to my dictionary of anatomy in a panic. Fortunately, I hadn't blown it."

Such books are among the basic references for science or health reporters. Here are a few others:

- Physician's Desk Reference, a book that tells all about drugs, their uses and side effects.
- Merck Manual of Diagnosis and Therapy, listing diseases and symptoms.
- A medical dictionary. Nowadays, some reporters consult these on CD/ROM.
- A science dictionary such as The American Heritage Dictionary of Science.
- A science encyclopedia, such as Van Nostrand's Scientific Encyclopedia or The Way Things Work: An Illustrated Encyclopedia of Technology.

JOURNALS AND MAGAZINES

Rogers regularly pages through *Nature* and *Science,* the two standards on the science beat. He also flips through an eclectic variety of a dozen other magazines, from his favorite, *New Scientist,* to *Presence,* a journal about virtual reality. He's discovered reading them is a way to get into the heads of scientists, to read what they're reading, to understand them better. Reading also nurtures story ideas.

"It's a total skim," he says, "I see a picture or headline, sometimes the ad can be as helpful as the article."

One day when he was looking through *Aviation Week and Space Technology,* his eyes picked up a Rockwell ad showing its computer-generated design for the X-33—the next-generation space shuttle. On the facing page he saw an article about Lockheed Martin's design for the same shuttle. The article said NASA would be deciding on the new project in a few weeks.

"I figured—corporate conflict, great art, time peg—sounds almost like news," he says wryly. "I pitched it to my editor and he gave me the go-ahead."

Medical reporters follow the same techniques. Two must-reads for them are *The Journal of the American Medical Society* and *The New England Journal of Medicine,* both of which publish cutting-edge research that is peer-reviewed. That means other scientists have screened the articles to make sure the researchers followed proper scientific practice, an important indicator of whether the scientific foundation of a report's conclusions is sound.

Rogers says he won't attempt to interview scientists until he's read their journal articles on a topic.

"It's OK to have read it and not understood a word," he says to beginning reporters. "Scientists love it when you say, 'I've read your piece.'"

After sorting through enough of these scientific papers, Rogers says, reporters can develop a sixth sense. "I can look at some and go, 'This doesn't sound right to me,'" he explains. "Maybe it's the way the questions are worded or the number of people studied."

When studies conflict, he admits to agonizing over how to report them. For reporters who don't yet have that "sixth sense," he suggests calling somebody who has more expertise.

"Luckily, scientists are never shy about criticizing each others' work," he says. "They often point me to flaws in methodology."

PUBLIC RELATIONS PACKETS

Keep that sense of skepticism when you go to your mailbox. Once word gets out that you're covering medicine, that box will be overflowing with press packets and, if you are in television, **video news releases** or VNRs.

These ready-made stories on tape are tempting to use. They often have quotes and sound bites from the researchers or video and still photos of a new technique or prototype. In other words, they have information that small-market reporters can't get access to.

Keep in mind, however, that these are the video equivalent of a press release. They tell the story from one organization's perspective. That is why Cara Birrittieri of *New England Cable News* says she'll never run a preproduced story as is.

"I'll do my own local interview and maybe use a sound bite from the VNR or some of the pictures," she explains.

For example, when she was producing a story about the benefits of zinc tablets in preventing colds, Birrittieri couldn't find the specific type of zinc lozenges in local stores. So she used the pictures of them off a VNR.

"But I'll rewrite the entire thing," Birrittieri says. "There's no way I would ever put my voice on somebody else's package [taped story]. It's not my work."

Like Birrittieri, print reporters don't use press packets without verifying everything in them and pushing well beyond their perspective of the news. No political reporters worth their salt would give only the Democrats' version of the truth without the Republicans' perspectives. Nor do science, medical or environmental reporters rely on the pronouncements of a single research institution, advocacy group or drug company.

DIGITAL CONNECTIONS

Scientists were the first to get wired. So an advantage in this beat is that these folks are adept at e-mail and the Web. That makes them easy to track through government and university sites.

Adam Rogers of *Newsweek* often tracks scientists down through the Internet directory **Yahoo!**. One day he was working on a story about human peak performance (how to get the most out of one's body) and wanted to talk with the well-known physiologist Reggie Edgerton. Somebody said he worked at UCLA. A few clicks from the Yahoo! universities link and Rogers had the phone number and e-mail address. When he has a name but no location, he types the name into a search engine such as AltaVista.

ETHICS **USING MEDIA PACKETS**

Suppose you're a TV reporter in a small-market station. With two reporters working dayside and one working nightside, you're always scrambling to fill the newscasts. The news director says medical news is very popular in your market and assigns you to do a medical feature each night, using video news releases and news feeds. The news director says they won't take long—you just read the script provided and the tape editor will cut the story with the pictures sent.

Is there a difference in whether you'd use a medical story from the following sources:

■ A network feed, such as one sent by *NBC*

■ A medical TV news service for which the station is paying

■ A satellite feed from a medical organization, such as the American Medical Association

■ A package for a new vitamin supplement, mailed by the public relations firm representing the manufacturer

Do you think it is ethical to use a VNR? Parts of it?

What policies would you set for judging which stories, if any, you'd voice?

Rogers thinks one of the best uses of the Internet is for finding people, but he prefers to read journals in hand, the old-fashioned way. Canadian free-lancer Michael O'Reilly likes to go online for journal articles. One of his favorite sites is **e-journal,** the *World Wide Web Virtual Library Electronic Journal List.* It links him to dozens of medical journals with abstracts or full articles online. Before he did interviews at two London, Ontario, hospitals, he used the Virtual Library to read up on the topic of his interviews: medical imaging.

"I used it to find out the state of affairs in the research," he said, noting he skimmed several articles off this site. "There's a nice search engine that lets you quickly pull out information."

MEDLINE, the database of the National Library of Medicine, is another of O'Reilly's favorites. It abstracts from about 3,800 biomedical journals but doesn't have full articles.

Science reporters like **EurekAlert!**, a one-stop shopping site run by the American Association for the Advancement of Science. It includes news releases, journals and links to many research institutions, government agencies and nonprofits. A reporter who types in *lake river pollution* on the EurekAlert! search page might find a news release about how University of Florida researchers are using DNA fingerprint techniques to determine who is polluting certain waters.

O'Reilly says while reporters can be enamored of the new technology that speeds such research, they shouldn't be blinded by it. He knows information isn't always what it purports to be. So he cautions inexperienced reporters to be sure to evaluate the quality of the information they pull off the Net.

"In the case of science and medicine, you're looking for some official recognition," he says. "If you're looking for medical research, I would look in the peer-reviewed category or official organization sites, like the National Institutes of Health, that have gone through an editing process."

He says the Net is as vital to him as his telephone. "It's not even an issue of, 'Well, I'll use the Internet for this story.' It's, 'Of course I'll use it.' It's a constant tool for me . . . part of the daily routine."

That routine includes scanning Net discussion groups for story ideas. One day he saw some offhand comments on a science newsgroup about how hard it was to practice medicine in rural areas. That triggered a story idea— the problems in attracting physicians to rural areas.

"I then posted a general query to Healthnet [another discussion group] and tracked down physicians all across North America to interview about the topic," says O'Reilly. "I got lots of information about being out of touch, the limited resources, and long hours which lead to some pretty scary statistics, even going to higher death rates for rural physicians."

He parlayed the information into stories for *The London (Ontario) Free Press* and a Canadian medical publication.

The Net can be a timesaver for reporters as well. Nobel Prize awards, announced over several days in October, are always big news. *NPR*'s Joe Palca used to have to run over to the Swedish embassy each day to get the press

CLIPBOARD   INTERNET SITES MENTIONED IN THIS CHAPTER

AltaVista	www.altavista.digital.com	InfoSeek	www.infoseek.com
Center for Science in the Public Interest	www.cspinet.org	Media Resource Service	www.mediaresource.org
The Chemical Backgrounder	www.nsc.org/ehc/ew/chemical.htm	MEDLINE	www.nlm.nih.gov/databases/ freemedl.html
e-journal	www.edoc.com/ejournal	Yahoo!	www.yahoo.com
EurekAlert!	www.eurekalert.org	For an update to this list, see http://web.syr.edu/~bcfought.	

releases. Now that the Nobel Prize Committee is online, Palca can trade a trip through D.C. streets for a quick hike on the information superhighway.

Net-savvy skills give the journalist an advantage when news breaks. Suppose a radio reporter calls in from the scene of a major traffic pile-up and says a tanker rolled over, spilling some of its contents, ethylene glycol, into a nearby stream. The news director back at the station can check **The Chemical Backgrounder** at the Web site of the National Safety Council's Environmental Health Center and tell the reporter that the chemical is used in aircraft de-icing and antifreeze. It can be toxic, and any spill must be reported to the national Toxic Release Inventory.

Usenet and discussion groups on the Net are valuable for finding victims, patients or people experienced on a certain topic—often a hard category of sources to find. Sue Landry of *The St. Petersburg (Fla.) Times* posted a query on a discussion list called Pain-L to find Floridians with chronic pain for a story on how some patients suffer needlessly because their doctors don't properly treat their pain.

BASIC STORIES

Science, a former *New York Times* reporter was fond of saying, is about the new in news. When his editors attempted to assign him a story, he'd pull out a list of 50 ideas he kept at his desk and say, "Pick one." He hated assignments.

Few reporters in print or broadcast, however, have that luxury. Assignments are part of the business, too, and in science, medicine and the environment, several types of stories tend to dominate daily assignments.

STORIES ABOUT RESEARCH REPORTS

Real cures come along about once every 10 years, says Tom Linden, who has worked as a doctor and a medical reporter. But cure stories seem to come out every week, he jokes.

Linden, now a professor at the University of North Carolina, for years has watched as cure stories come and go. You've seen and heard them: "A breakthrough tonight . . . ," "A new study out today shows that . . ." or "Scientists today announced they have just discovered . . ."

Linden grows weary of such stories. And he cautions reporters to be wary as well.

"It's poor reporting if you highlight in the lead that there's been a breakthrough in treatment of breast cancer, when the gene is only carried by a small fraction of people," he says. "It's misleading, it sets up the reader to be skeptical of you . . . it's like crying wolf."

Sometimes it's incumbent on science, medical or environmental reporters to downplay or qualify a story the boss thinks would be great at the top of the news. Linden says there's too much pressure in today's newsrooms to hype stories. Why? Perhaps it's because of the volume of information in the pipeline. Drug companies, research centers, advocacy groups, government agencies, even scientific journals shower newsrooms with dozens of news releases each week. Company spokespeople have learned to be as good at "spin" as the politicians. Even journals will cluster stories on a certain topic to get more attention.

There are vested interests at stake here. Publicity can mean a better image for the university, and that translates into more research dollars. Doctors who are profiled as being on the cutting edge of technology often get more patients, thus more income. The stock of a pharmaceutical company jumps when its lifesaving drug-in-the-making is announced.

In most cases the significance of such studies isn't black and white. So reporters learn to qualify. They use terms such as "this research suggests" or "the finding could indicate"—that is, of course, if the story is worth covering at all.

It is much easier for reporters to determine the validity of the latest advance if it's drawn from one of the top science or medical journals. That is why so many news stories appear on the day *The New England Journal of Medicine, Nature, Science* or *The Journal of the American Medical Association* come out. Studies that appear in these publications have been vigorously reviewed.

The best science writers, however, don't always wait to run with the pack. They write up studies delivered at scientific meetings or submitted by local researchers. They keep tabs on what's being studied at the state environmental lab and know about the test trials at the teaching hospital down the street.

Here is a list of common questions for the research report story:

- What has been discovered?
- Why is it significant?
- What is the evidence that leads to this conclusion?
- How does this advance or contradict previous research in the field (and who conducted it)?
- Who did the latest research and what's their track record?
- How large and representative was the sample or trial?
- Who funded the research?
- What do others in the field say about it?
- What's the next step?

Adam Rogers of *Newsweek* wrote a research report story about genetic links to Alzheimer's, based on a study published the week before in *The New England Journal of Medicine.* It began with this intriguing lead:

It is the great eraser. It tangles neurons and fills the brain with sticky plaques that choke off thoughts and memories. In the end, Alzheimer's disease leaves its victims with severe dementia. But while scientists know Alzheimer's effects, they still don't understand its causes. They can't even confirm its presence until after death.

Rogers elaborated on the study, which told how people with a gene linked to Alzheimer's show lower activity in certain areas of the brain. He then explained the impact of the findings:

This could be a sign of the disease's beginnings . . . the real significance of the study is the possibility that doctors might identify Alzheimer's before it does any damage, and perhaps improve their ability to treat it.

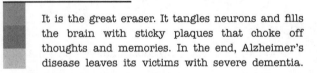

SUMMARY   RESEARCH REPORTS

1. Think ahead. Attend scientific conferences and talk to local researchers, but don't hype stories or fall for PR spins.

2. Put the most stock in studies that have been peer-reviewed.

3. Read abstracts at the beginning of a study and conclusions at the end to get the best overview.

4. Interview the authors.

5. Read the footnotes. All studies are built on previous research. Footnotes provide names of other scientists who can evaluate the work critically.

6. Explain the discovery as well as its significance.

His story followed the previous checklist of questions. In addition to quoting the lead author of the study, a psychiatrist at Good Samaritan Regional Medical Center in Phoenix, he added a quote about the research from a University of South Florida geneticist who wasn't involved. He also included some qualifications—the limitations of the findings and the fact that researchers would have to follow the patients for years to confirm their findings.

REGULATION STORIES

A new diet drug is found to have side effects and is pulled off supermarket shelves. Congress says hospitals must keep new moms for at least 48 hours. And the state attorney general tells a local business it has a month to clean up contaminated soil at the industrial park. Such events signal another standard story in covering the new frontiers—the regulation story.

Government controls a lot of what goes on in science, medicine and the environment. It churns out lots of laws and regulations, ideally to make people's lives better and safer. Each time, there are paper trails to follow, lobbyists to observe, hearings to attend and votes to tally (see box, Regulatory Sources, earlier in the chapter).

Russell Clemings, who covered the environment for *The Fresno (Calif.) Bee,* talks about "six flavors" to government regulation stories:

- Proposed action by an advocacy group or congressperson
- Hearings, where officials listen to various viewpoints
- Adoption of regulations by a legislative body
- Monitoring by a government agency
- Enforcement action taken by regulators
- Government inaction (often the best stories, Clemings notes)

Here's an example of a story from *The Dallas Morning News* about upcoming hearings on a proposed regulation:

A long-running battle over emissions from a cement plant that burns hazardous waste will heat up next week as public comment is sought on the plant's proposed permits.

Opponents say that emissions from the Texas Industries Midlothian plant, which has been burning the waste since 1987, have caused health problems in residents and farm animals and damage to the environment.

Officials of Texas Industries will argue that the elements of the proposed permit are appropriate and should be granted by the Texas Natural Resource Conservation Commission.

The Dallas Morning News

The reporter finished the story with the viewpoints of the commission staff, a time line for the process and advice on how citizens could voice their opinions.

Stories such as this, often written on deadline, just tell the basic facts. But the more interesting stories, whatever the "flavor" of regulation, don't focus on the processes, the fine print of the regulations or the "he said-she said" from hearings that drone on into the night.

"It's important to follow the regulatory process, but not to write about it directly," says Clemings. "Focus on the results of that process or the problems the process is trying to address."

He likes to find a human example and build a story around that. So when the federal government proposed putting 10 Sierra Nevada foothill plants on the endangered species list, Clemings did more than just outline the proposal for *Fresno Bee* readers. He traipsed through the countryside and talked with cattle ranchers whose animals grazed where the plants grew. His story chronicled their ire—and their fear if the regulation was implemented.

SUMMARY — REGULATIONS

1. In writing regulation stories, make the time line and process clear.

2. Humanize the process by keying on those potentially affected.

3. Explain why a regulation has been proposed.

4. Search out viewpoints on all sides.

5. Tell readers, viewers and listeners how they can have input.

6. In evaluating existing regulation (or government inaction), show the impact, again, in human terms.

STORIES ABOUT HAZARDS AND OUTBREAKS

When people are forced to flee their homes because a noxious gas is seeping out of a smashed tanker on the nearby freeway, they want to know what they've breathed in and whether it will hurt them. And when two cases of potentially deadly meningitis are reported at the high school, everyone wants to know what the risk is to other students.

At times of fear and uncertainty, the media can perform an important public service. It's easy to alarm, harder to educate. Reporters must balance their stories so they don't panic the public but also don't minimize the potential harm. Here is a checklist of questions to ask when a hazard or medical outbreak makes news:

- What is the status and time line? For example, is the tanker still leaking?
- What damage or illness has occurred or might occur?
- Who or what has been affected? Who might be?
- What is the science behind the hazard? For example, what is the chemical's name and what are its properties?

LEARNING FROM THE PROS — REPORTING ON RISKS

ABC-TV reporter John Stossel says the media too often hype unusual, rather than common or significant, risks. In an *ABC* special, "Are We Scaring Ourselves to Death," Stossel compared risks by measuring the impact a certain activity would have on the life span of a so-called average person. Here's part of his script:

> The biggest environmental killer, air pollution, is thought by some to kill 50,000 to 60,000 people every year. That would shorten your life by 61 days. Crime is still worse. Twenty-six thousand Americans are murdered every year—113 days off your life. Now compare all this to driving. Cars by far should be the bigger worry—43,000 deaths. That's 182 days off our lives.
>
> *ABC News*

Stossel told viewers the biggest threats turned out to be smoking, (five and a half years off the average life) and poverty (seven to 10 years).

Stossel's story raises a question: Do government staffers spend too much time and money regulating the minor threats while larger problems go unnoticed?

Stossel believed so and in the same special said:

> Stairs kill about 1,000 Americans a year, bicycles 700, and yet when seven people died taking poisoned Tylenol, Americans spent more than a billion dollars sealing products in tamper-resistant packages.

Reporting risk requires perspective.

HAZARDS AND OUTBREAKS

1. In breaking stories the goal is to educate not alarm.

2. Get the basic facts in, then look at the big picture and tell the implications.

3. Make clear what you don't yet know.

4. Explain the degree of risk: Choose the significant over the sensational.

- What can be done and is being done to solve or contain the problem?
- What isn't known yet?

The last question is very important. Too often, reporters are embarrassed to say they don't know something. Although the main goal in news gathering is to get the story, sometimes the whole story just can't be nailed down by deadline. In those cases, it is up to the reporter to answer the unanswered questions in the audience's mind by telling what officials or experts don't yet know or aren't saying.

The best reporters like to anticipate news rather than merely react to it. So they follow patterns and conditions that might turn into front-page news later in the month. For example, environmental reporters watch the snow melt and the rain gauge, looking for potential flooding. Heather Kahn of *NewsCenter 5* (*WCVB-TV,* Boston) warned viewers one spring that a mild winter meant more ticks and a greater risk of lyme disease.

In putting together stories on outbreaks and hazards, reporters usually interview an expert who can explain the big picture, including the risks. It is important to qualify the risks (see box, Learning From the Pros: Reporting on Risks).

CONSUMER HEALTH STORIES

Viewers of *NewsCenter 5* (*WCVB-TV,* Boston) see at least one story each week on health and wellness. It's part of the station's two-year commitment to "The Healthbeat Project."

"There's an explosion of medical news out there for consumers to look at," says producer Rhonda Mann. "These segments focus on how to use that information to keep ourselves healthy, to prevent illness."

As the producer for the medical unit, she doesn't appear on camera, but she does much of what a reporter does. She's in charge of the daily health segment: the research, reporting and responsibility for both the look and the content.

In one week, for example, she produced stories on how to recognize ear infections in young children, the rise in breast cancer and whether trendy new fabrics in exercise clothing really offer any benefits.

It doesn't take a stationwide project to take on the topic of consumer health. Such stories are everywhere.

Rhonda Mann (right), the producer of the medical unit at *WCVB-TV,* Boston, confers with health reporter and anchor Heather Kahn (left) on a story. In television, a segment producer and reporter often work as a team on stories.

"The first thing you need is a reason for doing the story," says Mann. "You need something in there that's newsy."

The calendar often triggers a story idea. July 4 approaching? How about a piece on how to grill food safely? Producers and reporters also watch for trends. Mann set up a story on the food snacks known as "power bars" after one of her colleagues mentioned she'd just seen lots of people eating them on the local bike trail.

Once she's settled on the topic, Mann works to find a person through which to show the story. She knows that such a miniprofile makes for good storytelling by personalizing the issue. It also gives her good visuals.

"You need to find the person who has decided, when it's January first, that he or she is going to lose weight," explains Mann, who found such a person and built not only one story, but several follow-ups, around her.

Volunteer organizations are one of the first places she turns to find such profiles. For a story on how to beat the heat during summer's dreadful days, she called the Visiting Nurses Association because she knew the nurses make house calls and teach people how to stay cool. If it's a story on cancer, she's likely to call the American Cancer Society. If it's a fitness story, she'll start at the local gym.

"I just ask around. I'll call friends," she says. "Sometimes I put up a big poster in the newsroom—'Do you know anybody with high blood pressure.'"

Interviewing experts adds credibility to the story. For a story called "Germ Warfare," a guide to preventing the spread of colds, Mann found an expert at the state health department who teaches classes in schools and day-care facilities about the proper method for washing one's hands.

Mann works hard to make sure she's giving viewers the best expert and the latest information. "We do a story every so often on infant safety—things like not leaving soft blankets in the crib or strings dangling that could choke the child. Each time we check with the American Academy of Pediatrics, the professional organization for the nation's pediatricians, to get a copy of the latest guidelines."

One time she found the academy had changed its recommendation after research found a link between sudden infant death syndrome and infants who sleep on their stomachs.

Mann says she tries to give viewers some type of guide or checklist to take away from her stories. She calls them bullet points. Here are some from a story on allergies:

> Close your windows—in both your home and car. It really does keep pollen out. Don't hang your sheets outside on the line to dry. Pollen does stick to clothing. And save yardwork until the day after a rain.
>
> *NewsCenter 5 (WCVB-TV, Boston)*

SUMMARY

CONSUMER HEALTH

1. Find a reason for the story—link it to the season, the calendar or a trend.

2. Tell the story through a person who is living it.

3. Find the best expert and the latest, accurate information.

4. Give the audience guidelines on what to do, but make sure those guidelines are agreed upon by experts.

5. Think visually and note details that will make the story interesting.

On television, such tips usually appear in colorful graphics on the screen to make them easily understandable. In newspapers, they are often boxed beside the article in a highlights box.

Mann tells beginning reporters to check these tips carefully because often they can be controversial. For example, head lice makes the rounds in elementary schools just about every year. In doing a story, Mann found the state health department and the Pediculosis Association, a national nonprofit group that studies lice, disagreed over whether consumers should use over-the-counter lice-removal shampoos. She gave both views.

Since she works in a visual medium, Mann says it's also essential to have good pictures.

"I'll always ask people, 'What will we see when we come there?'" she explains.

When she was setting up a story about protecting yourself from mosquitoes carrying encephalitis, she asked the researcher to describe the lab over the phone. Would there be actual living mosquitoes buzzing around? Would the camera be able to take pictures of them directly or through glass? Were there other visuals, such as maps of where each type of mosquito lives?

For print, a reporter would take careful notes to describe the cages, the insect's wings or the way the researcher clicked on a tiny vacuum cleaner to suck up a mosquito that escaped. Regardless of the medium, thinking visually is important.

ENTERPRISE STORIES

The basic stories outlined above, as well as other breaking news, often spur reporters to delve deeper into a subject and come up with in-depth and original stories. Such enterprise stories might measure promise versus performance, look behind a policy to see the forces that shaped it or take readers and listeners along on a scientific quest.

CAPTURING SCIENCE AT WORK

Enterprise reporting in health and science often takes an enterprising person, or at least an adventuresome one. Take Jane Stevens.

"I found myself in the middle of the biggest piece of nowhere I've ever been," says Stevens.

That "nowhere" was Antarctica. Whether it is a "nowhere" thousands of miles away or a tour inside the new high-tech lab down the street, enterprise reporters capture the process of science by taking the audience to the scene.

Stevens lived aboard an icebreaker research ship in Antarctica for 50 days to probe, with scientists, the mysteries of Antarctic sea ice and how it influences the Earth's climate (see box, Ethics: Reporter Involvement, in Chapter 12, page 209). A free-lancer with 25 years experience and a specialty in science and technology reporting, she turned her high-seas adventure into a magazine article for *National Geographic* and a 12-minute TV documentary airing on *The Learning Channel.*

She's an example of the journalist of the future—gathering the story as a whole, then slicing and dicing it for various media. Here's part of her TV script:

> Like explorers mapping their finds, we chart the thickness of the snow and ice. Then we take samples back to the lab, where experts study ice crystals and measure salt content. Our tools break through to the cobalt kingdom below our feet. It's breathtaking.
>
> But where are the tiny plants and animals? Here, in the ice itself. Tiny canals crisscross the floes supporting a veritable garden of algae—the first link in the Antarctic food chain. Melted, even a drop of sea ice yields a kaleidoscope of life. Enough biodiversity to rival a Mississippi bayou—without the mosquitoes.
>
> *National Geographic Explorer*

WRITING FOR THE NEW FRONTIERS

Here are some tips about writing for the new frontiers:

1. Make sure you understand the story before you try to write it.

Science deals in complexity and uncertainty. It is steeped in jargon. As a result, it offers a special set of challenges in reporting and writing. Most people know the purpose of a criminal trial; few may know the purpose of a double-blind research study. (It is to eliminate bias. This is done by telling neither a medical researcher nor a patient who is getting a drug and who is getting a placebo.)

Keep in mind: It's not good enough to quote someone saying something you don't understand. For one thing, your audience won't understand either. For another, you run a high risk of taking the quote out of context. As a re-porter, you've got to persist in your questions until you're sure you've got it straight.

2. Use analogies.

Because concepts about science, medicine or the envi-ronment are sometimes hard to grasp, many reporters find analogy is a helpful tool.

In a story about brain research, Joe Palca of *National Public Radio* used this comparison: "The cerebellum is a fairly large structure, about the size of your fist."

Newsweek's Adam Rogers used a well-understood weather concept to explain the onset of one disease: "Alzheimer's disease strikes with the subtlety of an ad-vancing fog bank, rolling in gradually to wipe out memory, reasoning ability, and eventually personality."

3. Add graphics or visuals.

In print, television and online, graphics can help explain dense information. Cara Birrittieri of *New England Cable*

News asked the cable channel's artists to draw the anat-omy of a goat to use when she was explaining how sci-entists are injecting goats with a certain gene in hopes of producing a helpful protein in goat milk.

4. Demonstrations can show a point.

Tom Linden once threw a football on the TV set. He did it to show the motion of the elbow in a story about football great Joe Montana's problem elbow.

Joe Palca of *NPR* took a ride on the Anaconda roller coaster at King's Dominion in Virginia to explain potential and kinetic energy:

> When we get to the top of the hill—which is about 20 feet away—we start down and we start gaining all the potential energy back as kinetic energy. Whoa! All right. It starts off pretty simple and then—holy smokes! Oh! And now I'm upside down and the G-forces are forcing me down in the seat. . . .

Print and online reporters use diagrams and words—**infographics**—to show how something works.

5. Qualify, qualify, qualify.

Writing about new frontiers requires careful qualifiers. Rarely does science offer a smoking gun. More often it provides a series of clues. Seasoned reporters know to use terms such as "suggest" and "indicate" rather than "prove." After all, in science, the decade ahead just might bring a change in understanding.

Stevens' tips for reporters doing enterprise, whether in multimedia or just one form: Be flexible. Before she went, she carefully planned out a checklist of information and pictures she needed each day. But once *en route,* she had to adjust to changing circumstances.

SCIENCE AND PUBLIC POLICY

New frontiers reporters sometimes pause to look at the public policy implications of the rapidly changing world of discovery. *Wall Street Journal* reporters Amanda Bennett and Anita Sharpe did just that in a story headlined "AIDS Fight Is Skewed by Federal Campaign Exaggerating Risks." The story, part of a packet of stories that won the coveted Pulitzer Prize, questioned whether government funds were being used appropriately in the fight against AIDS. Here's some of what the two women reported:

Increasingly [scientists and doctors] worry that the everyone-gets-AIDS message—still trumpeted not only by government agencies but by celebrities and the media—is more than just dishonest: It is also having a perverse, potentially deadly effect on funding for AIDS prevention.

. . . though homosexuals and intravenous drug users now account for 83 percent of all AIDS cases reported in the U.S., the federal AIDS-prevention budget includes no specific allocation for programs for homosexual and bisexual men . . .

Much of the Centers for Disease Control's $584 million AIDS-prevention budget goes instead to programs to combat the disease among heterosexual women, college students and others who face a relatively low risk of becoming infected.

The Wall Street Journal

Bennett says she and Sharpe set out to find the forest amidst the trees. They linked many disparate reports on AIDS and came up with the big picture. Bennett says such enterprise stories emerge when reporters learn to put aside their templates for seeing the world and look anew at the facts.

"Question your assumptions," she tells young reporters trying to find good enterprise stories. "The best stories often change the way people think."

Such stories don't come without controversy.

"A lot of reporters get scared when they see opposition," says Bennett, outlining her tips on enterprise reporting. "Your job is to try to shoot your story down."

So she set out to do just that. She had reports showing that people in low-risk groups had very little chance of becoming infected with HIV through one heterosexual encounter. But experts told her it was happening routinely.

"I spent weeks and weeks and weeks saying, 'Tell me who they are, give me examples, find them for me,'" she says. But no one could.

Bennett surmised that some cases existed but surely not in the numbers touted. It wasn't the widespread, growing epidemic that the government's public service ad campaign was suggesting.

Still, Bennett worked with great care to be responsible in telling her story. She wanted to make sure the story didn't mislead readers into thinking they were at little risk of getting AIDS. Likewise, she didn't want to "artificially scare people to accomplish someone's social goal."

LEARNING FROM THE PROS — TIME FOR ENTERPRISE

Wall Street Journal reporter Amanda Bennett says finding time to do enterprise stories isn't easy. It is essential. In hiring staff for the *Journal's* Atlanta bureau, she hears from a lot of reporters who want to work at the *Journal* but haven't worked enterprise stories enough to get there.

"I tell them I have 100 resumes on my desk of reporters in similar circumstances to theirs, who *do* make time for enterprise," says Bennett.

"If you're a reporter who has a regular beat, that beat will always consume you," she says. "Pick a day every so often, or a half a day and 'go skeleton.'"

What she means is put aside everything else, warn people away, hunker down and work your enterprise project. She coined the term after she jokingly put a skeleton from Halloween on her office door as a threat to people not to enter.

Everybody at the *Journal's* Atlanta bureau now "goes skeleton" from time to time.

One way she assured herself that she was being fair was to double-check the research that told her heterosexuals were at a low risk. She checked out the credentials of the scientists, interviewed them in depth about how they did what they did and checked their calculations.

"Then I felt comfortable with it," says Bennett, adding that it took almost two weeks just to do that. "I wanted to make sure I wasn't just taking some crackpot out there with his single theory."

Promise vs. Performance

You can bank on it. There's always a story in comparing how something is supposed to work to how it actually does. Computers can be the workhorses for such stories. Elliott Jaspin headed a team of *Cox Newspaper* reporters who conducted the largest computer-assisted reporting project ever, when they analyzed more than 100 million Medicare records.

The project made history both because of its size and its method—involving 30 reporters analyzing data at *Cox* papers across the country. It included an expensive six-month court battle just to get the records, weeks of deciphering the files on 200-plus magnetic tapes, and months of analysis, figuring out what story the data was telling.

Reporters won't tackle a big project like this until they are well-on in their careers, but the techniques the *Cox* staff used can be easily applied to smaller projects, such as how grant money was spent to immunize county children or clean up a local toxic waste site.

Here's the beginning of the *Cox* series in one paper:

While Medicare is going broke, enterprising doctors have turned to highly efficient assembly line medicine and aggressive marketing to gross more than $1 million a year from the program. That's about $20,000 a week, or roughly as much as the average American earns in an entire year.

Dayton Daily News

The series became, in essence, an audit of the federal Medicare program. Jaspin's team found it was difficult, if not impossible, to monitor the doctors' treatments to see if they were necessary. The team also found that the federal government employs far too few investigators to check up on payments to doctors.

Such enterprise stories on enforcement go to the heart of journalism, says Jaspin.

"One of our highest callings is that we make sure the government is doing the job they are supposedly being paid or elected to do."

SUMMARY   ENTERPRISE

1. Look for patterns and trends. Use breaking news as a starting point.

2. Stay flexible. Start with a framework, but be ready to adapt as you learn the story.

3. Look for what's not reported.

4. Try to shoot down your own story. When you can't, you know it's solid.

5. Learn computer-assisted reporting skills and try them out on small projects first.

6. Persevere. The good stories take much more time than you'd ever planned.

RECOMMENDED READING

Blum, D., & Knudson, M. (1997). *A field guide for science writers.* New York: Oxford University Press.

This is the official guide of the National Association of Science Writers. If you buy one book, this is the one. It's a compilation of articles on all facets of science reporting by three dozen of the best-known science writers in the United States. It covers writing for magazines, newspapers and broadcast as well as tips for those working for nonprofits, government agencies and industry.

Cohn, V. (1994). *News & numbers: A guide to reporting statistical claims and controversies in health and other fields.* Ames: Iowa State University Press.

Cohn, the well-respected reporter from *The Washington Post,* gives reporters the basics they need to know to cover science and numbers.

Logan, R. (1994). *Environmental issues for the '90s: A handbook for journalists.* Washington, DC: The Media Institute.

This handbook outlines the background and issues on major environmental topics and includes a directory of organizations and resources. It's very helpful background for the reporter new to the environment beat.

National Institutes of Health. National Library of Medicine. Bethesda, MD. [Online]. Available: **www.nlm.nih.gov**.

This is the Web site of the world's largest medical library. Here, a reporter finds all types of news and resources on biomedicine and health care. You can research databases for free, including MEDLINE, which covers 3,800 biomedical journals.

Society of Environmental Journalists. Environmental Journalism Home Page. [Online]. Available: **http://www.sej.org**.

This is the Web site for the environmental journalists organization. It showcases some of the best environmental reporting in its "gallery," produces the SEJ biweekly tip sheet, links to other sites by topic, and lists resources and contacts.

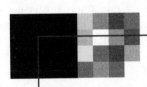

EXERCISES

A. RESEARCH

1. Define the following terms as you'd use them in a story:

   a. carcinogen

   b. chemotherapy

   c. comet

   d. effluent

   e. ecosystem

   f. global warming

   g. health maintenance organization (HMO)

   h. malignant

   i. morbidity rate

   j. osteopath

   k. ozone

   l. pathology

   m. toxic waste

2. The wires report that a meteor shower is due in your area next week. Name four people you'd contact for interviews. List three different angles for stories.

3. You get a wire story or VNR about a study being published tomorrow showing that exercise can significantly lower a woman's chance of developing a certain fatal disease. Write a memo listing

five questions you'd ask about the study before you decide if it's worth writing about. List three ways you'd go about finding a woman to profile if you did write the story.

4. A national fast-food chain has just announced it is rolling out new environmentally friendly sandwich packaging that will easily biodegrade. You're asked to localize the story. Write a memo listing four types of people you interview. Find their phone numbers. Also list either the graphics, video or audio you'd need to make a good story.

5. Find out the difference between Medicare and Medicaid. Write copy that concisely explains both. You may write for a newspaper, a Web site, a radio script or a TV reporter stand-up (the portion of the script delivered by the reporter on camera).

B. BASIC STORIES

1. Write a story about a research report that is released this week. It can appear in a journal or come from local scientists.

2. Talk to your local legislator or the staff at a regulatory agency about a proposed law or regulation that might affect your community or businesses operating there. Write a story about the impact, making sure you talk with people who would be affected by the regulation and people who hold opposing views about it.

3. Find a story about a local connection to the space industry. Perhaps it's a company that produces materials for the space shuttle, an astronomy professor who's doing federal research or a local engineering company that's bidding on a NASA project.

4. Write a consumer-oriented story about whether a diaper service is more economical and environment-friendly than using disposables.

5. Write a story about the latest developments in exercise and health for teens. Contact sports med-

icine experts, physical education teachers and area teens.

C. ENTERPRISE STORIES

1. Talk with emergency management staffers, risk assessment experts at a university and a local health official to find a potential risk—either health or environmental—that is facing your community. Write an article explaining the potential problem, what officials are doing about it and how consumers can be prepared should it occur.

2. Find out what happens to medical waste in your community. Track the volume, the cost, where it is going and whether appropriate precautions are being taken.

3. Find out from the county, state or federal environmental agency the name of one of the most polluted sites in your area. Get hold of studies that have been carried out on how to clean up the site and evaluate what has been proposed. Then write an in-depth story looking at the status of any cleanup. Interview regulators, consultants, neighbors, environmental groups and the offending company. Look at the public policy implications, past and present.

4. Talk with substance abuse counselors and police about the trends in drug abuse. Ask what drug is starting to appear more often. Then interview substance abuse experts about the drug, its impact on people and how people abusing it can find help.

5. Evaluate the quality and accessibility to medical facilities in your community—what is available and what is needed. For example, is there only one hospital doing heart bypass surgery or are there three competing units duplicating services? How far do people have to travel for specialized procedures? Who handles health care for persons on welfare, and is it adequate?

APPENDIX A   An Internet Primer

The Internet is a network of computer networks begun by the U.S. government in the 1960s as a way for researchers working on defense contracts to communicate. It has blossomed into a communications medium with thousands of librarylike sites full of information as well as advertising-bannered commercial sites.

Student reporters usually access the Internet directly through their colleges, but most reporters use a computer, modem and telephone line to connect to a commercial online service such as America Online or CompuServe. Such online services are actually hybrids—they offer not only an entry point to the Internet but also e-mail, chat rooms or forums and databases. Some reporters connect to the Internet through an Internet service provider, which is a smaller, regional version of a commercial online service. Others have direct connections.

However they get there, once on the Internet, reporters are linked to a wealth of information resources. A software program called a browser, such as Microsoft Explorer or Netscape Navigator, allows reporters to move around on the Net. They type in an Internet address, and the browser carries them to that Internet site.

There are many of ways of traversing this new information superhighway and various types of places to stop. Here are the most common functions reporters use:

- **Electronic mail:** This is how you send messages back and forth to other Internet users. E-mail addresses usually end in one of the following: *.com* (commercial site), *.edu* (educational institution), *.gov* (government), *.mil* (military), *.net* (computer network) or *.org* (nonprofit organization).

- **File transfer protocol (FTP):** This is a way to transfer, or download, information from a remote site to a desktop computer. FTP addresses begin with *ftp://*.

- **Forums or conferences:** These reside on commercial online services or at Web sites. They are similar to an electronic bulletin board where people with like interests post messages for others to read and respond to. One example is the journalism forum, JForum, on CompuServe. Another is a forum at the New York Times On The Web about Puerto Rico's destiny.

- **Gopher sites:** These are informational sites, but without any fancy graphics or pictures—just words. Many have been replaced by World Wide Web sites, but there are still some gold mines of information out there on gophers. The key to knowing you're at a gopher site is an address that begins *gopher://*.

- **Internet relay chat (IRC):** This is real-time message sending in which each person sees the other's comments as they are being typed. You load special software on your computer, dial in to an IRC server, and then select which discussion you'd like to join.

- **Mailing list discussions:** Think of these as the family Christmas letter—the same copy is sent out to lots of people who supposedly are interested in the subject. A person subscribes to a list on a certain topic (such as vegetarian food) and gets all the messages, called postings, from other subscribers via e-mail. Sometimes these are referred to as a listserv or an electronic discussion group. Many of these groups' names end in -L (for list).

- **_Usenet discussion groups:_** This is the Wild West of the Internet, the place where you'll find the most eclectic discussions on thousands of topics. Reporters subscribe (it's free) to groups in which they're interested. They use a special software program (sometimes a part of the Web browser) to go out on Usenet and read the postings, similar to reading a bulletin board. One example is _alt.rec.hockey,_ where hockey die-hards vent their steam.

  These newsgroups, as each discussion is called, begin with one of the following: _alt._ (alternative), _comp._ (computers), _misc._ (miscellaneous), _news._ (Usenet news, not current events), _rec._ (recreation) _sci._ (science), _soc._ (sociology) or _talk._ (talk).

- **_World Wide Web (WWW) sites:_** This is the most popular part of the Internet, complete with text, photographs, splashy graphics, audio and sometimes even video. The first screen you see at a new address is called the home page. If you have an address that begins _http://_—which stands for hypertext transfer protocol—that's a Web site.

The 3-R List: Reporter Research Resources

Here's a list of the best of the best Internet sites for research. Because site addresses and content change, update this list periodically from one of the author's Web pages: http://web.syr.edu/~bcfought.

ASSOCIATIONS

Associations Online	http://www.asaenet.org/gateway/onlineassocslist.html	A searchable database of associations run by the American Society of Association Executives.
National Charities Information Bureau	http://www.give.org	A quick reference to 400 charities.

MAILING LISTS/USENET

Deja News	http://www.dejanews.com	Search newsgroup postings here.
Liszt	http://www.liszt.com	Search mailing lists, newsgroups and IRC chat channels here.
Reference.com	http://www.reference.com	Search mailing lists, newsgroups and Web forums here.
Tile	http://www.tile.net	Search mailing lists, newsgroups and ftp sites here.

MEDIA

Alpha Complete News Index	http://www.select-ware.com/news	Megasite with links to international media.
AJR Newslink	http://www.newslink.org	Megasite from the magazine, *American Journalism Review,* linking to 8,000 media sites.
Electronic Newsstand	http://www.enews.com	Search for information about magazines by title or topic and link to their online sites.
MediaInfo	http://www.mediainfo.com/emedia/	A megasite from the people at *Editor and Publisher* magazine, linking to media by geography or type. Covers magazines, newspapers, radio, TV, syndicates and associations.

MIT Radio List	http://wmbr.mit.edu/stations/list.html	Megasite linking to 4,000 radio stations.
UltimateTV	http://www.ultimatetv.com	A megasite for television news and programming.
Vanderbilt Archives	http://tvnews.vanderbilt.edu	The archives for network TV news.

PEOPLE FINDERS (E-MAIL, PHONE, ADDRESSES)

E-mail: media	http://www.gugerell.co.at/gugerell/media	E-mail directory of addresses for international media, developed as a hobby by an Austrian Airlines pilot.
Four11	http://www.four11.com	A white pages directory from Yahoo!
Internet@ddress.Finder	http://www.iaf.net	Useful for finding names, e-mail and Internet video phone contacts.
Switchboard	http://www.switchboard.com	Searchable database for phone and e-mail.
Phonebook gateway	http://www.uiuc.edu/cgi-bin/ph	Connections to universities around the world to find faculty or experts.

REFERENCES

Research-It	http://www.iTools.com/research-it	An extensive list of dictionaries, thesauri and more.
THOR: The Online Resource	http://thorplus.lib.purdue.edu/reference	Purdue University's reference site.
Yahoo Reference	http://www.yahoo.com/Reference	A megasite of references from the Yahoo! directory folks.
Virtual Library: Albany	http://www.albany.edu/library/virtual/reference	A megasite of references from the University at Albany.

REPORTER HELPS AND GUIDES

Barbara's News Researcher's Page	http://www.gate.net/~barbara	Pointers from news librarian Barbara Gellis Shapiro.
The Beat Page	http://www.reporter.org/beat	A helpful list of resources by subject from Shawn McIntosh, reporter at *The Dallas Morning News.*
Facsnet	http://www.facsnet.org	A topical list of links from the journalism education organization, the Foundation for American Communications. Registration is required but is free.
Internet Journalism Resources	http://www.moorhead.msus.edu/~gunarat/ijr	Topics developed by Moorhead State journalism professor Shelton Gunaratne.
Megasources	http://www.acs.ryerson.ca/~journal/megasources.html	A thorough list developed by Professor Dean Tudor of the School of Journalism, Ryerson Polytechnic University, Toronto, Canada.

Search Engines

Amazing Inet Guide	http://www.sunstorm.com/amazing	A megasite linking to all search engines.

Other References

Mailing lists about communications	http://web.syr.edu/~bcfought	The Newhouse Net lists include links to numerous mailing lists and electronic newsletters about journalism and communications.
Journalism associations and organizations	http://www.cais.com/makulow/vlj.html	This comprehensive list is part of the World Wide Web Virtual Library: Journalism and is updated regularly by Internet trainer and journalist John Makulowich. It includes associations, centers, clubs, foundations, guilds, institutes and societies.

Sample Reports

The reports compiled by police and firefighters are key documents to help reporters understand the official version of a crime, fire or accident. For beginning reporters, who may not have seen such reports, the following pages give you samples so that you can become familiar with these reports before you're covering a story under the heat of deadline pressure.

- ■ *Police Incident Report.* This provides the name of the victim(s) and suspects(s), a summary description of the crime, and the date and place where it occurred. It gives the names, addresses and phone numbers of witnesses, some of whom may prove to be excellent sources. It also provides the name of the officer who filed the report.

- ■ *Accident Report.* This report gives the names of participants, the location of the accident and a description of what occurred. There's often a diagram that shows the path(s) of the vehicle(s) during the accident. Look in the officer's notes for signs of drinking, drugs, speeding or road hazards.

- ■ *Fire Incident Report.* Here you'll find the name(s) of the resident(s) and owner(s), the location, and details about how the fire started and spread. Check for any indication of arson or suspicious circumstances. Also pay close attention to the value of the damaged property.

- ■ *Search Warrant Return.* Law enforcement officials must get a judge to sign a search warrant before they search a property for signs of a crime or for evidence. Once the search is completed, the return lists what the police found or confiscated. Look for the location, time and place of the search. You'll also find the name of at least one officer involved, so you have someone to contact for further information.

Sample Crime Incident Report: Domestic Violence.

(Names and events are fictitious and for illustration purposes only.)

SYRACUSE POLICE DEPARTMENT Form 3.6 (Rev. 10/89)	CHAIRS INCIDENT REPORT	Beat/RA 452	Back of Report Y N	2. DR NUMBER: 99 123433

1. AGENCY: **01**

VICTIM

INVOLVED PERSON TYPE VI=VICTIM / MP=MISSING PERSON / CO=COMPLAINANT

3.TYPE VI	4. NAME (LAST, FIRST, MID, TITLE) Henry, Sally L.	5. STREET NUMBER AND NAME, BUILDING NO., APT. NO. 424 Water St,	6. CITY / STATE / ZIP Syracuse, NY

7. PHONE 4764466	8. DATE OF BIRTH 10 Jun 82	9. AGE 17	10. SEX F	11. RACE W	12. SKIN L M D	13. HGT 5'4"	14. WGT 134	15. HAIR Bro	16. EYES Grn	17. GLASSES Y N CONT	18. SOC. SEC. NUM. 082 54 9876

19. DESCRIPTION ----	20. SCARS/MARKS/TATTOOS ----	21. CONDITION ☐ Normal ☐ Drugs ☐ Alcohol ☐ Marks ☐ Bruises ☐ Illness ☐ Undetermined ☐ Handicapped ☐ Mental Disorder	22. NATURE OF ILLNESS OR INJURY bruised head/preg.

23. EMPLOYER/SCHOOL NAME Y-Med	24. STREET NUMBER AND NAME, CITY Harrison St	25. PHONE

INCIDENT

26. INCIDENT Dom/Harass	27. INCIDENT ADDRESS STREET NUM. AND NAME, BLDG., APT. 234 Oak St	28. CITY Syracuse	29. PREMISE NAME residence	30. ALARM NUMBER Harr

31. OCCURRED DATE 09 14 99	TIME 1630	32. TO DATE 09 14 99	TIME 1700	33. DISPATCHED TO ADDRESS same	34. DATE 14 Sept 95	35. TIME P	36. OFFENSE/CLASSIFICATION 1240261

37. TYPE OF PREMISE ☐ Residence ☐ Apt. House ☐ Unattached Garage, Shed ☐ Hotel/Motel ☐ Oth. Residential ☐ Street ☐ Conv. Store ☐ Public/Comm. Bldg. ☐ Gas Station ☐ Pkng Lot ☐ Public Garage ☐ Bank ☐ Other Commercial	38. WEAPON ☐ Handgun ☐ Oth. Firearm ☐ Knife/Cutting Instr. ☐ Explosives ☐ Oth. Weapon ☐ Strong Arm ☐ All Other	39. LARCENY ☐ Pocket Picking ☐ Purse Snatching ☐ Shoplifting ☐ From Motor Veh. ☐ Motor Veh. Parts ☐ Bicycles ☐ From Building ☐ From Coin Machine ☐ Motor Vehicle ☐ All Other	40. BURGLARY ☐ FORCE ☐ NO FORCE

41. CONTROLLED SUBSTANCE ☐ Cocaine ☐ Marijuana ☐ Synthetic ☐ Other	42. DOMESTIC VIOLENCE ☐ Wife by Husband ☐ Husband by Wife ☐ Child by Parent ☐ Parent by Child ☐ Oth. Family Relationship ☐ Comm. Law Wife by Husb. ☐ Comm. Law Husb. by Wife	43. ARSON PROPERTY ☐ Single Resid ☐ Oth. Resid ☐ Storage ☐ Industrial ☐ Oth. Comm. ☐ Public Bldg. ☐ Other ☐ Motor Veh. ☐ Oth. Motor Veh.	44. ABAND. Y N

INVOLVED PERSONS

INVOLVED PERSON TYPE CO=COMPLAINANT WI=WITNESS PR=PERSON REPORTING PG=PARENT GUARDIAN PH=PHYSICIAN OT=OTHER INVOLVED SP=SPOUSE

45. TYPE PA	46. NAME (LAST, FIRST, MI, TITLE) Donnell, Mary	47. STREET NUMBER AND NAME 589 Hartson St.	48. CITY / STATE / ZIP Syr NY 13204	49. PHONE 476 0987	50. AGE 35	51. SEX F	52. RACE W

SUSPECT

53. NAME (LAST, FIRST, MI) Harris, Thomas	54. STREET NUMBER AND NAME, BUILDING NO., APT. NO. 323 Maple St	55. CITY, STATE, ZIP Syr NY 13208

56. ALIAS/NICKNAME/MAIDEN NAME (LAST, FIRST, MI) ---	57. DATE OF BIRTH 4 Aug 82	58. AGE 17	59. SEX M	60. RACE W	61. ETHNIC HISP NON	62. SKIN L M D	63. HGT. 5'10"	64. WGT 150	65. HAIR Brn	66. EYES Blu	67. GLASSES Y N CONT	68. SOC. SEC. NUM. 08265 2345

69. WEAPONS, ACTION, ETC. punched and dragged victim	70. SCARS/MARKS/TATTOOS ---

VEHICLE

VEHICLE CODE 01=LOST 02=FOUND 03=STOLEN/NO PROS 04=STOLEN/PROS 05=RECOVERED 07=SAFE KEEPING 08=ARSON 09=DAMAGE
10=USED IN CRIME 11=IMPOUNDED 12=TOWED 13=REPOSSESSED 14=OBSERVED 15=ABANDONED

71. CODE	72. PLATE #	73. STATE	74. EXP.	75. TYPE	76. IMP PLATE Y N	77. VEHICLE ID NUMBER

78. YR.	79. MAKE	80. MODEL	81. STYLE	82. COLOR	83. VALUE	84. NUMBER OF OCCUPANTS

85. WEAPONS IN VEHICLE	86. SPECIAL VEHICLE FEATURES	87. TOWED Y N	88. TO / BY	89. RELEASE Y N	90. NCIC CHECK ☐ POS ☐ NEG	91. SCOFFLAW CHECK ☐ POS ☐ NEG

PROPERTY

PROPERTY CODE 01=LOST 02=FOUND 04=STOLEN 05=RECOVERED 07=EVIDENCE 08=SAFE KEEPING 09=ARSON 10=DAMAGE

92. CODE	93. QUAN	94. ARTICLE	95. SERIAL NUMBER	96. MAKE	97. MODEL	98. DESCRIPTION / COLOR	99. GUN CALIBER	100. GUN TYPE	101. VALUE

102. ***NARRATIVE HERE	TOTAL

On above date, time, location I was dispatched to location regarding a domestic dispute. Upon arrival I spoke to the victim who stated on 14 Sept 99 between 1630 hrs and 1700 hrs she and suspect Thomas Harris, with whom she shares an unborn child, became involved in a verbal dispute. The dispute got physical when she attempted to leave. The suspect punched her in the head and knocked her down

103. STATUS ☐ Open ☐ Unfounded ☐ Warr/Summ Applied For ☐ Cleared Arrest ☐ Cleared (Non-Felony Offense Only) No Prosecution	104. CLEARED AGES ☐ 18 & Over ☐ Under 18 ☐ Both

105. NOTIFIED / TURNED OVER TO ☐ Special Invest. Notified: ☐ Crim. Invest. ☐ Communications ☐ Youth Division ☐ Other	106. COPIES TO	107. TELETYPE ☐ SENT ☐ CANCELLED DATE	108. MSG #

109. False statements made herein are punishable as a Class A Misdemeanor pursuant to Section 210.45 of the Penal Law of the State of New York.
AFFIRMED UNDER PENALTY OF PERJURY

PRINT NAME Timeeka Sherman /SIGNATURE Tameeka Sherman 301	110. APPROVAL Sgt Jane Jones 224	111. Page 1 of ___

Sample Accident Report.

(Names and events are fictitious and for illustration purposes only.)

Local Codes
99-147673

New York State Department of Motor Vehicles
POLICE ACCIDENT REPORT
MV-104A (4/94)
DMV COPY

DMV USE

19

20

Accident Date	Day of Week	Time	No. of Vehicles	No. Injured	No. Killed	Non-Highway	Not Investigated at Scene	Left Scene	Police Photos
11 / 11 / 99	Thurs	☐ AM ☐ PM	2	—	1 —			☒	☐ Yes ☒ No

VEHICLE 1 ☒ **VEHICLE 2** ☐ **BICYCLIST** ☐ **PEDESTRIAN**

Driver Name–exactly as printed on license
unknown

DMV USE

Name–exactly as printed on license
Doe, Juan

DMV USE

21

Address (Include Number & Street) — Apt. No.

Address (Include Number & Street) — Apt. No.
234 High Road

City or Town — State — Zip Code

City or Town — State — Zip Code
Tully — NY

22

Date of Birth	Sex	Unlicensed	No. of Occup.	Public Property Damaged	State of Lic.
/ /		☐		☐	

Date of Birth	Sex	Unlicensed	No. of Occup.	Public Property Damaged	State of Lic.
09 05 75	M	☐	1	☐	NY

Name–exactly as printed on registration
unknown — Date of Birth / /

Name–exactly as printed on registration
S.K. Smith & Sons — Date of Birth / /

23

Address (Include Number & Street) — Apt. No. — Haz. Mat. — Code — Released ☐

Address (Include Number & Street) — Apt. No. — Haz. Mat. — Code — Released ☐
987 Prairie Ridge Rd.

City or Town — State — Zip Code

City or Town — State — Zip Code
Tully — NY

24

Plate Number	State of Reg.	Vehicle Year & Make	Vehicle Type	Ins. Code

Plate Number	State of Reg.	Vehicle Year & Make	Vehicle Type	Ins. Code
AB 9999	NY	92 White dumptruck		

Check if involved vehicle:
☐ is a commercial motor vehicle;
☐ is more than 95 inches wide;
☐ is more than 34 feet long;
☐ was operated with an overweight permit;
☐ was operated with an overdimension permit.

Check if involved vehicle:
☐ is a commercial motor vehicle;
☐ is more than 95 inches wide;
☐ is more than 34 feet long;
☐ was operated with an overweight permit;
☐ was operated with an overdimension permit.

25

ACCIDENT DIAGRAM

Rear End — Left Turn — Right Angle — Right Turn — Head On
1. — 3. — — 5. — 7.
Overtaking — Left Turn — — Right Turn — Sideswipe
2. — 0. — 4. — 6. — 8.

Rt 690 West

Rt 81 South ramp

VEHICLE 1 DAMAGE

26

27

☐ No Damage ☐ Undercarriage
By
Vehicle Towed To

VEHICLE 2 DAMAGE

☐ No Damage ☐ Undercarriage
By
Vehicle Towed To

28

Reference Marker	DMV USE ONLY	County Onon	☒ City ☐ Town	☐ Village Syracuse

Route No. or Street Name
on Rt. 690 West

☐ Miles ☐ N ☐ E
☐ Feet ☐ S ☐ W of
☒ At Intersection With
81 South ramp

29

TICKET/ARREST ☐ OPR 1 ☐ OPR 2 — Ticket/Arrest Number(s)
☐ PEDESTRIAN ☐ BICYCLIST ☐ OTHER — Violation Section(s)

Nearest Intersecting Route/Street

Accident Description/Officer's Notes Driver of vehicle #2 stated he was headed west on Rt. 690 in the left lane when vehicle #1, a small blue vehicle (no further information) cut in front of his vehicle from the cneter lane and struck vehicle #2. Driver of vehicle #2 stated vehicle #1 did not stop and continued west on Rt. 690 W. No further information.

30

USE COVER SHEET

K

		8	9	10	11	12	13	14	15	16	17 BY	TO 18	Names - If Deceased, Give Date of Death
ALL INVOLVED	A	1	1	uknown									
	B	2	1	X	1	25	M						Doe, Juan
	C												
	D												
	E												
	F												
	G												

SIGN HERE

Officer's Rank and Name	Badge No.	Department	Precinct/Post Troop/Zone	Station/Beat/Sector	Reviewing Officer	Date/Time Reviewed
PO. Sarah Jones	202	03301	TOP			11 Nov 99 13:00

Sample Fire Incident Report.

(Names and events are fictitious and for illustration purposes only.)

NEW YORK STATE INCIDENT REPORT
F-40-2

FDID	Department Name	Alarm Box	District	Time In	REVISED REPORT ☐
3 4 0 0 9	Clay	2 3 0		2 1 1 5	

Incident No. 980525

Exp.	Mo.	Day	Yr.	Day of Week	Alarm Time	Time Out	Arr. Time
	0 5	28	99	Fri	19 0 0	19 05	19 0 7

FIRE SERVICE RESPONSE

ALL CALLS

INCIDENT ADDRESS — Street: 1234 Caughdenoy Rd — Rm. Or Apt.

PERSONNEL: 30

City: Clay — ZIP 3 0 41 — Census Tract No.

ENGINES: 3

OCCUPANT NAME — Last, First: Smith, John M

MUTUAL AID (check one)

AERIALS: 1

OWNER NAME — Last, First: Smith, John M

1 ☐ RECEIVED

TANKERS: 0

OWNER ADDRESS — Street: 1234 Caughdenoy Rd

2 ☐ GIVEN

OTHER VEHICLES: 6

City: Clay — State NY — ZIP 3 0 4 1

IF HAZARDOUS MATERIALS ARE INVOLVED (see coding sheet)

PLEASE PUT APPROPRIATE CODE NUMBER IN BOX FOR EACH CATEGORY

CLASS

AMOUNT

METHOD OF ALARM FROM PUBLIC	TYPE OF SITUATION FOUND		TYPE OF ACTION TAKEN
1 Telephone	11 Structure fire	19 Fire/explosion not classified	1 Extinguishment
2 Municipal alarm system	12 Any fire outside a structure where the material burning has a value	20 Overpressure rupture (no combustion)	2 Rescue
3 Private alarm system		30 Rescue	3 Investigation
4 Radio	13 Vehicle fire	32 EMS only	4 Remove hazard — Primary 1
5 Verbal	14 Trees, brush, grass fire	40 Hazardous condition	5 Standby
6 Home dialer	15 Refuse fire (material burning has no value)	50 Service call	6 Salvage
7 Tie-line		60 Good intent call	7 Medical assistance
8 Voice signal: Fire alarm system	16 Explosion, no after-fire	71 False malicious	8 Fill in, move up — Secondary 2
9 Cable TV link	17 Outside spill, leak with fire	73 False malfunction	9 Cancelled en route
		74 False unintentional	

No. Incident-related Injuries — Fire Srv. 0 0 1 — Other 0 0 1

No. Incident-related Fatalities — Fire Srv. ___ — Other ___

Is juvenile involved in ignition? 1 ☐ YES 2 ☐ NO

Method of alarm: **1**

Type of situation found: **11**

IGNITION FACTOR (see coding sheet): Fuel spilled — **41**

FIRES

Fill in this section if "TYPE OF SITUATION FOUND" is 11, 12, 13, 16, 17, 19 ONLY (Refer to coding sheet)

		FIXED PROPERTY USE: one/two family dwelling	41
MULTI-USE PROPERTY COMPLEX: Dwelling	41	AREA OF FIRE ORIGIN: garage	47

EQUIPMENT INVOLVED IN IGNITION: portable heating unit — 15

FORM OF HEAT OF IGNITION: heat from gas fueled equip — 12

TYPE OF MATERIAL IGNITED: gasoline — 23

FORM OF MATERIAL IGNITED: interior wall covering — 15

IF HEATING EQUIPMENT INVOLVED, TYPE OF FUEL USED:
1 Kerosene 2 LPG 3 Electric 4 Wood 5 Coal 6 Oil 7 Natural Gas 8 Gasoline 9 Other

PROPERTY DAMAGE CLASSIFICATIONS

1 $1-99	6 $50,000-149,999
2 $100-999	7 $150,000-499,999
3 $1,000-9,999	8 $500,000-999,999
4 $10,000-24,999	9 $1,000,000 OR MORE
5 $25,000-49,999	0 NO DOLLAR LOSS

Value: **7**

Damaged: **4**

CONDITION UPON ARRIVAL	MOBILE PROPERTY TYPE	
1 Overheat	11 Automobile	20 Freight road transport
2 Smoldering	12 Bus	30 Rail transport
3 Open flame	13 Motorcycle, snowmobile	40 Water transport
8 Out on arrival — **3**	14 Motor home	50 Air transport
	15 Travel trailer	60 Heavy equipment
	17 Mobile home	70 Special vehicles, containers --
		99 Other mobile property types

Is property abandoned / vacant? 1 ☐ YES 2 ☒ NO

If Mobile Property -- | Yr. | Make | Model | St. | Lic. Number | Serial Number / VIN

If Equipment Involved in Ignition | Yr. | Item | Make | Model | Serial Number

STRUCTURE FIRES

NO. OF STORIES	EXTENT OF DAMAGE	
1 Single Story	1 Confined to the object of origin	
2 Two Stories	2 Confined to part of room or area of origin	FLAME 2
3 3 or 4	3 Confined to room of origin	
4 5 or 6	4 Confined to fire-rated comp. of origin	
5 7 to 10	5 Confined to floor of origin	SMOKE 3
6 11 to 20	6 Confined to structure of origin	
7 21 to 50	7 Extended beyond structure of origin	
8 Over 50	9 No damage of this type	WATER 2
9 Below Grade		

DETECTOR PERFORMANCE	1 ☐ PRESENT 2 ☒ NOT PRESENT
IF PRESENT, TYPE OF CLOSEST UNIT	1 ☐ SMOKE 2 ☐ HEAT
POWER SUPPLY	1 ☐ BATTERY 2 ☐ A/C

1 In room of fire: operated
2 Not in room of fire: operated
3 In room of fire: did not operate
4 Not in room of fire: did not operate
5 In room: fire too small to operate
9 Not classified

Detector: **4**

CONSTRUCTION TYPE (see worksheet)	SPRINKLER PERFORMANCE
1 Fire resistive	1 Equipment operated
2 Noncombustible	2 Equipment inservice, did not operate
3 Heavy timber	3 Equipment present: fire too small to operate
4 Ordinary	8 No equipment present in room/space of fire origin
5 Frame	9 Equipment not in service

BUILDING HEIGHT: **2**

LEVEL OF FIRE ORIGIN: **1**

Sprinkler performance: **8**

IF DETECTOR DEFECTIVE—Brand Name, Serial No.

FIRE REFERRED FOR INVESTIGATION TO:

ADDITIONAL FIRE DEPARTMENT INFORMATION (see coding sheet)

ITEM	CODE	ITEM	CODE	ITEM	CODE

Officer in Charge (name, position) | Date | Member Making Report (if different from Officer in Charge) | Date

REMARKS _____

DOS-348 (3/87)

Sample Search Warrant Return.

(Names and events are fictitious and for illustration purposes only.)

RETURN

STATE OF NEW YORK: ONONDAGA COUNTY

I and members of the New York State Police executed the Search Warrant at 123 Main Street, Dewitt, New York as was therein commanded on the _27_ day of May, 1999, by making a search in the place designated in the said Warrant for the property therein described by the taking of samples and photographs and find of the said property the articles described in the following inventory.

Dated: Syracuse, New York this
    _29_ day of April, 1999.

_____
(Executing Police Officer)

LASHAWN BARNES

INVENTORY

INVENTORY of property taken by me by virtue of the within Search Warrant made publicly: (list all items seized)

1. (6) Sample of soil and water by loading dock of 123 Main Street, Dewitt, New York.

2. Numerous photographs of the interior and exterior of the building.

Dated: Dewitt, New York this
    _29_ day of April, 1999

_____
(Executing Police Officer)

LASHAWN BARNES

News Organizations That Appear in This Book

National Media

ABC News
Associated Press
CBS News
The Christian Science Monitor
HotWired
Knight-Ridder News Service
Los Angeles Times Syndicate
The MoJo Wire
MSNBC
National Geographic Explorer
National Public Radio
Nation's Business
NBC News
Newhouse News Service
The New York Times
Newsweek
The Wall Street Journal
USA Today

Alabama

NBC13 Interactive Neighborhood (Birmingham)

Arkansas

Arkansas Democrat-Gazette
KHTV-TV (Little Rock)

California

The Fresno Bee
KCBS-AM (San Francisco)
KNTV-TV (San Jose)
KQED-FM (San Francisco)

Los Angeles Times
Marin Independent Journal
Mercury Center (San Jose)
The Orange County Register
The Sacramento Bee
San Francisco Chronicle
(San Francisco) Examiner
San Jose Mercury News

Canada

The London (Ontario) Free Press

Colorado

KMGH-TV (Denver)

Connecticut

The Hartford Courant

District of Columbia

The Washington Post
WRC-TV
WUSA-TV

Florida

(Fort Lauderdale) Sun-Sentinel
(Fort Myers) News-Press
The Miami Herald
The Orlando Sentinel
St. Petersburg Times
Tampa Tribune
WFLA-TV (Tampa)
WINK-TV (Ft. Myers)

Georgia

Atlanta Journal and Constitution

Illinois

Chicago Tribune
WBBM-AM (Chicago)
WBEZ-FM (Chicago)

Indiana

The Indianapolis Star

Iowa

The Des Moines Register

Kansas

The Wichita Eagle

Kentucky

The (Louisville) Courier-Journal

Louisiana

The (Baton Rouge) Advocate
The (New Orleans) Times-Picayune

Maryland

The (Baltimore) Sun

Massachusetts

5 Online (Boston)
Boston.com (Boston)
The Boston Globe
New England Cable News
WBZ-AM (Boston)
WCVB-TV (Boston)

Michigan

Detroit Free Press
The Detroit News
WDIV-TV (Detroit)
WWJ-AM (Detroit)
WXYZ-TV (Detroit)

Minnesota

KARE-TV (Minneapolis)
Minnesota Public Radio
(Minneapolis) Star Tribune
Star Tribune Online
St. Paul Pioneer Press
WCCO-TV (Minneapolis)

Missouri

The Kansas City Star
St. Louis Post-Dispatch
KSDK-TV (St. Louis)

Montana

KFBB-TV (Great Falls)

Nebraska

Omaha World-Herald

Nevada

Reno Gazette-Journal

New Hampshire

WMUR-TV (Manchester)

New Jersey

The (Bergen Co.) Record
(Morristown) Daily Record
The (Newark) Star-Ledger

New York

(Albany) Times Union
The Buffalo Times
(Middletown) Times Herald-Record
Newsday
Niagara Gazette
Rochester Democrat and Chronicle
Syracuse Herald-Journal
Syracuse Herald American
The (Syracuse) Post-Standard
WCBS-AM (New York)
WKBW-TV (Buffalo)
WTVH-TV (Syracuse)

North Carolina

The (Raleigh) News & Observer

Winston-Salem Journal

Ohio

Cincinnati Magazine

The (Cleveland) Plain Dealer

The Columbus Dispatch

Dayton Daily News

The (Warren) Tribune Chronicle

Oklahoma

The Daily Oklahoman

Oregon

The (Portland) Oregonian

Pennsylvania

The (Allentown) Morning Call

(Lancaster) Intelligencer Journal

The Philadelphia Inquirer

Tennessee

The (Nashville) Tennessean

Texas

Austin American-Statesman

Beaumont Enterprise

The Dallas Morning News

KHOU-TV (Houston)

KVUE-TV (Austin)

WFAA-TV (Dallas)

Virginia

The (Norfolk) Virginian-Pilot

Richmond Times-Dispatch

Washington

The Seattle Times

The (Spokane) Spokesman-Review

Wisconsin

The Milwaukee Journal

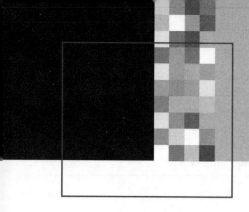

Glossary

acquitted Found not guilty.

actual malice The legal standard that must be met by a public official or a well-known public figure (and in a few states, a private person) who sues a reporter for libel. The litigant must prove that the media defendant knew information was wrong and printed it anyway or printed it with reckless disregard of whether it was right or wrong. *See also* negligence.

actualities Recorded interview segments that radio reporters edit into their stories. Sometimes called sound bites.

advances These are stories written before, or in advance, of a meeting or event to alert the audience to what will be discussed. They also are known as previews in broadcast.

angle A way of approaching a story that makes it distinctive or different from what has been said or written before.

answer In civil court cases, the written response to a plaintiff's complaint from the person accused of the wrong. *See* complaint.

archives The library of old scripts and tapes in broadcast newsrooms.

arraignment The initial court proceeding at which a judge tells the defendant the charges and sets bail.

arraignment files Also known as case files, these include information ranging from statements by suspects, witnesses and victims to a suspect's record of previous convictions.

arrest log Tells the name, address, age and charges filed against each person arrested. Also called the booking log.

arson The crime of deliberately setting a fire.

assessed value The basis on which a piece of property is taxed. *See* market value.

audits Reviews by independent evaluators of how particular programs or agencies are operating. Audits can be aimed exclusively at financial performance, but some also gauge how well a program is accomplishing its goals. These are called performance audits.

autopsy report A medical report following the examination and dissection of a dead body. It can give information about the cause and conditions of death.

beat An area of specialization developed by a reporter. Some reporters cover topical beats such as health, the courts or politics. Others cover geographical beats such as a neighborhood or town.

blotter Also called the desk log, this document catalogues the daily situations, by time and incident, to which police respond. It should always be available to reporters.

bookmarks A feature of a World Wide Web browser (*see* browser). It's a list of the WWW addresses of frequently visited sites, developed by a computer user to help reach those sites quickly.

brite A story intended to make the audience smile. In broadcast, this story is also called a talk-about.

browser A software program for traveling the Internet.

budget The blueprint used by any organization to plan for the year ahead. It balances expenditures (the amount of money going out) against revenues (the amount of money coming in).

burglary The act of breaking into a building.

civil case When one party or company sues another over a perceived wrongdoing not necessarily criminal in nature.

clips The name given to newspaper library files of old stories. Today these are electronic, but they used to be "clipped" and organized by topic.

close A television story's concluding, and lasting, image and script.

close-ended questions These focus on a specific answer, either a fact or detail or a confirmation or denial. *See* open-ended questions.

complaint In a civil court case, this document outlines the wrongs allegedly done to the person, organization or company filing the suit.

computer-assisted reporting Using a computer to analyze records that then become the basis of news.

contempt A legal term meaning disrespect for the court.

context Information about the background of an issue that is critical to understanding new developments.

criminal A person who has been convicted of or has pled guilty to committing a crime.

criminal case A court case, filed by the government, to prosecute a person for breaking a law(s).

databases Computerized collections of records.

daybooks Summaries of the day's news events either fed electronically by wire services or compiled by news managers. They serve as the basis of stories.

debt service The amount of money a government entity pays each year toward reducing its debt.

defamation The legal term for damaging someone's reputation either in writing (*see* libel) or speaking (*see* slander).

defendant Someone who has been formally charged in court with breaking a law.

depositions Transcripts of testimony taken under oath.

discovery The process during a civil court case in which plaintiff and defendant seek each other's records and documents.

docket The court schedule.

donut An edited television story run between a reporter's live open and live close. Also called an insert.

fairness A quality reporters strive to maintain by balancing their reports and avoiding intentional bias. Fairness dictates that reporters make a concerted effort to present various sides of stories rather than a single point of view.

false light The legal basis for a privacy lawsuit by people who believe they have been portrayed in a way that is untruthful.

felony A serious crime.

follow A story that further develops, or follows, a news event. Follows that elaborate on the news a day after a story breaks are called second-day stories or follow-ups.

future file A file, organized by month and day, used by reporters as a reminder of upcoming events and issues to cover. A notice of the next budget hearing, for example, would be filed under the date it is to be held.

general assignment Reporters who are not assigned a specific topic or beat to cover are considered general assignment reporters. They cover a wide range of topics.

grand jury A citizens panel that reviews evidence brought by the prosecutor and votes on whether a case should continue.

hits In database or Internet searching, this term refers to the number of potential records or sites that fit the parameters of a search for information.

home page The first page users see when they arrive at a World Wide Web site.

homicide Killing of one person by another. *See* murder and manslaughter.

incident report Written by police officers, it describes what happened at an accident, crime or police call and what witnesses recounted.

indictment A document listing a charge or charges against a defendant. It is returned by a grand jury after the grand jury has heard evidence from the prosecutor.

infographics Graphic material that through diagrams, words and pictures tells a story in and of itself. Some accompany stories and others stand as stories on their own.

injunctions   Orders from a judge that require or prevent a certain act.

Internet   A network of computer networks sharing information. The Internet has exploded from a government research system to a new communications medium.

interrogatories   Written responses from a witness or party in a civil suit.

intrusion   The legal basis for a privacy lawsuit by people who believe a reporter or photographer has intruded into their private space, often through use of hidden recorders, hidden cameras or long telephoto lenses.

investigative files   Records that detail the police follow-up and the status of an investigation; often compiled by detectives.

jail   A place where defendants are housed before trial and people convicted of lesser crimes serve short sentences. *See* prison.

larceny   Theft of another person's property. *See* robbery.

lead   The beginning of a story. In hard news, this typically is the first sentence or paragraph. It summarizes key information. In less hard-edged stories or those told in more narrative form, a lead can last several paragraphs.

lead support   Information that elaborates on the news summarized at the start of a story. In newspaper stories, lead support generally follows in the paragraph or two after the lead.

libel   Damaging someone's reputation in writing. *See* defamation and slander.

links   Highlighted words on a World Wide Web page that a person can click on to travel to a different layer of information.

localizing   News is "localized" when reporters look at international, national or state events from the perspective of their impact at home. If, for example, the federal government sets tougher standards for drinking water, a localized story would measure how the city's water utility and customers might be affected.

lurk   The practice of monitoring discussions on Internet mailing lists, discussion groups, chat rooms and forums without participating or identifying yourself.

mainstream   The process of seeking out all kinds of people to include in stories of everyday life.

The term applies to the inclusion of women and minorities in stories that aren't specifically about women or minorities.

manslaughter   The unlawful killing of a person, done unintentionally or in the heat of passion. *See* homicide and murder.

margin of error   The range of possible error in polls that results from applying random sampling to the population as a whole. Pollsters typically report that their findings will be within a three to five percentage point swing of what the general public believes. It is crucial to give the margin of error in reporting polls.

market value   The value at which a property might be expected to sell on the open market. *See* assessed value.

misdemeanor   A lesser crime.

murder   The unlawful killing of a person, done with premeditation. *See* homicide and manslaughter.

negligence   A legal standard that a person bringing a libel suit must prove. It requires proof that a reporter didn't exercise ordinary, professional care in determining the truth. In many states this is the standard used in a suit brought by a private person. *See* actual malice.

news feed   A syndicated or satellite service that feeds video or audio stories to television or radio stations.

news peg   An event or anniversary that makes coverage of an issue particularly timely.

news release   Also called a press release, this is a document, written in the form of a news story, that provides legitimate information but in a form that casts the organization distributing the release in the best light. News releases should never be reprinted as complete news stories.

news service   Also known as the wires, these organizations send stories from around the world to subscribers. Perhaps the best known news service is The Associated Press.

no bill   A term used when a grand jury decides there is no reason to continue a case brought before it. In such cases, the grand jury offers a no bill.

not for attribution   Information given to reporters in this way can be used in a story, but the person, or source, of the information can't be identified by name.

off the record Information gathered from sources under the guarantee that it will not be used in a story unless it is independently verified elsewhere. Sources who provide off-the-record information should not be identified in idle newsroom chatter either. They want to remain anonymous.

on background Another term for not for attribution.

on the record Everything told to a reporter in this way can be used in a story with the source's name and title attached.

open-ended questions Questions designed to draw an interview subject out. They begin with words such as "what," "how" and "why." They can't be answered with a single word or fact. See close-ended questions.

parole A conditional release under which the person has to follow certain rules and is supervised by a parole officer. See probation.

plea bargaining Negotiating with a defendant to lower a charge in exchange for a guilty plea.

previews See advances.

primary source A first-hand source, either an individual or document.

prison A place where people convicted of crimes serve their time. A prison is usually run by the state or federal government, whereas a penitentiary, a similar facility, is often run by a county. See jail.

probation An alternative to incarceration for persons convicted of lesser offenses who agree to follow specific guidelines to stay out of jail. See parole.

prospectus Detailed financial information that a publicly held company must issue under federal law before it can raise money.

PTAs or PTOs An acronym for parent-teacher associations or organizations. Members often play an active role in schools.

publication of private facts The legal basis for a privacy lawsuit when the media report intimate personal information such as medical tests.

random sampling This polling term applies to cross-sections of the population, drawn scientifically, to gauge popular opinion. Reporters should not confuse informal sampling with random sampling. A story based on interviews with every third person on the street corner is not random,

nor does it in any way reflect broader public opinion.

rap sheet A person's past criminal record.

reader A story read by a radio anchor that doesn't include sound-on-tape.

robbery Theft of money or property from a person through force or the threat of force. See larceny.

search engine A World Wide Web site with a searching function that hunts through the Internet for key words designated by a computer user.

search terms Words or phrases that can be used to find specific information in any electronic database.

search warrant Issued by a judge, this document authorizes police to search someone's property or possessions to gather evidence in a crime. See warrant return.

secondary source A person, article, tape or computer file that recounts someone else's information or work. This account is one step removed from the actual information.

sequester The act of isolating a jury in a high-profile case so that members can't read or view news accounts or be contacted by persons involved in the case.

slander Damage to someone's reputation through the spoken word. See defamation and libel.

sound bite Recorded interview segments that TV reporters edit into their reports.

sources A term typically applied to people who reporters turn to regularly for help with stories.

stand-up A portion of a TV story in which the reporter delivers an on-camera narration.

subpoena A legal document ordering a person to testify or to turn over evidence.

suspect Someone police believe may have committed a crime. All suspects are presumed innocent until proven guilty.

talk-about story See brite.

telnet A computer program that allows a person to log onto another computer to use programs there.

tips Information that sources supply to reporters to help them develop stories.

trend stories Stories that measure broad and sometimes subtle changes in society. Trend stories are rarely announced. They are noticed by observant and alert reporters. The trend may be a change in teen fashion, a migration pattern of more Americans to the Southwest or a spate of ordinances in adjoining communities to crack down on jaywalkers.

transitions Words that act as road signs, telling the reader or listener that a story is changing direction or theme. Contrasting words such as "although" and "however" are examples.

unions Associations that represent workers in negotiations over wages and working conditions.

vendors Commercial companies that provide databases for a fee.

video news releases Video or TV news stories, produced by companies and public relations agencies, designed to subtly promote a product, service or organization.

warrant return A court document that reports what police found during a court-approved search. *See* search warrant.

World Wide Web The most popular portion of the Internet. Users access it using a browser. WWW pages may include text, images and video as well as icons and highlighted terms that allow them to connect to other layers of information or other WWW sites.

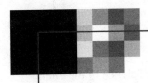

INDEX